Reason and Resonance

Reason and Resonance

A History of Modern Aurality

Veit Erlmann

ZONE BOOKS · NEW YORK

2014

ZONE BOOKS
1226 Prospect Avenue
Brooklyn, NY 11218

First paperback edition

Printed in the United States of America.

Distributed by The MIT Press,
Cambridge, Massachusetts, and London, England

Library of Congress Cataloging-in-Publication Data

Erlmann, Veit.
       Reason and resonance : a history of modern aurality
/ Veit Erlmann.
           p. cm.
       Includes bibliographical references and index.
       ISBN 978-1-935408-05-5
               1. Auditory perception. 2. Listening.
3. Sound. 4. Culture—Philosophy. 5. Hearing—History.
6. Audiology—History. I. Title.

       BF251.E75 2010
       128'.3—DC22
                              2009052201

I am the resonance and the tone.

—Michel Serres, *Les cinq sens*

Contents

The String and the Mirror

The great encyclopedist, essayist, and music amateur Denis Diderot had a penchant for strong analogies, such as this one from his *Entretien entre d'Alembert et Diderot*, written in 1769:

> The sensitive vibrating string oscillates and resonates a long time after one has plucked it. It's this oscillation, this sort of inevitable resonance, that holds the present object, while our understanding is busy with the quality which is appropriate to it. But vibrating strings have yet another property—to make other strings quiver. And thus the first idea recalls a second, and these two a third, then all three a fourth, and so it goes, without our being able to set a limit to the ideas that are aroused and linked in a philosopher who meditates or who listens to himself in silence and darkness.[1]

Diderot's scandalous assertion—so scandalous, in fact, that publication of the *Entretien* had to wait until 1830—seems to be at odds with the more commonplace image of the philosopher as someone who deliberates and ponders with cool detachment, who searches for the truth by completely withdrawing from the world, and whose intellect seems to be akin to a mirror.[2] Ever since René Descartes and John Locke invented an entity called "the mind," thinking has come to be understood as reflection. Just as the mirror reflects the light waves without its own substance becoming affected, the mind mimetically represents the outside world while at the same time remaining separate from it.

Resonance is of course the complete opposite of the reflective,

9

distancing mechanism of a mirror. While reason implies the disjunction of subject and object, resonance involves their conjunction. Where reason requires separation and autonomy, resonance entails adjacency, sympathy, and the collapse of the boundary between perceiver and perceived. Resonance is found in many areas, whether it is a current within an electrical circuit that surges back and forth in step with the frequency of a signal coming from the outside or the representation of a normal state of a molecule by a combination of several alternative distinct structures among which the molecule moves. Most importantly, however, resonance is also the mechanism that generations of scientists have taken to be at the base of how the human ear works. From the beginning of the seventeenth century to the early decades of the twentieth, the perception of pitch was thought to ensue from the selective response of certain structures deep inside the cochlea vibrating in phase with the oscillations of the outside air and the fluid filling the inner ear. Reason and resonance, one might say, belong to diametrically opposed realms. The mind and the ear are locked into a relationship of categorical alterity.

Or are they? How is it, for instance, that Diderot, in what appears to be a blatant reversal of the alleged visual bias of Cartesianism and the eighteenth century more broadly, privileged the ear over the eye? Whence the association of self-reflection and consciousness with something one might—in analogy to introspection—call "introaudition"? In some sense, this predilection for strings and resonance was of course the perfect illustration of the haphazard flow of fragmented sensations that Enlightenment thinkers took to be the raw material from which the rational self constructed itself. Such a self resembled, in the words of "Diderot's" interlocutor "d'Alembert" (who was of course none other than the mathematician and coeditor of the *Encyclopédie*, Jean le Rond d'Alembert, who had himself written authoritatively on strings), "a sort of musician who presses his ear against the vibrating strings and who makes judgments about their consonance or their dissonance."[3] In a sense, then, Diderot's "philosopher" is a passive self, one barely held together by the classic tripartite faculties of reason, memory, and imagination, and a distant ancestor, at best, of the post-Kantian self whose "stream of consciousness" William James saw as being controlled by an "innermost centre" or "sanctuary."[4]

But there is also another side to Diderot's lifelong obsession with sympathetic strings. The encyclopedist was not merely reaffirming what had been a well-established model of hearing for well over a century. He claimed that the intimacy between "idea" and "quivering" strings constitutes the very core of the enlightened self. He was, in fact, advancing a line of argument similar to the one I am pursuing in this book—that there existed a moment in Western cultural history when reason and resonance developed in contiguity, along strikingly parallel and hitherto largely unrecognized trajectories, and that these corresponding histories of reason and resonance are both a key element of modern cultural practice and at the heart of modern aurality. My argument proceeds from the assumption that the story most commonly offered about the making of modern rational selves as the progressive silencing of sensation and emotion as inherently incompatible with thought is only half the story. The other, untold half is one of a rich tradition of inquiry—Romanticism and twentieth-century phenomenology being just two of the better-known examples—that refused to let go of the simple fact that truth and knowledge do not exist independently of the way in which they are acquired and that subjectivity is not merely the impure other of objectivity. The acoustic and physiological phenomenon of resonance, I suggest, played a constitutive role in the history of modern aurality and rationality. It was, for all intents and purposes, modernity's second science.

Almost two centuries after Diderot's *Entretien*, another French philosopher, Jacques Derrida, castigated what he called philosophy's phonocentrism, the reduction of language and thought to the "absolute proximity of voice and being, of voice and the meaning of being, of voice and the ideality of meaning."[5] Only a handful of critics have taken Derrida to task for his phonopho-bia.[6] None, however, appear to have queried Derrida's concurrent demotion of the ear as an integral component of what he calls the "indissociable system" of "hearing (understanding)-oneself-speak," and by which "the subject affects itself and is related to itself in the element of ideality."[7]

This is where *Reason and Resonance* seeks to break new ground. The book attempts to chart a terrain in which "understanding" and resonance, hearing and the "meaning of being," physics and philosophy, enter into complex and intimate relationships with each other. But *pace* Derrida, this intimacy does not *eo ipso* negate philosophy's possibility. Nor can the coupling of reason and reso-nance always be subsumed under one principle, be it Diderot's human harpsichord alluded to in the passage from *Entretien* quoted above, the philosopher who "listens to himself," or Derrida's pho-nocentrism. How and why one era celebrates the union between "oscillation" and philosophical "meditation" while another can scarcely hide its deep suspicion of the "self-presence of the cogito, consciousness, subjectivity" made possible by the ear is not a ques-tion of static sensory "regimes" or "epistemologies," be they those of the eye or the ear.[8] And it is not a question of aligning, in his-toricist fashion, certain historical periods with the predominance of one sense over the others, similar to the still widely accepted dichotomy between a premodern, oral/aural era and a modern, visual/literate one. In fact, the unlikely union of reason and reso-nance is the hallmark of the very period that, at least on its own testimony, feared it most: modernity. With a precision rare in cul-tural history, the rise to prominence of philosophy as the "mirror of nature" and the parallel ascent of resonance theories of hearing can be determined as having occurred over a period stretching from 1633 to 1928. It is during those almost three centuries that two fields of knowledge—philosophy and otology (as I will call the study of the ear throughout this book)—were struggling to come to terms with a set of strikingly similar problems concern-ing the foundations of subjectivity, truth, and sensation.

Why 1633? It was in that year that yet another thinker put the finishing touches on a book in which he outlined a scientific rationale for his notorious assertion, publicized a few years later, that mind and body are two rather distinct kinds of things and that the only certainty a person can have of his or her existence derives not from sensing his or her body, but from the ability to reason. The thinker was none other than René Descartes, and the work in question his posthumously published *L'homme* (Treatise on Man). But—strange irony of history—the same work also marks the beginning of a new kind thinking on the physiology of hearing. In a brief section on the ear and in what might be described as the aural equivalent to his groundbreaking work on vision, the philosopher had reversed centuries of speculation during which hearing was understood to involve some form of arithmetic (or, even more mysteriously, humors and vapors) and had formulated the first theory of hearing couched entirely in terms of resonance. Over the course of the next two centuries, this novel concept would be modified and enlarged in two seminal texts: *Traité de l'organe de l'ouïe* (Treatise of the Organ of Hearing), published in 1683 by the anatomist Joseph-Guichard Duverney, and, above all, in Hermann von Helmholtz's towering *Die Lehre von den Tonempfindungen als Grundlage für die Theorie der Musik* (On the Sensations of Tone as a Physiological Basis for the Theory of Music), published in 1863.[9]

What about 1928 then? Descartes', Duverney's, and Helmholtz's resonance theories remained the dominant models for pitch perception until 1928, by which time the Hungarian communications expert and later Nobel Prize laureate Georg von Békésy had published a study on the patterns of vibrations of the basilar membrane, a fibrous plate inside the cochlea that is about 30 millimeters long and 01. to 0.5 millimeters wide and supports the organ of Corti. The key mechanism of pitch perception, Békésy argued there, is not selective resonance, but a traveling, nonresonant wave that affects a much wider area of the basilar membrane and the structures lining it than had been assumed.[10]

Seasoned travelers in the history of philosophy will immediately recognize the broader significance of the year 1928, for it was in 1928 that Martin Heidegger completed his *Sein und Zeit* (Being and Time). Much as Descartes' *L'homme* had set Western epistemology on a course of far-reaching impact, *Sein und Zeit* immediately became recognized as the most devastating attack yet on the Cartesian idea that indubitable knowledge is the only relation worth establishing to being. But this dramatic shift not only entailed a major reinterpretation of virtually every aspect of Western thought, it also called for a rethinking of the relationship between reason and the ear.

These chronological parallels are not meant to reinforce a monolithic concept of modernity. Nor do I have a brief in this book to frame the history of modern aurality in the binary terms of the seemingly defunct "great divide" theory put forth by the Annales school of history or in the work of Marshall McLuhan and Walter Ong.[11] (The latter scholars, it will be recalled, held that historical and cultural differences developed along an axis distinguishing a modern, image-saturated West from the sound-oriented, "tribal" societies of China and Africa.)

As a matter of fact, the "great divide" theory is alive and well.[12] The list of McLuhanesque/Ongian polar opposites can be extended ad libitum, verging on what Jonathan Sterne has aptly called a "litany:" vision is concerned with the exterior, hearing with interiors; vision is about intellect, hearing about affect; vision tends toward objectivity, hearing toward subjectivity; and so on.[13] The problem with the "litany" lies in the sense of totality and inevitably that it imputes to social processes. Or, as Sterne puts it, it "posits history as something that happens *between* the senses. As a culture moves from the dominance of one sense to that of another, it changes. The audiovisual litany renders the history of the senses as a zero-sum game, where the dominance of one sense by necessity leads to the decline of another sense."[14]

The present book adopts a different approach. Thus, on the one hand, it clearly seeks to cast the ear in a more central role on the European historical stage, hoping that such a shift in emphasis would lead to a different image than the prevailing one of modernity as an ocular era. Yet on the other hand, instead of linking the modern crisis to a body believed to have gone dumb and deaf, I also wonder whether it might make more sense to argue quite the opposite: that we listen only too well. In other words, instead of joining in the chorus of those who lament our era's alleged hearing loss only the better to dismiss the modern project all told, what is required is a more dynamic elaboration of the concept of modernity through hearing. The story of modern aurality, hence, is not one of a neatly delineated modern *acousteme*, equivalent to the Foucauldian *episteme*. It is rather one of a more heterogeneous field, a history that unfolds completely outside of the "great divide" and contrary to the static tableaux of "sensory cultures." And so, like the growing number of cultural historians, anthropologists, and cultural theorists who prefer to speak of modernity in the plural (as, for instance, in "alternative modernities"), this book traces the intertwined histories of reason and resonance between 1633 and 1928 as part of a more multistranded, nonteleological history of the modern West. Instead of limiting the space of resonance to that of "prescientific" magic (and thereby assigning to resonance a place in the historical imagination prior to the modern era), I consider resonance as being inextricably woven into the warp and woof of modernity. Likewise, instead of the absolute pivot around which modern philosophy, science, and ideals of selfhood orbit calmly, as the planets orbit forever around the sun, I see reason's autocratic status as the center of all modern virtues as constantly being threatened with implosion.

Not only do the twinned trajectories of reason and resonance clearly disrupt any homogeneous concept of modernity as either ocularcentric or logocentric, they also cast a different light on other binaries, as well. In what follows, I will review several of these, occasionally borrowing a leaf from visual studies' own book: especially from a series of theses and countertheses by, W. J. T. Mitchell, one of the founding figures (and, it seems, increasingly also one of the detractors) of the "pictorial turn" in the humanities.[15] One of Mitchell's concerns is the way in which the perceived opposition between the social and the natural underpins one of visual studies' core tenets—that is, the idea that vision is not a natural, but a socially constructed faculty. The study of visual culture, Mitchell counters, must abandon the mantra that "we see the way we do because we are social animals" and instead focus on how "our social arrangements take the forms they do because we are seeing animals."[16]

While students of visual culture have undeniably tended to give short shrift to the rich history of scientific discovery concerning the eye, Mitchell's call for a "dialogue with visual nature" does not easily translate into the auditory realm.[17] It is especially the concept of nature that needs to be questioned. Quite apart from the risk of locking auditory studies into yet another dichotomy—this time between society and nature—it is precisely "nature" or some other nonsocial entity that has been one of the attributes clinging most tenaciously to the sense of hearing. The equation resonates in Hanns Eisler's and Theodor W. Adorno's sweeping assertion that "ordinary listening, as compared to seeing, is archaic" and that "hearing has not adapted itself to the bourgeois rational and, ultimately, highly industrialized order as readily as the eye."[18]

The evidence presented in this book suggests that nothing could be further from the truth, that the line separating what is said to be natural about the ear from what is said to be social has been constantly shifting, always running alongside and frequently overlapping with other lines of demarcation between different conceptual and metaphorical registers of knowledge. Thus when the eighteenth-century *médecin-philosophe* Claude-Nicolas Le Cat voiced his admiration for the ear's delicate structure and used the analogy of a machine to explain its functioning, he was not claiming that hearing is a social artifact, nor was he solely interested in the ear as nature. Rather, the objective was to define new parameters for understanding one through the other, to foreground, as Jessica Riskin has written of the contemporaneous project of building lifelike machines such as Vaucanson's famous defecating duck, "both the sameness and the incomparability of life and machinery."[19]

To my knowledge, nothing comparable has been attempted in regard to the ear. Despite the recent flurry of studies on "auditory culture," the physical ear has maintained a strangely elusive, incorporeal presence.[20] In their eagerness to save the sonic from modernity's alleged condescension, students of auditory culture have focused almost exclusively on hearing as a metaphorical construct. In so doing, ironically, they have made common cause with the "visualist paradigm" precisely by obscuring behind a barrage of images and metaphors the bodily substance of our capacity for sensory experience.[21] Yet by focusing on the materiality of perception—that is, on such things as air, water, bones, membranes and the like—I do not merely seek to add a physical dimension to the prevailing concept of hearing as a "cultural construct." To talk about hearing in material terms is to acknowledge the fact, as Bruno Latour insists, that the material world always comes to us in cognizable forms.[22] It is to look for a deeper interpenetration of the biological and the cultural and to complicate simple tripartite sender-medium-receiver models that situate seeing or hearing somewhere in the middle between the polar forces of "nature" (or what Mitchell glosses as "genetically determined capacity"), on the one hand, and "society" (or, in Mitchell's phrase, a "programmed set of automatisms"), on the other.[23] But above all, an emphasis on the materiality of perception recognizes the fact that signifier and signified can no longer be kept apart as though there existed signs that are uncontaminated by what they signify. Because the signifier/signified dualism has all but exhausted its epistemological force, it makes sense to conceive of the act of hearing in terms outside of this dichotomy. One way to do this—the way I have chosen in this book—is to foreground the ear's rich physicality, independent of the signs and meanings that the organ may mediate.

17

One of the most important corollaries of the thesis of the social construction of the senses—it, too, to a large extent a thesis formulated by students of visual culture—is the concept that the development of modern forms of sensory perception has been fundamentally shaped by a long history of media technologies. For instance, the way we see today is not only determined by the rapid expansion of photography, film, television, and information technology. The historical boundary at which it makes sense to speak of visual media is also being steadily pushed back, with digital media now being seen as only a preliminary end point of a process the beginnings of which historians trace as far back as the eighteenth century and, in some cases, even the seventeenth.

Auditory studies is fast catching up. Thanks to the "archaeo-logical" efforts of Penelope Gouk, Wolfgang Scherer, Jonathan Sterne, and Siegfried Zielinski, an amazing array of devices and practices has been brought to light, some indeed dating as far back as the seventeenth century.[24] But perhaps auditory studies is catching up too fast. Thus, Sterne has issued what is probably the most historically informed warning to date against fetishizing audio technology. He writes that while it is through techniques of listening that "people harnessed, modified, and shaped their powers of auditory perception in the service of rationality," such techniques (and the technologies on which they are based) were culturally embedded. If the phonograph changed the way we hear, he says, it did so only because many of the "practices, ideas, and constructs associated with sound-reproduction technologies predated the machines themselves."[25] But Sterne's caveat does not go far enough. It excludes from critical scrutiny the condi-tions that must be given for something to become recognized, labeled, and valorized as audible in the first place. Why and how do certain orders of knowledge make some aspects of our audi-tory experience more worthy of attention than others? Under what conditions does it become necessary, socially acceptable, or just generally indispensable to what Lorraine Daston has called a "moral economy of science" to think about auditory perception in technical terms?[26] And when has it been considered to be more productive to foreground hearing's naturalness?

There are several possible answers to such questions discussed in various parts of this book. For instance, in Chapter 7, I argue that prior to tackling the (hitherto undertheorized) issue of rhythmic perception and the concurrent crisis of musical listening during the early part of the twentieth century from the vantage point of audio media such as the phonograph, it might actually make more sense to begin by examining the criteria for what constituted a medium around the turn of the twentieth century in the first place. Not only were such criteria hotly contested, they could also not be reduced to only one set of factors, whether these be cultural or technological. Rather, such criteria were contingent on what was considered as a "problem" of auditory perception. Key to this unorthodox approach is of course the hypothesis that it was not so much media's influence on rhythmic perception that was becoming a problem in the years around 1900, but the clear-cut distinction between subjects and media itself that had become contentious, and the growing significance of rhythm in fields as diverse as sociology, philosophy and psychology was one of the major arenas for this debate.

But we do not have to confine ourselves to the twentieth century to find examples of how the interaction between media and sensation was being thought of in more multilayered terms than those typified by processes of inscription. Equally instructive is Johann Wilhelm Ritter's attempt (discussed in Chapter 5) a century earlier to construct a nascent theory of sign-mediated hearing by linking up various parts of his anatomy with a voltaic battery. Yet although Ritter's self-electrocution may come as close as anything to corroborating the argument of technology's pervasive (and evidently quite painful) impact on how we perceive and think about sensory perception, there was more at stake. Ritter's experiments — to say nothing of his untimely reflections on music — were contingent on one of *Naturphilosophie*'s most important tenets. This was the notion that matter and mind, nature and technology, are interconnected by an invisible chain and that, hence, within this enormous electric circuit, everything is a medium and nothing, except the forever elusive Absolute, is unmediated. Thus, it was clearly not the invention of startling new technologies that was responsible for Ritter's "galvanic" theory of hearing, but the prior erosion of the conceptual opposition between mediation and nonmediation in the wake of the sea change that had occurred in the theory of hearing.

Finally, there is the example of how Johann R. Deimann's and A. Paets von Troostwyk's *Elektrisirmaschine* or "electrification machine" may have led Kant, toward the end of his life, to rethink the interplay of experience and transcendence at work during hearing. As Chapter 4 will show, the new concept of hearing—alongside a new way of thinking about musical works as autonomous—that came to prominence during the last two decades of the eighteenth century was not a consequence of Kantian aesthetics alone. It had every bit to do with the discovery of the connection between nerve endings and moist brain cavities made by the renowned anatomist Samuel Sömmerring, which in turn developed from novelist Wilhelm Heinse's *Sturm und Drang* fixation with all things liquid. Kant may well have had the *Elektrisirmaschine* in mind in trying to combine Sömmerring's quirky metaphysics with a sort of empirically enriched transcendentalism, but this does not mean that Deimann's and Troostwyk's apparatus at its birth actually foretold for the ear a new way of hearing.

There is another dichotomy that needs to be examined here. Even though it is not part of Mitchell's discussion, the notion that modern visual technologies have a pervasive impact on our ability to concentrate and that twentieth-century mass culture is fundamentally a culture of distraction has generated a tremendous amount of comment in film studies, art history, and visual studies generally.[27] The attention-distraction dichotomy has of course an aural equivalent or, rather, two equivalents. There is an anthropological version, according to which attention and distraction are historically invariable and sharply differentiated modes of perception to which we refer whenever we distinguish between listening and hearing. But there is also a critical version that sees the relationship between attentive listening and distracted hearing as having fundamentally been determined by capitalist social relations and the rise of mass cultural consumption. Needless to say, both versions of the attention-distraction theory permeate discourse about what is arguably one of the most important domains of auditory practice, music. Take, for instance, Roland Barthes' famous essay "Listening." Listening, Barthes remarks there, "speaks."[28] By this he means that the act of listening is essentially concerned with extracting meaning from the dispersion and "shimmering" of signifiers. As such, listening is a psychological act, distinguished from hearing, which is a purely physiological phenomenon. Although it was one of Barthes' main preoccupations to overcome the distinction between a language-driven experience operating within the confines of the Saussurian signifier-signified dichotomy and an unmediated, corporeal experience, the fact remains that he lacked the desire or insight to historicize the listening-hearing divide.

This was, without a doubt, the signal achievement of the Frankfurt School theorists.[29] Distraction, Walter Benjamin, Siegfried Kracauer, and Theodor W. Adorno argued, is as much the response that the commodity form of art imposes on audiences alienated from the means of cultural production as it is diametrically opposed to what Adorno would famously call "structural listening." Recent scholarship has followed Critical Theory's lead in enriching our understanding of both sides of the divide. The roots of auditory *Aufmerksamkeit*, or attention, for instance, can now be squarely traced to Kantian transcendental aesthetics and possibly earlier, to the invention of silent, motionless listening protocols during the German and French Enlightenment.[30]

Meanwhile, distraction is beginning to receive more nuanced treatment, no doubt in part as a result of Jonathan Crary's *Suspensions of Perception: Attention, Spectacle, and Modern Culture*.[31] Here Crary focuses on the remarkable parallels between the abrupt shifts in visual perception toward a focused, stationary stance and the rise of a more diffuse, vagrant way of looking prompted by Impressionist art. According to Crary, "modern distraction can only be understood through its reciprocal relation to the rise of attentive norms and practices."[32] Much the same may be argued for hearing. The modern era without question witnessed the massive dissemination of new patterns of sensory consumption marked by distraction and the atrophy of concentrated listening, but this new way of hearing was also the result of efforts to sharpen the ears of modern subjects and to turn them into more finely calibrated and ever-ready receivers of signals and codes. Put another way, the capacity to hear "correctly" in some domains is bound up with a more unfocused stance in other domains, and vice versa. Or, to put it in even more paradoxical terms: Ours is an era of the most accurate mishearing and of the most diffuse hearkening.

Inspired by these texts and the broader trend within the humanities toward sound and "auditory culture," some musicologists are also revisiting the rigid dichotomy between hearing and listening, both interrogating its Adornian roots and exploring a wide array of alternative or, as one pioneering collection of essays calls it, "postmodern modes of hearing."[33] Aside from the fact that here the listening-hearing dichotomy, unwittingly perhaps, slips back into the discussion, the range of listening stances beyond the attention-distraction divide is impressive, running the gamut from, to quote terms from some of the essays' titles, "uncertainty" and "disorientation" to "loss" and to "failure" and "a passion for the violent ineffable." Furthermore, such listening stances do not readily align with the power relations in force at any given time. While the structural listener's uncanny complicity with power has often been noticed, the reverse notion, that alternative modes of hearing might be any less implicated in power relations, does not appear to hold true. More often than not, both structural listening and "postmodern" modes of hearing are shot through with the same logic, whether this be one of control and submission, disruption and pleasure, or all of these at once.

One last dichotomy remains. It, too, is one of the most persistent stereotypes clinging to hearing—the cliché that in contrast to vision, which dwells on surfaces, hearing refers us to the interior. Like some of the other dichotomies mentioned earlier, this cliché has its origin in nineteenth-century ideologies of bourgeois subjectivity and, in the case of musical listening, in Romantic aesthetic theory. Like the other binaries mentioned, the image of the self-referential ear has generated a sizable literature, much of it aimed at uncovering inaudible interior sonic worlds. Obviously, the reader of this book will look in vain for descriptions of such worlds. For similar reasons, which have led Richard Taruskin to point out the limits of authenticity in the "historically informed" performance of early music, I am not after a "period ear."[34] Much as present-day performances of early music can be shown to be the product of a rich layering of meanings that people over time have invested in such music, filtering the past through modern sensibilities offers the historian altogether more attractive venues for exploring the interpenetration of these layers than any attempt to think, as it were, anachronistically. Just as cleansing renderings of Jean-Baptiste Lully's opera *Alceste* of recent additions (such as modern tunings or instrumental timbres) will not deliver the "authentic" listening experience of the seventeenth-century French courtier, we cannot divorce what people heard from the thick layer of speech genres and conventions of communication in and through which listeners report on their elusive inner experience.

And so, commensurate with the larger point of this book, I do not dwell much on how a person's "inner listening" may be socially and culturally conditioned. Instead, I focus on what it is about the ear—its structure, its elemental substances, its functioning— that allows such a person to speak of this experience as pertaining to his or her inner self in the first place. And instead of a history of behaviors tied to the ear or a history of ideas representing such behaviors my account of modern aurality is a history of the "listener function." Giving Foucault's famous concept of the "author function" an aural twist, one might say that the listener is not simply the recipient of an indefinite number of significations that fill his or her hearing, nor does he or she come after the work.[35] Rather, the listener is a function that fixes these meanings with the goal of circumscribing and prescribing the auditory ways in which individuals acknowledge themselves as subjects.

Clearly, the ear troubles some of our most entrenched clichés. Hearing unsettles the modern imaginary, just as modernity haunts the ear. It is connected to the deepest layers of our experience, but it is also articulated to science and reason. It is a physical reality, but it is also a cultural construct. And so, given the ear's fragile, albeit crucial position in the history of modern culture—as unstable as that of reason itself—it ought to come as no surprise that this elusiveness also has infused otology, one of the most fascinating, if severely neglected fields of modern knowledge. Although initially it consisted only of the anatomical study of the ear and until the late nineteenth century did not acquire the current, broader meaning of a branch of medical science that deals with all aspects of the ear and its diseases, modern otology offers fertile ground for studying more than just the growth of positive knowledge *about* the ear. The history of otology, from humble beginnings in the late Italian Renaissance to its coming of age in the late nineteenth and early part of the twentieth centuries, may be impressive (and as such well worth a fuller treatment than I can offer here), but it is not a heroic narrative of reason's triumph over myth, empirical observation over metaphysical speculation.[36] It is also closely intertwined with a slightly different narrative in which the focus is not on the ear as an object, but in which the ear figures as a form of embodied knowledge, as something we think *with*.

The reader will get a taste of this approach by glancing at the cast of characters peopling my account. For instance, most of the thinkers and texts being dealt with are situated well outside of the core territory that most historians of otology have mapped out. Many of these historical figures are also decidedly different moments in modern history, have been keeping each other company in ways that go beyond doctors' alleged superior musical sensibilities, such as when early modern gentlemen scholars used music to "naturalize" the marvelous, when possession of acoustic and musical knowledge became a mark of social distinction for members of Germany's educated elite, or when mid-nineteenth-century savants gathered in choral societies in an effort at furthering sociability, national identity, and, ironically, in the spirit of their seventeenth-century predecessors, at depersonalizing scientific practice by getting to know each other.[38]

Rather, I argue, what the work of the thinkers, scientists, novelists, pamphleteers, and musicians featured in these pages shows is that the road European societies travelled toward ever greater rationalization and modernization did not run in a straight line along ever higher and thicker walls separating the sciences from the arts. Throughout the modern period, scientific thinking and musical sensibilities merged on a higher plane, mutually shaping each other and advancing sophisticated arguments about the foundations of knowledge and personhood. This is why, apart from the detailed discussion of Hermann von Helmholtz in Chapter 6, I did not select Gottfried Herder or Novalis as crown witnesses for the much-quoted Romantic turn toward sound, but their near contemporary, Wilhelm Heinse, who, although largely (and somewhat unjustly) forgotten today, together with Sömmerring formulated one of the late eighteenth century's most ambitious and unabashedly metaphysical theories of hearing. For the same reason it is Le Cat, and not the Abbé de Condillac or the musically gifted, not to say more colorful Jean-Jacques Rousseau, who are the subject of Chapter 3 on Enlightenment otology. Le Cat's evolution from an adherent of Cartesian-style resonance theory into one of its early critics owed less to startling new scientific discoveries than, literally, to a change of heart that was as much inspired by Rousseau's views on morality and sentimentality as they in turn contributed to the emerging culture of sensibility. Or, finally, instead of dwelling on the work of Ernst

Florens Friedrich Chladni, who, in addition to being considered the "father of acoustics," also took a great interest in music and invented a number of musical instruments, I focus in Chapter 5 on Johann Wilhelm Ritter and Johannes Müller. Although the fields in which they excelled—electrochemistry and physiology, respectively—were only loosely interconnected, and both scholars only took a passing interest in music (Ritter is said to have played the piano passably, Müller to have enjoyed listening to his wife, a professional singer), their work is rich with reflections of a musical nature.

In sum, I follow these thinkers' example. Like Le Cat, Heinse, and Ritter, I do not consider art to be exterior to science, a prop that makes you think better. It is science's very essence. And as they did in their works, I see it as the ultimate goal of my book not only to give new vibrancy to a reason believed to have become rigid and unyielding, but also to renew a commitment to the ability of reason to resonate in us and through us.

CHAPTER ONE

The Great Entente:

Anatomy, Rationalism,

and the Quest for Reasonance

Let us follow René Descartes, the first modern philosopher and "founding father of the modernist visualist paradigm," into the depths of his famous thought delirium, otherwise known as *Meditations on First Philosophy*:[1]

> I shall consider that the heavens, the earth, colours, figures, sound, and all other external things, are nought but the illusions and dreams of which this [evil] genius has availed himself in order to lay traps for my credulity; I shall consider myself as having no hands, no eyes, no flesh, no blood, nor any senses, yet falsely believing to possess all these things....
>
> I suppose, then, that all the things that I see are false; I persuade myself that nothing has ever existed of all that my fallacious memory represents to me. I consider that I possess no senses; I imagine that body, figure, extension, movement and place are but the fictions of my mind. What, then, that can be esteemed as true? Perhaps nothing at all, unless that there is nothing in the world that is certain....
>
> That is why I shall now consider anew what I believed myself to be before I embarked upon these last reflections . . . in order that there may be nothing at all left beyond what is absolutely certain and indubitable....
>
> I shall now close my eyes, I shall stop my ears, I shall call away all my senses, I shall even efface from my thoughts all the images of corporeal things, or at least (for that is hardly possible) I shall

esteem them as vain and false; and thus, holding converse only with myself and considering my own nature, I shall try little by little to reach a better knowledge of and a more familiar acquaintanceship with myself.[2]

For generations of readers, this scene of bodily domestication has figured as the urscene of rationalism, coming on the heels of what is perhaps one of the philosopher's most notorious assertions made several years earlier: "je pense, donc je suis," I think, therefore I am. The struggle between soul and body, thought and sensation, reason and unreason staged in the *Meditations*—and, of course, the ultimate triumph of the former over the latter—has come to epitomize the cold, objectifying, ocularcentric and antisensual type of rationality that is said to have dominated Western thought for the last four centuries. But if it is true that seen and heard things for Descartes were but illusions, what sense does it make to invoke the French philosopher at the beginning of a book that does not conceive of modern aurality as having evolved in the shadow of reason, but within a larger context in which the history of reason and the history of the senses often run in parallel? And if the purpose of Descartes' thought experiment was to exclude the senses from the realm of cogito, and if primary qualities such as size, figure, and duration took precedence for the philosopher over secondary ones such as color, flavor, and sound, would a history of modern aurality not have to be framed as a critique of the very hegemony of reason made possible by the philosopher's act of ear closure?

The proposition of this chapter is that the tensions and contradictions of rationalism involved the ear in ways rarely accounted for in the prevailing image today of Descartes as the arch ocularcentrist. The philosopher conceived of the ear's relationship with rational mastery, knowledge, epistemological certainty, and, ultimately, the foundations of modern subjectivity in far more ambiguous terms than a superficial reading of the *Meditations* might suggest. Having stopped his ears did not prevent Descartes from taking great pains in elucidating the properties of sound and from studying the anatomy and physiology of the ear. And even though his interest in the ear never crystallized into a coherent theory, much less a major study along the lines of his groundbreaking optical work *La dioptrique* (1637), Descartes did ponder—if frequently in a rather roundabout manner and, to be sure, always with the broader problem of the mind-body relationship uppermost on his mind—the deeper association of *sum* with *sonus*. In fact, instead of the alleged exclusion of the ear from the search for truth, Descartes' philosophy enacts an uneasy truce between *cogito* and *audio*, a precarious entente between *entendre*, hearing, and *entendre*, understanding. More than a thought experiment, Descartes' nocturnal ruminations can thus be interpreted as a psychosonic exercise, setting off what one might call the philosopher's lifelong (and never quite completed) quest for "reasonance," for the joining together of reason and resonance in a new concept of personhood. In short, the *Meditations* must be decoded sonically, as the first in a series of experiments in self-fashioning that modern egos go through to this day: how to reason and resonate at the same time.

Cutio Ergo Sum

The quest for reasonance begins almost in passing, in a kind of acoustic blind spot. It begins in an enormously influential phrase that Descartes uses in the original Latin version of the passage quoted earlier: *inconcussum*. Although usually translated as "indubitable," *inconcussum* actually means "unshakable." Derived from the root *-cutere* (to shake violently), which itself is based on the Indogermanic *-kwat*, the term *inconcussum* is thus surrounded by a semantic field carrying, apart from the idea of violent motion, specific sonic and even cognitive connotations.[3] Yet, while the philosopher's desire for certainty thus clearly appears to be premised on the absence of sound, the rich etymology of *cutere* and its various ancient derivatives such as *percussio, concussio,* and *discussio* (along with more modern terms like *concuss* or *secousses*) suggest that Descartes was actually grappling with a more complex set of issues. These issues not only cast doubt on the philosopher's hidden claim that the sought-after certainty can only occur in a soundproof space free of the noise of the crackling fire and even that of the philosopher's own breathing, they entangle the philosopher's strategy of securing the ego by means of reasoning in a web of uncanny affinities with the very phenomenon of *-cutere* the strategy is meant to negate.

To disentangle this web of affinities it is useful to examine more closely the central place of the violent, "shaking" aspect of sound in the acoustic imagination of the sixteenth and seventeenth centuries. Terms such as *ictus*, *impulsio*, *percutere*, and *concutere* recur with remarkable frequency in three partly overlapping fields of inquiry: the aerial transmission of sound, the relationship between the frequency of vibration and pitch, and the theory of consonance and resonance.[4] To begin with the propagation of sound through air, until well into the sixteenth century, opinions were sharply divided over what exactly air is. During the Renaissance, for instance, the modern view that air is an amalgamation of various gases—plain matter, in other words—and that the propagation of sound is through this mix, was anything but commonly accepted. While there had been in place since antiquity the notion that air is matter and that as such air is a key ingredient in the phenomenon of sound, there were also those, such as the Florentine savant, translator of Plato, and music theorist Marsilio Ficino (1433–1499), who wove together Neoplatonism and medical pneumatology into a theory of musical magic in which sound was said to stem from the movement of a force that is at once spiritual and material.[5]

There was even less unanimity about how air moves. Two main strands of thought can be distinguished here, both inherited from antiquity and both influential until well into the early seventeenth century. The first consisted in the notion first put forth by Aristotle (as reported by the medieval theorist Boethius) that the propagation of sound is the result of a succession of condensations and rarefactions. The concept was adopted and enlarged by the Stoics, who argued that this succession occurs spherically, like waves on water spreading in concentric circles. The second strand, too, dates back to ancient Greek philosophy, to Plato and the atomists. Yet in contrast to Aristotle and his medieval interpreters, here, sound was not thought to be propagated in a wavelike motion of air, but as a stream of particles of air or even special atoms projected from the sounding body.

Ultimately, though, the differences between these competing views had little bearing on the question how the movement of air might be related to the perception of sound. In fact, it is precisely this absence of difference that throws the contrast between various strands of Aristotelian and Scholastic thought and Descartes' new acoustics into sharp relief. Take, for instance, the controversy that raged during the 1640s in Utrecht over the alleged anti-Christian implications of Descartes' philosophy and that pitted the French philosopher and his ally Henricus Regius against the theologian Gisbertus Voetius and his pupil Martin Schoock. Several years before the dispute took an increasingly acrimonious turn, the latter had published a work, *De Natura Soni, & Echus* (On the Nature of Sound and of the Echo), in which he distanced himself from the Peripatetics and, on a superficial reading, even adopted a mechanist view of auditory perception.[6] Sound, according to Schoock, is not a "sensible quality" (*qualitas sensibilis*), separate from the mechanical process of aerial transmission. If sound were a quality, then it would differ from the movement of the bodies themselves, and air in motion would be one thing and sound another. So what is the purpose of this quality, "as if air, when it is moved and prompted in a certain way, does not already itself move the eardrum?" What else is there to say about sound but that it is "air in motion itself" (*sonus sit ipse aër motus*), or rather, "repercussed air" (*repercussus*), that is perceived by the soul?[7]

Schoock's critique did not dispense with qualities entirely, though. If such qualities do not inhere in the material objects themselves, he wondered might there at least exist the theoretical possibility that they are produced by the motion of air? This,

33

Schoock declares, has to be denied. To his ears, the perception of sound was instantaneous; because the sound of a cannon is heard the moment it is fired, "who would say that sound, as a quality, is produced by a motion and fraction of the air when it has already been heard?"[8]

For Descartes, such a position was unacceptable. Although the philosopher does accept qualities and in his *Le monde* (The World) defines sound as a "certain vibration of the air striking our ears [*tremblement d'air qui vient frapper nos oreilles*]," such qualities reside entirely in the mind of the perceiver. What is more, such qualities also are not the result of a relationship of unmediated resonance between air and soul and therefore bear not the slightest resemblance to the physical force causing them. "A man opens his mouth, moves his tongue, and breathes out: I see nothing in all of these actions which is in any way similar to the idea of the sound that they cause us to imagine."[9]

Another area in which little consensus had been reached was the nature of musical pitch, with ancient concepts founded in arithmetic rather than physics enjoying widespread popularity until well into the seventeenth century and beyond. Ever since Pythagoras (ca. 570–497 B.C.), pitch had been determined by establishing the ratios of musical intervals in relation to the length of a string on a monochord. An interval was deemed most consonant when the number of divisions of the string necessary to obtain the consonance could be expressed by a "simple," inverted proportion. An octave, for instance, was considered the most consonant interval for the simple reason that it is produced by dividing the string into two halves, which gives a ratio of 2:1. A fifth, accordingly, corresponds to a ratio of 3:2, and a fourth to one of 4:3. By contrast, intervals such as the second or major third are obtained by dividing the string according to ratios of 5:4 and 9:8, respectively, and were therefore considered dissonances.

By the second half of the sixteenth century, the conception, as one anonymous ninth-century tract had put it, that music was "born of mother arithmetic" increasingly came to be regarded with suspicion.[10] One of the first attempts to link pitch to frequency was Girolamo Fracastoro's explanation of resonance in his *De sympathia et antipathia rerum* (Of the Sympathy and Antipathy between Things) of 1546. Pitch, the Veronese physician (and inventor of the term "syphilis") argued, depends on the frequency of impulses (*impulsiones*) transmitted through the air. Because air is "matter that is dense in itself," its forceful compression through a blow (*ictus*) results in the condensation (*addensatio*) where previously there had been rarefaction (*rarefactio*), the series of alternating condensations and rarefactions producing a wavelike motion (*more undarum*).[11]

It would take centuries before Fracastoro's assertion could be validated empirically. Though unproven the theory of condensation and rarefaction nevertheless signaled the possibility of a major reversal of Pythagorean dogma, paving the way for a new type of empirical inquiry into pitch in which the physics of vibrating bodies merged with the study of the perception of consonance and dissonance on the basis of coinciding pulses. Furthermore, as Hendrik F. Cohen has shown in his classic study *Quantifying Music*, the first serious attempts at defining consonance through coincidence were made at the same time as Descartes was elaborating his new epistemology.[12] Over a period of less than three decades, natural philosophers such as Johannes Kepler, Vicenzo Galilei, and above all, Galileo Galilei and Marin Mersenne, had all linked consonance to the observation that the ear judges those intervals to be the most consonant in which the pulses of air produced by two strings coincide most frequently. If a string of a certain length is plucked, Galileo Galilei, for instance, reasoned at the end of the First Day of his seminal *Discorsi* (1638), it regularly pulsates back and forth perpendicular to its axis, thus displacing — or "percussing," as he and other scholars preferred to call it — the surrounding air.[13] But since the frequency of these pulsating movements determines pitch, it follows that strings of varying lengths, tension, and thickness also "percuss" the air at different frequencies and, consequently, yield different pitches. When two strings of the same pitch (which is called "unison") are sounded together, their "percussions" obviously coincide at the same time, which is the beginning and end point of each complete swing. By contrast, when strings of different pitches are sounded together, their "percussions" coincide only in an inverse proportion to the respective length of the string. For example, if two strings are tuned an octave apart, the higher string will vibrate twice as fast as the lower string and therefore will have completed its first complete swing while the lower string has completed only half of its swing. Differently put, the pulses of two strings tuned an octave apart coincide every second pulse; in a fifth, they coincide after the higher string has completed three swings and the lower one two, and so on. Consequently, the pleasure we experience in hearing an octave is a function of the greater coincidence of "percussions," and the experience of dissonance in turn is a function of the greater scarcity of such coincidence.

Needless to say, sympathetic resonance is the key to this "coincidence theory," as Cohen labels all these findings. The observation that a plucked string is able to set in motion another string nearby tuned to the same pitch or a fifth higher was proof that the perception of consonance is based in "percussions." Of course, numerous inconsistencies remained, and opinions continued to be divided on such fundamental issues as the propagation of sound through air. Descartes' early mentor, the Dutch scholar Isaac Beeckman, for instance, argued that sound is propagated through corpuscles of air moving toward the ear and that pulses, accordingly, are the result of alternating phases of sound and silence. But regardless of these differences, the point is that in the early phase of the Scientific Revolution, a range of key acoustic phenomena was being conceptualized through the rich semantic field surrounding *cutere*. In fact, *cutere* had become one of the era's major scientific buzz words.

And so when Descartes set out to consolidate his *prima philosophia*, it must have been in full awareness of the cardinal role of *cutere* for the revolution underway in European science and letters that he defined thought as the *fundamentum inconcussum* of truth. But it is open to question whether the philosopher was equally sensitive to the conundrum that inevitably follows when taking into account the acoustic dimension of *cutere*. Let us again listen to Descartes "holding converse" only with himself. If there is no sky and no earth, and minds and bodies are "nought but the illusions and dreams," he goes on to wonder in the second meditation, "was I not then likewise persuaded that I did not exist?" Not at all, he says. "Of a surety I myself did exist since I persuaded myself."[14] Thought, clearly, does not occur in its own vibration-free sphere. *Res cogitans* remains tied to the laws of physics by some form of cavity resonance. The space the thinker traverses as he gains "acquaintanceship" with himself by estranging himself from the world reverberates with voices engaged in an inner dialogue, an internal *discussio*, a breaking down of the composite entity called "ego" (here specifically the ego called "Descartes") into a multitude of opposing memories, representations, beliefs, and persuasions. It is this *concussio* of voices inside the "thinking thing" that provides certainty. *Cutio ergo sum*.

The Compendium musicae *and the Limits of Rationalism*

Descartes' dilemma of stabilizing truth by soundproofing thought while simultaneously taking for granted the percussive nature of self-reflection did not start with the *Meditations*, though. It haunted his *prima philosophia* from the outset or, more precisely, from 1618 when the philosopher, barely twenty-two years old, wrote the *Compendium musicae*.[15]

Although it is one of Descartes' least-known works, the *Compendium musicae* is in many ways also one of his most important. Such an assessment may seem surprising, given the treatise's limited and for the most part unfavorable reception. Music scholars, for instance, have always been doubtful about Descartes' debut, writing it off as just another "elegant Renaissance model of a demonstrative musical treatise," saturated, like some of its more celebrated and, to be sure, more voluminous humanist models such as the Renaissance Italian music theorist and composer Gioseffo Zarlino's *Istutioni harmoniche* (1558), with numbers, ratios, and proportions.[16]

Meanwhile, biographers and historians of philosophy, usually without much further elaboration, have almost unanimously dismissed the *Compendium* as a mere footnote in the philosopher's larger trajectory, thus perpetuating a tradition started by Descartes' first biographer, Adrien Baillet, who characterized the work as a "crude piece" (*morceau brute*).[17] In 1619, they tell us, Descartes, received a series of dreams in which he saw the outlines of a "marvelous science," followed by the first full statement of its principles in his first published work, the *Discours de la méthode* of 1637. With the exception of a few letters written in the late 1620s, Descartes never again turned his attention to music, and in fact excluded aesthetics from the purview of *prima philosophia* altogether. As one publication summarizes the debate, the *Compendium* was neither "modern, nor very original, nor of any great musical competence."[18]

Not all scholars, however, share this negative view. Reading anew Descartes' early text, Brigitte van Wymeersch, for instance, has stressed its more consciously Janus-faced, even unabashedly modern character. The *Compendium*, she argues, marks a clear "epistemological rupture."[19] In addition to signaling a dramatic shift in the theory and aesthetics of music all told, the structure and style of reasoning organizing Descartes' account foreshadow the famous dreams of 1619 and even anticipate some of the key propositions of the *Regulae* of 1628 and the *Discours*. Thus, any reader familiar with the ponderous, rambling prose of Zarlino or Robert Fludd, the Elizabethan author of *De musica mundana*, will immediately be struck by Descartes' terse cadences. Not only does the title of the work come straight to the point, stating without further ado music's object — and thus also Descartes' object — to be sound (*huius obiectum est sonus*), the work is also shockingly short. Compared with his predecessors' works, which run into hundreds of pages, Descartes' barely comprises forty.

Also, in contrast with earlier treatises, Descartes does not open his text with the *laus musicae*, the standard rhetorical gesture that had been in vogue throughout the Renaissance and that mostly consisted of an evocation of cosmic harmony or a discussion of how Orpheus had tamed wild beasts with his lyre. Nor does he waste much time citing the works of ancient authors. Apart from one brief mention of Zarlino, no other work is discussed. And, last but not least, the fact that Descartes began the *Compendium* with a discussion of rhythm, rather than pitch, as prescribed by tradition, is perhaps also to be seen as a shrewd move. It enables the philosopher to posit a more direct, quantifiable link between physical cause and bodily effect without having to take a detour via ancient cosmology. In short, method and style *are* the content of the *Compendium*.

The most significant indication by far, however, of the philosopher's radical renunciation of received learning is a paragraph at the very end of the *Compendium* in which Descartes dedicates the work to Isaac Beeckman, under whose supervision many of the acoustic experiments reported in the *Compendium* had taken place. In dedicating the work to Beeckman, Descartes says, he had expressed only "some characteristics of my talent [*ingenij mei lineamenta*]."[20] The phrase has a markedly bold ring. Repudiating Scholastic-style reasoning laboriously winding through endless sequences of *concertatio* and *disputatio*, it kicks off the philosopher's lifelong battle against tradition as the sole authoritative source of knowledge.[21]

The structure of the *Compendium* breaks new ground, as well, fleshing out van Wymeersch's claim that it is the philosopher's first exercise in what are arguably the central methodological tenets of the "marvelous science": intuition and deduction. Descartes' discussion of consonance — which forms part of a longer section called "The Difference of Sounds in Regard to High and Low," which in turn follows the "Preliminaries" (*Praenotanda*) and a section on time — is the perfect illustration of this new approach. Descartes begins by reporting a phenomenon he had himself observed on a lute and that therefore, he insists, was not the product of "mere fancy" (*imaginarium*): the fact that a plucked string will cause a string of the same pitch (and sometimes even of a fifth above) to resonate sympathetically.[22] This, he concludes, proves a more general point: "Each string includes all strings that are shorter than itself, but not longer ones. Each pitch contains, therefore, all higher pitches; but lower pitches are not contained in a high pitch. It is therefore clear that the higher pitch of a consonance must be found by division of the lower one."[23]

Although it is ultimately meant to confirm the Pythagorean mathematical proportions, the simple observation of the sympathetic resonance of strings here signals a remarkable break with past scholarship. Using the "characteristics" of his *ingenius*, Descartes proceeds from the "intuition" of what he took to be simple, observable facts to statements about ever more complex phenomena.

The originality of this sort of reasoning becomes even more apparent in the next paragraph. Here Descartes, in the first of two divisions, divides a string into six consecutive, equal divisions in order to establish the octave, fifth, fourth, major and minor third as consonances, just as they had been recognized by Pythagorean tradition. But in contrast to his predecessors, Descartes limits his division of the monochord to six on notably different grounds. Whereas for Zarlino, for instance, the number six, or *senario*, as he called it, carried metaphysical value, because there were six planets, six days of the Creation, and so forth, Descartes refused to consider further divisions—which would have yielded the major and minor second—"because the ear's imbecility [*imbecilitas*] prevents it from distinguishing greater differences of pitch without effort."[24] In short, it was by turning Pythagoras on his ear, by combining the sensory experience of sound with arithmetical reasoning, that Descartes determined consonance, not by invoking a symbolic or metaphysical foundation.

Of course, Descartes' division is not free of inconsistencies, the most glaring perhaps being the ambiguous terminology used to describe what is "easiest for the ear to perceive."[25] In the original Latin text, the sympathetically vibrating higher strings are said to tremble (*tremunt*) and, like the octave produced on an overblown flute, to be the result of resonance (*resonare*).[26] Yet if one adds to this the term *concutiet* ("will set in vibration," that is, *concutere*) that the philosopher uses to describe the same phenomenon several pages later, one not only sees how the same words are invoked to explain two quite different phenomena (overtones and resonance), but more importantly, one begins to sense the perilous instability inherent in the "epistemological rupture" invoked by van Wymeersch.[27]

The same reservations apply to an alternative or secondary division that Descartes proposes in order to accommodate the ambiguous status of thirds and fourths in early modern musical practice (figure 1.1). Although a fourth was generally felt to be less pleasant than a major third (4:5), it was considered a more perfect consonance because of its simpler ratio of 4:3. In a move that many musicologists consider to be the only redeeming aspect of an otherwise old-fashioned treatise, Descartes here attempted to reconcile the two perspectives by introducing an altogether novel distinction between consonances that are generated "directly" and those that are generated "by accident." The "direct" consonances, or consonances "per se," are obtained by further subdividing previously generated divisions of the string, and not by dividing the entire string into equal sections. By contrast, consonances "by accident" are those that originate solely as a "residue," according to the principle that, as Descartes puts

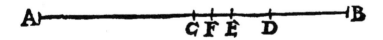

Figure 1.1. René Descartes, "Secondary Division," *Compendium musicae*.

it, "a sound which is consonant with one tone of an octave must also be consonant with another."[28] More particularly, when the segment of a string (AB) that is divided to obtain an octave (CB) is subdivided further into two equal segments (CD and DB) the consonance that results between the first division (AC) and the second (AD) is a fifth—a consonance "per se." The remaining segment (DB) between the second division and the octave is a consonance "by accident."

On a superficial view, this "secondary" method of determining consonances, quite apart from several factual errors, might easily be dismissed as Scholasticism—Descartes even goes as far as reviving the old Pythagorean notion of "sonorous number." At the same time, the discussion of thirds and fourths allows sound to become subject to a discourse that owes its cohesion only to itself, rather than to a place within an immense network of numerical correspondences.

In another noteworthy attempt to highlight the *Compendium*'s modernity, Jairo Moreno has invoked Michel Foucault's episteme of representation to support a reading that stresses Descartes' use of hearing to figure a new subject-object relationship.[29] Going over a slightly different range of passages than van Wymeersch, Moreno claims that the objective of the *Compendium* is not to determine the nature of sound per se, but to outline a new method for the construction of a different type of ego. The work is therefore less a treatise *more musico* than a user's guide for listeners striving to become modern subjects. There are numerous examples of this will to representation, as we may call it. One of the most striking is Descartes' beginning with a discussion of meter and rhythm, as mentioned earlier, adroitly using it as a rhetorical device designed to buttress the author's claim to intellectual independence.

> This division is indicated by the bar or measure, as it is called, to aid our imagination, so that we can more easily apprehend all the parts of a composition and enjoy the proportions which must

prevail therein. This proportion is often stressed so strongly among the components of a composition that it aids our understanding to such an extent that while hearing the end of one time unit, we still remember what occurred at the beginning and during the remainder of the composition. This happens when the entire melody consists of 8 or 16 or 32 or 64 units, etc., i.e., all divisions result from a 1:2 proportion. For then we hear the first two units as one, then we add a third unit to the first two, so that the proportion is 1:3; on hearing unit 4, we connect it with the third, so that we apprehend them together; then we connect the first two with the last two, so that we grasp those four as a unit; and so our imagination proceeds to the end, when the whole melody is finally understood as the sum of many equal parts.[30]

For Moreno, Descartes here is subtly shifting the emphasis of musical theory away from the object perceived to the perceiver. Yet far from being crude subjectivism or a sign of the growing inwardness of late Renaissance listening practices, the synthesis that takes place in the imagination of the listener between the different sense impressions is essential to Descartes' larger project of reconfiguring the relationship between subject and object and, indeed, to the very way philosophy thinks its other. What matters to Descartes is not the nature of the perceived object per se, but the epistemological foundation of truth.

There is of course no denying the fact that the dissolution during the late Renaissance of what Foucault called the "uniform layer in which the seen and the read, the visible and the sayable criss-cross endlessly" also had parallels in the acoustic realm, opening a space for a subjectivity that defines itself not in contiguity with, but in opposition to a world of sounds.[31] Yet van Wymeersch's and Moreno's readings work only if one accepts a priori dichotomies such as those between "modern" and "premodern," "reason" and "unreason," and "physical" and "metaphysical." In fact, one might perceive in such readings a distant echo of Foucault's famous interpretation of Descartes' *Meditations* as a silencing of madness. The argument that Foucault put forth in his *History of Madness* is, in a nutshell, that the purpose of Descartes' thought experiment was to draw a sharp distinction between errors and dreams, on the one hand, and madness, on the other. Whereas the former are still based on truth as their condition of possibility, madness does not grant reason the same privilege, "for madness is precisely a condition of impossibility for thought."[32]

As is well known, Jacques Derrida subjected Foucault's argument to a scathing critique in which he highlights two major points of disagreement.[33] First, unlike Foucault, Derrida sees no principal difference between madness, dreams, and ideas derived from sensory perception; all are excluded from the realm of truth because they offer insufficient ground for asserting the existence of a reality exterior to consciousness. The inner voice that excludes madness from the field of reason therefore raises a "feigned objection," one that Descartes merely "echoes" by insisting that he is no less mad than "you," that is, the hypothetical interlocutor, the "other" inner voice of feigned objection, or just simply the reader.[34] For Derrida, then, there is no principle difference between Descartes' "internment" of madness by reason and Foucault's "reappropriation of negativity": "To all appearances, it is reason that he interns, but, like Descartes, he chooses the reason of yesterday as his target and not the possibility of meaning in general." In short, Foucault's book is, quite simply, "a Cartesian gesture for the twentieth century."[35]

The second area in which Derrida differs from Foucault concerns the project of a history of madness as a rational endeavor. This, Derrida contends, is an impossible project because the crises of reason are always in complicity with the crisis we call "madness." Philosophy is no less hyperbolic and audacious than madness itself. Not tied to any historical moment, such as the division emerging in the "classical age" between reason and unreason, philosophy's fundamental gesture of gaining a point of certainty by simultaneously thinking and escaping the totality of being is the condition of all histories, no less than of philosophy, and

44

shares this gesture with madness's questioning of what exists.[36]

If method and reason do in fact dominate the *Compendium*, and if the ensuing certainty, accordingly, is seen to reside in a separation of the perceived object from the perceiver, what is being silenced and interned by Descartes? Conversely, what is it that becomes just another case of thought? In short, what about "reasonance?" At this point of my discussion of the *Compendium*, it will come as no surprise that the work is indeed littered with remarks in which Descartes repeats the quintessential gesture of exclusion of the material and irrational that also structures the *Meditations*. Thus Descartes gives us little reason to assume that he saw perception as anything more than a bodily reflex. For the philosopher, auditory perception, in particular, bears the mark of delusion, error, even madness (*imbecilitas*). In the opening paragraph, for example, after having specified music's object (sound), end (to delight and move), and means (pitch and duration), Descartes declares that the quality of sounds and the natural cause of aural pleasure are "the domain of physicists." Yet in the paragraph immediately following this gesture of exclusion, Descartes seems to make an important exception for the human voice. Echoing a remark in Girolamo Fracastoro's *De sympathia*, he writes:

> The human voice seems most pleasing to us because it is most directly attuned to our souls. By the same token, the voice of a close friend is more agreeable than the voice of an enemy because of sympathy or antipathy of feelings — just as it is said that a sheep-skin stretched over a drum will not give forth any sound when struck if a wolf's hide on another drum is sounding at the same time [*lupina in alio tympano resonante*].[37]

At the end of the *Compendium*, in the dedication to Isaac Beeckman cited earlier, Descartes returns to this theme of friendship. Again, instead of excluding the sensuous, sympathetic and, hence, irrational qualities of sound, here, friendship and sympathy seem to frame reason, even embrace it. "I see land and hurry ashore [*terram video festino ad littus*].... I permit this immature offspring of my mind to reach you although it is as uncouth as a new-born baby bear, to serve as a token of our friendship and as unmistakable proof of my love for you."[38]

Descartes scholarship tends to be notoriously selective, marginalizing those facets of the philosopher's work that do not fit the neat image of masterful clarity that posterity has crafted of it. That is why most commentators have either ignored the passages above or, like the editors of Descartes' *Oeuvres*, dismissed them as "strange."[39] Yet there is also more to these passages. Their logic is the logic of resonance—the same logic, in other words, that enabled Descartes to reason his way toward a modern concept of consonance as rooted in the coincidence of "percussions." We thus cannot totally exclude the possibility that by positioning these remarks at the beginning and end of the work, Descartes may actually have intended them to play a more prominent role in the overall textual design. It is as though these passages were meant to enclose the *Compendium*'s rational core in friendship, sympathy, and resonance. Hence, it is not rational discourse that surrounds, confines, or contains its other. Rather, in a logic not dissimilar to philosophy more broadly, rational discourse is incorporated into resonance. For what is philosophy, other than, literally, friendship and intimacy: a resonant, amorous relationship between the subject and the truth?

At the same time, Descartes' injunction that Beeckman refrain from publishing the book—which follows the passage cited—gives additional salience to the lesson of the *Compendium*. The work is more conversation than book. Its traces of inscription are accidental and exterior to it. That is why the phrase "terram video festino ad littus," which Descartes most likely took from Erasmus's *Adagia*, does not so much point to Descartes' personal circumstances at the time of his writing as it grounds the text in an order in which friendship relates to knowledge as land relates to the open sea.[40] Love and reason do not exclude each other, nor does one intern or silence the other, as Foucault believed reason to silence its other. Rather, the boundary between reason

46

and unreason is forever fluctuating, like the tides. The ultimate lesson of the *Compendium* might thus be said to be of a maritime kind: It names the perils of being adrift on the sea we call truth, of reasoning without resonating.

"Tympan"

Derrida's relationship with the ear was of an intricate, even obsessive quality. Recall, for instance, the intellectual energy that Descartes' twentieth-century nemesis mustered in *Of Grammatology* toward upsetting the proximity of ear and logos by foregrounding writing and *différance*. Or consider his project of an otobiography; the somewhat less well known encounter with the hermeneutics of Gadamer; the discussion of Hegel, aurality, and bells in *Glas* or the early essay "Tympan"—all of which reveal an intense preoccupation with hearing and, at the same time, a profound distrust of a metaphysics of the "third ear."[41] In the last mentioned text, for instance, Derrida argues that the position of the tympanum at the border between the ear canal and the labyrinth is emblematic of philosophy's effort to "think its other."[42] Because the eardrum "equalizes" the inner and outer pressure of air, it becomes the chief organ of proximity, of "absolute properness." It controls the difference between what is proper to oneself and what is the realm of the other. In this way, one might say, the ear assumes two roles crucial for projects of self-constitution. It helps the self to recognize the other in terms known to the self and thereby constitutes philosophy's principal means for the "metaphysics of presence," its entente with its outside. But by the same token, the ear also excludes the possibility of the self knowing what remains irredeemably alien to its own terms, the true other that forever remains outside. To hear another is therefore to always hear oneself.

Hence, a philosophy that refuses to ground itself in the inherent self-referentiality of the ear can mark a margin for itself only if it avoids frontal opposition between itself and the other. But such a philosophy must not just be oblique, like the eardrum. Like

Nietzsche's project of philosophizing with a hammer, it must also shatter philosophers' ears. It must pierce the tympanum, unbalance the pressure on either side of the membrane, and open itself up to tympan, to writing. Deconstruction, in other words, has to be resonance-proof.

Derrida's analysis is marked by a surprising (for a meticulous thinker as Derrida at any rate) anatomical blunder. Strictly speaking, the eardrum is incapable of equalizing inner and outer pressure. This is the role of the Eustachian tube, which connects the labyrinth and the mouth cavity. Derrida's lapse is all the more surprising, since he also invokes a variety of more conventional metaphors to argue his case, metaphors we have previously encountered in the context of the discussion of *concutere*: "The *proprius* presupposed in all discourses on economy, sexuality, language, semantics, rhetoric, etc., repercusses its absolute limit only in sonorous representation.... A quasi-organizing role is granted, therefore, to the motif of sonic vibration (the Hegelian *Erzittern*) as to the motif of the proximity of the meaning of Being in speech."[43]

If we permit ourselves to understand this passage as implying that vibration is indeed at the heart of the metaphysics of presence and that some form of resonance links the exterior to the inner ear, then the tympan constitutes a far more porous, unstable border than Derrida seems to admit. Its limit is less absolute, and reason is linked to the vast landscape of madness, emotion, dreams, and errors in myriad ways.

Beyond Derrida's contradictory stance on the eardrum as the control organ of difference and, at the same time, the medium of equalizing resonance, the question is how the tympan becomes "tympan," the emblem of philosophy's arrogance, in the first place. Whence the privileged status of this tiny bit of anatomy? When we say "tympan" to refer to the border between reason and resonance, are we merely invoking a convenient metaphor? Or are we are using a term coined by the sixteenth-century pioneer anatomist Gabriele Falloppio and, in so doing, are we at

48

the same time inserting the discourse about philosophy's other into a history of how the concept of truth began to acquire its specific "tympanic" form? Two interrelated factors contributed to this history: the reconfiguration of the part to the whole and the emergence of a theory of the sign. Both were integral parts of anatomy's rise as the early modern period's master discipline and of the birth of otology at the end of the sixteenth century.

Throughout much of the Middle Ages and well into the early modern period, the body had been seen as just one element, albeit a central one, in a vast cosmic web in which everything was thought to relate to everything else in perfect harmony. The body was a "little world"—a microcosmic replica of the macrocosm.[44] But this relationship between things, human bodies and invisible realms was far from abstract. It was seen in more palpable terms as the ability of each and every element to be affected by and in turn to influence all the other elements by similitude, adjacency, antipathy, and sympathy.

Just as there was no clear-cut division between the body and its environment, inside the body, the same micro-macro relationship obtained. For centuries, learned discourse had followed the doctrine of ancient physician Galen that the body is split into three zones. In that doctrine, a lower zone, comprising the intestines, kidney, spleen, and stomach, was said to serve a nutritive function. It was separated by the diaphragm from a middle zone containing the heart and the lungs, whose function was said to be to vitalize the body. The third zone, finally, separated from the middle zone by the neck, was the head, whose main function was said to be to ensoul the body. As the illustration from Robert Fludd's *Utriusque cosmi* shows (figure 1.2), these zones were not only interconnected through a busy traffic of humors and pneuma, they were also connected to the macrocosm beyond. Thus, the four elements—water, earth, air, and fire—corresponded to the four humors blood, phlegm, black bile, and yellow bile located in the intestinal region, which in turn mirrored the *coelum elementarum.*

49

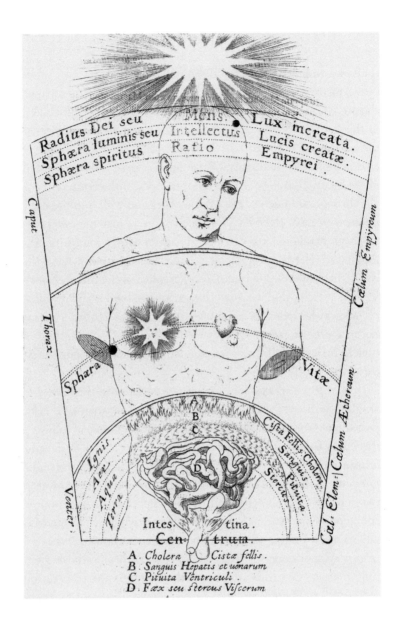

Figure 1.2. Robert Fludd, *Utriusque cosmi majoris scilicet et minoris metaphysica* (courtesy of Harry Ransom Humanities Research Center, University of Texas at Austin).

Not coincidentally, the sense organs also were part of this cosmic metonymy, occupying an indeterminate, liminal position. According to ancient and medieval pneumatological theory, sensory perception was supposed to take place not on the skin, at the borderline demarcating the person and the world, but somewhere less clearly circumscribed, in the interstices of the effluvia being ejected from and moving toward the body.[45] But this to-and-fro also placed the sense organs in an intermediary position with regard to the world beyond, as the association of the ears with Aries and, hence, with masculinity and dryness in Fludd's *Utriusque cosmi* shows. Individual body parts, in other words, take their place in the order of the entire body by dint of a larger meaning extraneous to either.

By the mid-sixteenth century, Galenic anatomy had begun to fall into disrepute. Much of this decline was due to a sudden upsurge in a broad range of cultural practices involving the opening of human bodies. From embalming by evisceration, forensic autopsies, Caesarian sections, and the cult of relics of saints to the dismemberment of executed criminals and the opening up of the wombs of women who had died in childbirth, starting around 1300, Europe was in the throes of a veritable anatomical craze that yielded and was bolstered by a flurry of lavishly illustrated anatomical atlases, books about the "little world," and poetry celebrating the body.

Yet while the sheer quantitative growth of these practices is beyond question, historians differ as to the cultural significance of this shift. Two aspects of the debate are of interest here: the notion that the emergence of dissection marked a radical turning point in the way people acquired a sense of what it meant to know and, ultimately, a major shift in how they made sense of their own selves. What use, for instance, was the new technique of dissection to a medicine traditionally concerned with controlling the patient's regimen and evacuations of blood and other humors, other than to generate a more abstract and hence more modern type of knowledge?[46] Is it mere happenstance that beginning around 1600, dissection seeped into the thesaurus of truth and reason itself, with the phrase "to anatomize" becoming something of a staple in the English lexicon, roughly equivalent in its meaning to our modern verb "to analyze?"

While there can be no doubt that dissection was crucial in giving late medieval to late Renaissance ideas of selfhood and (self-) knowledge an unfamiliar anatomical inflection, recent scholarship has convincingly demonstrated that early modern dissection and anatomy also continued to function within long-standing networks of kinship and family, on the one hand, and power and religion, on the other, and were thus anything but breeding grounds of modern science.[47] The range of emotional responses to postmortems, for example, cannot be easily classified as being indicative of either premodern or modern ways. Well before a throng of onlookers followed Andreas van Wessel's (aka Vesalius) (1514–1564) dissection of an executed woman with a mix of curiosity, stupefaction, and revulsion, there existed during the late Middle Ages a contrast between the deeply engrained notion that a person is her body and what Caroline Walker Bynum calls the "medieval capacity simultaneously to abhor, deny, and delight in bodily partition."[48] As she explains further, it was not what happened to the body physically that determined the emotional response and gave meaning to the process of division. What mattered was the moral standing of the person being dissected, eviscerated, tortured, depicted, or preserved in reliquaries. That is why fragmentation was both horrifying and educative. The severed quarters of a traitor displayed on castle walls, according to the logic of the synecdoche, stood in for the broken integrity of the community in much the same way as devotional representations of Christ's wounds as individual body parts reminded the congregation that each fragment of Christ's body is the whole of God, that *pars* not only stands *pro toto*, but that the part *is* the whole.[49]

On the other hand, Victoria Nelson has taught us what happens when metaphysics is on the wane and is replaced with a world of man-made, soulless machines that can be assembled and disassembled at will.[50] The divine and the spiritual return with a vengeance in grotesque and at times brutal, terrifying form. In medieval times and during the Renaissance, illustrations of individual body parts were, if not wholly unfamiliar, rare, in part because the church looked with disapprobation on the public display of dismembered bodies other than those of criminals. Consequently, medieval and Renaissance anatomical illustrations for the most part showed entire bodies.[51] But by the beginning of the seventeenth century, the body that haunts the mind from which it was severed had turned into one of the era's most persistent themes, one that is perhaps reflected most strikingly in a new role of body parts that operate outside the synecdochic relationship with a whole. It is then that, for the first time, luxation and dismemberment become pervasive tropes, infiltrating the entire order of knowledge. It is from the early seventeenth century onwards that errant body parts such as "petulant" tongues take on lives of their own; that lifeless hands begin to twitch mysteriously during dissection, and that, above all, individuals no longer knew their bodies as so many microcosmic replicas of the macrocosm, but as made of parts similar to another person's remains. Worse, the spectacle of fragmented, monstrous bodies in which the whole is no longer greater than the sum of its parts also tugged at the indivisibility of the soul. If the body could be shown to be composed of so many parts, what was to prevent one from considering that the mind, too, could be split into innumerable pieces? And if the self was so easily dismantled, what else was stable?

Troubling questions, these. The responses they elicited from the seventeenth century onward varied widely, from more conservative, moralizing efforts such as the newly invented literary genre of *blazons*, which reminded readers of the transience of human life, to John Donne's epic poem *Devotions* (1624) and Phineas Fletcher's *The Purple Island* (1633), where coherent bodies are invoked as metaphors for the ideal body politic.[52] At the other end of the spectrum, in period illustrations of individual sense organs, for instance, a different kind of synthesis emerges, one involving a complete rethinking of the status of the particular in the larger order of knowledge. Here, the rationalist project of preserving the integrity of the soul by securing its supremacy over the body begins its triumphal procession by, first and foremost, making the body "contribute, as a material, to the science which is to dominate it."[53] Or so it may seem, judging from the sheer wealth of detail bursting forth from the engravings. Instead of standing in for the hidden secret of things, as the different body organs had traditionally done for the four elements, the four humors, the spheres, or the planets, bones, fibers, membranes, and nerves now signified the opposite: the lifting of all secrets under the unifying gaze of the scientist.

But there is also another dimension to the synthesis being attempted in the new-style anatomies of the late Renaissance and early seventeenth century. As such, this dimension is, in a sense, invisible and has therefore not been subject to the same degree of scrutiny that scholars have applied to the often rich frontispieces, ornate cartouches, spectacularly flayed bodies, and other more conspicuous aspects of early modern anatomical atlases. Amid all the body fragments beckoning the reader to risk another look or two, the stability that the new anatomies strove for rested not so much on the claim that simple things seen from up close are more true than vast phenomena dimly glimpsed from afar. Rather, it was that the concept of the singular as the basis of truth was now synonymous with that of the fact *as* the singular.

All this, as Foucault argued long ago, was determined by a new status of the sign. Because beginning around 1600 signs no longer derived their relationship to the objects from a preset meaning, their only fuction resided in what Foucault called the representation of their representing.

> There will therefore be no theory of signs separate and differing from an analysis of meaning. Yet the system does grant a certain privilege to the former over the latter; since it does not accord that which is signified a nature different from that accorded to the sign,

meaning cannot be anything more than the totality of the signs arranged in their progression; it will be given in the complete *table* of signs. But, on the other hand, the complete network of signs is linked together and articulated according to patterns proper to meaning. The table of the signs will be the *image* of the things. Though the meaning itself is entirely on the side of the sign, its functioning is entirely on the side of that which is signified.[54]

Several examples from early seventeenth-century otological atlases illustrate Foucault's argument well, even as some still represent the body parts in relation to larger entities. In Helkiah Crooke's *Mikrokosmographia* (1601) and Johann Remmelin's *Catoptrum microcosmicum* (1619), for instance, eyes, ear ossicles, and a cochlea float freely in the corners of the page, their truth emerging from an iconography ambiguously blending anatomy and biblical mythology. Another example is Giulio Casseri's *Tabulae anatomicæ LXXIIX, omnes noua nec ante hac visa* (1627), in which a human figure is allegorically depicted amid a bucolic scenery of passing clouds, ruins, and a derelict column emblazoned with an eye, ear, and nose (figure 1.3). Even more radical than these depictions is a plate from the same author's *De vocis auditusque organis historia anatomica* (1601, figure 1.4).[55] Here, the anatomist, in a comparative vista of human and animal ear ossicles, strips the bony structures of any symbolic dimension, rearranging them in such a fashion as to reveal Foucault's "*image* of the things." And, finally, the same binary theory of the sign underpins the plates "de Auditu" and "Figurarum auris explanatio" by Fabrici Acquapendente (1533–1619), both from his seminal *De visione, voce, auditu* (1600, figures 1.5 and 1.6). With its simple list of terms without any elaboration or meaning other than their relation to their referent, *Figurarum auris explanatio* names the parts depicted (and, for that matter, the totality of which they form part, the ear) not on the basis of a meaning anterior to the signs, but on the basis of a meaning that emerges only, to cite Foucault once again, from "the totality of the signs arranged in their progression; it will be given in the complete *table* of signs."[56]

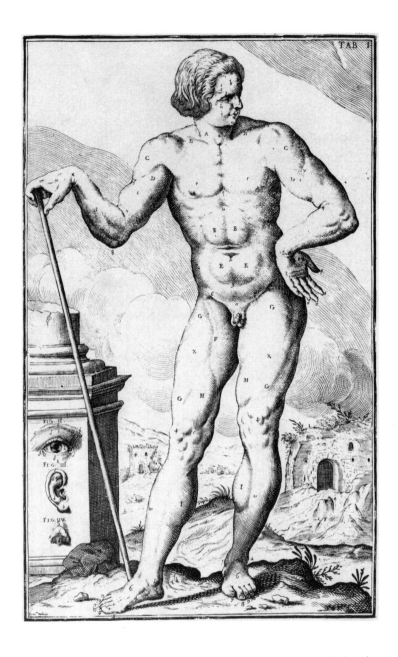

Figure 1.3. Giulio Casseri, *Tabualae anatomicæ LXXIIX, omnes noua nec ante hac visa*, fig. I (courtesy of Thomas Fisher Rare Book Library at the University of Toronto). Casseri's anatomical atlases were among the most well known of their time. Of the ninety-seven plates in *Tabulae anatomicæ LXXIIX* (also known under the variant title *De humani corporis fabrica libri decem*) only a handful are close-ups of individual body parts.

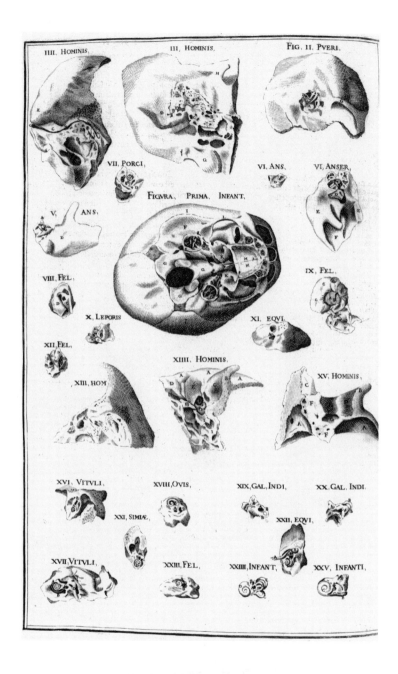

Figure 1.4. Giulio Casseri, Organi Avditvs, *De vocis auditusque organis historia anatomica*, fig. 10 (courtesy of Thomas Fisher Rare Book Library at the University of Toronto). Casseri was probably one of the first comparative anatomists in his field, as is evident in this figure. It was made by an engraver who is said to have lived in Casseri's house.

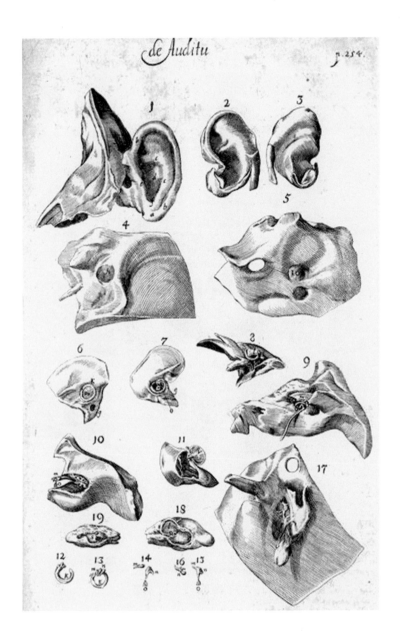

Figure 1.5. Fabrici Acquapendente, *de Auditu* (*De visione, voce, auditu*) (courtesy of Service Interétablissements de Coopération Documentaire des Universités de Strasbourg, Départment du Patrimoine). Aquapendente was one of the first anatomists who departed from the tradition of presenting the body against animated backgrounds and to depict clean, isolated parts.

254 HIERONYMI FABRICII PARS I.

XIX. FIGURARUM AURIS
EXPLANATIO.

Prima Figura auriculam totam integram exhibens.
a. Inferior auriculæ pars λόβος dicta.
b. Auriculæ circumferentia helice dicta.
c. Protuberantia auriculæ, qvam anthelicen dicunt.
d. Concha auriculæ.
e. Hircus ſive tragos, conchæ videlicet adnata eminentia. f. Antitragos.
2. Anteriorem auriculæ faciem excoriatam pingit.
3. Poſterior auriculæ facies excoriata.
4. h. Meatus auditorius in oſſe ſqvamoſo exſculptus.
5. i. Membrana Tympanum dicta.
6. g. Os oblongum pyramidalem figuram exhibens.
i. Tympanum. K. Annulus oſſeus.
7. g. Os Pyramidalem figuram referens.
K. Annulus oſſeus.
l. Cavitas concha dicta. o. Stapes.
8. K. Annulus oſſeus.
l. Cavitas concha dicta. o. Stapes.
9. m. Malleus.
o. Stapes.
10. m. Malleus. n. Incus. o. Stapes.
11. i. Tympanum. m. Malleus. n. Incus.
12. K. Annulus oſſeus.
13. K. Annulus oſſeus.
m. Malleus.
n. Incus.
14. m. Malleus. n. Incus. o. Stapes.
15. m. Malleus. n. Incus. o. Stapes.
16. m. Malleus.
17. r. Muſculus nuper inventus.
18. l. Concha, cavitas.
o. Stapes.
19. s. Protuberantia in media cavitate.

Figure 1.6. Fabrici Acquapendente, *XIX. Figurarum auris explanatio* (*De visione, voce, auditu*) (courtesy of Service Interétablissements de Coopération Documentaire des Universités de Strasbourg, Départment du Patrimoine).

And so the table that seventeenth-century anatomy labored to fill with signs such as "tympanum," "malleus," or "chorda tympani" became the image of the ear solely because the fragmentation and reification of the body in the new anatomy was itself seen as the very epitome of reason. And only because seventeenth-century visual representations of the sense of hearing redefined the broader relationship of the particular to the universal can there be what Foucault called "duplicated representation," a "bond established, inside knowledge, between the *idea of one thing* and *the idea of another*."[57] Last and most significantly, only because the pact between reason and the sign enabled the latter to lay claim to the different parts of the ear, could the tympanum become emblematic of philosophy's effort to think its other.

Resonance against All Odds

If, then, "tympan" is not the privileged signifier of the operation of equilibration we call "philosophy," but the product of the particular and the sign merging into a new style of scientific reasoning, Derrida's denunciation of the ear as the central organ of the metaphysics of presence must be revisited in the light of sixteenth-century theories of hearing.

The development of these theories—and especially the place of Descartes' otology within them—proceeded along three axes: theories of the conductive mechanism in the middle ear, the concept of "air implantatus," and, most importantly, the physiology of auditory resonance. Its basic outlines having been in place since Galen, the anatomy of the middle ear had been consolidated by the second half of the sixteenth century. To name but the most significant figures and their discoveries, more detailed knowledge of the middle ear (and the origin of many of the names connected with its parts such as "malleus") started with Vesalius. His contemporary and founder of the Italian school of anatomy, Gabriele Falloppio (1523–1562), also counts as a pioneer of otology due to a whole series of discoveries, the first description of the cochlea and the discovery of the aqueduct (the bony passage in the temporal bone through which the facial nerve passes) now named after him, being just two of the more important ones. Falloppio also coined the term "tympan," which, tellingly, he labeled the *tertium comparationis*, that is, as the common link enabling us to see the signifier in the signified. Meanwhile, Bartolomeo Eustachio (1510–1574), in many ways Falloppio's equal in the scope of discoveries made, provided the first detailed descriptions of such important components as the tensor tympani (a muscle attached to the hammer that increases tension on the eardrum in response to intense sound), the membranous labyrinth, and the tube linking the middle ear to the throat named, after him, the Eustachian tube. Falloppio's student Volcher Coiter (1534–??) in turn published the first monograph on the ear, *De auditus instrumento* (1573) and must therefore be credited with having established otology as an independent field of study.[58] Two other noted otologists we encountered earlier are Fabrici Acquapendente, a student of Falloppio's, and, bringing the golden era of Italian anatomy to a close, Giulio Casseri (ca. 1552–1612).[59]

The history of the concept of the air implantatus is much more protracted. Known since the pre-Socratics, the air implantatus was thought to fill the entire middle and inner ear. Its origin, Plato held for instance, was in the uterus, and its substance was said to be of a more ethereal kind, different from ordinary air and more akin to the *pneuma* blowing through the universe. Doubts about this special quality of the air implantatus were first voiced by Coiter, who argued that because of its direct communication via the Eustachian tube with the outside air, the air implantatus must be just plain air after all, ill-suited for the pneumatic, Platonic qualities attributed to it. Still, even when stripped of its metaphysical connotations and despite some minor objections put forth by Günther Schelhammer (1649–1712), the air implantatus retained its role in accounts of audition as the single most important agent of sound transmission until the discovery of the endolymph by Domenico Cotugno in 1760.

Early modern otologists for the most part conceived of the

mediating role of the air implantatus in mechanical terms, as a form of action and reaction, combined with the transmission of Aristotelian "forms," "species," or "images." Coiter's description of the process proved particularly influential in this regard and must be quoted here in full:

> To have a sensation of anything, there must be a mutual action and being affected (actio et passio) between the sentient thing and the thing sensed, and for this there must be mutual agreement between the two. Whence it follows that when the external air acts, the internal or implanted air (air internus sive implantatus) is affected, the internal air receiving the alteration of the external air and being moved in the same way from outside. But this does not happen immediately, but through the interposition of the membrane and of certain ossicles wonderfully designed by nature, as follows. The external air affected by the quality of sound meets the myringa membrane, the pulsating myrinx moves the ossicles attached to it, these in turn strike a certain nerve [the chorda tympani] extended across the membrane, and this nerve or cord then rebounds against the membrane. From this the enclosed air receives the alteration and the sounds, but the sound is carried through the twisting and turning windings [the labyrinth and cochlea] of the ears without any disturbance, and reaches the auditory nerve. By means of this passage and agency, the image of the sound (strepitus imago) is at last transmitted to the seat of sensation (principium sentiendi).[60]

Here Coiter clearly excludes resonance as a factor, assuming like many scientists after him that the cochlea prevents echoes by absorbing surplus sound.

Descartes most likely did not possess first-hand knowledge of these works, even though he frequently refered to Fabrici's other writings in a section of L'homme dealing with the formation of the fetus. But he was familiar with Institutiones anatomicae, a compendium of anatomy compiled from numerous sources, including Coiter's work, by Gaspard Bauhin (1560–1624), Fabrici's student and a professor of anatomy at Basle University.[61] Descartes not

Figure 1.7. René Descartes, *Excerpta anatomica*. During his extensive anatomical studies Descartes made a series of sketches, copies of which were later made by Leibniz and
published under the posthumous title *Excerpta anatomica*. The sketch shown here is of
the cochlea.

only quotes extensively from Bauhin's work, there is also in his
Excerpta anatomica a half-page description of the ear, accompanied by several rather crude drawings of the cochlea and the
ossicle attached to the cochlea called "stapes" (figure 1.7).[62] Yet
while the philosopher was thus clearly aware of the existence of
the cochlea, the description he gives of the inner ear in *L'homme*
omits this vital organ entirely.

> As to the filaments [*filets*] that serve as a sense organ of hearing,
> they need not be as thin as the preceding [of the nose]. It suffices
> instead to suppose: [A] that they are so arranged at the back of the
> ear cavities that they can be easily moved, together and in the same
> manner, by the little blows [*secousses*] with which the outside air
> pushes a certain very thin membrane [the tympanum] stretched
> at the entrance to these cavities; and [B] that they [these filaments]
> cannot be touched by any other object than by the air that is under
> this membrane. For it will be these little blows which, passing to
> the brain through the intermediation of these nerves, will cause the
> soul to conceive the idea of sound.[63]

How does one reconcile this description with Bauhin's far more
detailed account? And why does the philosopher here seem to fall
behind his considerably more advanced otological knowledge as

63

revealed in his *Excerpta*? As a closer look at the passage reveals, there is something more original and potentially more far-reaching in this text, despite its awkward prose and weak empirical base. First, Descartes structures his argument in complete neglect of the logic of the *pneuma* or any other idea from the Galenic tradition. Second, the argument also does away, in one bold stroke, with the Renaissance *episteme* of semblance and the logic of representation. The tympanum, again, is the site for this remarkable shift. Note, for instance, that unlike Falloppio, Descartes does not seem to think of the eardrum as a *tertium comparationis*. Nor does his concept of the tympan appear to be part of a theory of the sign in which the relationship between signifier and signified is anchored in an abstract, arbitrary correlation between two entirely unrelated fields. Instead, the eardrum remains unnamed, unmarked. "Stretched" and receiving the *secousses* of outside air, it is incapable of any action of its own. There is no equalization or correspondence of any kind between the actions of the air outside and the air inside that is mediated by the eardrum.

Finally and most importantly, the absence of the cochlea is less a sign of ignorance on the philosopher's part than it serves to buttress Descartes' larger project of reconciling resonance with reason. As a reader of Bauhin's works, Descartes must have come across the latter's highly idiosyncratic, not to say incongruous views on the physiology of hearing. Thus, in his *Theatrum anatomicum*, the Basle professor had claimed that the tympanic cavity functions like a resonator. Because the cavity contains openings of different shapes and sizes, resonance is selective: Lower tones are received in the larger spaces, higher tones in the small, narrow ones. The cochlea, for its part, is said to play more of an ancillary role, damping the vibrations and thereby preventing undesirable reflections from confusing the echoes in the tympanic cavity.[64] Elsewhere, however, Bauhin leaned more toward the views of André du Laurens and Casseri, who argued that the proper organ of hearing is not the cochlea as such, but the endings of the auditory nerve in the cochlea.

Both theories were of course inadequate from a number of viewpoints, even though the latter enabled Descartes to give his broader theory of nerve action a specific, acoustic inflection. To Descartes, nerves were tubes, which he called *filaments*, that were filled with very thin threads that transmitted physical motion to the brain, where small pores would open containing the *esprits animaux*, or animal spirits. These, in turn, would move back to the muscle that first experienced the sensory stimulation, inflating it and thus causing it to move. But although in this theory nerves generally were held to be passive matter and, hence, just another form of *res extensa*, as the main operators in the interchange of body and mind, they also occupied a somewhat more liminal position between physiology and psychology, a position crucial for Descartes' later work on the biology of emotions. The auditory nerve, however, had an even more ambiguous status. With the eardrum having lost its pivotal position in the Renaissance *episteme* of semblance, the auditory nerve now became an example of what Hans-Jörg Rheinberger has called an "epistemic thing," that is, a biological entity or function embodying as yet unsecured knowledge.[65]

Descartes' understanding of the auditory nerve provides important clues as to how his concept of hearing may involve some form of resonance. Thus, the first feature to be noted about the auditory nerve is that apparently there is not one nerve, but many. Second, these filaments are agitated by the *secousses* of air "together and in the same manner." Third and finally, to produce the idea of pitch, the soul selects the sensations it receives by arithmetically matching the frequency of the vibrations to the concepts of order lodged at its core.

There are clear advantages to this theory, sparse though it may be. What Descartes is arguing for is, I believe, a resonance theory in which a great deal more autonomy is granted to nerve fibers than in his theory of filaments generally. Contrary to the concept of the nerves as passive transmitters of animal spirits and the subsidiary idea that, much as the top of a quill pen moves during writing, the entire nerve responds to a stimulus, the philosopher seems to entertain the possibility of the auditory nerve being subject to an altogether different form of action. As he had argued in the *Meditations*, nerves produce the same sensation regardless of the point at which they are stimulated. Since the nerves in our feet go "right up to brain," we feel pain even if these nerves are touched in some intermediate parts, such as the calf or lumbar region, and "the more distant part does nothing."[66] In one sense, this statement might simply be regarded as reiterating Descartes' stated view of the simultaneity of sensory stimulus and its perception in the brain and therefore as clashing with the assertion made in *L'homme* that the *secousses* of air "pass" to the brain in some form of temporal sequence. But in another sense, the reverse notion that sensation is identical regardless of the actual source of stimulation may also give additional significance to the auditory nerve as a major "epistemic thing" in Descartes' larger quest for reasonance.

In fact, despite Cartesian physiology's broader thrust, the philosopher's ambivalence (or, at any rate, my interpretation of his model of nerve action as a site of epistemic ambiguity) may be said to prefigure Romantic physiology's concept of the nervous system as a self-referential system rooted in what Johannes Müller in 1826 would call "sense energies." Like Müller, Descartes seems to unhinge sensation from the external object causing it. If the nerve linking the foot and the lower back (the sciatic nerve, in modern nomenclature) is "pulled" in the lumbar region, it will produce the same pain as when it is affected in the calf. Analogously, the auditory nerve will produce sound, no matter whether it is struck by "blows" of air, at its endpoint in the tympanum or somewhere else along its path toward the brain. In both cases, the ensuing sensations of sound will fail to provide reliable information on the exact nature and location of their respective source.

We would be missing the disturbing implications such non-reflexive, self-referential nerves no doubt pose to Descartes' concept of the disembodied mind. But at the same time the philosopher's inkling of a self-referential form of aurality casts an entirely different light on his musical aesthetics. Contrary to his alleged ocularcentric rationalism, the author of *L'homme* uses auditory perception to secure the *fundamentum inconcussum* by balancing, however obliquely, his aspirations for a *mathesis univeralis* with the aesthetic relativism rehearsed at the beginning of his career in the *Compendum musicae*. The summary of the theory of coincidence, following the discussion of the resonant action of the auditory nerve fibers quoted above illustrates the point:

> Note that a single such blow will be able to cause nothing but a dull noise which ceases in a moment and which will vary only in being more or less loud according as the ear is struck with more or less force. But when many [blows] succeed one another, as one sees in the vibrations [*tremblements*] of strings and of bells when they ring, then these little blows will compose one sound which [A] the soul will judge [to be] smoother or rougher according as the blows are more or less equal to one another, and which [B] it will judge [to be] higher or lower according as they succeed one another more promptly or tardily, so that if they are a half or a third or a fourth or a fifth more prompt in following one another, they will compose a sound which the soul will judge to be higher by an octave, a fifth, a fourth, or perhaps a major third, and so on. And finally, several sounds mixed together will be harmonious or discordant according as more or less orderly relations exist [among them] and according as more or less equal intervals occur between the little blows that compose them.[67]

We need not obsess over the question what status the soul has in this passage, most likely culled from Galileo Galilei's *Discorsi*. It suffices to note that it is of considerably lesser importance than the all-powerful role that the soul gains at the outcome of the psychosonic experiment called "meditations" carried out several years earlier. The soul of the listener envisaged above is much less imposing. Rather than being the arbiter of how "several sounds mixed together" match up with the absolute truth enshrined in the mathematical proportions of musical harmony outside of such sounds, its main purpose is simply to monitor the "according as," to ensure the "structural" equivalence, beyond its ultimate reference point in absolute truth, between the objective mechanics of resonant hearing, on the one hand, and the subjective experience of consonance and dissonance, on the other.

In sum, the place of otology in Descartes' lifelong pursuit of reasonance is quite patently at odds with some of the philosopher's more full-throated claims about the supremacy of the mind over the body, as well as with their late appropriation for the history of modern musical aesthetics by musicologist Heinrich Besseler. Descartes, the Heidegger disciple asserted, was the first thinker who linked the idea of the "listener" to a new and ultimately triumphant concept of subjectivity, one that proceeded "not from the music itself but from the listener."[68] In keeping with Heidegger's concept of the age of the "world picture" in which Man had become the center of all Being, Besseler envisaged seventeenth-century listeners as being "in the lead." It is the listener who "connects the corresponding components of the music with each other" and "to whom after 1600 not only points an isolated feature such as solo song, but music in its entirety."[69]

Besseler's claim may be doubted. Descartes' gesture toward resonance derives its far-reaching significance from nothing quite so extravagant as "Man." More than the effect of the philosopher's alleged youthful cognitive ambivalence displayed in the *Compendium* or the aesthetic rationalism of his mature period, Descartes' theory of hearing was one of the central sites of his lifelong quest for the great entente of reason and emotion. Grappling with the impossible proximity of reason and resonance, he simply gave the ear a chance to cast its lot with either.[70]

CHAPTER TWO

Point of Audition:

Claude Perrault's *Du bruit* (1680)

and the Politics of Pleasure

in the Ancien Régime

When it comes to seventeenth-century French culture and politics, the Louvre is always a good starting point — a much less noticed part of the Louvre than the *Mona Lisa* or the spectacular glass pyramid in the courtyard, that is: an elegant row of double columns at the eastern end called the "colonnade." When the Louvre was built, architecture did not know such rows of double columns, and in the eyes of many seventeenth-century beholders, the slender structures may well have "flirted with precariousness."[1] The evenly spaced regularity that characterizes classicist architecture is here disrupted and accentuated at the same time by a fragile arrangement that allows the spaces between the individual columns to contract and expand, as if a rippling movement had pushed them against each other.

The colonnade (as well as the elevation shown in figure 2.1) is said to be the work of Claude Perrault (1613–1688), one of France's most prominent intellectuals during the reign of Louis XIV. Brother of the celebrated author of fairytales Charles Perrault and of the pioneer of modern hydrology, Pierre Perrault, Claude Perrault designed the Observatory, translated the work of the ancient Roman architect Vitruvius into French, and authored the widely read essay, *Ordonnance des cinq espèces de colonnes selon la méthode des anciens* (Ordonnance of the Five Kinds of Columns after the Method of the Ancients, 1683), commonly considered to be one of the founding texts of modern architecture.[2] But Perrault was also one of the last all-round scholars, whose activities

Figure 2.1. Claude Perrault, *Louvre* (courtesy of Bibliothèque Nationale Française). Although no definitive proof of Perrault's authorship of the colonnade has been found, this elevation is said to be from his own hand.

covered a stupendous range of scientific and artistic subjects beyond architecture. A physician by training, Perrault conducted extensive zoological studies, "compiled" the first volume of the pioneering *Mémoires pour servir à l'histoire naturelle des animaux* (1671/1676), and became a founding member of the Académie Royale des Sciences. And as an astute cultural observer, he also weighed in on the infamous "Querelle des Anciens et des Modernes," one of the modern era's first culture wars, which was sparked by the premiere of Jean-Baptiste Lully's opera *Alceste* in 1674 and pitted "moderns" such as the Perrault brothers against "ancients" such as Racine and Nicolas Boileau.

Perrault's real passion, however, was the ear. It was in a book entitled *Du bruit* (Of Sound) that he first outlined what may well be his most influential contribution to the epistemology of life: the "animist" conception that the animal body is not a machine, as Descartes had taught, but a self-generating organism.[3] Tucked away in Perrault's multi-volume *Essais de physique* (1680) and having long been neglected by art historians, cultural historians, and musicologists alike, *Du bruit* is more than one of many early modern treatises in otology however.[4] It is a key document of the late seventeenth-century avant-garde and of considerable significance to the larger story told here about the intertwining of reason and resonance in the history of modern aurality.

Compressing, Decompressing

We owe a delightfully warm portrait of Claude Perrault and his brothers to the eminent evolutionary biologist and historian of science Stephen Jay Gould. By crossing the boundaries between letters and science, Gould suggests in *The Hedgehog, the Fox, and the Magister's Pox* (his last book, written before his untimely death), the Perrault brothers had become models for the "modern liberty to move on."[5] Even though posterity denies to Claude Perrault the status of near sanctity that it accorded to Newton, William Harvey, or Descartes, the architect-zoologist-physician might be regarded as a representative of the "vernacular" modern:

an everyday kind of epistemology that, as Gould puts it, "often surpasses the stellar as a source of insight about the main thrust of a movement."[6]

Perhaps Gould has a point. Claude Perrault's *Du bruit* undoubtedly provides us with a fascinating opportunity to examine the meaning of "liberty" during a period that, in many ways, may be said to have invented the idea of the "modern," but that also witnessed unprecedented levels of bloodshed, famine, and intolerance. Above all, however, the strange intermingling of architecture, opera, and otology pervading Perrault's work invites us to revisit some of the more expedient constructions of seventeenth-century culture. The idea, for instance, that the era witnessed the emergence of a new nexus between music, the ear, and a triumphant modern form of subjectivity is firmly entrenched in current musical writing, dating back, as we have seen in the previous chapter, to Heinrich Besseler's claim that beginning around 1600, music in its entirety "points" to "Man." And as even a cursory survey of the standard literature on early modern music and aesthetics shows, this new subject, "Man," is usually—and for the most part, without much further elaboration—equated with the Cartesian ego, representation, and absolute power.[7]

There are a few exceptions though. In what is one of the most thought-provoking discussions of early modern opera to date, Gary Tomlinson for instance, has brought new life to a debate that, if it did not ignore the broader philosophical implications of early modern opera altogether, has tended to subsume seventeenth-century musical aesthetics under the precepts of *Affektenlehre* or "Doctrine of Affections."[8] Working from a Foucauldian perspective, Tomlinson detects in the vocality pioneered in Lully's operas a new type of metaphysics. The recitative, perhaps Lully's most momentous accomplishment, he argues, not only became a source of expressive power, it also created new "conditions of subjectivity."[9] Faced with the disintegration of the Renaissance *episteme*, Lully struggled to regain some measure of semiotic predictability by means of musical stock formulas, standardized personae, and a whole arsenal of dramatic conventions, signs, similes, and chimeras. The fruit of his labors, the *tragédie en musique*, conjoined music and words in order to achieve a new unity of mind and body constituted through the fixity of representation or, as Tomlinson puts it, "habituation."

A similar account of Cartesianism's relationship with early modern aurality is offered by Georgia Cowart in *The Triumph of Pleasure: Louis XIV and the Politics of Spectacle.*[10] Focusing on the opera-ballet and comedy-ballet of the latter half of the seventeenth century, Cowart is concerned with the pivotal—and increasingly counterhegemonic—role that pleasure was beginning to play in the spectacles staged by and for Louis XIV. While during the early part of the monarch's long reign elite audiences were expected to identify with and submit to the heroic images of absolute power projected by the court ballet, beginning in midcentury, strains of resistance began to emerge. Audiences insisted on indulging in the sonic and visual delights afforded by these spectacles on terms of their own choosing, preferring a more egalitarian, everyday kind of libertinism over the martial manifestations of royal might. In short, as Cowart compellingly shows, early modern spectacle could be said to be one of the terrains on which Gould's "modern liberty" began to assert itself.

Neither Tomlinson nor Cowart question the larger Cartesian framework however. Thus, while Tomlinson's adumbration of the Lullian recitative as "habituation" indeed may open up a space for envisaging a new, albeit somewhat passive type of listener, the aural sovereignty achieved through such "habituation" remains firmly anchored in Descartes' mind-body dualism. Georgia Cowart, similarly, sees the weakening of the quasi-mystical correspondence between king and state power during Louis' final years and the potentially unruly kind of aurality increasingly being espoused by upper-class audiences as mediated by the rise of Cartesian mechanism.[11] And as in Tomlinson's account, the new alliance of pleasure and liberty for her manifests itself first and foremost within the space of representation: in plots and allegorical figures, but much less so at the level of bodily sensation.

However, it is precisely here, in the concept of an aurality operating outside the confines of the Cartesian mind-body dualism, that Perrault's unique contribution to the pursuit of "modern liberty" lies. Contrary to the notion that the groundswell of antiaristocratic sentiment and the rise of alternative, "proto-Enlightenment" visions of leadership and society were fueled by the growing acceptance and aesthetic relevance of Cartesianism, Perrault's position was a more ambiguous one.[12] The pursuit of "modern liberty" for the architect-zoologist-physician Perrault began at the interstices of reason and resonance. It began in the cochlea, in a new concept of hearing.

There is a glitch however. Historians of otology differ as to whom is due the honor of being the true pioneer of the resonance theory of hearing. Is it Claude Perrault, as the eighteenth-century inventor of iatromechanist medicine Herman Boerhaave held, or was it rather Perrault's young friend, Joseph-Guichard Duverney, a professor of anatomy at the Jardin du Roi and like Perrault a member of the Académie and a rising star on the French medical scene? Three years after *Du bruit*, Duverney had published *Traité de l'organe de l'ouïe*, a work that historians generally consider to be one of the milestones of modern otology and the first major statement of cochlear selective resonance.[13] The *lamina spiralis*, Duverney argues there, is

> wider at the beginning of its first revolution than at the end of its last, where it finishes in a point, and its other parts diminishing proportionately in width, we may suppose that since the wider parts may be vibrated without the others participating in that vibration they are capable only of slower undulations which consequently correspond to the low notes; and that on the contrary when its narrow parts are struck their undulations are faster and hence correspond to high notes, in the same way as the wider parts of a steel spring make slower undulations and correspond to low notes and the narrower

parts make more frequent and faster undulations and hence cor-
respond to high notes; so that, finally, according to the different
vibrations in the spiral lamina, the spirits of the nerve, which spread
through its substance, receive different impressions which in the
brain represent the different appearances of pitches.[14]

To be sure, modern science now locates pitch perception in the
opposite direction of what Duverney claimed: The perception
of low pitches occurs at the apex of the cochlea and that of high
pitches near its basal end. Still, Duverney's skills as an anatomist
(as an anatomist of the inner ear, at any rate) surpassed those of
Perrault, as a comparison between Perrault's and Duverney's
plates shows. Unlike Perrault's rather crude depiction of the
cochlea (figure 2.2) Duverney clearly depicted the "spiral canal"
(AA) and the "spiral membrane" (BB) next to it (figure 2.3), where
1, 2, and 3 mark the bony lamina and 4, 5, and 6 the basilar
membrane.

The real difference, however, between the two scientists lies
in the way in which they both distanced themselves from Cartesian mechanism and in so doing supported similar concepts of
listenership and subjectivity that one might call off-Cartesian.
In the third section of his *Traité*, for instance, Duverney offers
the first scientifically plausible theory of *tintement*, or tinnitus.
This, he writes, consists of the "perception of a sound that does
not exist, or of a sound that exists inside." The cause of this sensation, he argues, does not reside, as the ancients had believed,
in the mystical air implantatus ("the air inside the ear"), in
divine inspiration or in some form of mental defect, but in the
nature of the auditory nerve. It makes no difference whether its
fibers are affected (*ébranler*) on the side of the ear or on the side
of the brain: "The result will always be the same sensation."
The *tintements*, then, are "veritable sounds" that are perceived
"such as they are, yet the ear is unable to relate them to an
exterior object."[15]

Like Descartes, Duverney does not call into doubt the
existence of an exterior "reality." The idea of reality is still

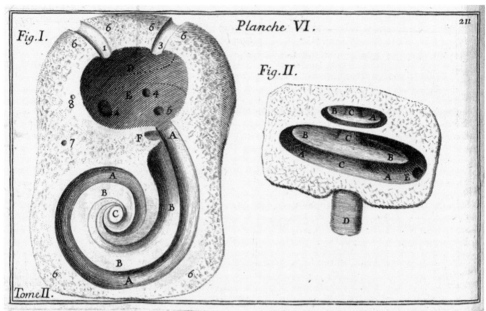

Fig.I.

Fig.II.

Tome II.

EXPLICATION DE LA PLANCHE VI.

Figure I. Elle reprefente le Labyrinthe entier, à la referve du canal horizontal , dont on ne peut rien voir non plus que des parties fuperieures qu'il a fallu enlever pour faire voir le dedans, il a une grandeur beaucoup au delà du naturel.

A A. le Canal fpiral appellé le Limaçon. B BB, la Membrane fpirale. D E, le Veftibule du Labyrinthe découvert, de mefme que le commencement des canaux verticaux & du Limaçon , par une fection qui forme le plan marqué 6.6,6,6. I. Le commencement du canal Vertical conjoint découvert. 2, l'entrée qui luy eft commune avec l'horizontal. 3. le commencement du vertical feparé découvert. 4. l'entrée inferieure du canal vertical feparé. 5. l'entrée particuliere du canal horizontal.

Figure II. Elle reprefente le canal fpiral du Limaçon couppé perpendiculairement au plan marqué 6, 6, 6,6. dans la I. Figure. A A A. le dedans du canal fpiral qui fait le Limaçon. B B B. la membrane fpirale. C C C. le noyau auquel la membrane eft attachée. D. le nerf de l'ouïe qui paffe dans le noyau & le penetre. E. l'entrée du Veftibule du Limaçon marquée A dans la I, F.gure,

Figure 2.2. Claude Perrault, *Essais de physique*, fig. 6 (courtesy of Bibliothèque Nationale Française). *Left*: in this figure from Perrault's *Essais de physique* is a cross section of the labyrinth, with AA being the cochlea, BBB the lamina spiralis, and DE the vestibule. *Right*: shows the same part perpendicular to the axis 6 6 6 6 on left. D represents the auditory nerve.

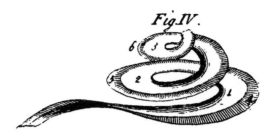

Figure 2.3. Joseph-Guichard Duverney, *Traité de l'organe de l'ouïe*, fig. 4. A close-up of the lamina spiralis.

inextricably linked to the object world. But he differs from Descartes in that a sound that is "veritable" and yet "does not exist" is less a logical impossibility than the admission of a parallel interior, subjective reality. In this reality, sensations of things exist that do not necessarily fit in with the master philosopher's pronouncement that they are illusions of the body.

In a similar vein, Perrault's animism, although it does not sever the link between the external world and the subject's representation of that world quite as radically as does Müller's law of sensory energies, can be said to undermine reason's power in safeguarding the integrity of that link. Thus, while Duverney's theory of selective resonance provides the perfect scientific rationale for a physiology and aesthetics that see auditory perception as a passive reflex and that, on that ground, might rightly be called a Cartesian theory of subjectivity mapped on to the sense of hearing, Perrault's animism points toward a new type of subjectvity—to modern liberty. Indeed, *Du bruit* is the first work to highlight the central role of hearing in the making of that off-Cartesian, as one might call it, subjectivity.

How, then, did Perrault's argument in *Du bruit* unfold? The work is divided into three parts. The first two parts contain a lengthy, if rudimentary summary of the velocity of sound, echo, vibration, sympathetic resonance, and other acoustic phenomena, but they also show, more importantly, Perrault embracing the corpuscular theory of air motion according to which sound is carried by subtle, elastic particles of air moving toward the ear. There then follows a third part on the ear that is further subdivided into four chapters. The first of these chapters presents a copiously illustrated, if rather unreliable discussion of the anatomy of the ear, while the remaining three chapters treat the comparative physiology of hearing. It is these latter chapters that form the most speculative, albeit most interesting part of the book, because they provided Perrault with the framework within which to promulgate his broader critique of the Cartesian mechanism.

The basis of this critique was the idea that solid bodies possess two essential qualities: hardness and spring, or in present-day usage, cohesion and elasticity. These were said to be as much due to internal factors such as the material and shape of the object as the result of external factors such as the pressure exercised by the surrounding air. Consequently, it was thought to be the natural propensity of bodies to resist separation and to tend toward cohesion, a feature Perrault, using an ancient Greek term, labeled *péristaltique*. In a like vein, human bodies were held to exist always in a state of tension. Muscles and membranes are naturally flexed, and the action of the animal spirits "destined for movement does not consist in operating contractions...but, quite to the contrary, to produce relaxation in the muscles opposed to those contracting."[16]

Although this concept of muscular motion was novel, the underlying physics was not. It was essentially a mechanistic concept, and as such, like all seventeenth-century physics, was modeled on the Cartesian machine metaphor, the predominant paradigm of European scientific thought. But Perrault's notion of peristaltic movement differed from Cartesianism in one crucial respect. For Descartes, movement could occur only if an external force acts upon inherently inert matter. As the famous illustration in *L'homme* had shown, for Descartes, the role of the animal spirits was to convey the sensation they had transmitted

to the brain back to the body organ that experienced the sensation and thus cause it to move. If a fire were about to burn a foot,
the animal spirits would transmit the feeling of heat back to the
muscle so that it would contract and remove the foot from the
source of danger. Similarly, the animal spirits would fill up the
muscles attached to the eye, shortening them, and thus cause the
eye to move left or right. For Perrault, quite the opposite was the
case. Instead of a chain reaction in which each part of the body
machine transmits its movement to the next part, the peristaltic
interaction between cohesion and elasticity was something that
Perrault considered to be dispersed throughout the entire body
machine.

This revision of Descartes' notion of inert matter inevitably
posed a dilemma for Perrault's attempt to understand auditory
perception. Though the *Essais de physique* are full of machine
analogies — the eye is compared to a telescope, the lungs of an
ostrich are depicted next to a pair of bellows, and so on — sensation for Perrault ultimately could be only another form of *péristaltique*. But how to demonstrate the way the tension between the
antagonistic forces of cohesion and elasticity plays itself out in the
ear? Once the vibrating air gets past the eardrum and meets with
rigid, bony structures, what happens to peristaltic action? *Du
bruit* is remarkably lapidary here. Since particles of air, Perrault
wrote, have elasticity and therefore, like all matter, tend to return
to their original position — thus displacing other particles that
had since taken their place in a continuous series of "impulsions"
finally reaching the ear — it followed that the organ of hearing was
agitated in "about the same manner."[17]

The problem with this statement is that there simply is no
air in the inner ear. And so, by holding on to the age-old idea of
the air implantatus, Perrault failed to apply the full potential of
the notion of peristaltic action to hearing. The ear, to be sure,
no longer quite functioned on the model of Descartes' rumbling
pulleys and wheels, but at the same time, it had not fully acquired
the plasticity of living matter that Perrault assumed to operate

79

throughout the rest of the body, either. As a consequence, Perrault's physiology could only fall back on analogies.

It is instructive to follow Perrault's analogical argument more closely, because although later rejected by Duverney, it remained extremely influential until well into the late eighteenth century, throwing into sharp relief the predicament facing the late seventeenth-century and eighteenth-century physiology of hearing. Basically, what Perrault argued for was a qualitative link between the physics of sounding bodies and the ear, the result being an anatomy in which only those components mattered that maintained a specific physiological relation to the object perceived. This sort of reasoning drew on a rather simplistic analogy between the ear and the eye. "I am looking for parts in the organ of hearing that have some analogy to parts in other senses, in order to see if by analogy they might have the same function," Perrault wrote.[18] What the Greeks and Romans used to call "imago" (image) and the Scholastics misinterpreted as species, he went on to say, might in fact be a useful way to conceptualize the analogy between seeing and hearing and to argue that sensory impressions are caused by identical processes, be it in the eye or in the ear:[19] As light rays are bundled by the retina, the labyrinth focuses the vibrating air. In addition, all sense organs are ultimately attached to the nervous system through nerves with the same substance and an almost similar delicacy.

If each sense organ, then, had something in common with the other sense organs, it followed that the different sensory impressions received by these organs had to be caused by some parts that were unique to this organ. The highly polished, watery surface of the retina, for instance, shares with the optic nerve some of its fluidity so as to ease the passage of the mirror images. Likewise, the consistency of the basilar membrane rests somewhere between the softness of the auditory nerve and the hardness of the cochlea. Because it made sense to assume, said Perrault, "that dryness is one of the conditions most required for bodies to be able to produce sound, so the same quality must also be present in the organ sensing the movement that caused the sound."[20] The connection was so close that he even attributed the fact that the auditory nerve is exceptionally harder in lions and sheep to these animals' "very dry temperament." And, in a similar vein, certain pathologies such as poor hearing had to be caused by the moist winds of southern France, which diminished the dryness of the membrane.[21]

Obviously, all of this was not only pure Aristotle (in the sense that perception was thought to be mediated by "qualities"), it also fell well short of Perrault's broader peristaltic claims. Having reached the limits of mechanical explanation, Perrault therefore set out in the third chapter to advance an ambitious, if somewhat circuitous theory of auditory perception and, ultimately, an entirely different metaphysics of the subject. Although still conceived in the long shadow of Descartes, significant parts of this theory also resonated more closely with late seventeenth-century cultural practice than with Cartesian dogma.

One of the major points separating Perrault's views from Descartes' reflexological theory concerned the role of the soul. Whereas Descartes had denied that the soul has any impact on the working of the body, Perrault believed that the relationship between the mind and the body, and more particularly between the mind and the sensory organs, could not be explained without assuming the agency of some kind of "reasoning" force in every part of the animal organism. He arrived at this conclusion by way of a complex argument that led him to query the central role Descartes had accorded the brain in judging sense impressions. How can the brain, Perrault wondered, handle two contrary sense impressions at the same time without getting confused? How can the rays of light that meet the eye in a straight line reach the brain undisturbed when the optic nerve itself is bent? And, finally, since nerve and sense organ must form a homogeneous whole, as they do in the retina, wouldn't the opacity of the optic nerve obstruct the delicate vibrations being received by the transparent humors of the retina and thus hinder them from reaching the brain? The solution to these quandaries, according to Perrault, could lie only in the rejection of Descartes' wax-seal theory of sensation. Or put differently, instead of figuring the body as a robot, a "new system" would have to assume the existence of "interior senses" that function independently of the body organs reserved for exterior sensation.[22]

The reason for this hypothesis was that the soul, by virtue of it being linked to all body parts, did not need the brain to ponder (contempler) these impressions. It could perfectly scrutinize them in each organ, where they were present in the moment of sensation. The role of the brain, in this view, was thus a more limited one — to prepare the animal spirits necessary for the exterior senses to be properly disposed for perception. Likewise, memory was not located in the brain, as Descartes' theory of traces would have it, but in every part of the body. In short, in contrast to a wound-up clock, the Perrauldian body consisted of fibers that were animated by a living, superior force lodged within it. The human body, if it was a machine at all, was capable of "doing something different from what it is made for."[23] Living matter had the innate ability to adapt.

Perrault had little difficulty in finding evidence for this stunning reversal of Cartesian mechanism. Having dissected countless animals from the royal menagerie — one infected specimen of which, a giraffe, is said to have caused his death — he was convinced that the operation of such a "reasoning" faculty could be easily observed in a horse, for instance. If Cartesian dogma was correct in imagining the movements of a horse to be only the quasi-automatic effect of a series of successive sense impressions devoid of any autonomous reasoning, why was the animal able to recombine these impressions in the reverse order and thus use the same path on its way home? Likewise, how was it possible that a viper whose head had been cut off not only continued to move, but also found the way back to its favorite hiding spot, if not through the memory stored in its sentient organ of touch?

At this point in the argument, oddly, Perrault denied the

difference between voluntary action guided by the soul and those movements that occur without the active participation of the soul, such as the beating of the heart, or movements that even defy the soul, such as illness. Instead, he argued for two types of thought: a "distinct" way of thinking, unique to humans and meant for "the things that we attend to with care," and a "confused" way of thinking, shared by humans and beasts and designed "for the things which habit has made so simple that they no longer require express and exact thinking." One example of the former was the regularity and vital importance of the cardiac contractions, which simply persuade the soul not to interrupt them. Ailments, by contrast, result from the soul's occasional failure to pay sufficient attention to the body's interior functioning.

Distinct or confused, the larger point Perrault was pressing here was of course that the functioning of the eye and ear would remain incomprehensible without "assuming a judgment and reasoning no machine would ever be able to attain, no matter how subtle and well-constructed one may imagine it to be."[24] Because there are two types of thought, the senses also are governed by two kinds of judgment that help them to correct errors to which they might otherwise be prone. The sense of touch, for instance, is much more easily deceived and consequently more in need of "distinct" judgment than sight and hearing, where "habitual and confused [judgment] are almost always adequate."[25] Thus, the ear as a rule has no difficulty in distinguishing a male from a female voice, just as it is seldom deceived by ventriloquist trickery. Some exceptions do, of course, exist, such as when the ears are cupped by the hand and a noise is heard like that of a waterfall, or when a piece of iron attached to a string that in turn is wound around a finger stopping an ear produces a bell-like sound. On the whole, however, Perrault proclaimed, the ear is capable of an admirable "certitude and discernment."[26]

Here *Du bruit* ends, leaving the present-day reader startled and frustrated at the same time. One is startled because animism, one of the key paradigms of seventeenth-century natural science, whose significance extended well into the eighteenth century, is premiered in a text that, contrary to the taken-for-granted hierarchy of the five senses, takes not vision as its testing ground, but hearing. At the same time, the dramatic shift from Cartesian dogma to a more flexible mind-body relationship or vital materialism, as one might call it, seems mired in contradictions. Perrault, it appears, was unable to reconcile the innovative thrust of his broader theory with his views of auditory sensation articulated toward the end of *Du bruit*.

To recapitulate: according to Perrault, a "reasoning" faculty resides throughout the body, not just in a soul separate from the rest of the body. Every body part, in other words, is animated, including the ear, which is furnished with an "internal sense" making it capable of "confused" thought and protecting it from error. But how would the same ear, now emancipated from crude mechanism, distinguish between different pitches? And, most importantly, how could the theory of the "animated," peristaltic ear be applied to the much-noted phenomenon that seventeenth-century audiences were prepared to accept as consonances intervals that theory deemed to be dissonant? In other words, what was the relationship between the physics of sound, on the one hand, and the physiology of hearing and aesthetic pleasure, on the other? And of course, looming over all these questions, was the much larger issue how the ear could become the site of "modern liberty."

The early beginnings of French opera less than a decade before the publication of *Du bruit* and the controversy surrounding the new form of spectacle, the *Querelle des anciens et des modernes*, provided Perrault with the ideal forum in which to tackle these issues head-on.

Folie de l'Écoute

In 1672, Perrault had attended a performance of the "pastorale" *Les peines et les plaisirs de l'amour* (1672) by Robert Cambert, one of the pioneers of French opera. The event inspired him to draft a text titled "Sçauoir si la musique à plusieurs parties a esté

84

connüe et mise en usage par les Anciens" (Whether Part Music Was Known to and Used by the Ancients).[27] Meant to serve as an introduction to another, much more ambitious essay titled "De la musique des anciens" (Of the Music of the Ancients) that he later appended to the *Essais de physique*—and which we will explore further below—"Sçauoir" was published only as recently as 1914, without it having been possible to determine why Perrault decided to withhold its publication. One reason might be that its key propositions had become superseded during the period leading up to *Du bruit* by the much sharper criticism Perrault advanced in his Vitruvius translation and, most crucially, as part of his embroilment in the Querelle des Anciens et des Modernes.[28]

Another reason for Perrault's decision not to publish his early text might be the same flirtation with "precariousness" that had shaped his colonnade project earlier. While, on the surface "Sçauoir" foregrounds the contrasting "ancient" and "modern" positions on the emerging musical theater, the listening stance that Perrault advocates in this text is much less clearly circumscribed, bordering perilously close on a concept of subjectivity that diverges significantly from Cartesianism and, by the same token, might be seen as undermining the increasingly repressive politics defining Louis XIV's late period.

What, then, is "Sçauoir" about? Perrault recounts a dispute he claims to have overheard between two spectators at the start of the performance of Cambert's "pastorale." At first, the disputants, Paleologue (Expert on Things Ancient) and Philalethe (Lover of Truth), quarrel over the value of the novel type of spectacle. Philalethe, who had been present at the work's premiere, is utterly ravished. Showing no interest in the author and composer of the piece, much less in finding out about the designer of the stage machinery, his only concern is "to know how someone was able to produce such surprising things" *de scauoir comment on pouuoit faire reüssir des choses si surprenantes*. Paleologue, meanwhile, declares that the only thing he is amazed about is how people who have seen Italian opera in Venice can "admire so little."[29] But as the curtain rises and the violins begin to intone the overture, something unexpected happens. Unlike the raucous spectators around them, who continue with their conversations and care only about the names of the female singers, the two antagonists suddenly find themselves transfixed by the interplay between different voices and the accompaniment of instruments, the "symphonie." Even the obstinate Paleologue becomes more "docile," listening with "less contempt" than he did at the start of their conversation:

> He even entered, in a way, into its "feelings" [*il entra mesme en quelque façon dans ses sentimens*] when the piece was finished and they remained in their place a little longer while the crowd dispersed. He [Paleologue] drew his [Philalethe's] attention to all the things that made the piece that has been played so marvelous [*merueilleuse*] and so much superior to the spectacles of the ancient in terms of intellect [*esprit*] and ingenuity [*inuention*].

The marvelous, Paleologue goes on to elaborate, consists mainly in a "shrewd economy" (*oeconomie iudicieuse*):

> in the clever way in which the composer introduced ballet episodes and machinery that are "necessary" to the topic at hand; the variety of characters represented by the different roles that provide an opportunity to broach both happy and sad subjects; the use of two familiar genres of song like the drinking song and the love song; the way the plot of the fable, with its intrigues, is made comprehensible by the concatenation [*enchainement*] of songs that ordinarily must also contain propositions of a general nature; the abstention from the recitative, which is devoid of charm [*grace*] when sung; the technique of having sing together several characters who are in conversation; and, finally, to have all this go on for three hours without being boring and notwithstanding the inconvenience all music, no matter how good, becomes subject to when it becomes insufferable because of its long duration.[30]

At first glance, the passage reads like a laundry list of all the things early modern audiences found to be either remarkable or objectionable in the marvelous effects, *le merveilleux*, so central to the new form of spectacle. But the passage is also interesting because it wrestles with some of the potentially more troubling implications of the marvelous for the nascent project of an off-Cartesian theory of hearing and subjectivity. At stake in this brief text is nothing less than the irrational side of the "animated" body.

One phrase, in particular, should give us pause: "he even entered in a way into its feelings," "*il entra mesme en quelque façon dans ses sentimens.*" It stands in marked contrast to the tenets of Cartesian representation and the aesthetics of *Affektenlehre*, both of which do not call for immersion and identification, but distance and mirroring, and as such it merits more detailed disucssion. For instance, it is not entirely clear whether *ses* refers to Philalethe's feelings, which Paleologue had earlier sought to resist, or whether, by contrast, the possessive noun points to the remainder of the sentence, "when the piece was finished and they remained in their place a little longer while the crowd dispersed," "*lorrsque la piece estant acheuée ils demeurent encore quelque temps à leur place pendant que la foule se retiroit*" and, hence, to the piece (*la piece*) itself.

Equally, if not more ambiguous is the word *sentimens*. What is the space of emotion in early modern opera? What exactly was the meaning of sentiment during the middle of the seventeenth century, and how did it relate to, according to classical dogma, the tripartite division of man's mental faculties into memory, imagination, and reason? And finally, what did Perrault mean by the phrase "he entered" (*il entra*)? To understand this remark, it is helpful to take a brief look at the plot of *Les peines*. The prologue has the Muses order Apollo to follow the rule of the steely Jupiter and to abandon love. Apollo, however, refusing to obey Jupiter, casts his lot with the Graces, asserting love's supreme power to transform pain into pleasure. This course of action, in turn, enrages the Muses, who denigrate Cupid and castigate the fruits of love as pains, only to see the ultimate defeat of the Muses and the triumph of love.

As would be expected of a "pastorale," the *sentimens* that the disbelieving Paleologue eventually "enters into," leads to the ultimate triumph of love, of pleasure over pain. But as Cowart rightly points out, there is a subplot that adds an altogether more defiant tone to *Les peines*. In aligning the Muses with Jupiter's (read Louis XIV's) ruthless rule, the work invokes, much like Molière's and Lully's *Le bourgeois gentilhomme* produced two years earlier, the "metaphor of the transformation of pain into pleasure as the means by which a utopia of spectacle could serve as the model for a new society."[31]

Equally helpful in understanding Paleologue's immersive moment might be to revisit some of the older scholarship of the "marvelous" and contrast it with more recent attempts to elucidate early modern spectacle in terms of its perceived parallels with postmodern or "Neo-Baroque" forms of affective immersion, virtuality, and the madness of sensory perception.[32] In the literature on French early modern opera, the marvelous has largely been framed in terms of its relationship to the precepts of "classical" theater. While in the spoken tragedy — Racine's *Phèdre* (1677), for instance — the supersensible realm is banned from the stage, opera thrives on presenting a world filled with supernatural characters, magic moments, and scene changes, all made possible by intricate machinery and music. In fact, in the eyes of some contemporaneous commentators, music's role in the lyrical theater was essential to the privileged place of the spectacular. In the *tragédie en musique*, Jean-François Marmontel wrote, "everything is false, but everything is in agreement; and it is this agreement that constitutes truth. Music gives charm to the marvelous, the marvelous in turn gives credibility [*vraisemblance*] to music."[33]

Yet spoken tragedy and opera are also united by a more hidden link, beyond the obvious opposition between what is not shown and, hence, exterior to the text, in the tragedy, and what is recovered and integrated into the text, in the case of opera. There is, in fact, a "familiar strangeness" between the two genres, as Catherine Kintzler, the foremost authority on French scenic aesthetics of the classical era, writes: "Opera treats the exteriority of the theater as though it was not exterior." It does so "by not only integrating this exteriority into the plot, but above all by bringing the poetic rules of the classical drama to bear on it, by treating this exteriority as a theatrical element in its own right."[34]

Exteriority is not merely exhibited, then, but truly repatriated and interiorized at the heart of the theater. In this way, exteriority narrows the gulf between opera and theater by bringing, in a perverted manner, what "should distance opera from theater in principle . . . closer to it."[35] The key to this coexistence of the two genres within the same aesthetic frame and thus also the guarantee for the effect of the marvelous to succeed is of course, as Marmontel was well aware, verisimilitude, *vraisemblance*. The supernatural events must be plausible. They must refer to a quasi-nature, one that if it is not accessible to the senses of ordinary mortals, at least might be possible if only one had access to it. Thus, when a supernatural being performs a magic act, this act becomes plausible only when it is part of some sort of intermediary chain of then "known" natural causes: the appearance or disappearance of a God can be accompanied only by an earthquake, a thunderstorm, or a meteor; the murder of Sangaride in Lully's opera *Atys* (1676) occurs in a moment of dementia brought about by the fury Alecton; and so forth.

Verisimilitude also depended on a subtle interplay between illusion and reality, distance and immersion. On the one hand, the assumption that the realm of the supersensible in the *tragédie en musique* is plausible depends on a separation of this world from the ordinary world of the spectator. Nature as the ultimate reference point of poetic representation is present, but only as a nature whose probability is mediated by the marvelous. The typical audience response corresponding to this distanced stance, typified in

89

part by Philalethe's interest in the "surprising" effects of Cambert's "pastorale," is thus one in which the object of wonder and the concomitant desire for rational mastery of this object are less about the marvelous itself than about the ambiguous relationship between the rational and the irrational: "How did they do this?"

Conversely, the principle of verisimilitude functions only when the suspicion that the communication between separate realms is the result of artifice is at least temporarily suspended. Only when the process of mediation between the ordinary and the marvelous is somehow naturalized can early modern opera work its magic. Contemporaries of the *tragédie en musique* commented at length on verisimilitude's ability to produce an enchanting effect on the audience, but as a rule failed to dwell on the specific musical qualities of this *enchantement*. Yet it is precisely here, in the physical linkages between sound and the body, that for a present-day observer such as Kintzler, music's genuine role and indeed necessity for the lyrical theater resides. More than a mere mode of expression proper to mythical characters such as Orpheus or the Sirens, music constitutes the very element in and through which deities, demons, and inspired poets act. But, she cautions, the way music imparts this sense of the ordinary extraordinary to the audience is not by some mysterious spiritual or psychological force, but by virtue of it being a "natural (and, hence, probable) sounding box for a number of passions or situations being dealt with in the work." Music finds itself in mechanical conformity with those passions as a result of the "sympathetic transmission of vibrations."[36] In short, the naturalization of the marvelous, for Kintzler, is a question of resonance.

A similar interaction of verisimilitude and the marvelous underpins opera's instrumental sounds. Such music, Kintzler suggests, must be understood as an excerpt of nature or as an approximation of nature, not as nature appears in its teeming variety, but as it truly is. It is through this principle of truth to nature (itself a key concept of early modern science), by concentrating on what is essential about the sounds of nature — the "rolling" of thunder rendered in a drum roll, the flash of lightning imitated in a single stroke of the tympani, the running brook made audible in the rapid runs of the woodwinds, and so on—that music transforms the ordinary and physical into the true. At the same time, however, this passage from noise to musical sound, this poetization of noise not only fictionalizes reality, it is itself fundamentally fictional, drawing the audience into the simultaneously real and fantastic realm of the sounds heard in opera.[37]

Music, of course, is not a natural language, and what legitimizes music's presence on the classical stage is therefore its insertion into the play of rhetorical tropes or, as Kintzler calls it more generally, the "hysterization" of music.[38] Music's ability to make the inaudible audible depends on the familiarity with a code, such as when a composer wishes to render the phrase "trembling with cold," he does so by adding a tremolo to the tone accompanying the word "cold."

Kintzler's adumbration of the *tragédie en musique* as a genre that oscillated between a pathetization and a hysterization of music is a powerful one, no doubt. Nonetheless, there are several problems with her interpretation. There is, first of all, Kintzler's terminological confusion. The use of the term "sounding box" (*caisse de résonance*) as a metaphor for music all told (rather than for specific acoustic aspects of it) is fanciful, at best. Another, perhaps more damaging problem is of a methodological nature. Many of the sources Kintzler adduces in support of her argument are culled from the writings of Abbé Dubos and Jean-Philippe Rameau, that is, from the mature period of the *tragédie en musique*. This move is problematic for the following reason. As is well known, Rameau's theory of harmony, expounded with great persuasion in his *Génération harmonique* (1737), was due in no small part to his discovery of the work of Joseph Sauveur (1653–1716) on harmonic partials published in 1701 and to his acquaintance with the scientist Jean-Jacques Dortous de Mairan (1678–1771).[39] As early as 1722, Rameau had allowed himself to be instructed in acoustic matters by Mairan, finding especially fertile ground for his theory of harmony in Mairan's concept of the *corps sonore*, or sounding body that transmits its vibrations to the perceiving ear, and in the concomitant idea that the ear perceives pitch on the basis of the sympathetic vibrations of the basilar membrane discovered by Duverney.[40] Harmony, Rameau confidently begins his treatise, "is a natural effect, the cause of which resides in the air agitated by the percussion of each individual *corps sonore*."[41]

Of course, neither the famous "Proposition 3" of *Génération harmonique*, in which Rameau acknowledges his debt to Mairan, nor Bernard de Fontenelle's "Extrait des Registres de l'Academie Roïale des Sciences" that he proudly appended to his work, mention Duverney's theory of hearing. Still, it is clear that Rameau's work relied on a much more sophisticated knowledge of acoustics and the physiology of hearing than the one attained during the period that saw Cambert's pastorals and Lully's first *tragédies en musique*. And so to apply this theory retroactively to the naturalization of the marvelous through resonance during the formative period of the *tragédie en musique* half a century earlier is simply bad history.

Returning to "Sçauoir," Perrault's objective was, of course, first and foremost, to grant "modern" harmony superiority over ancient Greek monophonic music and thus also to ground nascent French opera's legitimacy vis-à-vis the classical drama in the claim that not only had there to be a space for dealing with *le merveilleux*, but that opera was that space. Yet at the same time, the marvelous exerted a more ambiguous fascination on him, as is exemplified by Paleologue's magic transformation as he "enters" into the *sentimens* of the opera. Harmony's effects, Perrault wants to suggest, similar to those of the monophonic music of ancient Greece, are located at an emotional level, to be sure. But modern harmony differs from the simple cause-effect relationship underpinning ancient music, as he saw it, because it is predicated on a richer sense of multiply crisscrossing correlations between subject and object.

And thus the affective communion with music's *sentimens* generated by harmony does not so much depend on the stable interchange between two vibrating systems (music and the ears) guaranteed by the laws of nature as on a coming to sound — or, better still, a remaining in sound. The ideal listening stance that Perrault seems to impute to his two opera lovers is not one based on a fixed vantage point vis-à-vis an object mechanically transmitted via sympathetic resonance. Nor, in fact, are these listeners asked, as later audiences during the early eighteenth century were, to engage with the theatrical figures emotionally, through mimetic mirroring. Rather, Philalethe's and Paleologue's preoccupation with the marvelous can be described as involving what one might call, borrowing a phrase from Kaja Silverman's work on male subjectivity, which itself draws on Max Scheler's *Wesen und Formen der Sympathie* (The Nature and Forms of Sympathy) (1923) "exteriorizing" identification.[42] These spectators' theatrical experience always teetered on the brink of ecstasy, even madness; a delirious form of listening, a veritable *folie de l'écoute* similar to the visual frenzy or *folie du voir* that Christine Buci-Glucksmann has located at the heart of "Baroque" aesthetics.[43]

It does not take much, of course, to note the marked contrast between the instability of this identificatory position, this auditory frenzy, and the subordination of the senses to the mastered clarity of Cartesian representation generally held to be the sole basis of early modern arts. Instead of the containment of the object of representation within an optical frame or a system of stable signifiers, early modern *folie de l'écoute* can be said to liberate its object from any frame and, in a sense, even erase the object altogether. It is in this latter sense that Buci-Glucksmann adumbrates early modern opera as akin to "'Baroque' poetry's phonic multiplication of the signifier and as ruins of language, lacking any hermeneutic dimension."[44] And of course, this is also what Perrault's Paleologue has in mind when he discredits the sung recitative as being "devoid of charm."

As a corollary to this, it makes sense to rethink the status of the perceiving subject. Early modern opera, one might say, instead of excluding the perceiving subject from the space of representation and reducing him or her to the role of a stable, if largely passive observer, stages the act of seeing and hearing itself. Listening to the *bruit agréeable* of Cambert's pastorale here comes to be understood in the larger sense of the ear becoming absorbed by its own potential for the infinite expansion of the audible — as the possibility of gaining untold access to an unheard, yet eminently representable world.[45]

The idea of the *folie de l'écoute* erasing the object of audition and the concomitant concept of a listening devoid of a subject are not meant to denote some form of personal idiosyncrasy or pathology. Rather such objectless and subjectless perception is part of a broader logic of perception typical of the early modern period, which Gilles Deleuze, in *The Fold: Leibniz and the Baroque* (1993), has termed "fold-in."[46] The affective content of early modern opera, Deleuze contends, is not the result of a binary correspondence between text and music, which would be rather arbitrary and, one suspects, more in keeping with the Cartesian roots of *Affektenlehre*. Instead, the text is enveloped by harmony, as though the melody of the voice is inflected by the harmonies so as to render the text's affective dimension.[47]

There are several ways to read Deleuze's cryptic depiction of early modern opera as a fold-in. One of these would be to see in the operatic voice a tool for multiplying and ultimately destroying in an act of sheer folly the sphere of meaning and replacing it with pure sound. Another reading would proceed more from the standpoint of the listener and see in the Deleuzian fold-in of music and text the attempt to oppose a more off-Cartesian notion of the subject to that of Descartes' own, all too confident subject predicated on stable patterns of signification. In this view, it would have been Deleuze's goal to destabilize listening subjects such as Perrault's Paleologue and Philalethe by containing them in a potentially endless series of folds without a content or frame, thereby thwarting any claims to substance or coherence. Subjects such as these, obviously, do not so much perceive *from* a perspective as they "come to" or "remain in" one.[48] In short, theirs is a relationship to the world that is not determined by semiotic stability, but is mediated through a more resonant type of knowledge, or what Deleuze calls "point of view."[49]

It is tempting to draw a parallel between Deleuze's "point of view" and what film sound scholar Rick Altman, in a by now canonic collection on film sound, has termed "point-of-audition," or POA, for short.[50] From a mere technical standpoint, POA sound is akin to the "point-of-view" shots ubiquitous in Hollywood cinema. Like these, it is the dominant model of the Hollywood soundtrack during the 1930s and a major form of subject placement. For instance, when in Howard Hawks's *Only Angels Have Wings* (1939) Noah Beery's plane takes off into the night, the soundtrack for the next shot of Cary Grant and Jean Arthur is that of the sound of the (unseen) airplane motor fading into the distance. POA sound, in other words, here is used as a type of sound that would be heard from a point within the film's diegesis by a specific character. As such, it is a common way of positioning the spectator in a specific relationship to the plot on screen.

But POA sound is also highly fictional:

> Point-of-audition sound always carries signs of its own fictional audition. As such, point-of-audition sound always has the effect of luring the listener into the diegesis not at the point of enunciation of the sound, but at the point of its audition. Point-of-audition sound thus relates us to the narrative not as external auditors, identified with the camera and its position...nor as participant in the dialogue (the standard situation of the "intelligible" approach), but as internal auditor.[51]

Of course, POA sound in film is primarily produced by the montage of different patterns of volume and reverb. Yet even though in the context of early modern opera listening was not subject to film's more advanced technique of manipulation, Perrault's model of listening predicated on "exteriorizing" identification bears a striking similarity to what Altman calls "perfect interpellation." He writes: "We are asked not to hear, but to identify with

95

someone who will hear for us." Point-of-audition sound "inserts us into the narrative at the very intersection of two spaces which the image alone is incapable of linking, thus giving us the sensation of controlling the relationship between those spaces."[52]

POA sound thus enables a widening of the subject's sphere of imagination. But at the same time, this act of hubris threatens the same subject with the possibility of its own dissolution. Losing themselves in the phantom space of *sentimens*, Perrault's spectators do not restrict their auditory experience to the sounds and the affects represented by them under the rules of *Affektenlehre*. Their hearing takes place entirely outside the dichotomy of the subject and the phenomenal world, or better still, parallel to it.

One understands why listening to the marvelous might take opera audiences at midcentury down a slippery path. And one sees the cause of the uncertainty into which Perrault releases the reader at the end of *Du bruit* and, especially, why Perrault needs to invoke the ear's quasi-inbuilt "certainty" of judgment. Yet for all the fascinating parallels between Perrault's "Sçauoir" and Deleuze's and Altman's work, the question remains how the unstable, fantastic form of early modern listening and the uncertain subject-object relationship attendant on and mediated through such listening are embedded in the empirics of the ear. What might late seventeenth-century otological knowledge tell us about the era's attempts to fathom a less mechanical and more flexible ear-constituted subject? Here we need to turn to an aspect of seventeenth-century conceptions of hearing in which the interplay of otology, philosophy, and the "vernacular modern" project of grounding liberty in a new form of subjecthood becomes evident in all its precariousness. This is the association, current in seventeenth-century learned and popular discourse, of hearing with titillation.

The Ticklish Subject

Tickling is a double-edged sword. Pleasant one minute, it can turn into an unbearable experience the next. No wonder, then, that when we refer to something or someone as being "ticklish," we mean that it (or the person) is, to quote Samuel Johnson's *Dictionary of the English Language* of 1755, "tottering; uncertain; unfixed." What may be less obvious, yet what a quick look at French dictionaries from the era such as Robert Estienne's *Dictionaire francoislatin* (1549) and Antoine Furetière's *Dictionnaire universel* (1690) reveals, is that words such as "tickle" or "ticklish"—or rather, the equivalent French term, *chatouiller*—are relatively recent additions that came into more frequent use only from the late fifteenth to early seventeenth centuries.[53] And perhaps we may be even less aware that during this period, "to tickle," along with words such as "to touch," were also often used in direct association with the ear, heart, lungs, blood, or "spirits."

So whence this strange modernity of the tickling sensation? And what is so new about the haptic dimension of hearing, when none other than Aristotle had already reduced all forms of sensation to the sense of touch? Generally speaking, prior to the Romantic era, tickling posed a challenge to a thinking accustomed to the idea that sensations such as pain and pleasure are as sharply separated as day is from night. Hence, during the seventeenth century, such thinking was at pains to accommodate "mixed" feelings such as those caused by tickling. At the same time, there existed in the Western imagination a long tradition associating music with lasciviousness. Early modern letters are replete with descriptions of music's titillating effects being attributed to the ear's winding, turning structure, which prevents airy music from forcefully penetrating the interior of the body.[54] But by the same token, such titillation could also turn into *ravissement*, understood as the spiritual transport to a higher realm, or into sexual violence such as rape, also called *ravissement*.[55]

Yet the ear's ambiguous position at the borderline between sexual pleasure and sexual violence, pleasure and pain, all mediated by titillation, did more than inspire early modern painters, poets, and composers to rich explorations of the erotic, licentious, and even violent. The fascination with *chatouillement* also reverberated through more prosaic realms, such as the emerging fields of acoustics and otology, infusing them, in true early modern fashion, with philosophy's never-ending quest for the linkages between mind and body, reason and sense. And so the question one might ask is this: What is the relationship between such widespread (and more often than not, derogatory) descriptions of music as mere titillation, on the one hand, and more ambiguous or, as I have called them, off-Cartesian notions of personhood, on the other? What, in other words, is the connection between the ear and the "ticklish subject?"[56] As always, it is Descartes' work, especially his frequent use of the term *chatouiller*, that provides a useful point of entry.

In October 1631, Descartes wrote to his friend the Jesuit polymath Marin Mersenne: "Sound is nothing but a certain trembling of the air that comes to titillate our ears (*qui vient chatouiller nos oreilles*)."[57] This statement—repeated almost verbatim in the philosopher's *Le monde* written between 1629 and 1633—comes in the midst of a prolonged argument between the two scholars on the nature of sound, in the course of which Descartes ever so insistently reiterated the position he had taken as early as 1618 in his *Compendium musicae* that the perception of harmony is a purely subjective phenomenon. Mersenne had annoyed him, he wrote, "by asking me how much more agreeable one consonance is than another, as if you would ask me how much more agreeable I find it to eat fruit than fish."[58]

> Concerning the sweetness of the consonances two things should be distinguished: namely, what renders them simpler and more accordant, and what renders them more agreeable to the ear. Now, as to what renders them more agreeable, that depends on the places where they are employed; and there are places where even diminished fifths and other dissonances are more agreeable than consonances, so that one could not determine absolutely that one consonance is more agreeable than another. One could indeed say, however, that, normally speaking, the thirds and sixths are more agreeable than

the fourth; that in cheerful songs, major thirds and sixths are more agreeable than minor ones, and the opposite in sad [songs], etc., in that there are more occasions where they can be employed agreeably. But one can say absolutely which consonances are the most simple and the most accordant ones; for that depends only on how often their sounds unite, and how closely they approach the nature of the unison; so that one can say absolutely that the fourth is more accordant than the major third, while ordinarily it is not so agreeable, just as the cassia is definitely sweeter than olives, but not so agreeable to our taste.[59]

The terminology may be confusing, but what Descartes refers to by "accordant" and "agreeable" is the fact that to seventeenth-century ears, thirds sounded just as consonant, that is, "agreeable," as an octave or fourth, although these intervals were mathematically more "accordant." The philosopher's fit of anger might thus be read as a man's desperate attempt to separate subjective taste from rational judgment and to put an end to a debate that had started much earlier and that, in many ways, can be considered to lie at the origins of modern acoustics and psychoacoustics. As H. Floris Cohen has shown and as we have seen in the context of the earlier discussion in Chapter 1 of concutere, the entire debate hinged on the idea that consonance and dissonance are caused by the coincidence (or lack of coincidence) of pulses of vibrating strings.[60]

The first and rudimentary "coincidence theory" was that of Giovanni Battista Benedetti (1530–1590), formulated in a letter to the composer Cipriano de Rore.[61] A plucked string, Benedetti had observed, regularly "percusses" the surrounding air, producing waves of air similar to the ones brought forth by throwing a stone into the water. When such a string is sounded together with another string that is half as long, there results what he called a "cotermination of percussions:" The pulses of the longer string coincide with every second stroke of the shorter string sounding at an octave above. Accordingly, in the case of a fifth — where the proportion of the string lengths is 3:2 — coincidence occurs only on every third pulse, or when the higher string has performed three pulses and the lower one two. The main point about this observation is that Benedetti, in closing his letter, combines the Zarlinesque "wonderful proportion" of string length and pitch with a new focus on vibration and auditory sensations of pleasure and pain: "Now the pleasure [*voluptas*] that the consonances give to hearing comes from their softening [*leniunt*] the senses, while, to the contrary the pain [*dolor*] that originates from the dissonances is born from sharpness [*asperitas*]."[62]

Benedetti's prescient theory of coincidence more than likely remained unknown until the rediscovery of his letter in 1961. The same cannot be said of Galileo Galilei's last work, *Discorsi*, published in 1638 and one of the most widely read works of its time. Here, in a compact discussion of the "Reasons of the Wonderful Accidents of Sound," the Pisan scholar writes:

> The irritation from [dissonances] is born, I believe, of the discordant pulsations of two different tones that strike on our eardrum all out of proportion; and very harsh indeed will be the dissonances whose times of vibrations are incommensurables.... Those pairs of sounds will be consonant, and heard with pleasure, which strike the eardrum with good order; this requires first that the impacts [*percosse*] made within the same period are commensurable in number, so that the cartilage of the eardrum need not be in a perpetual torment of bending in two different ways to accept and obey ever-discordant beatings.[63]

Galileo's elaboration of Benedetti's theory, despite a number of mathematical flaws and notwithstanding its limited experimental scope, is extremely interesting for our focus here on titillation. What the determination of consonance and dissonance by hearing, rather than by number, implied is a sliding scale on which clear-cut distinctions were becoming increasingly blurred and consonance could be defined only relatively, as a function of the frequency of coinciding pulses. Thus, while an octave was taken as the most consonant interval because the *percosse* of the two strings coincided on every pulse, in a fifth, this would happen only in every sixth, in a fourth every twelfth, and in a major sixth every fifteenth pulse. Interestingly, on this logic, the latter interval would also have to be considered as more consonant than the major third, where the coincidence occurs only on every twentieth pulse, thus contradicting standard musical practice in which the third was considered to be the more consonant interval. In a nutshell, for Galileo, the perception of harmony was conceivable only in terms of a remarkably prescient psychophysics — of an erotics, even — in which a fifth produces a "tickling and teasing of the cartilage of the eardrum so that the Sweetness is tempered by a sprinkling of sharpness, giving the impression of being simultaneously sweetly kissed, and bitten."[64]

The line of inquiry started by Benedetti and Galileo Galilei continued to dominate acoustics until well into the second half of the seventeenth century, with only slight adjustments being made by Mersenne and Isaac Beeckman.[65] And there is little evidence that these thinkers' "philosophical" bent compelled them to explore the broader epistemological and cultural implications of aural titillation for the rational self that was meant to emerge from and to be maintained by the new scientific practices they established. Quite the contrary. Mersenne, for instance, only grudgingly assented to Descartes' insistence on separating the objectivity of "accordant" intervals from their subjective "agreeability." So resolutely in fact did he remain fixated on the idea of matching objective ratio and subjective perception that he resorted to an analogy with vision. Music, he wrote in 1634, is "the perspective of the ear, like perspective is the music of the eye."[66]

Not so Descartes. For him, there was more to the consonance-dissonance relationship than mere taste and vibrating air. At stake was a whole ethics of titillation. The point of departure for this theory is, naturally, the philosopher's brief synopsis, in *L'homme*, of the coincidence theory of consonance that follows the description of the ear and that we encountered at the end of Chapter 1. The sensation of consonance and dissonance, Descartes explains there, is a function of the "more or less equal intervals" occurring between the "little blows *(secousses)* that compose them."[67] As the little diagram accompanying his discussion shows (figure 2.4), "if the divisions of the lines A, B, C, D, E, F, G, H, represent little blows that constitute as many different sounds, it is easy to judge that those that are represented by the lines G and H cannot be as smooth to the ear as the others." Likewise, one must note that "A and B joined together, or ABC, or ABD, or even ABCE, are more concordant than are A and F, or ACD, or ADE, and the like." All of which shows, the philosopher concludes, "that it is not absolutely the smoothest things that are most agreeable to the senses, but those that titillate them in the best-tempered way: just as salt and vinegar are often more agreeable to the tongue than fresh water. And it is this that makes music as receptive to thirds and sixths and even sometimes to dissonances as to unisons, octaves, and fifths."[68]

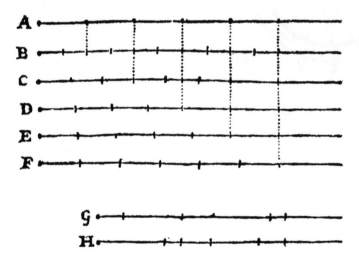

Figure 2.4. René Descartes, *Traité de l'homme*. Descartes's illustration of what H. F. Cohen later termed the coincidence theory of consonance. Similar diagrams remained popular until well into the eighteenth century.

One only has to compare this passage with Galileo's *Discorsi* to see that while Descartes adopts the explanation (and visual representation) of coinciding pulses, he eschews the Italian's openly sexual connotation of titillation. But Descartes not only excludes aural (and, to be sure, sexual) pleasure from the sphere of the cogito, he does so by attributing to *chatouillement* a stabilizing role, conducive to virtue and moral uprightness. The most striking formulations in this regard are perhaps those found in the philosopher's final work *Les passions de l'âme* (The Passions of the Soul). Here, Descartes differed from most of his moralizing contemporaries in insisting that the passions are necessary to human action and self-preservation and as such are neither good nor bad in themselves. They exist independent of the soul and acquire moral significance solely by dint of a critical judgment being brought to bear on them. The interesting twist is that Descartes, in what looks like a complete turnaround on his earlier anti-aesthetic stance, invokes tickling as a way to distance himself from the moralist critique of theater and the denial of the cathartic function of art that was being articulated ever more vehemently during the second half of the seventeenth century. He accepts the aesthetic experience as an essential condition of the search for a moral foundation of personal being and in the process reinstates Aristotelian dogma by widening it. In a section devoted to the question "How the passions are excited by goods and evils which only respect the body; and wherein consists tickling [*chatouillement*] and pain," he writes: "A man naturally takes delight to feel himself moved to all sorts of passions, yea, even sadness, and hatred, when these passions are caused only by strange adventures, which he sees personated on a stage, or by such like occasion, which not being capable to trouble us any way, seem to tickle the soul by touching it."[69]

But why does this *chatouillement* please us? Not simply because the action on stage obviously does not threaten or concern us directly or because there is no resemblance between the tickling sensation and what causes it. Rather, Descartes argues, the tickling sensation puts to the test the power of the soul to over-ride a sensation that under normal circumstances would cause it discomfort. For example, when a husband mourns his deceased wife, mixed in with his feelings of sadness, pity, and even love may be a "secret joy" at the thought that she will never return. Similarly,

> when we read strange adventures in a book, or see them person-ated on a stage, it sometimes excites sadness in us, sometimes joy, or love, or hatred, and generally all the passions, according to the diversity of objects that offer themselves to our imagination. But withal we take a delight to feel them excited in us and this delight is an intellectual joy, which may as well spring from sadness, as all the rest of the passions.[70]

Descartes' sarcasm aside, aesthetic experience clearly takes on a positive function. If we could only imagine ourselves in a the-ater each time misfortune befalls us, Descartes seems to suggest, the ensuing sadness would be turned into pleasure. In legitimiz-ing the delight in the sights and sounds of the theater — of the spoken theater, that is, not of the degraded forms of amusement such as Italian opera — as an essential conduit toward rational mastery of the passions and as a mirror of ethical conduct, Des-cartes redefines the aesthetic experience as an enactment of the search for a moral foundation.[71]

Which brings us, at long last, back to Claude Perrault, "Sçauoir," and *Du bruit.*

A Matter of Taste

Perrault must have sensed the vagueness of his early text, for he appended to *Du bruit* the aforementioned postlude entitled "De la musique des anciens," in which he distanced himself even fur-ther from the claims and cultural models of the "ancients." But in so doing, Perrault not only accentuated the relativist stance of "Sçauoir," he also placed it on a more solid footing by ground-ing it in the concept of good taste. Originally conceived as a response to Giovanni Battista Doni's account of ancient music *De Praestantia musicae veteris* (1647), "De la musique des anciens" is a blistering attack on the idolization, current throughout the seventeenth century, of ancient Greek music. This idolization, Perrault argued, was simply based on a misreading of the ancient sources. The word *symphonia*, for instance, did not mean that ancient Greek music was the sophisticated polyphonic music modern audiences took it to be. Quite the contrary, it was monophonic and monotonous, little more than a "rhythmic grumble," a "noise fit for the infancy of the world."[72] To understand the linkage between Perrault's anti-Hellenic criticism and his otological pursuits, we have to retrace our steps and return to the Louvre and Perrault the architect.

In 1673, Perrault had translated into French Vitruvius's *De architectura, libri decem* (Ten Books of Architecture).[73] Rediscovered during the Renaissance, Vitruvius for two centuries had been the undisputed authority on architecture, aligning in Pythagorean fashion the proportions of buildings with the ratios governing musical harmony. Although by the late seventeenth century such precepts were no longer taken at face value, the idea that musical harmony might in and of itself lend solidity and aesthetic unity to edifices still carried considerable, if not practical ideological weight, as is evident in the concurrent publication of *Architecture harmonique* (1679) by none other than the *maître de musique* at the Sainte-Chapelle in Paris, René Ouvrard, and *Cours d'architecture* (1675–1683) by the director of the Académie Royale d'Architecture and one of Perrault's fiercest critics, François Blondel.[74] Using the intervallic proportions obtained on the monochord as his yardstick, Ouvrard had been dreaming up buildings that would function as vast resonators solely by dint of the harmonic proportions underlying their construction. Blondel, for his part, insisted that the ancient architect's proportions were in agreement with the laws of nature and, like music, were grounded in what he, following Vitruvius, called *eurythmie*.

Perrault's extensive footnotes to Vitruvius's text leave little

doubt that he considered his Roman predecessor's views as hopelessly outdated. It may thus well be argued that by the time he
wrote "De la musique des anciens," Perrault had already fixed his
attention on the full-blown assault on Grecophile architecture
he would soon launch in *Ordonnance*. The music essay, then, was
but an opening salvo in the culture wars of the late seventeenth
century, a prelude to the broader project of challenging not just
the hegemony of ancient Greek architecture, but that of antiquity
and the foes of "modern liberty" all told. If, Perrault reasoned,
it could be shown that the ancients were "a little ignorant in
precisely the science [music] in which they took the most pride,"
not only would the exalted place of the ancients in the history of
music become untenable, the very usefulness of musical ratios for
determining the sizes and proportions of buildings would also
become open to doubt.

It was precisely this musical argument that served as the
jumping-off point for Perrault's new theory of architecture. The
latitude ancient architects had taken in determining the dimensions of buildings, he stated in the opening paragraphs of *Ordonnance*, show "just how ill founded is the opinion of people who
believe that correct architectural proportions were as certain
and invariable as the proportions that give musical harmony its
beauty and appeal — proportions that do not depend on us but that
nature has established with absolutely immutable precision and
that cannot be changed without immediately offending even the
least sensitive ear."[75]

A proper comparison between music and architecture
demanded consideration of more than harmonic proportions.
Individual and national differences would come into play, as
would, perhaps more significantly, epistemological factors. For all
their structural homologies, the eye and the ear do not perceive in
quite the same manner. Whereas the eye is able to convey to the
mind the effect of proportional relationships through knowledge,
the ear cannot provide such knowledge.[76] Still, Perrault mused,
why is it that even though the eye is capable of producing positive

knowledge, we often appreciate proper proportions without actually knowing their reason? Are such preferences grounded in something objective, such as musical harmonies, or are they merely founded in custom? Antedating some of the propositions set forth in Charles Perrault's (ultimately more influential) *Parallèle des anciens et des modernes* (1688), Claude Perrault supposed two kinds of beauty to inform our judgment: a beauty based on convincing reasons and an arbitrary sort of beauty. While the former he claimed to be easily apprehended by everyone, he saw arbitrary beauty as entirely based on external associations, such as the patterns of speech or certain forms of aristocratic *couture* that, although unattractive in themselves, were deemed beautiful because of the "worthiness and patronage of people at court." Thus, it is not reason that forms the basis for aesthetic judgment, but power.[77]

The same holds true for architecture which displays both positive beauty and beauty that is only arbitrary. Yet far from denying the existence of classical proportions, Perrault considered that these sorts of "positive" beauty belong to the realm of *bon sens*, or common sense proper. Arbitrary beauty, by contrast, is the object of what he called *bon goût*, good taste. Thus, although it takes only common sense to realize that a large edifice built of precisely cut blocks of marble is more beautiful than a small stone house "where nothing is plumb, level or square," only the architect — or, more broadly, the *honnête homme*, the man of distinction — has the knowledge of arbitrary beauty required for *bon goût*.[78]

With this notion of good taste, Perrault plainly put himself at variance with the prevailing opinion that the beautiful has its origin in the natural proportions inherent in musical harmony and in architecture and that, hence, in Nicolas Boileau's famous dictum, "rien n'est beau que le vrai," "nothing is beautiful but the truth." But the anti-Vitruvian, anticonservative criticism was not the only point behind the issue of good taste. Its significance went beyond architecture, broaching a new sense of art as an autonomous sphere. Nowhere does this become clearer than in one of the key propositions set forth in *Ordonnance*, which directly links Perrault's aesthetics to his scientific research on hearing and sight. This was the idea, fundamental to Vitruvian dogma, that in order to allow the truth of harmonious proportions to appear, the architect has to take into account the optical distortions of dimensions that arise when statues on top of buildings are viewed from a distance and, consequently, have to be slightly tilted forward. Perrault systematically refuted this theory, arguing—as he had in fact shown in his *Du bruit*—that hearing and sight are "not as susceptible to surprise and deceit as people claim."[79] Aesthetic pleasure, in other words, is acquired pleasure, or, as Descartes had taught, it is the result of habituation and reflex.

How, then, did Perrault frame the specifically musical component of his argument? The point of departure, once again, was the perennial question of whether or not the music of the ancients was superior to that of Perrault's day. Like Descartes fifty years earlier, Perrault was prepared to grant ancient Greek music exceptional powers. And like the celebrated philosopher, he believed the penchant of Greek musicians for what he called "excessive transport" to reside in the fact that "all they put their effort into was to touch the heart and the senses, which is quite a lot easier than to satisfy the intellect [*esprit*]." Small wonder, then, that the ancients "did not endeavor to look for another genre of perfection, since it would have been to the detriment of their goal of pleasing the multitude, which is usually more easily moved by the senses and the heart than by the intellect."[80]

And so it was with "modern" music:

> Those who do not possess an intellect capable of being touched by what is admirable in the diversity and beautifully arranged consonances of part music [*musique à plusieurs parties*], but instead only have ears to judge the clarity and intonation of the voice and a heart to love the gaiety of a cadence or the plaintive sweetness of a sad mode, will prefer a beautiful voice or a sweet flute solo to a music in parts whose beauty remains unknown to them. A musically

informed mind, by contrast, will be ravished with admiration upon hearing an excellent counterpoint, poorly sung though it may be.[81]

Two terms in this passage require explanation: "counterpoint" and "part music." Both are closely related and highlight the ambiguity of theoretical thinking about music — or, for that matter, any theorizing — before the consolidation of tonality in Rameau's "theory of harmony" nearly half a century later. In Perrault's case, the use of these terms is further complicated by the fact that the composers he singled out as exemplars of *musique à plusieurs parties* — the sixteenth-century Italian Orlando di Lasso being one of them — by the end of the late seventeenth century had definitely become passé and thus stood in jarring contrast to Perrault's dissenting architectural views and his professed status as a "modern" more broadly. At the same time, it must be remembered that throughout the seventeenth century, a triadic conception of harmony and a more polyphonic notion based on composite intervallic relations governed by rules of individual voice leading existed side by side, without one necessarily connoting a more "modern" stance over the other.

The association of taste with social status highlights the precariousness of Perrault's project of grounding aesthetic relativism in anatomical "animism." Having repudiated Pythagorean musical dogma no less than Cartesian physiology, Perrault struggled to anchor the compatibility of sense and reason within the larger framework of absolutism's "modernizing" agenda. The simultaneously resonating and "reasoning" cochlea, while potentially enlarging the subject's sphere of liberty, also threatened to undermine the established order. Taste, always a good way to end an argument, bridged these conflicting strands of late seventeenth-century point of audition. But even as Perrault's work straddled several aesthetic, political, and scientific projects without resolving the contradictions inherent in either of these projects, it is precisely the everyday, "vernacular" character of his modernity that lends his theory of hearing a compelling force. Even in hearing it appears, to "move on," one sometimes has to go back.

Figure 3.1. Claude-Nicolas Le Cat, *La théorie de l'ouie* (1757), frontispiece (courtesy of the Bancroft Library, University of California, Berkeley). The engraving depicts Le Cat (in the lower left corner) overlooking a scene of putti, ear ossicles, various acoustic instruments, and an organ. The female figure at the center holding a lyre and stave of radiating light sits astride a huge, cochlea-shaped mound: Reason and resonance united and, literally, supported by the ear.

CHAPTER THREE

Good Vibes:

Nerves, Air, and Happiness

during the French Enlightenment

In 1751, in a provincial town north of Paris, there appeared a small pamphlet whose cover bears the following seemingly interminable inscription: *Discours qui a remporté le prix à l'Académie de Dijon, en l'année 1750: sur cette question proposée par la même Académie; si le rétablissement des sciences & des arts a contribué a épurer les moeurs. Nouvelle édition, accompagnée de la réfutation de ce discours, par les apostilles critiques de l'un des académiciens examinateurs, qui a refusé de donner son suffrage à cette pièce* (see figure 3.1).[1] In its thirty or so pages, the anonymous "examining Academy member" takes issue with the propositions that a certain "citoyen de Genève" had made in an essay submitted to the Academy in Dijon the previous year and that had won first prize. How could there be any truth, the author of the "refutation" writes, to the Genevan's assertion that the sciences, letters, and the arts "wrap garlands of flowers around the iron chains" that men wear and that stifle in them "the sentiment of that original liberty for which they seem to have been born, make them love their slavery, and turn them into what is called civilized peoples?" Was not slavery, on the contrary, the fruit of "tyranny established by violence, *the reason of the stronger*, inevitable consequence of barbarism?" he asks.[2] And what of the prizewinner's audacity of opposing the morals of the American savages to those of his own century, polished as they were, precisely because of the sciences and the arts? In short, wasn't all the talk about pure nature, simple nature, and a golden age little more than "flowery turns of phrase," which in the end "comes down to knowing whether the *trees* which formerly were in our countryside are bigger than those of today?"[3]

The "citizen of Geneva" was of course none other than Jean-Jacques Rousseau, and the "*pièce*" was his stunning *First Discourse*. As for the anonymous author of the "critical apostilles," there can scarcely be any doubt that it was Claude-Nicolas Le Cat (1700–1768). Although he is today overshadowed by luminaries such as Théophile de Bordeu (1722–1766) and Albrecht von Haller (1708–1777), in his time, Le Cat was a highly acclaimed physician and, if we are to believe Voltaire, a "very great *philosophe*."[4] And indeed, the recipient of numerous honors and prizes and the author of works on topics as varied as geophysics, astronomy, geology, archaeology, history, and *beaux arts*, Le Cat embodied the best of the Age of Reason. For instance, in his 1765 *Traité de la couleur de la peau humaine en général & de celle des nègres en particulier* (Treatise on the Color of the Human Skin in General and of the Negroes in Particular), he denounced the "folly" of looking at black skin color as "a punishment for blasphemy," declaring pigmentation to be caused instead by a substance located in the membrane surrounding the tips of nerve cells, a substance that he called "ethiops."[5] And mirroring the era's ethos of self-improvement and anti-aristocratic altruism, he was convinced that "to keep ourselves occupied is the only means of rendering ourselves useful to ourselves and others."[6]

Le Cat also wrote on the ear, with two volumes of otology bearing his name: the *Traité des sens*, originally written in 1739, and a supplement of 320 pages to the *Traité des sens* entitled *La théorie de l'ouie*, written in 1757. (Both works were later revised and appeared in the second and third volume, respectively, of Le Cat's *Oeuvres physiologiques*, published in 1767.)[7] At first sight, though, these texts seem unlikely candidates for the project of charting enlightened otology. Compared with the almost contemporaneous discovery of the endolymph in 1760 by Domenico Cotugno (1736–1822) or the seminal descriptions of the round window published four years after Le Cat's death by Antonio

Scarpa (1747–1832), Le Cat's otological findings, if they figure
in the annals of otology at all, are usually dismissed as insig-
nificant or, as in Adam Politzer's authoritative *Geschichte der Ohrenheilkunde* (History of Otology), lacking in "clarity of reasoning."[8] Also, Le Cat's musical and philosophical acumen paled in
comparison with the breadth and intensity of the prolonged (and,
more often than not, acrimonious) debates between Rousseau,
the composer Jean-Philipe Rameau, and the mathematician Jean
de la Rond d'Alembert over such diverse issues as Italian music,
musical acoustics, and music theory.[9] Above all, however, Le Cat's
work does not comfortably fit into some of the binaries we have
become accustomed to in making sense of the dramatic changes
affecting the sciences, arts, letters, and philosophy in France
during the middle of the eighteenth century. For instance, in the
otology of the era, the contrast between an older, cool-headed,
mechanistic worldview that looked down upon the human body
as a mere machine and that scorned the senses as untrustworthy
sources of knowledge and the radical, new concept of *sensibilité*
that exalted sentiment and physical sensation as essential to the
pursuit of empirical knowledge, civic virtue, and art was far less
evident than in other fields such as optics, the study of electricity,
social theory, or music.[10]

Yet Le Cat's ambiguous position at the intersection of numerous competing paradigms, oddly, predestines his otological work
for closer study of the three-century tenure of sympathetic resonance at the heart of the physiology of hearing, precisely because
it complicates any attempt to plot mid-eighteenth-century otology's development along the kind of axis often held to be typical
of period medicine more broadly, with the mechanist doctrines
of Descartes, William Harvey, or Herman Boerhaave (1668–1738)
at one end and the sentimental vitalism of the Montpellier school
at the other.[11] The idea, for instance, that our ears perceive tones
passively, that is, as the result of a mechanical synchronism
between vibrating air and oscillating cochlear structures, might
be seen as clashing with Bordeu's vitalist credo that the "reign

of feeling or sensibility is among the most extensive; feeling is involved in all the functions; it directs them all."[12] But at the same time, the prominence of resonance in eighteenth-century debates also reflects what Jessica Riskin has called the "mutually transformative intimacy of natural and moral science" within the larger Enlightenment project of moral and political self-fashioning.[13] Straddling several fields of inquiry at once, resonance was thus eminently compatible with sensibility's fundamental tenet that the animal body, social communication, art, and even humanity's highest aspiration for happiness all operate on the basis of sympathy.

There are numerous domains where this sentimental aspect of sympathetic resonance could be seen at work. In medicine, for instance, it was not a one-way street leading from a single cause to an effect that was thought to make the body work, but the sympathetic interrelationship of different parts resonating in mutual dependence. It is "this communication that body parts have with one another," the article "Sympathie (Physiolog.)" in the *Encyclopédie* declared, that produces an enchainment of pleasant sensations, just as, conversely, it "transports to one part the pains and illnesses that afflict the other."[14] And as the author of the article, the Chevalier de Jaucourt, insists, it is not membranes touching each other that bring about sympathy, but nerves that are to be understood as autonomous, interacting forces, rather than as mere channels with only one discrete function.

Another area in which the notion of sympathy held sway was musical aesthetics. Enlightened audiences from the middle of the century on increasingly enlisted their ears as active partners in the ambitious project of grounding the subject in what Frédéric-Melchior Grimm, one of the chief ideologues of sensibility and an ardent defender of Gluck's operatic reforms, called "the intimate relation between our sentiments and our sensations."[15] Instead of attuning themselves to what music imitates, midcentury listeners were enjoined to confirm in their own emotions the truth of the stories told in Gluck's operas. And instead of allowing music's sound simply to wash over and subdue them, these listeners felt an inexplicable personal affinity with Gluck's tender melodic strains, their ears leaning in sympathy toward the music and, above all, other listeners next to them.[16]

And finally, and again perhaps more paradoxically, the ubiquity of sympathy was also felt in the more lofty domain of philosophical discourse, where it touched on a host of "moral" issues. One, if not the most vital of these issues concerned enlightened notions of subjectivity and happiness.[17] In eighteenth-century thinking, or at any rate among the more philosophically inclined, happiness had supplanted spiritual salvation in the other world as humanity's highest aspiration, and like all "moral" aspects, such a more worldly concept of happiness depended on the interaction between body and mind sympathetically conjoined through what Helvétius called the pleasures of movement and "spring."[18] Yet because the semantic field surrounding *bonheur* overlapped with otologically pertinent phenomena such as "vibration" and, hence, like all natural phenomena, now was conceived along Newtonian lines, the ear's role as part of a new, self-generating self was ambiguous. How could there be a self that was simultaneously happy and autonomous when otology taught that listening is subject to resonance's benign, yet indomitable rule? How did "good vibes" and the *moi* go together? How might a sensibilist conception of sympathy become the basis for a process of self-fashioning in which, to use Fritz Breithaupt's apt phrase, the individual is under the constant pressure to be, and the I comes to "hold the monopoly on selfhood?"[19] In short, what choice did the new sensibilist ego have, other than to listen, to be, in fact, a happily vibrating self?

"Sentir c'est penser": Otology and Sensibility

Le Cat's preoccupation with the ear, as we have seen, evolved over a period of several decades. And although he called *La théorie de l'ouie* a mere "supplement" to the earlier *Traité des sens*, significant differences exist between the two works, especially in the concluding sections on the physiology of hearing, in which Le Cat addresses the key questions of the Enlightenment concerning the seat of sensation and the transformation of sensory impressions into ideas. Some of these differences are symptomatic of the discontinuities of style, epistemology, and subject matter that marked popular and scholarly discussions of the ear during mid-century. For instance, while the *Traité* hectically shuttles back and forth between remarks on Italian music, a discussion of the structure of the labyrinth, deafness, and a peculiar Italian ritual during which the bites of spiders were treated with the help of music, the *Théorie* follows a more orderly line of reasoning. It begins with a discussion of the outer ear and the vestibule, from which are then drawn more general conclusions on questions such as the "features of good music." Similar differences are observed with regard to music's more general healing powers beyond those of curing spider bites. Elaborated in great detail in the *Traité*, they receive only passing mention in the *Théorie*.

By far the most telling difference, however, between the two works lies in how Le Cat in the *Théorie* rebuts one of the most commonplace tropes of enlightened zeitgeist: *l'homme-clavecin*, the human harpsichord.[20] Although the idea that the human body may be compared to a string instrument dates back to Pythagoras's derivation of cosmic harmony from the intervallic proportions obtained on the monochord, and the harpsichord itself came to prominence only around the late fifteenth century, it was Descartes who first anthropologized the string metaphor by describing the animal body in purely mechanical terms. And so by the time the harpsichord had come to acquire unique status as both cultural capital and a show piece of the bourgeois household, with its light, silvery sound being seen as emblematic of inner refinement and delicacy, enlightened probes into the mind's mysterious inner workings increasingly involved some sort of analogy between fibers and strings. Cartaud de la Vilate, for instance, asserted that humans "are like harpsichords that tremble harmoniously."[21] Meanwhile, the Abbé Jacquin, in one of the many vade mecums offering medical knowledge to France's ever-growing reading public, counseled:

> To form an idea of the passions, it is good to consider our individual as some kind of musical instrument whose strings, struck in greater or lesser chords, produce more or less harmonious sounds and thus excite either pleasure or ennui. The nerves, which for the most part take their origin in the brain...are divided up into an infinity of fibers spread across the whole body, covering even its surface. Those are the keys and strings of the instrument.[22]

The fascination with *l'homme-clavecin* even went beyond the realm of popular health manuals and works of moral and aesthetic edification, appealing to more prominent intellectuals, as well as to trained scientists. As early as 1734, Montesquieu, for instance, had described a close relationship between muscle fibers and reason. The more flexibility there is in the nerve fibers, he claimed in comparing nerves to harpsichord strings, the better one is able to think.[23] Naturalist Charles Bonnet, meanwhile, was adamant that the brain fibers are "a kind of key or hammer designed to render a certain tone."[24] And last, but not least, and perhaps most notoriously of all, Julien Offray de la Mettrie conjectured that the "organ of hearing, and even the entire human body, may be regarded as such [stringed] instruments."[25]

At the same time, there is something odd about the popularity of the harpsichord metaphor. After all, the harpsichord is not a very touch-sensitive instrument. Because its jack-mounted plectrums pluck the strings, it is not possible to vary the instrument's loudness appreciably, nor for that matter to produce a vibrato. The sounds of the harpsichord are delicate, to be sure, but also somewhat incorporeal and insensate, a fact that the composer François Couperin was well aware of when he complained that it has "appeared almost impossible to maintain that one could give any 'soul' to this instrument."[26] But if the lack of tactile responsiveness and harpsichord music's modest potential for *sensibilité* made the instrument a rather inept signifier for the caressing of the filmy network of nerves and spirits, its very rigidity also conveyed some of the mechanistic inevitability at the heart of Enlightenment notions of the interplay of body, mind, and environment.

Diderot's lifelong obsession with the harpsichord as both musical instrument and metaphor is a case in point. From early beginnings in the *Principes d'acoustique* (1745), still written under the influence of Rameau's notion of the *corps sonore*, and the *Encyclopédie* article "Affection" (1751), to *Entretien entre d'Alembert et Diderot* (A Conversation between d'Alembert and Diderot) and *Rêve de d'Alembert* (D'Alembert's Dream) (both 1769), Diderot deployed the harpsichord metaphor throughout his work. Yet each time the metaphor is pressed into service, it is meant to illustrate a different concept of the subject. In the *Principes d'acoustique*, for instance, strings underscore the traditional notion that a "beautiful life," like musical pleasure, rests on proportions and harmony. In the "Affection" article, by contrast, Diderot sets up a correlation between the "mechanism of the body" and the sensibility of an individual—a correlation akin to the strings of a musical instrument producing different pitches when played with a bow. In the *Entretien*, finally, the instrument becomes the master metaphor and organizing principle suffusing everything: nature, individual, society, and even the text itself.[27] Whether as "keys that are pressed by nature around us," as "keys that often press themselves," as a set of two harpsichords mounted with identical strings, or even as harpsichords that are both instrument and player at the same time, it is an inexorable totality and completeness of organization that lends a hermetic closure to both the subject and the discourse about the subject. Of course, while the differences between these texts may well speak to the paradigm shift from mechanistic models to vitalism, the metaphor of the resonant strings remains the same.

But there were exceptions. As early as 1746, the Swiss physician Albrecht von Haller had declared himself unable to detect in the "red slime" of the sympathetic nerve a tension that "bore the slightest resemblance with a musical string."[28] Le Cat, for his part, entertained similar doubts. To assume the existence of such things as a Platonic World Soul or sympathetic resonance, he argued, was to give in to "pure suppositions."[29] Even more problematic was the nature of the analogy between lifeless matter and the realm of sound and sentiment. What facts have permitted anatomists to "transfer to the system of the nerves the mechanism reserved for the art of the likes of [composers] Lully and Rameau," he wondered. And "where in the animal economy are the strings analogous to those from which the likes of [violinists] Gaviniés and Mondonville draw such touching sounds?"[30]

Yet Le Cat's skepticism did not amount to a wholesale rejection of resonance. Rather, what he questioned was the assumption that because the entire body was thought to function along the lines of the sympathetic vibration of strings, the physiology of hearing, too, had to be modeled on the harpsichord metaphor. Le Cat's critique was two-pronged. In a first broadside against what he called the *sistême* of Cartesian mechanism, he urged a model of perception in which it is only certain parts of the ear, such as the basilar membrane, and not, as systematic philosophy taught, the human body in toto, that are subject to resonance. Other parts he believed to be based on a different principle. As he had indeed shown in his *Traité de l'existence, de la nature et des propriétés du fluide des nerfs* (Treatise on the Existence, Nature and Properties of the Nerve Fluid), nerve action differs from the movements of a string, because nerves are not "filaments," as Descartes had described them, but are filled with a liquid that allows them to act independently of outside stimuli.[31]

The same applied to different parts of the ear, of course. The basilar membrane, for instance, instead of "distinct, separate" harpsichord strings, consists of clusters of tissue that can hardly be said to vibrate freely. Similarly, the acousticus, like nerves generally, is "attached to various points, embedded and enfolded in fat, flesh and around various vessels." Hence: "Is this the condition of the strings of a bass viola?"[32]

The second line of attack in Le Cat's rebuttal of the harpsi-chord metaphor, unlike the first, anatomically grounded one, is based on a fusion of natural knowledge with "moral" sentiment, of physics with aesthetics. Contrary to the claim that the *Théorie* was meant to appeal to the "mind only," sentimental imagery, analogies, and metaphors pervade the book.[33] Such sentimental-ism and Le Cat's credo that "sentir, c'est penser," "to feel is to think," thus bear out the view that Enlightenment science and the culture of sensibility mutually influenced each other and that, consequently, works such as Le Cat's *Théorie* were not merely sober scientific works *about* sensation and feeling, but exercises in sentimentality as a style of investigation.[34] At the same time, the eclectic mix of "moral" science and aesthetics contravenes Ernst Cassirer's classic claim that France's *éclairés*, unlike their British counterparts, who favored an aesthetic approach, tackled rationalism's hegemony on purely physiological terrain.[35]

There are several significant, albeit highly contradictory con-cepts that Le Cat draws on to advance his sensibilist claims. The first is harmony. Arguing along Aristotelian lines that it is the essential office of sense organs to be proportionally predisposed toward their objects, he saw it as the role of the ear to vibrate in unison with the particles of the air implantatus at its center. Because of all the ear's constituent parts, he goes on to state, the cochlea is the only "machine" capable of such a relationship, and because the elasticity of the basilar membrane dividing its two channels decreases relative to its diameter, there is no point at which the "insensible gradation" of tones would not encounter its counterpart vibrating in unison. In short, the cochlea is the "organ proper of harmony."[36]

The term "gradation" (*gradation* in French) is difficult to unpack. Le Cat uses it repeatedly, and in light of his critique of a simplistic concept of resonance, it might be read as potentially undermining the Cartesian physiology of hearing. Derived from the Latin *gradatio*—that is, from the realm of rhetoric—the con-ceptual history of *gradation* is closely intertwined with the rise of antimechanist paradigms in philosophy, science, and art. By the late eighteenth and early nineteenth centuries, "gradated" phenomena were increasingly thought of as those phenomena that are in constant flux. They typically were found in fields where clear-cut divisions are lacking and imperceptible transitions and thresholds predominate; in other words, fields such as biology, chemistry, and painting.[37] By the time Le Cat was busy revising his earlier views, however, static Cartesian concepts of sensory perception still held sway and were only gradually being displaced by more dynamic models stressing the discontinuities between the endlessly differentiated physical phenomena and our perceptions, rather than the differentiations themselves. Several French dictionaries of the era reflect this terminological ambiguity. While during the middle decades of the century *gradation* was largely understood to mean "rhetorical figure," from around 1780, the term (in most European languages) also encompassed things such as the scales on a barometer, the color shadings in a painting, an imperceptible intensification of movement, or, especially in the emerging Romantic *Naturphilosophie*, the shifting boundaries between the material and the spiritual.

There can be little doubt that Le Cat's critique of *gradation* in the *Traité des sens* in part remained anchored in the older idea, fundamental to enlightened epistemology, that the natural world could be broken down into discrete, clearly delineated entities and that these world bits would be faithfully reflected by an apparatus equipped with the same crisply demarcated channels of transmission of sensory data. By this logic, human agency, if not completely absent, was reduced to a mere effect of mechanical causes, and listening, in turn, was less the act of an autonomous will than something that ensued from the sympathetic relationship between two orders of *gradation*: "gradated" tones, on the one hand, and the "gradated" fibers of the basilar membrane, on the other.

But this is only one possible reading. Even as Le Cat fails to offer a more detailed definition of *gradation*, one cannot but wonder about the tremendous impact the discovery of imperceptible thresholds must have had on the imagination of a man trying to come to terms with the consequences of midcentury music's delicate strains for the theory of hearing. Here, another term that Le Cat invokes frequently might offer some clues, *progression*. Although it, too, presupposed a difference between clearly demarcated objects, what is striking is not so much this difference as such, but the sheer quantity of acoustic phenomena that the ear now needs to distinguish. Le Cat counts no fewer than 9,632 "types of vibration of musical tones," a number he possibly computed from Joseph Sauveur's intricate logarithmic divisions of *mérides*, *eptamérides*, and *decamérides* (1/43, 1/301, and 1/3010 part of an octave, respectively), first introduced in his landmark study *Traité de la théorie de la musique* (1697). Be this as it may, the figure stands in marked contrast to Descartes' theory of hearing, which, as we have seen, recognized only a handful of intervals and partials as perceptible by the human ear. Seen in conjunction with the adjectives "imperceptible" (*insensible*) and "innumerable," the term *progression* thus seems to take on a new meaning, pointing toward a radically different concept of sensation, embodiment, and experience.[38] When tones or fibers become more fine grained to the point of losing their contours and dissolving into one another on an endlessly progressing scale, their objectlike character gives way to amalgamation, glissandi, crescendi, and diminuendi. So, too, one has to conclude, would auditory perception become more fluid. It would focus more on the energy inherent in such "imperceptible" transitions and the experience of *sensibilité* afforded by them, rather than on how to ground the ear's presumed authority as the arbiter of truth in its ability to rationally discern even the finest harmonic distinctions.

Of course, it would be several decades before the early Romantics took the notion of gradation and intensity to a new level. For Le Cat, meanwhile, neither concept—the more dated one of the cochlea as the organ of harmony nor the more dynamic idea hinted at in terms like *gradation* and *progression*—can gloss over the fact that his reasoning runs up against a fundamental hurdle. Can the mind assume sovereignty over itself in a vacuum, outside of the mechanical sphere of sympathetic resonance? Le Cat seems to wonder. And if the fibers of the basilar membrane are able to "receive" all 9,632 tones, but do so only "when necessary," that is, when the law of sympathetic resonance requires it, what is there left for the mind to do? Is harmony, according to this scheme, thus not grounded in mere physical necessity, and is the perception of harmony, accordingly, the result of a selection made by nature, not by an autonomous feeling subject? There can be no doubt, then, that if the sensibilist critique of the Cartesian *sistême* and the principle of selective resonance mutually exclude each other, so, too, do the lingering traces of Cartesian mechanism in Le Cat's *Théorie* grate against a sensibilist concept of hearing that would take into account a broader range of nonmechanical factors such as listeners' intentions and experiences.

Another factor preventing Le Cat from articulating a full-blown antimechanist theory of hearing was his stubborn adherence to the principle of mimesis infusing eighteenth-century musical aesthetics, that of Rousseau and his followers included. For instance, it went without saying that the composer's role was to imitate, rather than invent. The music of Lully, Le Cat claimed, was the perfect example for music's imitative powers. Since it was born from the happy congruence between natural laws and what the composer Jean-Philippe Rameau had famously called "our instinct for harmony," it was only natural that Lully's music, unlike the astonishing (though hardly touching) melodic "cascades" of Italian composers, went straight to the heart.

Also, Le Cat's turn to aesthetics lacked the rhetorical élan and critical force of Rousseau's contemporaneous critique of the canonization of harmonic theory at the hands of Rameau. Dubbed the "Isaac Newton of music," the latter had revolutionized seventeenth-century concepts of chord progression by mechanizing them. Once considered mere intervallic qualities situated along a

continuum, in the wake of Rameau's work, consonance and dissonance increasingly came to be thought of as sharply distinguished
categories. Just as matter can exist only in either a state of movement or a state of repose, dissonance and consonance, according
to Rameau, are related to each other "mechanically," dissonance
pushing the flow of harmonies toward resolution. Dissonance,
in other words, is as vital to consonance as external force is to
inert matter.[39]

Le Cat, who knew Rameau's music and may well have read the
composer's theoretical works, agreed with this position, albeit
complementing it with what he took to be a novel physiological
explanation. Dissonances, he wrote, are "mechanically disagree-
able" because their sensation is caused by the damping of freely
vibrating fibers: "Chords are made of tones that are relatively
distant from each other; they thus set in motion those sections
of the membrane that are separated by a reasonable distance;
which in turn will produce in those sections of the tissue that are
affected by the chord the same number of undulations as there are
tones in the chord." However: "Insert a dissonant tone into these
chords and . . . you raise that space in the nervous tissue that must
be depressed or almost tranquil. Those intercalated oscillations
thus hinder the adjacent ones."[40]

At the same time, dissonances involve more than mere physical
necessity; they were also useful in accounting for the emerging
rupture between sound, human anatomy, and subjective experience by bringing a "moral" perspective to bear on the interaction
of body and mind shaping auditory perception. Dissonances, Le
Cat insisted, have the virtue of goading the soul into taking active
control over the body. Because they presuppose a "fear of privation," that is, the fear of being deprived of a routinely experienced
pleasure, dissonances, on the one hand, operate on a principle
"common and generally necessary to man." But on the other
hand, by temporarily "spicing up pleasure," such dissonances
also teach humans to act sensitively and in socially responsive
ways. In the same way that the mouth becomes accustomed to

bitter coffee, the nose to tobacco, and the ear to Baroque arias, conditioning the senses by "fear of privation" highlights the value of social harmony. "One cannot enlarge the realm of harmony enough," Le Cat declares. "One cannot be careful enough with resources so honorable, both for the relaxation of laboring men and of the boredom devouring so many idle people."[41]

Another major "moral" factor affecting the physiology of hearing was the fact that music stirs the passions. Before he acquired speech, "Man" possessed the art of expressing himself through melody, Le Cat echoed Rousseau—the same Rousseau whose work he had blasted seven years earlier as "elegant babble." Hence, music is the true universal language, so universal, in fact, that it touches only those whose tastes have not yet been corrupted by false fantasies, such as Le Cat's own three-year-old daughter, who shed tears while listening to the "sweet accents of a tender melody played on an excellent violin."[42]

But the reverse equally held true. Our passions—which Le Cat understood in their Cartesian sense as bodily states—also influence our hearing. Hence, it is not only the ear that listens; so, too, do the ganglia, the eighth pair of cranial nerves, and even the solar plexus. There are no longer passive strings waiting to be set in motion by external "impulsions." Instead, our entire rich interior world also acts in response to the ear, subtly inflecting the automatism of auditory resonance. The physiology of hearing, then, during the middle of the eighteenth century, entailed a double recognition: of the changed musical styles and audience expectations that called for a more personal, emotional involvement in the act of listening, but also of listening as a total process connecting highly localized mechanisms to the body at large. In "moralizing" the physiology of hearing, Le Cat became the first otologist to shift the focus of inquiry from homologies, equivalences, and distinctions to the mutual interdependence of sensation and sentiment in flows of nerve liquid, tears, and melody.

Moral Effects and Physical Agents: Ébranlement, Air, and Happiness

Movement, especially when it entails pleasure, played a pre-eminent role in eighteenth-century French cultural practice and thought. It came in various forms, but none was as crucial as *ébranlement*. More than a mere "Baroque" relic and having been in circulation since at least the seventeenth century, the term encompassed a wide spectrum of meanings. Gilles Ménage's *Origine de la langue françoise* (1650), for instance, derived the root *branler* from Latin *vibrare*, to vibrate, while most seventeenth and eighteenth-century dictionaries list synonyms such as to "move," "to touch," and "to shake." Yet whichever of these meanings may have asserted dominance, and regardless of the area, discourse, text, or debate invoking the shimmering term, *ébranlement* offered a fertile metaphorical ground for the Enlightenment's relentless search for the material "hinges" between body and soul, ideas and sensory perception. As Diderot's and d'Alembert's *Encyclopédie* summarized the debate, through the word *ébranler*, "moral effects are set in relation to physical agents."[43]

If *ébranlement* was the main factor in establishing a happy balance between body and mind, one "agent" was particularly crucial: air. Mediating between the bodily interior, the environment, and the forever untraceable soul, air until the discovery of oxygen in 1774 had remained an elusive, albeit metaphysically highly potent substance. Air was said to be, literally, everywhere. It was in the lungs and in the blood, it penetrated the most minuscule pores, and it circulated in the microscopic interstices between the fibers and solids. Air also possessed all the known attributes of physical matter: gravity, elasticity, temperature, and so forth. As such, it could be measured by a whole panoply of newly invented instruments, such as the manometer, barometer, and thermometer, and it could be pondered, classified, and made "philosophically" pertinent under the umbrella of such newfangled disciplines as pneumatology (a combination of chemistry, medicine and social reform), eudiometry (an early attempt at measuring air quality) or aerometry (the science of air). Furthermore, air was also connected to a set of rather more pressing practical concerns arising from two interrelated aspects of eighteenth-century daily life: the sporadic resurgence of the plague and the deteriorating hygienic conditions of France's rapidly growing urban centers. In fact, the question of how all the stench may have contributed to the spread of epidemics was one of the era's most hotly debated, stimulating a whole spate of climatological studies, from Jean Astruc's *Dissertation sur l'origine des maladies épidémiques* (1721) to John Arbuthnot's *Essai des effets de l'air, sur le corps-humain*, originally published in English in 1733.[44] Meanwhile, philosophers, eager to map the olfactory component of Enlightenment sensualist epistemology, also strained to take measure of all the malodors, fragrances, and perfumes impinging on cultured noses, along the way revitalizing a whole range of seemingly outdated concepts ranging from Stoic *pneuma* and vapors, to Newton's aether, to a nebulous mix of gases, effluvia, scents, and miasmas.[45]

Some of these thinkers were even of the view that air is an important, if not decisive factor shaping the arts. One of the earliest examples of this new open-air aesthetics is *Réflexions critiques sur la peinture et la poésie* (Critical Reflections on Painting and Poetry) (1719) by the Abbé Dubos.[46] Although the work is better known as a milestone in the shift from rationalist aesthetics toward subjectivism and sensibility, the Abbé not only devoted more than fifty pages to air and other, more mysterious phenomena such as telluric "exhalations," he even argued for an intimate connection between aesthetics and air.[49] Claiming that the *génie* of nations derives from the quality of the blood that mixes with the air they breathe, Dubos deftly wove macroclimatic changes, temperature fluctuations, and geography into an intricate mélange of subtle empirical observation and racial prejudice. It was only natural, he maintained for instance, that France's temperate climate had produced some of the greatest artists, whereas the frigid climates of the North only brought forth "savage poets, crude versifiers, and cold colorists." The same went, of course, for too extreme a climate. "Does not everybody agree in attributing the stupidity of the Negroes and the Lapps to the excessive heat and excessive cold?" the Abbé wondered.[50]

Dubos's ideas would take on more openly political, albeit no less racist tinge several decades later in two works by none other than Montesquieu: *An Essay on Causes Affecting Minds and Characters* written between 1736 and 1743, and his chef-d'oeuvre *The Spirit of Laws* (1748). In the latter work, in particular, Montesquieu declared the "empire of the climate" to be paramount.[51] Unfolding an imposing panorama of people, climates and institutions from China to Russia to Malabar, he suggested that the arid climates and vast plains of Central Asia, for instance, almost inevitably brought in their trail despotic rule and, perish the thought, polygamy.

Whereas Montesquieu for the most part was content to limit his reflections to temperature, a short work entitled *Dissertation ou l'on recherche comment l'air, suivant ses différentes qualités, agit sur le corps humain* (Dissertation on How Different Qualities of Air Act on the Human Body) (1753) by the Montpellier-educated physician François Boissier de Sauvages (1706–1767) focused more on the oscillations of air. Coming on the heels of a monumental (and, due to Foucault, now mostly derided) work on nosology, Sauvages in this essay ambitiously invoked a broad range of "physical" and "mechanical" analogies between the isochronic vibrations of the elastic molecules of air and the pulsating liquids and solids of the human body, the goal being to account for the interface between matter and mind. "Everything in the human body beats, the heart, the ears, the arteries, spreading over all the sensible points in the body, and thus also the meninges and the elastic fluids that are found everywhere."[52]

Hence, Sauvages went on to assert, to "impress different ideas" on the mind, "the elasticity of the nervous fluid must be brought to bear upon by the vibrating air, so as to produce a certain correlation with its fundamental or some of its harmonics." But apart from a material correspondence between the vibrating air that reaches the ear and the tonus of the fibers inside the body, there is also a quasi-magic homonymy between tonus — the tension inherent in all matter — and "tone." In fact, the connection between soul, air, and musical sound all told becomes patent in the double meanings of the very word *air* itself: "Energetic people such as Italians and Languedocians, take pleasure in melodies [*airs*] whose movement is rapid, because the swift vibrations of the air [*air*] impress a parallel movement on their organs, which keeps them in a condition natural to them."[53]

The mix-up of air and melody, tonus and tone, was not Sauvages' alone. It recurred in many other works written at about the same time as Sauvages' *Dissertation*. Thus, Jean Laurent de Béthizy de Mézières, in *Effets de l'air sur le corps humain* (Effects of Air on the Human Body) enlarged Sauvages' reflections on air into a sweeping critique of French opera. Music, he argued, has a strong "moral" and curative effect because of the *ébranlement* the air transmits to our organs. Much the same argument was put forth in 1758 by Sauvages' colleague in Montpellier, Joseph-Louis Roger, in his *Traité des effets de la musique sur le corps humain* (Treatise on the Effects of Music on the Human Body) and by Charles Lorry in his 1765 *De melancholia* (Of Melancholy).

All this, on a superficial reading, has a certain fatalistic ring to it, and as d'Alembert caustically remarked, indeed amounted to little more than "the physics of Descartes applied to politics."[54] But even though the impact of climate appeared to be couched in rather immutable terms, the broader thrust of these works was toward a more emancipatory, anthropological notion of human self-fashioning and self-regulation. Thus, Dubos allowed for some historical variation (usually for the worse) in the atmosphere's impact on the arts. The arts of the modern city of Rome, he proclaimed, in a presciently "green" vein, were but a pale reflection of their ancient glory, the reason for this decline being a gradual warming of the atmosphere. The breakdown of the city's ancient sewer system, the gaseous "exhalations" streaming forth from the depths of abandoned mines, and the pestilent air emanating from the swamps of Ostia all had contributed to a degenerated state in which latter-day Romans bore but a superficial resemblance with their illustrious ancestors.

Even Montesquieu, whose notion of nature, according to Jean Ehrard, shared with the rest of the era's natural philosophy a certain blend of "finalism" and optimism, conceded that the expression "empire of the climate" was little more than a metaphor, and that his book was really "a permanent triumph of morals over climate, or more generally, over the physical causes."[55] Like Le Cat's determinism, for which it was the model, Montesquieu's was based on a conflation of a moralized nature and naturalized morals. It was an attempt to give to individuals the freedom to adjust to the nature of things because nature, as defined by Enlightenment doctrine, is good. And in the same vein, Sauvages' acknowledgment of cultural and regional differences as categories of positive knowledge also undermined universal biological norms, gradually replacing necessity with reason as the basis of freedom.

Finally, a concern with the vibratory foundations of freedom and happiness also pervades David Hartley's massive *Observations on Man, His Frame, His Duty and His Expectation.*[56] In this work, a French translation of which had appeared in 1755, the English physician took it upon himself to provide a mechanical explanation for everything from sexual desire and ulcers to sleep and hearing by combining Locke and Newton into a wide-ranging theory of the associative formation of consciousness through, in his terms, "vibrations." These, he observed, resemble "the Tremblings of the Particles of sounding Bodies" and are conveyed to the medulla by the external senses and nerves. Like Newton, Hartley believed ether to play a key role in this all-encompassing vacillation, causing the entire body to be set in motion "in the same manner as the Vibrations of the Air in Sounds agitate many regular Bodies with corresponding Vibrations or Tremblings."[57] And since "tremblings" are the only form of movement in which an object returns to its original position, they are capable of forming lasting impressions. The latter were said to be of two types: first, "simple ideas of sensation" caused by basic bodily sensations such as pleasure and pain. These ideas were "simple ideas" because they are seen as differing only in degree, their relationship to each other resembling a sequence of slower vibrations that are superseded by more "vigorous" vibrations. By contrast, a more complex type of "ideas" or "cluster" of ideas was said to arise from the combination or association of several simple ideas and was thus more properly equated with the intellect. In short, simple ideas and clusters of ideas were seen as sharing the same material base—vibrating air—their only difference residing in the degree of complexity.

Several consequences of Hartley's theory are noteworthy. First, complexity may result in greater intellectual refinement and hence a greater "hygiene of association," Hartley's term for the policing of the carnal elements of sensation. But such "hygiene" does not therefore automatically lead to a much higher goal, happiness. This, Hartley believed, is achieved only by a process of entropy in which Nature, thanks to an all-knowing and all-benevolent God, tends to restore an equilibrium between the greater intensity of painful conditions and the more numerous "sensible Pleasures," thus ultimately reducing "the State of those who have eaten of the Tree of Knowledge of Good and Evil, back again to a paradisiacal one" or to "pure ultimate spiritual Happiness."[58] Furthermore, because "vibrations," by virtue of their material base in air, sympathetically affect everybody, it follows that "if one be happy, all must."[59]

Second, despite its heavy theological slant, Hartley's theory of resonance and collective happiness is essentially conceived within a thoroughly secular and modern framework. In much the same way that Dubos' climatology had formed the basis for an antirationalist, subjectivist aesthetics, the rationale behind Hartley's theory of association was to craft new forms of communication out of the self-reproducing, playful interactions among the forces of the imagination. Little wonder that, meanwhile, a spruced-up concept of the aesthetic experience also formed part of this broader nexus of air, *ébranlement*, and the ear. Given humanity's push toward everlasting happiness, and in light of the entropy of painful and pleasurable vibrations, "more harsh Discords, are perpetually required to give a Relish, and keep the Sweetness of the Concords from cloying."[60]

Without question, the "moral" implications of vibrating particles of air were enormous, involving every part of the body and touching on the enlightened subject's most deep-seated desires. But if, as I have argued, of all these body parts the ear was seen as the one most susceptible to vibration, and happiness in turn was regarded as constituting the ultimate goal of human endeavor, one question remained: the question how the project of granting the ego "the monopoly on selfhood" might draw on mid-eighteenth-century subjects' heightened aural sensibility when, at the same time, the laws of physics underlying aural perception constrained the freedom of the ego in the first place.

Here I wish to suggest that rather than simply concocting a hodgepodge of theological and medical oddities or regurgitating the basic tenets of Cartesian physics and the classicist aesthetics of affect, mid-eighteenth-century concepts of aurality actually set a precedent for the emerging depth psychology of later decades. Essentially couched in the conventional terms of sympathetic resonance, this theory of auditory perception not only paralleled the broader Enlightenment project of crafting new individuals, it also matched the way in which visual evidence during the eighteenth century increasingly lost its stigma as mere marvel-mongering legerdemain and came to be accepted as a major source of knowledge, teaching the virtues of objectivity, observation, abstraction, and most importantly, self-reflexivity.[61] In fact, as eclectic and metaphor-laden as the elements making up this new auditory awareness undoubtedly are, they tell us more about modern aurality at midcentury than many of the condescending constructions of early eighteenth-century music and culture as somewhat late-blooming instances of an otherwise exhausted "Baroque."

Curing Spider Bites

The push toward new mental and sensory frontiers was ushered in with unprecedented force. The extraordinary mushrooming of texts concerned with music's healing powers was no exception to this, their intensity and frequency contributing every bit as vigorously to the saturation of Enlightenment culture with the somatic, the sensory, and the sensual as all the visual metaphors, optical technologies, and treatises on vision. In particular, it was through medicine that discourses on hearing between 1700 and 1800 were disseminated into a wider field of inquiry, for the first time addressing, and in many ways even creating, a mass audience of ever more varied composition. A random sample of the more than two hundred books, articles, dissertations, and dictionary entries that, in a conservative estimate, appeared during these 100 years, reveals the close interconnections between the rekindled interest in music's medical effects and a broad spectrum of institutional settings, languages, and literary genres.

At first sight, though, the novelty of this discourse does not become readily apparent, often being buried under a barrage of references to Greek mythology and bulky quotations from the works of the seventeenth-century Jesuit polymath Athanasius Kircher, particularly from those concerned with a phenomenon known as *tarantisme*. In the southern Italian region of Apulia, Kircher had reported, a dance ritual was customarily performed with the intention of curing patients who have been bitten by the poisonous tarantula spider. A music called *tarantella*, so his informants had told him (and notations of several examples of which he included in his account), was essential to the process, illustrating the intimate correlation between vibrating strings and the nerves of the victims.[62]

Present-day commentators take a rather dim view of the ritual and its eighteenth-century apologists. Gushing over the latter's "literary platitudes" and denouncing them as remnants of an ossified tradition mired in Neoplatonism, these commentators tend to overlook the important place the discourse on tarantism held in the larger project of compulsory self-fashioning through the ear.[63]

As always, Diderot and d'Alembert's *Encyclopédie* is useful in decoding tarantism's complex and hidden modernity. As is well known, the colossal compendium was one of the first reference works to apply the new technique of cross-referencing systematically, the term *tarentula* appearing in dozens of articles, sometimes with a cross-reference, sometimes without. But the key articles that illustrate best the enormous relevance of tarantism for promoting the Enlightenment's modernizing agenda are the ones authored by Rousseau, the Chevalier de Jaucourt, and above all, the editors Diderot and d'Alembert themselves.[64] One of these articles is "Ame" (Soul), written by Diderot in 1749, halfway between Le Cat's *Traité* and the *Théorie de l'ouie*. Although the term *tarentula* does not figure in this article until the very end (and then only as a cross-reference), what is striking about this reference is the fact that musical therapy occupies an important place in an entry as crucial for Enlightenment ideology as "Soul" in the first place. Thus, to illustrate the "effects of the soul on the body and, conversely, of the body on the soul," Diderot toward the end of the article offers the following description of a musical healing:

> A famous musician and great composer had been attacked by a fever that grew stronger and ever more persistent. On the seventh day, he fell into a violent and almost uninterrupted delirium, accompanied by cries, tears, terror, and perpetual insomnia. On the third day of his delirium, one of those strokes of instinct that are said to make sick animals look for appropriate herbs had him ask for a little concert in his room. Though his doctor acquiesced only reluctantly, cantatas by Bernier were sung for him. No sooner had he heard the first chords than his face took on a serene air, his eyes became tranquil, the convulsions ceased completely, and he shed tears of joy and from then on felt for the music a kind of sensibility that he never experienced before and that he was never to feel again since. He was without fever for the whole concert; but as soon as it

was over, he lapsed back into his prior state. So without hesitation, recourse was taken again to a remedy that had worked to such sudden and fortunate effect. The fever and the delirium still subsided during the concerts...and [thus] ten days of music cured him completely, without any other remedy than a bleeding of the foot—the second he received—which was followed by a great evacuation. See TARENTULA."[65]

The rigor of this account (the substance of which Diderot had taken from a report published by Denis Dodart half a century earlier and that in turn echoed Plato) is striking. It seems that the text is organized around a series of strict binaries and symmetries. Thus, ten days of crisis—which mirror Hippocratic medicine's penchant for the numbers seven and three—are followed by ten days of musical treatment. The ten days of musical therapy, in turn, are marked by similar contrasts, such as the opposition between the patient who asks for a "little concert" and the reluctant doctor. Then there are the tears during the crisis and the tears of joy upon the first signs of recovery. Finally, the timing of the entire procedure, too, is subject to the same binary logic: The curative effect of the music sets in as instantly (after "the first chords") as it stops abruptly ("as soon as it was over").

Of course, all this stiltedness is not the stylistic faux pas of a writer as accomplished as Diderot. Rather it is consonant with the broader aim of the article, that of rebutting the Cartesian separation of body and soul by demonstrating the reciprocal relationship between the two. But despite its predictability, Diderot shies away from dogmatically reading a lifeless, machinelike quality into the interaction between ideas and the body, insisting on what he calls the "organized" nature of this interaction.

Occurring, like "symmetry" and "rigor," throughout the "Soul" article, "organization" is a fascinating term. On the one hand, it suggests the strong influence of iatromechanist medicine on Diderot's early work. But at the same time, like much else in the turbulent phase under consideration here, "organization" had no stable meaning and could be used for rather different purposes.

In "Soul," Diderot still uses the term fairly conventionally, in order to characterize the relationship between "what thinks in us" and the living body. "However one conceives of what thinks in us," he says, "it is certain that its functions depend on the organization and the actual state of our body while we are alive." But by 1749, iatromechanical medicine's influence on Diderot was already beginning to wane, and terms such as *organisation*—not to mention the lone appearance of the term "sensibility" in the musical episode above—were acquiring a new meaning as key markers in the extraordinary paradigm shift in French medicine from Cartesian mechanism to what eventually came to be known as "vitalism."[66] And it is precisely this sprawling vagueness of the "organized" body, running on principles situated halfway between mechanism and vitalism, that Diderot seems to have in mind when he concludes "Soul" with the following annotation: "It is rather curious to see how in a man for whom, in a manner of speaking, music after a long and continuous process of habituation has become the soul, the concerts restored little by little to the spirits their normal course."[67]

What Diderot outlines here, rather purposely, I believe, is an altogether more paradoxical type of individual. His is a subject that straddles two different worlds and in whose innermost structure facts of nature and facts of culture intermingle in ever-changing configurations. One is a world of instincts and reflexes in which the subject exists solely as a point of intersection between physical and physiological coordinates and in which, in the end, the odd is always evened out. The other world is one in which rest and movement, the orderly and the unruly, are kept in constant suspension—in short, a world of "sensibility" in which the "organized" subject always finds itself in jitters and the site at once of a drawn-out process of self-modeling and of abrupt fits of delirium and chaos.

What, then, is the relationship of this vignette with the Apulian spider and the strange ritual cross-referenced at the end of Diderot's article? What does the article "Tarentule" (not

"Tarentula" as announced in Diderot's cross-reference) tell us about the strange intertwining of "morals" and matter? Authored by the Chevalier de Jaucourt (1704–1779), one of the principal medical contributors to the *Encyclopédie*, who is also responsible for the articles "Ouïe" (Hearing) and "Résonnance" (Resonance), the article in essence refutes as fabrication several key texts that had appeared during the first half of the eighteenth century in the wake of Kircher's account. In particular, Jaucourt takes exception with the notion advanced in 1702 by the Montpellier-educated physician and chemist Etienne-François Geoffroy (1672–1731) that the spider's poison increases the nerves' normal tension, thus causing them to resonate sympathetically with a certain note played on a musical instrument, which in turn forces the animal spirits to resume their normal flow through the nerves.[68] This, Jaucourt interjects, does not make any musical sense, because it is precisely what musicians playing for the ritual do not bother with. And it does not make any medical sense, either, because the same animal spirits that are supposed to be trapped by the overwrought nerves, according to general consensus, are also responsible for stretching the nerves.

Surprisingly, Jaucourt's critique does not lead him to renounce outright the possibility of music's therapeutic effects. Apulians, like most people, feel a natural aversion toward spiders, he writes. But because the tarantula is a truly venomous creature, and Apulians, apart from to a dry, sanguine temperament, have irritable nerves that make them prone to fits of delirium at the slightest harm, it is only understandable that they imagine themselves having been bitten by the spider. Furthermore, since traditional methods such as antitoxins and sweating cures are impractical, given Apulians' overall impulsive temperament, it is contrary remedies—rest, fresh air, beverages, and soothing music—that are being put to use. Reflecting the growing acceptance of anthropological theories of culture, Jaucourt here quite readily replaces the nerve-string analogy and its cognate theory of sympathetic vibration with a broader cultural explanation, all the while maintaining the speculative thrust and logic of binary opposites that structured Diderot's article of fourteen years earlier. Thus, a dry temperament requires liquids in much the same way as an agitated state is obviated by rest. And echoing Diderot's article, music occupies a privileged — though profoundly ambivalent — position by virtue of the fact that Apulians, like Diderot's musician, "love it passionately."

It is the textual structure of Diderot's anecdote and Jaucourt's discussion of tarantism, then, that lends the relationship between the sensory stimulus (music) and the mind an inevitable, compulsive quality. Whether this relationship is thought of in strictly physical terms or, somewhat less inexorably, as the product of a peculiar *organisation* and local forms of knowledge, it is hard to escape from it either way. Individuals, if they figure at all in Jaucourt's Apulia or Diderot's France, must ultimately adjust to the normal course of things.

It is somewhere between the positions staked out by Diderot and Jaucourt that eighteenth-century authors before and after the hypothetical watershed of 1750 began to define the relationship between music and medicine. It is the ambiguous space of homologies and anthropological empiricism that enabled Pierre Desault, for instance, to declare that music could heal rabies and phthisis (the eighteenth-century term for tuberculosis), quite aside from providing comfort and entertainment to the bitten patient.[69] And it is by linking seemingly disconnected domains as harpsichord music and afflictions such as phrenitis (encephalitis), ischias (sciatica), and the gout that Charles de Folard, Gerard van Swieten, Jean Pierre Burette, and a host of lesser French medics came to carve out a space for what Foucault termed "the endless task of understanding the individual."[70]

It is important to realize that eighteenth-century physicians did not harbor the slightest doubt about the rationality of such claims. Rather, what was "bizarre and absurd," the widely read *Nouveau dictionnaire universel et raisonné de médecine, de chirurgie et de l'art vétérinaire* (1772) noted, were the once-admired curings of ancient Greece: Marsilio Ficino's Neoplatonic musings, Giovanni Baptista della Porta's musical magic, or Kircher's speculations.[71] At the same time, it must be remembered that the real goal of these perhaps imaginary therapies was not a modern one in the sense of repairing the bodies and minds of full-fledged, albeit traumatized subjects. Rather, claims such as the one put forth by Pierre-Joseph Buchoz in his *Mémoire sur la manière de guérir la mélancolie par la musique*, that in cases of "dry" melancholia, one has to begin by exposing the patient first to lower notes and then "imperceptibly" raise the pitch to the highest level, thus flexing the rigid fibers accustomed to the different degrees of vibration, hinted at the possibilities of a hermeneutic of the compulsively self-fashioning subject. Likewise, when Philippe Hecquet argued for an intimate relationship between diseases of the digestive tract and music's ability to "rectify" irregularities in the oscillation of the nerves by bringing a person's intestines into "accord" and "cadence," he was outlining the first in a chain of "spatializations" that Foucault invokes in his account of the birth of modern medicine.[72]

The first of these, what Foucault calls primary spatialization, might be likened to Boissier de Sauvages' massive nosological classification system and hence be called a nosology of music. In primary spatialization, disease is situated "in an area of homologies in which the individual could receive no positive status."[73] Here, as in Diderot's discussion of tarantism, certain diseases and certain categories and parameters of music enter into contact with each other, not as part of a causal relationship, but solely by dint of shared affinities. What Foucault refers to as "secondary spatialization," on the other hand, which requires "an acute perception of the individual" in which "doctor and patient are caught up in an ever-greater proximity, bound together" by the doctor's "penetrating gaze" and the "qualities" that have roamed freely over the patient's body, might be at play in a disease such as phrenitis—and the music thought to be the most effective in treating it.[74] Prior to the birth of modern brain neurology, phrenitis was considered to be part of a larger group of diseases that were associated with certain forever-changing points on the body and that thus had no firm location. Its symptoms—fever and "delirium," primarily—wandered about the various parts of the brain, where they would mutate into any number of cognate diseases: mania, lethargy, melancholia, or some sort of generic "folly." In the words of the *Encyclopédie*, the cause of phrenitis was no longer, as in the old Hippocratic model, "a metastasis of humors from one organ to another or the transmission of the febrile matter inside the brain," but the swelling of the blood vessels in the brain and the meninges. Hence, all causes that led to the enlargement of these parts were of the order of the phrenitis, as were, among others, chagrin, pain, anger, love, and even "nymphomania" (*fureur utérine*).[75]

And so it went for music. Just as the body's organs themselves come to be seen as mere sites on which various lesions, dysfunctions, and inflammations manifest themselves, the chief purpose of music is said to be to allow its features to affect the afflicted organ viscerally, through a causal link that is at once external to the diseased body and determined by qualities extraneous to the music. Consider, for instance, the following passage from the *Encyclopédie* article "Délire" of 1754, in which Diderot summarizes Austrian Empress Theresa's physician van Swieten's views on music's role in healing phrenitis. "One sometimes has to take recourse to extraordinary and unusual means such as musical instruments, chanting, dance, erupting noise, even noise, light, etc. in order to substitute new and stronger ideas... for those constituting the delirium, thus always setting contrary affects against those that are dominant."[76]

Although the article itself can be seen as the perfect illustration of Foucault's second spatialization, in which the space of the disease—its place in a classificatory system—and the space of the body no longer coincide, Diderot's concern here is not with determining for music a new place in the reconfigured relationship between disease and the organism. Nor does he evince any interest in the medical effect of music per se. In fact, although it was written after the putative turn of French medicine toward vitalism, the text does not subject the "flat" homological space of nosological classes to a more radical questioning of the kind Foucault calls the "tertiary spatialization" of disease, "all the gestures by which, in a given society, a disease is circumscribed, medically invested, isolated, divided up into closed, privileged regions, or distributed throughout cure centres."[77] To grasp this shift and the role of the ear within it we need to turn to the relationship between music and melancholia—next to the plague, possibly the eighteenth century's most dreaded illness.

Melancholia, Pain, and the Performance of the Self

True, melancholia was not a new phenomenon. Like phrenitis, it had long been considered as an affliction to be, if not cured, at least alleviated by musical means.[78] But by the eighteenth century, melancholia acquired a new meaning, encompassing a wide range of subvarieties and symptoms, from hypochondria—which carried overtones of delusion and madness—to a more vaguely circumscribed everyday languor and exquisite ennui. In fact, melancholia was not seen as just a mental disorder to begin with. Conditions such as the spleen or the "vapors" were almost invariably regarded, as one of many fashionable late seventeenth-century tracts on melancholy put it, as "Distempers of the Body, rather than Faults of the Mind."[79] Melancholia was a matter of physics, then, of a disturbed humoral balance, of blocked bloodstreams and unstrung fibers. Eighteenth-century melancholia was also a more class-specific ailment than what we now call depression, primarily afflicting the upper echelons of society. It was precipitated by the pressures and pleasures of a class whose members felt perennially besieged and replenished at the same time by alluring new goods, pastimes, sights, and sounds. Thus, while eighteenth-century diaries and letters are replete with complaints about ennui, languor, and indolence, for Voltaire, melancholia was quite simply one of two more general states making up the human condition. Man is born to live in the "convulsions of distress or in the lethargy of boredom," Martin declares in Voltaire's *Candide*.[80]

But there was one aspect of melancholia that made it a truly modern disease, striking at the heart of a whole range of Enlightenment articles of faith, such as the liberating role of the mind, the nature of pleasure, and the purpose of happiness. This was the fact that the very existence of diseases of the mind was incompatible with one of the Enlightenment's most cherished principles: the power of reason to penetrate the veil of myth and superstition that prevents people from seeing themselves and the truth. If clear thinking is the only effective antidote to the diseased ancien régime, the argument went, a lessening of one's mental abilities raises the specter of political impotence and self-imprisonment. Underlying melancholia as a social phenomenon was thus what one might call a *horror inertiae*, an all-pervasive fear of stagnation and entrapment that threatened to obstruct the forward thrust underlying Enlightenment ideology. The ability of the individual to feel and enjoy himself or herself move constituted an important source of happiness, but the mind was in even greater need of movement.

In light of this ban on apathy, it is little wonder that pleasure and *divertissement* ceased to be reproachable aberrations and instead became acceptable and indeed inevitable accommodations to life. Good health, happiness, and the pleasures of the imagination merged in a triad for which nature itself was both model and motor. "The condition of the machine that causes pleasure," Le Cat opined, "is a certain state of health, a certain tonus of the pericardial plexus and the nerves that gives a great amount of freedom of movement to the fluids. It seems that one feels oneself alive and tickled inside by the harmonious movement of the fluids, just as the ear usually is [tickled] by the pearly cadences of an excellent violin. This vague tickling or this well-being that is not easy to determine, is opposed to that misery experienced by melancholics."[81]

There is, then, a stark antagonism between melancholia,

languor, and pain, on one side, and pleasure, happiness, and movement on the other. But there is another dimension to the melancholia-music nexus. Just as melancholia constitutes a threat to the very sense of modernity that engendered it, so, too, are the specific parameters of the music supposed to bring about relief from the modern malaise, the products of a new kind of aesthetic thinking. Dissonance, as we have seen, was one of the most important of these parameters — as vital to consonance as external force is to inert matter. But while the significance of dissonance for the musical aesthetics of the first half of the eighteenth century is well documented, its deeper association with disease, disruption, pain, and violence has been less systematically studied. Seventeenth-century thinkers such as Descartes were still struggling to reconcile the public's newly awakened desire for the hideous, monstrous, and dissonant with the reformulated Aristotelian maxim that the affective power of art resides in the represented objects themselves and that, hence, only a beautiful object or a harmonious melody could bring about pleasure, whereas a horrifying event or a dissonant chord would cause discomfort. Consequently, these thinkers were at a loss when it came to describing the strange delight audiences took in watching the horrors of a sea battle or in listening to the increasingly dissonant strains of the *tragédie lyrique*.

This situation was to change dramatically during the first half of the eighteenth century. Although much of the debate on *douleur agréable* or *terreur agréable* focused on theater, poetry, and painting, and the discussion of musical dissonance, meanwhile, occupied its own discursive sphere, these art forms were closely intertwined in that they all celebrated the newly discovered ambiguity of pain and pleasure. Relishing a thunderstorm, peering cheekily into a mountain gorge, coolly watching a murder on stage, or hearing a "shocking" dissonance were all key to the modern condition.

Mobilizing dissonance in a deliberate attempt at energizing the diseased, apathetic body languishing under a corrupt absolutist

regime, it was again Dubos who set the tone for this new understanding of a more "sexy" kind of pain. Inspired by Locke, for
whom the "displeasure of want" was the main force driving
human desire, Dubos openly advocated that the pleasure (*volupté*)
felt in view of horror is a necessary means to combat ennui and
languor. But while public executions, gladiators, and bullfights
can have side effects such as nausea or, even more disturbingly,
leave behind corpses, the arts, luckily, are incapable of inflicting
real pain, arousing only "artificial" passions instead. With this
notion of artificial effects, Dubos patently distanced himself from
Aristotelian theories that called for profound ethical purifica-
tion. The aesthetic shock therapy administered to the upper-class
clientele of melancholic courtiers and bored *salonniers* does not
reach nearly as deep as Aristotelian catharsis. Much as medicinal
baths had originally been thought of as a mere cooling device for
overheated bodies, declares Dubos, so the antimelancholic effects
of the arts are meant to stay at the "surface of the heart."[82]

But if Dubos' concept of an ethically indifferent art may be
said to have released the spectator-listener from the iron grip
of classicist rules, such seemingly unfettered audience behavior
is not therefore any less obsessive than the fear of stagnation
that necessitates this sort of art of the surface in the first place.
Quite to the contrary. Using the arts as a weapon, Dubos' contemporary, the naval officer André-François Boureau-Deslandes
(1690–1757), in a work called *L'art de ne point s'ennuyer* (The
Art of Not Getting Bored), ventured that the upper echelons of
French society were engaged in a "new kind of hidden war."[83]
Although for the brave captain these arts were confined to more
inoffensive pastimes such as big-city life, good food, conversation,
dames, and music, the bellicose metaphor also points toward what
was at stake in reshaping subjects according to more enlightened
designs. The new craving for sweet terror, even at its most aestheticized and ethically inconsequential, was an essential ingredient in the struggle for the individual. In a way, it was through the
cultivation of a specifically aural type of *frisson* that enlightened

audiences came to experience themselves as subjects in the first place. Two areas in which these aural encounters with pain and violence are particularly illuminating are opera and, once again, musical treatments of melancholia.

Dubos does not linger on horror and divertissement in the short section on music that concludes his *Réflexions*. But in a discussion of the merits of instrumental sounds—which he calls *symphonies*—in opera, horror is being hinted at. Using the ancient motif of the ship wreck, Dubos argues that instrumental sounds have a more visceral effect than verbal expression, because they more or less directly imitate the "noise" of the storm. Still, he cautions, "the *symphonie's* impression could not be as genuine as the impression that the true storm would make on us," thus implying that the aestheticization of horror, so central to the classical stage, should primarily occur in language or sung speech.[84] In many ways, this conclusion is born out by the different approaches taken to the representation of violence in the early modern *tragédie sanglante*, the classical theater of Racine and Corneille, and some of Rameau's operas. While the former had gloried in the unabashed staging of atrocity in which the spoken word doubled the effect of the gory events on stage, the tragic stage of the classical age had sublimated horror into morally productive *terreur* by banning violent effects to a past merely narrated by the characters on stage. The *tragédies lyriques* of the middle of the eighteenth century, finally, aestheticized horror by "singing" it, by making violence "tolerable" through the (mostly stereotyped) musical representation of violence.

I am deliberately substituting the term "singing" for "saying" (*dit*), the word Catherine Kintzler uses in her remarkable discussion of violence in early modern French opera in order to highlight a crucial difference in scholars' interpretation of acts of violence in the *tragédie lyrique*.[85] The difference these interpretations posit is that between an aesthetic and a moral mandate. In terms of the former, the horrifying effects of violent acts are said to be brought under control by harnessing them in logos.

According to the latter interpretation, by contrast, opera's moral mission rests on the purposeful production of powerful visceral effects.[86] While the first interpretation is favored by Kintzler, the second is being advanced in Downing Thomas's analysis of the famous "Trio des Parques" from Rameau's first opera *Hippolyte et Aricie* (1733).[87] There, Rameau deploys a whole battery of chromatically descending harmonies, a jarring eleventh chord, and a jagged continuo pattern to convey the horror of the three Fates as they announce to Theseus that he will not really escape Hades, because he will find it again in his home. As Thomas's careful analysis shows, by exploiting the enharmonic genre — a genre that Rameau insisted derives its shocking effect from the use of quarter tones — Rameau had actually found a way to, in his own words, "inspire repulsion and horror." He had thus managed "to produce jolts of somatic response in the spectator."[88]

Somatic jolts and intellectual stability — two conflicting interpretations, to be sure, but perhaps also two extremes on the continuum of mid-eighteenth-century culture and aesthetics. But above all, it is in the specific formulation of violently clashing sounds as antidotes to ennui, in the perceived ability of dissonance to jolt bodies and at the same time keep in check the effects of such violence through aestheticization, that mid-eighteenth-century concepts of auditory perception transcended the obsolete aesthetics of affect and began to articulate a concept of the listener as an ego.

This becomes perhaps even clearer in my second (and final) example: the combination of musical shock therapy and the aestheticization of medicine in the thinking of Jean-Jacques Menuret de Chambaud (1733–1815). Like Boissier de Sauvages a product of the renowned medical school at Montpellier, and, together with the Chevalier de Jaucourt, one of the most prolific medical collaborators on the *Encyclopédie*, Menuret was the author of dozens of articles on infectious diseases, "semiology," and psychology, but also of major entries such as "Pouls" (Pulse), "Respiration," "oeconomie animale," and "Maladie." The main articles of interest here are the ones on "Manie," "Mélancolie," and "Musique, effet de la" (Music, effect of), all of which were published in 1765, three years before Le Cat's *La Théorie de l'ouie*.[89] In these articles, Menuret specifies a whole spectrum of therapies for patients suffering from mania, melancholia, epilepsy, or nymphomania—all of which aim at a "révolution générale dans la machine," a "general change in the machine." But the precise working of such therapies, despite the mechanist imagery, remains vague. From shock therapies, such as immersions in cold water, to transfusions and gentler *plaisirs*, such as horse riding, spectacles, and concerts, through to a broad range of dietic treatments, such as travel, fresh air, rubbings of the belly, and "venereal activities," Menuret vacillates between conventional iatromechanist prescriptions targeting the body and a psychological approach centering on the mind.

The article "Musique, effet de la" advances Menuret's argument most forcefully. Here, the encyclopedist formulates one of the era's most cogent blueprints for systematizing the individual by forcing it into the self-conscious, aesthetic role of an active listener. There are three types of musical effects one has to distinguish in conceptualizing this listener: effects on crude bodies, effects on animals, and, most importantly, effects on "Man in his Relations to Morals and Medicine." In the latter category, one must further distinguish between the miraculous effects of music during the "centuries of barbarism and ignorance"—in other words, in Greek antiquity—and the numerous instances reported with increasing frequency since around 1700 in which patients suffering from melancholia, phthisis, and epilepsy have been cured with the help of a kind of music that is "linked to the sensibility of the human machine."

The term "sensibility" is of course crucial. Even though Menuret does not offer any definition of it, much less grant it the same relevance as in Montpellier medical thinking more broadly, what is interesting is how he foregrounds a certain performative element in accounting for music's healing powers and how he thereby sets himself into marked opposition to some of his contemporaries' notion of the *moi* as a mere stage where perceptions pass and glide. First, Menuret sets up an analogy between the "organization of our machine" and "good music." Appreciation of such music, he posits, does not so much require "knowledge" rooted in Pythagorean numbers as a "mechanical" reaction according to the coincidence of pulses. Because a "poorly organized" person cannot appreciate good music, such a person, in addition to "lively airs that briskly stir [*rémuent*] the springs that nature, usage, and habit failed to render subtle," requires consonances between higher notes. Such notes "strike the soul more often," since in them, the "vibrations coincide more frequently."

So far, of course, all of this was old hat, familiar to those in the know from the days of Galileo and Descartes. But the next step takes Menuret's argument in a very different direction. Invoking, paradoxically, Athanasius Kircher's theories of modal affects, Menuret suggests that "the composer must make his melodies conform to the condition of the patient" before he next focuses the attention of the patient on pleasant objects and thus diverts him from the ailment afflicting him. In this way, music "adds to the illusion and makes it complete," removing the anxiety (*frayeur*) often accompanying such illnesses and thereby attenuating the real pain.

In the entry on melancholia, Menuret accentuates the illusory nature of antimelancholic cures even further, recommending that a whole theater be staged for the patient. Thus, a person who is convinced that an animal is living inside his body must be tricked into believing the opposite by presenting him the offending creature in a pot. Similarly, a "delirious melancholic" who is convinced that he has no head must be persuaded of the contrary by placing a painfully heavy cannonball on his head, while a person taking himself for a hare must at all cost be spared the sight of a dog and be entertained by music instead.

Quixotic as it may seem, this repair work on traumatized subjects did serve an "enlightened" purpose. As Menuret insists, the "prudent physician knows how to gain the trust of the patient." He must accommodate himself to the patient's delirium, appear convinced that things are as the melancholic imagines them to be. The treatment, then, would take on a more complex, almost fictional character. By maintaining the patient's affective milieu, the treatment creates a space in which the physician represents the individual to the individual, thus in turn allowing the patient to experience his or her own uniqueness. It was thus no longer a question of schematically fitting disease and music into a preset structure of analogies and oppositions, but of creating a complex dramatization of illusions, voices, and narratives convincing the patient of the centrality of his or her own self, rather than that of a preordained set of spatializations. By taking into account "the nature of the illness [and] the tastes of the patient" and by constantly monitoring and, whenever necessary, adjusting the musical cures administered, the physician would invite the patient to enact a plot, to become, in fact, listener, spectator, and actor all in one. This move into performativity and reflexivity alters the self from a mere object of *ébranlement* into a subject that must will itself into existence.

CHAPTER FOUR

Water, Sex, Noise:

Early German Romanticism

and the Metaphysics of Listening

The story of the Romantic ear begins—like so much else both ominous and auspicious in European history—on the river Rhine:

> It is as if a world of water were rolling out of nature's laws into the abyss. [It] is the highest force the fiercest storm of the grandest life that human senses are able to grasp. As even the most detached philosopher is obliged to admit, it is one of the most immense effects of gravity the human senses will encounter. It is a gigantic storm what thunderous booming what a storm raging through my entire being! Holy! Holy! Holy! it roars through bone and marrow. Come let nature present you another kind of opera, with a different architecture and different colors and different harmonies and melody. One stops hearing and feeling for oneself the eye no longer sees and merely allows an impression to be made upon it thus is one smitten and stirred by a feeling never before experienced. I am becoming an abyss to myself, and eventually one becomes impatient at being such a small fixed mechanical fragile thing, unable to get in.[1]

The location is the famous Rhinefall at Schaffhausen and the rush of words—scarcely disrupted by punctuation marks—that of Wilhelm Heinse (1746–1803), written while he was on a cultural pilgrimage to Italy in 1780. Shamefully neglected by musicologists and cultural historians alike, Heinse was an accomplished musician and author of a sizable literary oeuvre framed by two key texts of modern aurality: the early *Musikalische Dialogen* (Musical Dialogues, 1776) and a novel, *Hildegard von Hohenthal* (1795).

Today, though, Heinse is mostly remembered for the early erotic bestseller *Ardinghello* (1777) and the passage just quoted, one of the earliest examples of German *Frühromantik*. And what could be more Romantic than the river Rhine, what more intoxicating and luxuriantly sensual than the image of the world as a cataract tumbling into the inner self as into an abyss? Is a more telltale denial of the Enlightenment conceivable than the numbing of the senses and drowning of all thought in an oceanic feeling of holiness?

Compare this passage with another text, this written sixteen years later and further downstream in Mainz, where the Rhine flows at a more leisurely pace. Like Heinse's text, it, too, is concerned with water and sound. But instead of a loss of hearing, here the focus is on a sharpened auditory awareness:

> When Heinse, guided by manifold experience and deep reflection, pertinently—and as far as I can see—for the first time asserts that "the ear is clearly our most exact sense," I believe I am in a position to provide the physical grounds for the truth in this novel assertion. For, as I have demonstrated above, among all the nerves, none is in so direct, so naked and bare a contact with the moistness of the brain cavities, and hence affects so directly the common sensorium [than the auditory nerve].[2]

The passage is from *Über das Organ der Seele* (On the Organ of the Soul), written in 1796 by Samuel Thomas Sömmerring (1755–1830). A close friend of Heinse, Sömmerring was Germany's most renowned anatomist at the turn of the nineteenth century and a key figure among Europe's new breed of thoroughly empirically minded scientists.[3] Or so it seems. For although the physiology of hearing was central to Sömmerring's overall argument, it was not—as the title of the short work indeed suggests—the author's only concern. In mapping out the densely packed landscape of auditory nerve, brain cavities, and the ventricular fluids, Sömmerring had set himself a more ambitious goal: to offer final and irrevocable proof not only that the soul exists, but that it has an exact location, too.

What is so noteworthy about a waterfall, one might ask? Have not the poets of all ages and zones mused about cataracts and rapids?[4] Likewise, what does an anatomist's foray into the misty world of metaphysics have to do with another man's urge to surrender his "Ich" by diving headlong into the abyss? And what does it all have to do with music and listening, anyway? Although the passages quoted may be said to foreshadow the Romantics' celebration of self-loss, sensory excess, and pure sound, the true significance of works such as *Über das Organ der Seele*, the Rhine epos, or *Hildegard von Hohenthal* lies elsewhere. The jumble of otology, anatomy, aesthetics, and metaphysics in these texts is more than a mere anecdote in the larger narrative of the origins of Romanticism in the idealist aesthetics of the sublime. Rather, this juxtaposition of fact and fiction, empirics and speculation, allows us to trace a lineage far less rectilinear than the one said to stretch from Kant to Hegel to Schopenhauer. In much the same way that Claude Perrault and Claude-Nicolas Le Cat had sought to keep materialism and metaphysics in a precarious balance by granting reason and resonance an illicit intimacy, Heinse and Sömmerring, while still laboring in Descartes' shadow, likewise struggled to restore to listening a role in the genesis of the subject that is as physical and primordial as it is cognitive and spiritual. And so it is, once again, the endolymph, the texture of the auditory nerve, the complex linkages of audition to the vocal tract and phonation—in short, the infinitely subtle microworld of the auditory periphery—that will take us into the heart of that strangest of subjects, the Romantic ego.

"Our most exact sense:" Samuel Thomas Sömmerring and the Unity of Consciousness

The anatomy of the brain, prior to Franz Joseph Gall's ground-breaking discoveries in the early nineteenth century, had been known only in its basic outlines. The brain is notoriously difficult to dissect because of its spongy, rapidly decomposing substance, which is why much of its furrowed structure (including the ventricles and their fluid contents) had remained terra incognita for centuries. It is here, in particular, that Sömmerring's work broke new ground. In a detailed summary taking up much of the first half of *Über das Organ der Seele*, the anatomist introduced two discoveries of capital importance. The first, the liquor cerebro-spinalis, he claimed, is integral to a healthy brain and not merely, as conventional wisdom has had it since antiquity, a consequence of its corrosion after death. Second, this watery substance is not only of vital importance to the brain's functioning, but also the point at which all spinal nerves end.

The latter fact, in particular, was of more than anatomical significance, raising a wide-ranging, "philosophical" issue: the question, that is, of the seat of the soul or *sensorium commune* and, hence, the foundation of the subject. All through the seventeenth and eighteenth centuries, the *sensorium commune* had been under-stood as a somewhat elusive entity, situated somewhere between a material, bodily aggregate state known, under its Cartesian name, as *res extensa*, and a more intangible condition called *res cogitans*. And even though the attempts at localizing this strange hybrid proved inconclusive and scientists increasingly disparaged those looking for "material mind images," the *sensorium commune* continued to bear on a whole host of cultural issues, including what status music and the sense of hearing would come to hold in the emerging Romantic imagination.

How, then, did Sömmerring tackle the "philosophical" issue of the soul? Simply put, by drowning it—by drenching it in some sort of immaterial H_2O. Not only does the cerebrospinal fluid wash around the nerve ends, he argued, it is also a "special kind of juice." In fact, it is none other than the *sensorium commune* itself. The reasoning behind this striking about-face on centuries of hunting for the soul in a solid part of the body, Sömmerring ventured, was "a priori" evident. Water, without a doubt, is the source of all life: "From the first hours and perhaps days after conception, the entire force of our real individuality—our I—is really and truly contained in a droplet of delicate liquid."[5] And even though a mollusk such as the sea slug *Doris laevis* (now *Cadlina laevis*) is nothing but an "animated slime" barely distinguishable from the glaucous sea in which it lives, all lower organisms possess structure, spirit, and vitality. Even higher organisms such as the human body were supposed to contain humors that—although entirely undifferentiated and translucent—serve a specific purpose other than moisturizing the body. For example, Sömmerring claimed, the liquid inside the labyrinth of the ear (discovered in 1760 by Domenico Cotugno) in all likelihood has its own special composition that is essential to the effect of sound on the auditory nerves. So why should the cranial juice not also possess a structure indicative of a primal life force animating the individual?[6]

The reference to the ear is crucial. Faced with the growing fragmentation of the enlightened unified subject, granting the ear a pivotal role in a clearly ordered sensory apparatus allowed Sömmerring to invoke, one last time, the notion of an undivided soul. This he did with the help of two interrelated lines of argument. The first proceeded from a shrewd (if scientifically dubious) analogy between what Sömmerring called the "organization" of the cerebrospinal fluid, on the one hand, and the transmission of sound waves, on the other. In the same way as water simultaneously transmits to the different senses sensations of heat, taste, odor, and sound, so, too, does the cranial fluid "permit all five senses distinct sensations without disruption."[7] The evidence for this assertion, Sömmerring informed his readers, had been provided by Ernst Florens Chladni's discovery in 1787 of the so-called *Klangfiguren* or "sound figures"—geometric patterns that become visible when a glass plate covered with sand is set into vibration with the help of a violin bow.[8] Although Chladni's main concern was to improve on the earlier findings of Daniel Bernouilli, Leonard Euler, and Jacopo Riccati by determining the properties of bodies with elastic curved surfaces such as bells and bowls, and thereby discovering, almost in passing, the longitudinal waves in solid bodies, Sömmerring and other Romantically

155

inclined intellectuals seized more on what they and the general *Bildungsbürgertum* perceived to be the spiritual implications of the sound figures.[9] Because the latter, Sömmerring reasoned, reveal beyond any doubt that each tone has its own "form of oscillation," it followed that each "sense organ was capable of transmitting its own forms of oscillation, different from those of the other senses, to the ventrical fluid."[10]

The point about the "organization" of water and the "form" of sound vibrations of course mirrored the mix of vitalist medicine, chemistry, and Goethean morphology that had come to pervade scholarly discourse during the latter decades of the eighteenth century. But oddly enough, the antimechanist implications of this notion did not impress on Sömmerring the equally urgent desire to engage Duverney's resonance theory of hearing promulgated more than a century earlier and still in force at this time. Nor did he evince a strong wish for strengthening his "philosophical" argument by drawing on his extensive research on the auditory system, published in 1806 in the still exemplary *Abbildungen des menschlichen Hoerorganes* (Illustrations of the Human Organ of Hearing).[11] Sömmerring had set his sights on higher goals.

And this is where the second, perhaps even more questionable pillar of Sömmerring's ear-centered metaphysics becomes significant. Inspired by Heinse's assertion, put forth the previous year in the novel *Hildegard von Hohenthal*, that the "ear is clearly our most exact sense," Sömmerring not only believed he had found evidence that "of all the nerves, none is in so immediate, so naked and bare a contact with the humidity of the brain cavities" as the auditory nerve, but that the optical and auditory nerves also touch the brain cavities at opposite ends, thus preventing the "movements" transmitted by them from becoming confounded and thereby ultimately preserving the unity of the conscious mind.[12] To hear, to have a soul, even to live, according to Sömmerring, were one and the same.

The reception of *Über das Organ der Seele* was far from even. Leading scientists such as Johann Friedrich Blumenbach and

Georg Christoph Lichtenberg either chose to ignore the work altogether or, like Karl Rudolphi and the young Schelling, criticized it as being too speculative and philosophically unsound. Even Sömmerring's longtime acquaintance Goethe, with whom he had corresponded about such weighty matters as elephant skulls, took exception to the mingling of science and philosophy. Not only had Sömmerring "not brought any advantage to his cause," he wrote, but "special objections" had to be brought forward—at some later stage—against the exaltation of the ear in paragraphs 37 and 39 of his tract.[13]

While Goethe, as far as we know, never got around to specifying his "special objections," Immanuel Kant (to whom Sömmerring had dedicated the work) meanwhile found fault with Sömmerring's argument on more substantial, epistemological grounds. Reiterating the notion first advanced in the *Critique of Pure Reason* that the "I," as a thinking entity, is an object of the internal sense called "soul," Kant insisted: "Now while the soul can perceive itself only through the internal sense, it can perceive the body only through the exterior senses. Thus it cannot determine for itself a location, because for that it would have to turn itself into an object of its own external apperception and externalize itself outside of itself—which contradicts itself."[14]

But Kant, prudently, also left the door open to another explanation, one that would acknowledge Sömmerring's undisputed authority as anatomist and, more importantly, preserve the notion of a unitary consciousness. What, he intriguingly suggested, if one thought of the ventricular fluid as a special kind of liquid, as a kind of substance that, instead of operating mechanically, is "organized" without being "organized?" By this he meant that, obviously, not only is the cerebrospinal liquor not animated, but as chemists had recently found out, water is also not a substance as such. If it was possible to separate oxygen from hydrogen electrolytically, Kant went on to speculate, why should the nerves not also be able "to break down the water of the brain cavity into such primary elements and in this manner, by releasing one or the other of those elements, bring into play different sensations." And, above all, what would be the consequences for the notion of the transcendental subject if one further assumed that these elements reunite as soon as the sensory stimulation has stopped, that the nerve ends, in other words, "perceive the sensory world and in turn react back on it?" Clearly, the self-reflexive subject and its basis in "a collective unity of all sensory impressions in a common organ" would remain unassailable.[15]

"Ear Physiognomy" and the Erotics of Listening

The rejection of Sömmerring's tract was not universal, however. The inextricable unity of soul and sound was, literally, music to the ears of a group of fiery (and mostly very young) poets and thinkers. Novalis, for instance, was fascinated by Sömmerring's transcendental liquor cerebrospinalis because of the affinity it must have suggested with his own notion of the intermingling of the organic, unbounded fluidity of poetry and the watery World Soul.[16] Another enthusiastic reader was the young Franz von Baader, who was later to become instrumental in transmitting seventeenth-century mysticism to Hegel and the philosophers of the Tübinger Stift. Von Baader greeted Sömmerring's discovery as evidence that "nature had assigned to the innermost of each living organism fluidity as the material proper of life."[17] Friedrich Hölderlin, finally, saw Sömmerring as a high priest whom Germans were unable to follow into the sanctuary.[18]

Yet the most fervent supporter of all, and, as it turns out, the one sticking closest to the auditory core of Sömmerring's argument, was Heinse. The humid significance with which the anatomist had invested the sense of hearing made the deepest impression on a poet who, after all, had been obsessed with water and hearing from as far back as the 1770s. But Heinse's vindication of Sömmerring's aurally based "transcendental physiology" was also significant on two further grounds. By defending Sömmerring's work, Heinse furnished to a whole generation of younger poets a scientific rationale for their experimental poetry. He thus bridged, in a way, the mimetic aesthetics and physiology of the Enlightenment and the attempts by poets such as Wilhelm Heinrich Wackenroder, Ludwig Tieck, and Novalis to craft a new autoreferential poetics.[19] Furthermore, Heinse's eulogy of the ear and his endorsement of *Über das Organ der Seele* provided a strong stimulus to a new brand of philosophy that was beginning to frame the work of Germany's intelligentsia in the years before and after 1800.

This philosophy went under the name of *Naturphilosophie*.[20] Two intertwined assumptions of *Naturphilosophie* were to prove particularly enduring and as such help shed light on the convergence of aesthetics and the life sciences underpinning Heinse's and Sömmering's auditory metaphysics. The first assumption was that nature is purposively organized. The idea of nature's organization was rooted in the medicine of the Montpellier school and the emerging biology of the second half of the century, both of which assumed nature to be essentially self-generating and obeying organic, rather than Cartesian and Newtonian principles. In this view, nature could no longer be taken to be inert, inanimate matter: Natural phenomena were their own cause and effect. More important, organisms also had a history and a goal. From the most rudimentary, seemingly undifferentiated substances such as water to the human body, nature's course was one of *Bildung*, of development toward perfection. The parts of a living organism, then, were not determined by the functioning whole: Each part must contain a design within itself.

The second, somewhat less frequently noted cornerstone of *Naturphilosophie* posited that scientific comprehension of the natural environment and aesthetic judgment are compatible. Nature and art are alike, the Romantic poets argued, in that they are the outgrowth of creative, vegetationlike forces, rather than the effect of a mechanical process. The purposive organization of plants—together with their organic structure—is thus akin to art, because plants and works of art are based on a preexisting ideal and sprout forth by dint of the creative powers of imagination giving them direction and purpose. If nature has its own poetry, so, too, does art have its natural laws, they claimed. It was thus only as a logical consequence that by adopting an aesthetic relationship to the natural environment—in other words, by studying the forms inherent in nature—we would be able to lay bare the fundamental forces operating within nature.

With all this, the *Naturphilosophen* differed from Kant, at least to a certain degree. The "old man," as they liked to call him, in his *Critique of Judgment* (1790) had allowed for certain parallels between aesthetic judgment and the way we grasp an organism whose parts are determined by the purpose of the whole. He would, however, make one crucial distinction. Since for Kant a purpose presupposes a freely acting, intelligent being, and nature, clearly, is not an intelligent being, to speak of a purpose in nature would be possible in only a metaphorical sense, *as if* nature were a freely acting creature. All living organisms, then, are really a kind of *Zweckmässigkeit ohne Zweck*, purposiveness without purpose, and our understanding of such organic nature accordingly is entirely subjective, grounded in the faculties of human consciousness alone. A teleological judgment is thus, in essence, always an aesthetic judgment.

The Romantics took these "virtual" connections between aesthetic judgment and teleological judgment *à la lettre*, thereby taking Kant's reasoning, in a sense, to its logical conclusion. If Kant was correct that logic and order reside in human consciousness alone, the structure of natural organisms is to be grasped solely by analogy with the structures of consciousness. In other words, works of art are *like* natural organisms, and natural organisms only bear a *resemblance* to works of art.

Heinse's position, too, diverged from Kantian idealism, albeit on radically different grounds. From as early as 1774, Heinse had been casting a critical eye on the idealization of classical Greek visual arts rampant in mid-eighteenth-century German culture, a development that would eventually lead him to fall foul of the orthodoxy of Gotthold Ephraim Lessing, Moses Mendelssohn, and Johann Winckelmann. Thus, where Winckelmann—the "learned pedant," as Heinse called him—had elevated the "noble simplicity and calm greatness" of Greek art to an absolute norm, Heinse saw only "knowledge without pleasure." Where Mendelssohn had sought to distinguish the divine Venus from the mundane Venus, Heinse defiantly declared the "true Venus to be the same everywhere."[21] And, finally, in contrast to the famous statue of Apollo—in which he missed "Greek soil" and "plenitude"—Heinse celebrated the works of disparaged "Baroque" artists such as Caravaggio, Titian, and Rubens as exemplars of an art in which color matters more than design and immediacy of effect is more important than representation.[22] In short, beauty does not reside in an absolute ideal of which all art other than classical Greek sculpture can be only an imperfect reflection. It is to be found in the endless variety of life itself: "All art is human, not Greek!"[23]

Heinse's reading of Greek art—and thus also his penchant for the sensual and the aural—echoes the views of Friedrich Justus Riedel (1742–1785), one of his early philosophical mentors. The author of a widely read *Theorie der schönen Künste und Wissenschaften* (Theory of Fine Arts and Sciences) (1767) and of a collection of essays on Gluck's opera *Iphigenia*, Riedel differed from the equally popular Johann Sulzer, who in his *Allgemeine Theorie der schönen Künste* (General Theory of Fine Arts) (1771–1777) had considered some sort of mental process to be an integral part of the aesthetic experience. Riedel's work owed more to the British sensualists than to French theorists. Drawing on Shaftesbury and Hutcheson, he excluded any kind of cognitive process from the aesthetic experience and flatly denied the criteria for beauty to reside in reason.

Another early source of Heinse's anti-Kantian rancor may have been the novelist and philosopher Friedrich Heinrich Jacobi. Heinse had lived in Jacobi's house in Düsseldorf for extended periods while serving as editorial assistant to Jacobi's brother Johann Georg, editor of the journal *Isis*. It was at the Jacobi's that he came to share their interest in the pre-Socratics. Thus, readings of Heraclitus nurtured in him the view of the world as a never-ending conflict between antagonistic forces, while Empedocles' panvitalism and the idea of an *arche*, or elementary life force, awakened Heinse's Romantic instincts. Above all, however, Heinse was drawn to the erotic dimension in Empedocles' work, the belief that *Urstoff* and *Urkraft*, primal matter and force, relate to each other sexually. They desire each other, pull toward each other, reject each other. Or, in the more prosaic terms of the bourgeois ménage: "Love, wedding, marriage, and divorce—this is what constitutes the world."[24]

This concept of cosmic copulation in time would become the primary source of Heinse's aesthetics, finding expression in an endless stream of pornographic images and voyeuristic scenes in which longingly gazed-upon female bodies stand in for primal, prereflexive immediacy. In fact, female flesh not only became the dominant metaphor evoked throughout his work, it eventually merged with Heinse's celebration of the ear, linking, in a mystical, almost Dionysian hypertrope, hearing with sex. Of course, the notion that the act of musical listening is heavily imbued with eroticism and that, in fact, the ear itself, if not a kind of sexual organ, is one of female conception was among the world's most archaic beliefs.[25] But in the context of Heinse's adulation of the ear, the convergence of sex, sound, and sensualist philosophy took on an entirely novel significance. Thus, when Heinse describes the singing heroine in one of the most notorious episodes of the *Hildegard* novel as a "voluptuous" young "sorceress" with her hair let down and her breasts exposed, we are not merely dealing, as early critics such as Goethe or Johann F. Reichardt charged, with a provocative expression of "coarse sensuousness and raw passion."[26] Similarly, the singing of the young women at the *Ospedale dei Mendicanti* in Venice—along with their "tender skin" and "lascivious smile"—may have produced in Heinse an orgiastic feeling of dizziness that made one "savor one's existence away."[27] But the real meaning behind such erotically charged (and, to be

sure, chauvinist) moments of aural bliss lies elsewhere: in the tri-
als and tribulations inherent in the unworking of the boundaries
between society and nature, body and mind, music and language,
threatening the post-Revolutionary, post-Enlightenment subject.

One instructive example of this double-edged nature of
Heinse's aural eroticism is the way he used Sömmerrings's anatomical plates of the ear and the voice to structure the three parts
of the first edition of the *Hildegard* novel. Each of the three parts
of the first edition of the work is framed by vignettes of the ear
and the vocal organ: the beginning and end of Part One feature
Sömmerring's plates of a "well-formed" female ear, while Parts
Two and Three are framed by those of the male and "human"
hearing organs, respectively (figure 4.1). As Christine Lubkoll
has shown, the sequence of images underscores a central, albeit
highly contested goal of late eighteenth-century aesthetic theory:
the formation of the artistic subject and its grounding in specific, gendered acts of creativity.[28] The progression from female
ear to male voice and, finally, to the "human" ear mimics the
ontogenesis of what Heinse called "ear physiognomy."[29] At the
same time, the sequence parallels the development of the plot as
it culminates in the completion and triumphant premiere of the
main protagonist and composer Lockmann's opus magnum, the
opera *Achille in Sciro*. Its source nestling deep inside the female
body—that is to say, in Hildegard's "enchanting pubescent figure" and "nightingalelike" voice—the opera (read: the work of
art) takes shape only through an act of acoustic insemination,
a fusion of the male imagination (*Phantasie*) and female magic
(*Zauberisches*) that is symbolized by Lockmann's inscription of the
finished score with the pseudonym "Passionei." But it is only in
the moment of "delivery," in the frenetic acceptance of the work
(and by implication, of Heinse's novel) by the "human" ears of
the public, that the utopian promise of the work—of all works of
art—is to be realized: the fusion of the deepest sense of interior-
ity with the greatest possible universality.

The primal act of audiosexual creation remains fraught with

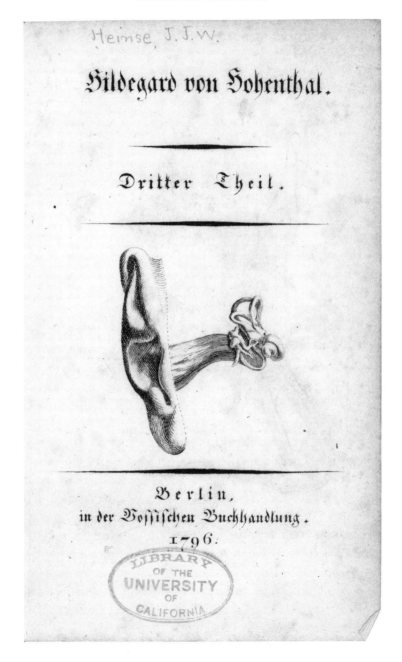

Figure 4.1. Wilhelm Heinse, *Hildegard von Hohenthal. Dritter Theil*, cover (courtesy of the Bancroft Library, University of California, Berkeley). Each of the three volumes of Heinse's novel bears on its cover a plate by the artist Christian Koeck. Together with other plates these later became the basis of Samuel Sömmerring's *Abbildungen des menschlichen Hörorganes* (1806).

risk fully sanctioned by the public sphere though it may be. To be sure, by frequently glossing music as a "siren's art" or as sounds "streaming forth from sweet lips," Heinse draws on some of the most clichéd (and thus, in a sense, safest) tropes for linking sound with sexuality, femininity, and water—recall all the Undines, mermaids, nymphs, Melusines, and Rhine daughters that would come to populate countless poems, novels, and opera plots from Goethe to Richard Wagner to Aribert Reimann. But in so doing, he also conjures up another, more precarious possibility. Lurking behind the synthesis of music and language encoded in Hildegard's bursts of postcoital gibberish (which in Heinse's secret diaries are glossed less squeamishly as "jubilant cooing and cheering cries of an excessive love itch going through all nerves" (*jubelndem Girren und jauchzendem Schrey des Uebermaßes von Liebesjucken in allen Nerven*) are self-loss and death.[30] To grasp this darker side of Heinse's audioeroticism we must return to the Rhinefall.

Rauschen, *the Sublime, and Vertigo*

It is in the foaming floods of the Rhinefall—in fact, in water generally—that the aural and the erotic converge in a precarious fusion of subject-enabling and subject-dissolving forces. Two essential properties of water in particular highlight this ambiguity of the Heinsean antitranscendental subject. The first of these, the deep and long-standing linkages of water with femininity and sexuality, we saw reflected in Heinse's sensualist brand of *Naturphilosophie* and, to a lesser degree perhaps, in the central metaphysical role of water in Sömmerring's physiology. Just as the latter took the ventricular fluid to be the soul's veritable emulsion, Heinse's panvitalism rested on the notion that water is the quintessential *fluidum vitale*. And where Sömmerring suspected Leibniz's, Newton's, Euler's, and Kant's ether to be just plain old water, Heinse echoed pre-Socratic thinker Thales of Miletus in supposing the origin of the divine to be in the water.

Fluidum vitale, downward-rushing cataracts—the sexual connotations of water weighed heavily on Heinse's imagination. As a "stream will forever remain the most lovely image of copulation," he wrote, so the Rhinefall, longing to unite with the depths of Mother Earth, dissolves "in the fire of love."[31] Farther south, on Italian shores, the roles may have flipped, in that this time, the water stands in for femininity, but it is still the same wet embrace. "It is as if one always had the naked body of Venus before oneself," Heinse mused as he rested his eyes on the Bay of Naples.[32] And in the same way that the Mediterranean sea aroused Heinse's voyeuristic instincts, it also cast an acoustic spell on him: "When the waves crash into the harbor and roll up on its high wall, over the roofs of the houses, and foam and sea come rushing down like a thunderstorm that unites—smack—with the newly arriving, swooshing [*herbey rauschend*] vehemence to a whirling dust: how nature comes alive in my senses and with its music catches hold of my being."[33]

Here, the second function of water in symbolizing the conflicting elements of Romantic subjectivity becomes apparent: its association, particularly since the late eighteenth century, with noise and euphoria. The term "herbey rauschend" that Heinse uses to describe the powerful, simultaneously threatening and exhilarating effect of the sea, merits more detailed discussion. Etymologically and phonetically, the words "noise" and "intoxication" are closely related—at least they are more noticeably so in German than in the English language, where the etymological link necessitates a detour via *nausea*, the Latin word for seasickness. A noise is called *Geräusch*, while too much wine, opulently scored music, or, for that matter, a rousing sexual encounter may result in the experience of *Rausch*. But there is also a third term that, at first glance, seems to have more in common with noise than with a state of intoxication—*rauschen*. As a verb, the term usually signifies the sound made by such things as rivers, brooks, and leaves, and thus might be translated as "rustling." The noun *Rauschen*, in contrast, more specifically stands for "white noise." If these English terms are all correct or, at any rate, perfectly acceptable translations, in the context of early Romanticism

Rauschen carried a number of less crisply circumscribed (and hence perhaps less readily translatable) meanings. Hovering on the borderline between a whole range of aesthetic, philosophical, and scientific projects, such polyvalent meanings mirror the era's complex and fluctuating relationship with the unencoded, the unknowable—in short, with Kant's noumenon.

Before the 1770s, *Rauschen* had usually provoked mixed feelings. From Klopstock to Albrecht von Haller to Hieronymous Grimm, alpine travelers in the first half of the eighteenth century reacted with horror to the region's many waterfalls. Even as late as 1775, Goethe, on his first trip to Switzerland, found himself repulsed by the "desolate" alpine landscape and most notably by the noise of its waterfalls, the "Gerausch des Waßer falls."[34] The aversion to *Rauschen* was particularly pronounced when such sounds were somehow being depicted in music. Thus, in 1722, Johann Mattheson condemned as "empty sound games" the rendering of the "trembling shine of the playful waves" in Handel's *German Arias* and urged composers to avoid words that "do not allow for a pleasant sound, as are hissing, yelling, etc."[35] Even as late as 1771–1774, Johann Georg Sulzer would still empathize with listeners overcome with "disgust" on hearing runs that *rauschen* "up and down" over an entire octave.[36] And it would not be for another three decades that writers were able fully to redeem the dizzy sensation from its inferior status. The "constantly changing movements of a foaming waterfall surging downward [*herabrauschend*] or of the floating sea," Christian F. Michaelis, for instance, declared in 1801, "as well as in a wild music evenly welling up and down—all these pull at our imagination with such force that it is unable to grasp it all, calling upon reason to furnish the idea of eternity." In other words, sounds such as these were "stuff for the sublime."[37]

The concept of the sublime, or *das Erhabene*, Michaelis referred to, was of course neither his nor was it new. It was at the base of the transcendental aesthetics elaborated in Kant's *Critique of Judgment* a decade earlier—as was, fascinatingly, the image of the thundering waterfall that inspired the feeling of the "dynamic sublime" in the person watching from a safe distance. But if for Kant music lacked "urbanity," occupying a lower position in the hierarchy of the arts a place somewhere — in his words — between the "merely pleasant" and the beautiful, by the late 1790s and not least because of its association with waterfalls, music suddenly came to be regarded as the most sublime of the arts. If all art, as the nineteenth-century critic Walter Pater famously suggested, aspires to the condition of music, after Heinse, all music would aspire to the condition of *Rauschen*, disrupting the dual Cartesian system of exchange, representation, and error-free thinking.[38]

Heinse rejected Kant's hijacking of the unpleasant, shocking experience of waterfalls for aesthetic — and ultimately moral — ends. Kant's was a "system of ignorance," he growled: "verbiage" (*Wörterkram*) and "waffling" (*Gewäsche*) that "pricks out a man's eyes, crushes his nose, deafens the ears, burns the tongue, and hardens all feeling."[39] But it was not only Kant's scorn for the senses to which Heinse objected. Human reason itself, he charged, had "thought everything but the sun into dust and driven all spirits from nature."[40] The gap that Kant's philosophy upheld between the subject and a forever unknowable world was the product of a civilization that had estranged humanity from nature. And so the contrast between Kant's aesthetics — geared toward higher goals such as "moral independence" — and Heinse's more hedonistic, not to say morbid desire to "get in" with the roaring waters of the Rhine, clearly cannot be starker. Instead of Kant's and Sömmerring's consciously sublimating subject, here we have the suspension of the *principium individuationis*, the letting go of the self in fits of religious rapture. In place of distance, we have almost complete immersion; instead of boundaries, the gradual dissolution of such boundaries.

The opposition to Kant, I believe, is also one of the reasons for what appears, at least superficially, to be the persistence of dated mimetic principles in Heinse's musical thought. In much the same way that Sömmerring's attempts to locate the soul were oddly out of touch with the medical and scientific consensus of the 1790s, many of the reflections Heinse had penned during his Italian travels and subsequently worked into the *Hildegard* novel were rather quaint, even by late eighteenth-century standards. For instance, Heinse disliked instrumental music. "Mere instrumental music," he wrote, echoing the views of many of his contemporaries, is "often nothing more than an empty flattery of the ear [and] a fanciful imitation of opera scenes."[41] Throughout his copious notes on the opera of the period, the postulate of verisimilitude reigns supreme, music's role being subsidiary to the dramatic structure or, as Heinse put it, to the "total impression," the "profound effect of the whole."[42] A scene in Gluck's *Iphigenia auf Tauris*, for instance, depicted a thunderstorm, while the ascending runs in that opera's overture signified the "raging people."[43] In fact, music generally is a "wide ocean," with specific works conjuring up a remarkably diverse waterscape. Here the human voice sounds like pure spring water, there massed choirs have the same effect as "the waves and waters of the sea." And in Gregorio Allegri's much-revered *Miserere* (1638), there is a "sublime harmony, ever swelling like a stream of countless springs and creeks and agitating the hearts in floods of delight and vortexes."[44]

If, by 1796, positions such as these had clearly become passé so too had many of the musical works Heinse took as reference points for his aquatic aesthetics. During his Italian travels, he had become an ardent admirer of the work of Niccolò Jommelli (1714–1774), at one time heralded as one of Europe's most illustrious composers. Jommelli's prolific output of operas and religious works—not to mention a prolonged period of employment at the court at Stuttgart—had exercised considerable influence on the Mannheim school and attracted a huge following throughout Europe. Audiences relished his harmonic boldness and crescendo effects, and his intricately constructed arias were all the rage at opera houses in Naples, Stuttgart, Venice, and Vienna. In short, Jommelli's works were part of the avant-garde—until the composer's death in 1774, that is. By the time Heinse published his

Hildegard novel, Jommelli's music had already lost much of its pull, so much so that Mozart found it "beautiful, but too clever and old-fashioned for the theater."[45]

Although, clearly, the antiquated nature of Heinse's personal tastes is beyond question, it would be a mistake to conclude with an older scholarship that his aesthetics amounts to little more than a "modified mimetic principle."[46] Rather, the penchant for *opera seria*, the music of Palestrina and Leonardo Leo (1694–1744), vocal music generally, and even the erotic connections of music were all hallmarks of the Romantic concept of modernity.[47] Likewise, the numerous references to water allow us to detect a different strand of Heinsean thought. In associating music with water, Heinse did not regard Gluck's operas as mere sonic visualizations of oceans, rivers, or waterfalls. The water metaphor was meant to tie the listening experience to a quasi-prenatal, oceanic feeling. It conveyed a certain simplicity and naturalness of the musical process as it followed its own course, unencumbered by words and verbal syntax. Having distanced himself from the rationalist theories of his patron Christoph Martin Wieland and the sentimentalist views of Rousseau, Heinse advocated a more mystic, almost maternalistic notion of music, one prefiguring *Naturphilosophie*'s and even twentieth-century music theorist Heinrich Schenker's credo that nature and art are living organisms.[48] The beauty of music, he claimed in his early *Über einige Gemälde der Düsseldorfer Galerie* (On Some Paintings in the Düsseldorf Gallery, 1776), comes "from the womb of the night, the invisible." Music represents not objects, but "masses and their movement."[49] And in the same way that Chladni's sound figures for Sömmerring bore out the discreteness of each sensory channel, Heinse was convinced that the "secret of music" is revealed in a simple experiment: a small stone, thrown into a lake, produces a high pitch and a uniform movement in "gentle masses." A big stone, by contrast, yields a low pitch and spreads a movement of "stronger masses."[50]

Heinse was one of the first theorists to promulgate the concept of music as a form of energy, anticipating similar ideas advanced by Wackenroder and Tieck almost a decade later. More significant, though, than the leading role he took in using the image of *rauschend* water to articulate the avant-garde (and soon to be canonized) notion of music as autonomous form is the fact that Heinse's auditory stance cut against the grain of the prevailing Kantian aesthetics of "disinterested pleasure." The hearing that Heinse envisaged was not a listening for concrete objects such as waterfalls, any more than such hearing was meant to afford glimpses of absolute truth transcending all subjective purposes. It was simply a listening for its own sake, stripped of the pretensions of the Absolute. The pleasures of this kind of hearing lay in the promise of immediacy available only from a musical work that undermines its own meaningfulness by not being anything other than it says and by not saying anything other than it is.[51]

However, we would be misrepresenting the ambiguous status of Romantic listening if we were to interpret Heinse's views as subjective idiosyncrasy, as the sign of a torn genius. On the contrary, instead of liberating Romantic poets, composers, and listeners from the straitjacket of grammar, the incongruities of the early Romantic ear reflect the broader reconfiguration of sensory perception taking place in the decades before and after 1800, illustrating just how deeply the ear was implicated in the new transcendental subject's predicament, caught between a world of unknowable noumena and the abysmal depths of the emerging self, both of which threatened the integrity of the rational subject. Two examples may illustrate this.

The first example involves the striking parallels between the Romantic fascination with *Rauschen* and a phenomenon that was increasingly commanding the attention of physicians, philosophers, and psychologists: vertigo. Although it had been known for thousands of years, vertigo toward the late eighteenth century acquired a completely different set of connotations as the focus of aural sensibility and musical aesthetics shifted toward sublime *Rauschen* and European societies edged ever more closely toward crisis. Thrown into sharp relief by the paroxysm of the French Revolution and the collapse of the established political order following in its wake, the causes of this crisis resided much deeper, under the skin, as it were, of the troubled body politic. Instability and ambiguity had become constant features of everyday life, invading the newly liberated subjects' every nook and cranny. The senses were not exempt from this more permanent crisis. In fact, it might even be argued that it was the emerging neurophysiology of perception of the mid-eighteenth century that had laid the foundation for this crisis in the first place. As the Cartesian machine body with its machine ears and machine eyes came under a cloud, the transmission of sensory stimuli was broken down into a sequence of more diffuse, protodigital signals with no isomorphic link to reality.

The impact on the idea of the modern subject of this shift from the nervous system as a neutral channel to an autonomous system was profound, finding expression in a rapidly expanding body of literature lamenting the growing fragmentation and dismemberment of the social body—the fact that, as Heinse put it, "these days, hardly anybody is a whole person any longer."[52] One of the most remarkable, if undervalued texts within this tradition is *Versuch über den Schwindel* (Essay on Vertigo) of 1786 by the physician-"philosopher" Marcus Herz (1747–1803). Setting forth a theory of vertigo that speaks as much to the era's upset sensory order as it lays out the rudiments of a media theory of perception and, implicitly, of Romantic listening, Herz imagined vertigo to be a corporeal as well as a mental affliction. Its truth, therefore, did not reside in mechanical causes such as topsy-turvy animal spirits, as older medical authorities had asserted, but was a consequence of a complex set of processes involving nerve fluids, the sensitivity of the sense organs, and especially the velocity of sensory impulses. Perceptions, as Herz echoed vitalist doctrine, do not leave imprints in the soul: A certain color or sound do not bear the "slightest resemblance with the preceding vibration of the retina or tympanum."[53] Rather, such perceptions had to be seen as what Herz called *Fertigkeiten*, or abilities. Essentially immaterial, these "abilities" denote the soul's capacity to process sensory stimuli with varying degrees of facility by drawing on memory and association. As a result, the soul does not contemplate wax-sealike impressions, but the ebb and flow of more or less intangible stimuli transported by the nerve fluid. Most important, however, for the orderly functioning of this chain of signals and thus for the maintenance of proper perception was what Herz—elaborating on an idea first put forth by John Locke—called the *natürliche Weile* or "natural interval." The soul, he argued, requires a certain amount of time in which to grasp a sensory impulse clearly before it is absorbed by the next impulse. Thus, an uncluttered perception depends as much on the nature of the stimuli received as it does on the perceiving sense organ. Different olfactory signals, for instance, linger for a long time in the soul and therefore can be distinguished only if they are separated by a longer interval. Different sounds, by contrast, because "they touch only the surface of the soul, and disappear with the presence of the object," can be grasped without much effort and during the shortest *Weile*.[54]

But what, then, is the cause of vertigo? Herz listed several factors that adversely affect the natural interval peculiar to each sensory input and sense organ, from too stark a contrast hindering the smooth transition between stimuli to novelty. What he believed to matter about these factors, however, were not their material qualities as such, but the relative degree of deviation from the normal *Weile*. Thus, a series of stimuli slower than the natural interval would result in boredom, a series above this threshold would cause vertigo.

Herz's analysis did not factor in disorders of the semicircular canals (whose balancing function was discovered only in 1824 by the French neurologist Marie-Jean-Pierre Flourens) as possible causes for vertigo. And he barely touched on the social causes of vertigo, allotting only a footnote to the idea that the "ability" to process sensory stimuli with varying degrees of facility might be due to the growing division of labor. "The study of a certain scientific discipline or skill in a certain occupation may well make the progression of ideas peculiar to this science or that type of labor more familiar to a person and a prevailing principle of his association," he posited. Mathematicians, for instance, would be most comfortable with those "relationships of ideas" that bear some resemblance to numbers and figures. By contrast, a person who has read nothing but poetry would prefer to write and speak figuratively.[55] Similarly, one suspects a rather more contemporary notion of the individual to be the true rationale behind Herz's even more sweeping claim that humans choose sound as the preferred medium for communicating their ideas. They do so, he suggested, because hearing poses the least obstacle to the mind "busying" itself to grasp and communicate the greatest amount of ideas in the shortest time possible.[56]

By all appearances, then, vertigo was the downside of the euphoria caused by the newfound freedom of the "busy" transcendental subject. More troubling still, vertigo also strongly hinted at the possibility that the mind, the crowning achievement of God's creation, no longer ensured a stable correlation between signifier and signified, between physical cause and effect. Overwhelmed by the dizzying flood of disconnected physiological signals and the potential obliteration of meaning following in its wake, the subject finds itself caught between two conflicting desires: the need to assert *amid* the jumble of signals the law of pure reason, on the one hand, or the desire to surrender itself to a pure language *behind* all the interference, on the other. Clearly, late eighteenth-century intellectuals, even as they remained acutely aware of the blindness of an age that had fragmented the very sensory abilities it had sought to liberate, scrambled to preserve the integrity of the rational subject.

The Naked Ego, the Voice, and the Speaking Machine
The second example illustrating how the ear—or, at any rate, Heinse's ideas of a *Rausch*-filled, self-referential listening—

became implicated in the quandaries of the Romantic self are the sweeping changes in the theory of speech. As we have seen, Heinse prized vocal music over the emerging instrumental sounds of the Viennese avant-garde, believing that singing and living are equivalent to being naked: "When a person sings," composer Lockmann declares in *Hildegard von Hohenthal*, "it is as if he threw off all his clothes at once, revealing himself in his natural state."[57] But as with Heinse's audioeroticism generally, the image of the naked body emitting melodious sounds should not (at least not exclusively) be mistaken for plain sexism. Rather, it is one of the key images of what Jacques Derrida has famously called "logo-centrism," a prime example of the proximity of voice, hearing, and being. More important perhaps, in this specific eighteenth-century association of voice with nakedness, pure being, or "pres-ence," it is only one of several competing discourses informing late eighteenth-century notions of hearing as a form of Romantic self-modeling.

There were two such competing discourses on the voice: the emerging speech physiology of the early eighteenth century and the pioneering work in acoustic phonetics and signal processing of the latter part of the eighteenth century and the beginning of the nineteenth century. Speech physiology had first caught Heinse's attention in the early 1790s. While working on the *Hildegard* novel, Heinse had chanced upon two seminal works: "Sur les causes de la voix de l'homme & de ses differens tons" (On the Causes of the Human Voice and Its Different Sounds) (1700), by Denis Dodart, and "De la formation de la voix de l'homme" (On the Formation of the Human Voice) (1741) by Antoine Ferrein.[58] Before Dodart, the human voice had been regarded as a kind of wind instrument. As in a flute or organ pipe, the air contained in the trachea was thought to be the main cause of phonation. Dodart refuted this analogy, assigning the main role in the vocal apparatus to the glottis, with the buccal cavity and the larynx merely assuming auxiliary functions. It is the vibrating lips of the glottis, he argued, that cause the air column inside the larynx to sound. Although Dodart's assertion was important in that it shifted the focus from an articulatory to an acoustic phonetics, it was still little more than a hypothesis. The empirical basis for the new science of the voice — the discovery of the function of the vocal cords — would be provided only half a century later by Antoine Ferrein. Experimenting on the vocal apparatus of dogs and deceased prisoners, Ferrein (who later became the inspiration for the figure of Dr. Orcotome in Diderot's novel *The Indiscreet Jewels*) took Dodart's findings one step further. The vocal cords, he argued, are like the strings of a harpsichord. In much the same way that the latter can be tuned by altering their length, so phonation depends on the tension of the vocal cords. Unlike harpsichord strings, though, he claimed, the vibration of the vocal cords is not the result of them being plucked, but of being struck by the exhaled air.

Both theories had their quirks. By isolating the glottis and the vocal cords from the rest of the vocal apparatus, Ferrein limited the scope of his phonetic model to the study of tones. Voiceless sounds such as hissing, which are produced in the buccal cavity, could not be accounted for. Similarly, neither Dodart nor Ferrein saw any difference between the physiological foundations of speech and those of song. Finally, and perhaps most interestingly of all, Dodart clung to the rationalist notion that harmonic proportions somehow play a role in the production of vocal sounds. "Distant" harmonic proportions, he believed, connect the shape of the buccal cavity — the part that modern acoustic phonetics calls the "acoustic filter" — and phonation.

Heinse's annotations to these two texts illustrate how he fused Dodart's vocal rationalism and Ferrein's mechanism into his own eclectic brand of phonocentrism. Like the French anatomist, he assures himself of the pervasiveness of harmonic proportions, hears an "inner music," and invokes "perennial vibrations of the vital nerves." And similar to Dodart, Heinse does not differentiate between speech and song, the latter simply being (another nautical metaphor!) a kind of speech boat cruising "under full sail" (*alle*

Segel der Sprachwerkzeuge aufgezogen). Finally, even where Heinse acknowledges the superior detail of Ferrein's work, he sees no contradiction with Dodart's fundamental claim about the vibrating glottis. Because in Ferrein's model, he figured, the vocal tools contain "more of the living mass in man," *mehr Masse vom Lebendigen am Menschen*, his theory simply made things "more sensuous."[59]

But if the physiology of the vocal tract indexed, in true Enlightenment fashion, "Man," acoustic phonetics was a different and altogether more troubling story. Like Herz's associationist psychology, acoustic phonetics, too, harked back to the uncertainties of the listening, "busy" subject. Rooted in the numerous attempts made throughout the century to produce speech artificially, acoustic phonetics ironically reached its apogee at precisely the moment when Heinse appropriated for himself Dodart's and Ferrein's findings on the voice as an instrument of "autoaffection." It was in 1791 that Wolfgang von Kempelen, an engineer who had acquired notoriety for his fraudulent "chess Turk" a decade earlier, had published a lengthy description of a device he called a "speaking machine"[60] (figure 4.2).

An intricate assembly of pipes, levers, and bellows-shaped artificial lungs, this machine was devised to mimic the human vocal apparatus with an unprecedented degree of fidelity and to prove the point that speech can be produced synthetically, to utter whole words and even short sentences. In its broad design, von Kempelen's invention consisted of a large, rectangular box with two holes on the longer sides and a bellows simulating the lungs that was operated with the right forearm at the end facing the person operating the machine. Inside the box was another, smaller box called the *Windlade* or "wind box" (figure 4.2, A), to which were attached several *Nebentheile* or "secondary parts" that simulated the mouth: three levers used for the production of vowels (*s, sch, r*) and, facing the end where the air flow entered the wind box (x), the "mouth," made of rubber (c). A third component consisted of two holes in the cover of the wind box that represented the nostrils (*m, n*) and that had to be covered with

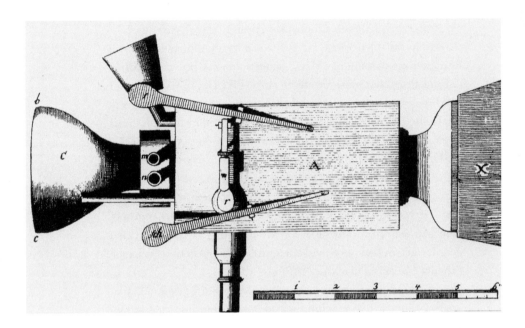

Figure 4.2. Wolfgang von Kempelen, *Mechanismus der menschlichen Sprache nebst der Beschreibung seiner sprechenden Maschine*, fig. 24 (Vienna: J. V. Degen, 1791). Von Kempelen's speech-machine with the outer box removed.

two fingers unless a nasal was to be produced. The flow of air into the "mouth" was by way of the *Stimmritze*, or the glottis, here simulated by an oscillating reed, complemented by a narrow shunting tube that adjusted air pressure in the "mouth cavity" in order to produce unvoiced speech sounds. Using his left hand, the person operating the machine controlled the resonance properties of the "mouth," and hence the production of vowels and some consonants, by varying the size of its opening. As for the vocal cords, they were simulated by a slamming reed made of ivory that, although adjustable, during a "performance" was able to produce only one pitch. The three levers, finally, were activated by the remaining fingers of the right hand, with two of them serving the production of the fricatives [s] and [ʃ] as well as [z] and [ʒ] by releasing air into two separate, hissing whistles attached to the side of the wind box. By pressing down the third lever, the operator dropped a wire on the "glottis" which resulted in a [R].

Of course, despite the fact that the speech machine was considered a genuine technological advance over the many "speaking heads" on display throughout Europe, the simulation of natural articulation that von Kempelen aimed for was far from being perfect. Since the shape of the mouth of the machine remained constant, some vowels, and especially the consonants [d], [t], [g], and [k], could only be feigned. Likewise, an [l] could only be approximated, by putting the thumb into the "mouth."

Troubling questions also vex von Kempelen's broader epistemological claims. According to the first of these claims, the machine was to yield new scientific insights into the nature of human phonation by drawing on general acoustics and by modeling actual processes of articulation. But although the point of von Kempelen's device was to enhance scientific knowledge of the interplay of different functions of the vocal apparatus, its heuristic value was diminished by the fact that the synthetically produced sounds were the result of a feedback between the activity of the operator's fingers and his auditory perception of these sounds. "Playing" the machine entailed a subjective component, as when someone knows their actions by their outcome, not their cause. Or as von Kempelen's predecessor Christian Gottlieb Kratzenstein, referring to his own version of a speaking machine introduced several years earlier, had written, "we act on our bodies like someone born blind [playing] on an organ whose structure he does not know."[61]

But this intrusion into the experimental setting of the subjective factor does more than undermine the scientific value of von Kempelen's invention and thus his status as a pioneer of phonetics. It dovetails nicely with von Kempelen's mildly heretical (even by late eighteenth-century standards), but not any less questionable claim that "language was not necessarily the gift of the Creator, but had been gradually invented by humans."[62] The machine actually displaced "Man" from his central position in the operation called speech by casting the operator in a far more ambiguous, not to say inhuman role: as part of a larger man-machine circuit that involved his auditory apparatus in a subtle interplay of attentive listening and deceptive autoaffection. To operate the machine, on one level, a finely tuned ear was required. But by the same token, the process of synthetic speech production was contingent on the operator's acceptance of ersatz sounds for the sake of the autoaffective production of the subject.[63] In other words, von Kempelen's machine is a quintessential example of the technological a priori of Derrida's phonocentric "hearing (understanding)-oneself-speak" and an illustration of the precarious position of early Romantic aurality as one of the major touchstones of modern subjectivity.

The Soul, a Loop

It is unclear whether Heinse or Sömmerring were among the audiences witnessing von Kempelen's machine. But they may have been familiar with a device that complements von Kempelen's maching from its auditory end, as it were, highlighting the dilemma inherent in the larger Romantic project of grounding

"Man" in a self-referential aesthetics and the purity of an Edenic soundscape. A closer look at this predicament takes us back, one last time, to water, the soul, and Kant.

As we have seen in his response to Sömmerring's *Über das Organ der Seele*, Kant drew on Antoine Lavoisier's electrochemical decomposition of water in order to conceptualize the interface between nerve endings and ventricular fluid. Lying beneath the "decomposition and regrouping of given sensory impressions," he argued, is an "ability of the nerves... to decompose the water of the brain cavities into its primary substances."[64] This in turn would not only allow the nerves to perceive the sensory world, but also to "react back on it." In other words, by recasting Sömmerring's *medium uniens* as mere H_2O Kant assimilates the soul to an experiment that had been carried out by Paets von Troostwyk and Johann R. Deimann in 1789 with the help of an *Elektrisirmaschine* or electrostatic generator (figure 4.3).[65] Basically, the experiment consisted of two glass tubes that were filled with distilled water. At its closed bottom, the first tube was fused with an electric wire that ended in the enclosed water. At the opposite, open end of the tube, another wire was inserted that in turn was connected to a second glass tube also filled with water and fused, at its bottom, with another wire leading to the *Elektrisirmaschine*. After sending shocks generated by the machine through the wire, the two scientists noted that gas began to rise to the surface, and that once the gas had reached the end of the upper wire, it ignited and then disappeared, thus starting the whole process over again.[66]

The aspect that most intrigued Kant about the *Elektrisirmaschine* was of course less the fact that water could no longer be considered a substance, as he had claimed prior to Lavoisier's findings, but that it allowed the electrolytic decomposition and synthesis of water to occur in a never-ending loop. The device's design was thus strikingly akin to the way Sömmering and Heinse imagined the interaction of (auditory) nerve endings and ventricular fluid in some kind of ear-soul. At a deeper level, however,

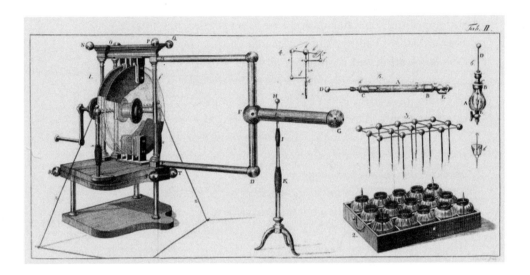

Figure 4.3. John Cuthbertson, *Beschreibung einer Elektrisirmaschine und einigen damit von J. R. Deimann und A. Paets von Troostwyck angestelten Versuchen*, fig. 2 (courtesy of Niedersächsische Staats- und Universitätsbibliothek Göttingen). Although in this drawing the emphasis is on the production of electricity through friction, the parts of interest here are the glass spheres and the system of electric wires depicted in the lower right corner.

Kant's cautious turn toward the materiality of thought also had ramifications for the Romantic concepts of aurality and thus implicitly for the theory of the modern subject. Conceiving of listening and reasoning in terms of chemical processes, rather than the mechanics of resonance, enabled the philosopher to evade, as he had put it in the third *Critique* the "barbaric" concept that aesthetic pleasure requires the "addition of stimuli [*Reize*] and emotions [*Rührungen*]."[67] Yet while this departure from mechanism strengthened the aesthetics of "absolute" music, that is, music that is not explicitly "about" anything, it also undermined one of the core elements of the aesthetics of the sublime. More than half a century before Hermann von Helmholtz declared hearing to be a form of Fourier analysis and thus the ear to be its own medium, Kant's bold reconfiguration of the soul as an electrolytic *perpetuum mobile* cut the ground from under the Romantic project of using the sense of hearing to take us beyond what Friedrich Schlegel called "the tyranny of the physical object."[68] But it did so, paradoxically, not by creating a more "idealized" (*idealisch*) space for "the passions to breathe in a purer ether," as Friedrich's brother August Wilhelm Schlegel had hoped, but simply by transforming the production of ideas into a form of data processing.[69] Operating in the "liquor" of reason, Kant's artificial soul organ, converts the subject into a mere medium.

CHAPTER FIVE

Hearing Oneself Hear:

The Autoresonant Self

and the Expansion of the Audible

In 1936, there appeared in Switzerland a slim volume entitled *Deutsche Menschen: Eine Folge von Briefen* (German Men and Women: A Sequence of Letters).[1] In it, one "Detlef Holz" had assembled a series of letters written between 1783 and 1883 by such giants of German intellectual history as Friedrich Schlegel, Johann Wolfgang Goethe, Georg Büchner, and Georg Forster. Detlef Holz was none other than Walter Benjamin. Although the Jewish intellectual had fled Germany in 1933, he stubbornly clung to the belief that Nazi barbarism could be countered by appealing to the enlightened roots of the Romantic era. *Deutsche Menschen* was to be a testimony to this tradition, speaking, as the inscription on the first page indicates, "of honor without fame, of greatness without glory, of dignity without pay." One of the letters Benjamin included in the collection was a letter by a young physicist by the name of Johann Wilhelm Ritter (1776–1810).

To historians of science, Ritter is no stranger: He discovered nothing less than ultraviolet light and invented the dry-cell battery. But Benjamin's interest in Ritter was fueled by a completely different aspect of Ritter's work, one that does not bear a direct relationship to science or in fact to Ritter's presumed humanism. The Jena physicist had been on Benjamin's mind ever since he had begun exploring the close parallels between "Baroque" allegory and the modern era in his first major completed book,

Ursprung des deutschen Trauerspiels (The Origin of German Tragic Drama), published in 1928.[2] There, Benjamin invokes the "brilliant Johann Wilhelm Ritter" to demonstrate the elective affinity between Romantic notions of music, language, and writing and the "self-indulgent delight in sheer sound" in the "Baroque" *Trauerspiel*.[3] But above all, it was a passage from Ritter's posthumously published *Fragmente aus dem Nachlasse eines jungen Physikers, ein Taschenbuch für Freunde der Natur* (Fragments from the Posthumous Papers of a Young Physicist, a Pocket Book for Friends of Nature) that caught Benjamin's attention. In that passage, according to Benjamin, Ritter had "involuntarily" commented on Ernst Florens Chladni's sound figures noting that "it would be beautiful if what became externally clear here were also exactly what the sound pattern is for us inwardly: a light pattern, fire-writing."[4]

Ritter's fascination with Chladni's sound figures (which we will explore in more detail below) was of course far from involuntary. Nor was Benjamin's own interest in Ritter limited to the relationship between sound, image, and music in the tragic drama. Benjamin was drawn to Ritter's esotericism because the "free play of sound" and phonetic tension he had found in the language of seventeenth-century theater led directly to the Romantics' concept of music as the "opposite of meaning-laden speech."[5] The musical philosophy of the Romantic writers, with its "self-indulgent delight in sheer sound," he argued, resonated with music's role in the work of Shakespeare and Calderón. More than merely filling functional, theatrical roles, music here transcended the separation between oral and written language, subject and object.[6] And it is this, music's and indeed sound's almost messianic potential, its resonant, yet nonmimetic character, that Benjamin believed Ritter to have embraced. And it is the same central position of music as "the last remaining universal language since the tower of Babel" that he hoped to work into the mix of German idealism, Jewish mysticism, and Marxism that was beginning to shape his critique of modern rationality.

Yet the messianic dimension that Benjamin believed to have

found in Ritter was only one aspect of his interpretation of Romanticism. In Benjamin's doctoral dissertation, *Der Begriff der Kunstkritik in der deutschen Romantik* (The Concept of Criticism in German Romanticism), published in 1917, the focus is more on the subject's formation through reason and self-reflexivity. In addition to more familiar motifs such as the Romantics' penchant for aphorisms, their belief in magical perception, and their insistence on the autonomy of the work of art, Benjamin here highlights several less obvious aspects of Romanticism, such as calculation, irony, *Witz*, and, most importantly, the idea that form is the preeminent medium for the reflexivity of the work of art.[7] While there can be no doubt that Benjamin's early theory of Romantic art contains the seeds of his later aesthetics of *choc* and "awakening," it also marks a milestone in the emergence, many decades later, of critical theories of modernity in a wide variety of fields beyond philosophy and literature.

One of these fields is the "new" musicology of the last couple of decades. But among the scholars writing within this paradigm, few, if any, have adopted Benjamin's theory wholesale. Between the two poles of Benjamin's analysis of Romantic art—sonic excess, on the one hand, reflexivity on the other—it is the latter category that has most preoccupied scholars. Whether through formal aspects such as irony, fragment, and narrativity or as the articulation of diverse sexual, ethnic, racial, and increasingly also slightly uncanny identities, Romantic music is seen to organize subjectivity along the lines of Benjaminian reflexivity.[8]

A completely different (and musicologically far less influential) take on Romantic music—on Robert Schumann's music, to be precise—is that of Roland Barthes, the French critic, who loved Schumann and who returned to his music throughout his writings. Barthes' love of Schumann's music was, literally, eccentric. It was a relationship in which many of our metaphysical fetishes—the soul, logos, or the sign—relinquish their accustomed role at the center of our fascination with music and begin to make room for the body. Schumann's music exudes violence,

Barthes says. It "beats," and therefore it needs to be heard not so much with the mind, but with the feet, the hands, and the blood streaming through the heart.[9] Slavoj Žižek, for his part, also seems to have a special predilection for Schumann's music. Like Barthes', Žižek's interest proceeds from the recognition of a deeply problematic subjectivity at stake in Schumann's music, one whose modernity does not derive from the subject having achieved completion as much as its never having begun to do so in the first place. The subject of Schumann's music is an impossible or barred subject.[10]

There thus appear to be two main strands in our thinking about Romantic music. There are, on the one hand, those who want us to hear Romantic music as form, irony, and the articulation of transcendental subjectivity. But there are also, on the other hand, Barthes and Žižek, for whom Romantic music is the correlate of a thwarted, utterly failed subjectivity, a music to which one does not merely listen with one's ears, but that one simultaneously endures and enjoys with one's whole body. Yet as sharply distinguished as these two strands are on one level, and no matter how the listening subjects that are being envisaged through them might differ from each other, there also exists a deep connection between Benjamin's concept of Romantic art as reflexivity and Barthes' and Žižek's more skeptical readings of Schumann. In neither approach is it solely the hypertrophic, self-reflexive ego, or, for that matter, the absent ego of pure bodily immanence, that are at stake, but a more ambiguous type of subjectivity, one that is self-reflexive and self-resonant at the same time. To grasp this double figure of the autoresonant listener, we first need to review the state of otology around 1800.

Electric Ears

The physiology of hearing around 1800 was in a state of flux. Propelled by the breathtaking momentum of fields such as biology and chemistry, the medical sciences had taken a decidedly anti-Cartesian turn, increasingly drifting toward organicist, antimechanistic concepts of life. Otologists, too, as we have seen, had been harboring doubts about the ear functioning mechanically, like a stringed instrument, for decades. Yet despite these doubts, and even though critics increasingly came to think of music as having emancipated itself from mimetic representation and of musical listening as being mediated by some kind of inner sense, alternatives to Cartesian mechanism were far and few between.

Consider the case of Chladni. One of the era's most systematic thinkers and a pioneer in acoustics, Chladni was at pains to free the physiology of hearing from the shackles of Cartesianism. His second book, *Die Akustik* (Acoustics) may illustrate the point. Published in 1802 and considered to be the first modern acoustic study, the work builds on Newton's work on the speed of sound, Leonhard Euler's research on vibrations in bells and membranes, Jean le Rond d'Alembert's and Daniel Bernoulli's writings on vibrating strings, and, last but not least, on Chladni's own groundbreaking acoustic experiments with sound figures published more than a decade earlier in the *Entdeckungen über die Theorie des Klanges* (Discoveries in the Theory of Sound).[11] Yet for all the work's brilliance, its concluding chapter on the physiology of hearing is disappointing.

As a medically untrained physicist, Chladni here relied entirely on secondary sources, particularly Domenico Cotugno's *De aquaeductibus auris humani* (Of the Aqueducts of the Human Ear, 1761) and Antonio Scarpa's landmark studies *Anatomicae disquisitiones de auditu et olfactu* (Anatomical Inquiries into the Sense of Hearing and the Sense of Smell, 1789) and *De structura fenestrae rotundae auris et de tympano secundario, anatomicae observationes* (Anatomical Observations on the Structure of the Round Window, 1772).[12] But even though Scarpa, in particular, had finally laid to rest the rationalist notion that the geometric proportions of the semicircular canals are congruent with music's harmonic partitions and that the auditory nerve transmits sonic vibrations to the brain, he had precious little to say about what might replace the older mechanist model of hearing. No wonder that Chladni's physiology lagged considerably behind his own pioneering acoustic work. The sensation of pitch, he argued in a vein reminiscent of Sömmerring and drawing on Euler's and d'Alembert's work on the pressure equilibrium in fluids, occurs in every fiber of the auditory nerve lining the inner ear. In other words, Chladni rejected Duverney's theory of sympathetic resonance in favor of the notion that the acoustic impulses are being sensed by all nerve endings at the same time. The purpose of this, he believed, is to produce the "greatest variety of movements and impressions."[13]

It would be a mistake, though, to dismiss Chladni's physiology (like the physiology of hearing during the early decades of the nineteenth century more broadly) as mere Romanticism and therefore as being of dubious scientific merit. In much the same way that Perrault's and Le Cat's attempts to come to grips with resonance provide more than the sources of scientific information *about* their respective era's musical sensibilities, early nineteenth-century theories of hearing have much to tell us about how empirical science and culture reciprocally shaped each other in ways not accounted for by objectivist histories of scientific discovery. By the same token, we would miss the enormous significance that the larger Romantic project of crafting new and supposedly more harmonious subjectivities had for early nineteenth-century otology and for the sciences all told if we overlooked the rich acoustic vocabulary to which literary scholars have long alerted us, a vocabulary centering on echo, resonance, and oscillation.[14] Johann Ritter's work is crucial here, sitting at the crossroads of both developments.

Like many young scientists of his generation, Ritter had little regard for Cartesian-style mechanism. And like these, he preferred the organicist epistemologies championed by Friedrich Schlegel, Schelling, Novalis and the swarm of intellectuals he was in contact (and often friendly) with in Jena, where Ritter was living. Thus, no sooner had Luigi Galvani, Alessandro Volta, and Alexander von Humboldt discovered "animal electricity" than Ritter's tranquil life as a pharmacist's apprentice took an obsessive and ultimately tragic turn. Like the European public witnessing electrocutions of frog legs, Ritter was enthralled by this new and mysterious force so patently at odds with the claims of either Galvani or Volta. In his first published book, *Beweis, dass ein beständiger Galvanismus den Lebensprocess in dem Thierreich begleite* (Proof of a Constant Galvanism Accompanying Life in the Animal Kingdom) he offered evidence on three points: that galvanism is not an innate, "spontaneous" force, as Galvani believed; that it is qualitatively distinct from electricity, which, following Volta, he understood as the result of two different metals being brought into contact with one another; and, finally, that galvanic activity is continuous as long as a voltaic circuit remains closed.[15] But above all, it was "animal electricity's" broader epistemological implications that Ritter was after, the "metaphysics of frog legs," in Friedrich Schlegel's wonderfully tongue-in-cheek phrase.[16] Here was a natural phenomenon that defied Newtonian dogma, fusing the hitherto isolated mechanical forces of nature into what Ritter's close ally Schelling called a "great association" that interwove the "magnetic, electrical, chemical, and finally even organic phenomena."[17] Nature was seen as a coherent whole, with Volta's electric pile being but one element in a long chain joining the organic and inorganic. In fact, the cosmos itself was seen as an immense battery and galvanism as the "key to the entry into innermost Nature."[18]

This idea pervades Ritter's entire work, but perhaps nowhere more so than in his experiments on the ears—his own ears! From 1798 on, following in the footsteps of the ever so intrepid Alexander von Humboldt, Ritter had been subjecting himself to a series of self-experiments in which, as he called it, he "married" his battery by sending electric shocks of up to 50 volts through his genitals, eyeballs, and ear canals.[19] At first, the latter part of these experiments proved unsatisfactory, yielding only "unspecific" results. Unlike the galvanic treatment of the tongue, which resulted in a bitter, alkaline sensation, unlike that of the eyes, which produced a burst of flashes, geometric shapes, and colors (to say nothing of the results of the treatment of the "organs of procreation"), in the electrocution of the ear canals, no auditory reaction ensued. The reason for this, Ritter surmised, was that present methods of galvanization did not allow for a "rapidly oscillating transformation of the dynamic relations of the finer parts of the ear."[20]

Several years later, however, by which time Ritter's health had been wrecked by the barrage of electroshocks and the drugs consumed to ease the pain, a completely different picture emerged. Depending on the metals used, the size of the battery, the part of the ear being galvanized, and most importantly, whether the circuit was closed or open, he noticed an extraordinary variety of tonal sensations. Chief among these was a difference in pitches and in the range of tones accompanying certain main tones. Thus, while a slap on the ear usually produced a g′ (in modern nomenclature), which at times seemed "sandwiched" between the octaves d′–d″ or c#–c#″, a galvanic circuit between the left earlobe connected to the silver end of the battery and the right hand connected to the zinc side resulted in a slightly higher tone, situated somewhere between g#′ and a′. And when the polarities were reversed, and the earlobe was connected to zinc and the hand to silver, Ritter heard an f′.[21]

And so on. These experiments continued for several years, until in 1809 an entirely novel theory of hearing appeared on the horizon. In the text that so excited Walter Benjamin, Ritter writes:

> It would be nice if, similar to what is externally evident [on Chladni's glass plates], it would also become clear what the sound figure is to us internally: figure of light, figure of fire [*Feuerschrift*]. The electrical processes accompanying the origin of the tone inside the ear are part oxidation processes, part deoxidation or hydrogenic processes. And so we are not sure yet whether in the end they also are not accompanied by light.... Thus, each tone carries its own letter directly with it; and the question is whether indeed we only hear writing—read, when we hear, see writing! And is not every act

of seeing with the inner eye a form of listening, and hearing a seeing from and through the inside?[22]

The passage is less cryptic than it seems. Goethe, Johann Gottfried Herder, and Novalis at some point or other had all hoped to recuperate some form of urwriting by reviving the ancient concept of the world as *liber mundi*, a book born of the interpenetration of God and Word and to be read in search of knowledge. Although Ritter, too, would revel in this mysticism, the concept of a figure of fire (and the emphasis on writing more generally) also hinted at an altogether more sober concept. This concept essentially paved the way for a theory of hearing in which the perception of sound through resonance was displaced by or at any rate became secondary to a more complex type of interaction between galvanic current and some sort of higher, nonresonant intellectual activity.

This interaction was mediated by signs. Drawing on the work of the Danish physicist Hans Christian Ørsted (1777–1851) on electric sound figures, Ritter conceived of the *Feuerschrift* as emerging out of a blend of oscillation and electricity. Ørsted, whom posterity likewise remembers only as a pioneer of more "useful" things such as electromagnetism (and not as the author of philosophical works and writings about music, for instance), had found that when the glass plate carrying Chladni's sound figures was turned upside down, some particles (especially fine iron filings or seeds of club moss) clung longer to the plate than others.[23] Typically, the particles that clung longest to the plate were those that were finer and positively charged and, hence, when shaken off by vibrations, the ones that tended to stick to the negatively charged heaps of dust at the center of each sound figure, where the vibration of the plate was strongest.

There was, then, no vibration without electricity. But while such electric activity could be made visible on things such as glass plates, the constant flow of electricity inside the human body remained largely hidden from view. This is where Ritter's experiments on his sense organs proved to be of enormous use. Because the circuits connecting his eyes and ears to the voltaic battery were but a small link within a larger chain uniting spirit and nature, and because, consequently, the "theory of sound and the theory of inner motion are one and the same," he anticipated important consequences for the theory of hearing. If, for instance, a vibrating string can be said to alternate between a positive and a negative charge, and the "compression and the consequent expansion which take place in every sound wave produce a similar electrical alternation," then "such an alternation between electrical states must also take place in the ear."[24] The perception of sound, consequently, would be less a result of resonance than of a rapid succession of electric shocks.

Which brings us back to the *Feuerschrift*. The faster these electric shocks follow each other, Ørsted goes on to state, "the more perfect a continuum they form": "Just as the fiery path described by a twirled brand constitutes an unbroken line more perfectly, the faster the rotation takes place, the tone also acquires more solidity, unity, and individuality, the closer its elements move towards each other. The less all this takes place, the more ordinary, indefinite, dissolved, even deeper the tone seems to be."[25]

The implication here is that the formation of each tone in the ear is mediated through signs. Because the electric shocks (of a vibrating string or a mass of oscillating air) follow each other in such quick succession that the mind cannot grasp them, the only reason the listener can hear a tone at all is because these imperceptible jolts crystallize into a *Feuerschrift*. Just as the "fire path" produced ("described") by the twirled brand resembles a line or the tone generated on Chladni's glass plate "carries its own letter directly with it," inside the ear, the discontinuous series of electric shocks transmutes into writing.

The notion of listening as a kind of reading was not meant to denote a synesthetic relationship between seeing and hearing, as many commentators have argued. Rather, it enabled Ørsted and Ritter to displace earlier resonance theories that had assumed audition to be caused by the sympathetic resonance between the air implantatus and the spiral lamina. This seems all the more

striking since German Romantic letters are rich in a vocabulary stemming from the increasingly popular, yet still poorly
defined field of acoustics — terms such as *Mitklingen* (cosounding),
Mitschwingen (sympathetic vibration), *Nachklang* (reverberation),
Widerhall (echo), or *Stimmung* (mood, tuning). And although the
frequency of these terms is congruent with the anticlassicist
denigration of vision current at Ritter's time, he and Ørsted were
wary of the power mechanisms intrinsic in the resonance model,
suspecting it to be little more than a thinly veiled attempt at perpetuating the Cartesian project of fine tuning the individual for
the established order.

And so the image of the *Feuerschrift*, as Ørsted was well
aware, not only contradicted "all the received opinions about the
auditory organ," it also forced a rethinking of the relationship
between auditory perception, thought, and subjectivity.[26] Once
the auditory process (and indeed sensory perception all told)
now came to be understood, in Novalis's terms, as "final effects
of inner processes," what certainty was there that the *Feuerschrift*
corresponded to external reality?[27] The most suggestive, albeit
inconclusive answer to this question was given by Ritter himself.
Consciousness, he claimed, if it is to be preserved at all, is maintained not through the unencumbered sympathetic flow of data
between the sense organs and the mind, but through interference. As his experiments on the tongue, eye, and ears had shown,
sensations lingered as long as the voltaic circuit remained closed.
And since such closed circuits traverse the entire body in a dense
neural network, a constant stream of mostly unconscious sensations would run through the healthy body, ensuring "unity in the
system" and "harmony of actions." Awareness of such sensations,
consequently, could occur only when this unity was disrupted
and a "disharmony of such actions" set in. Only then do we
"know that we are warm, that we are cold, only then do we smell,
taste, hear, see, feel."[28]

Consciousness as disturbance: Not until Johannes Müller's
promulgation of the law of specific sense energies two decades

later, and possibly not even until Ernst Mach's *Beiträge zur Analyse der Empfindungen* (Analysis of Sensations) of 1886, would disturbance and flow be seen in quite such radical terms—as essential to life. But Ritter even goes one step further. He defines sensory perception entirely in functional, quantitative, even asemantic terms, as resulting from a difference in degrees of galvanic disturbance. Thus, when we say we have heard a tone, what we really refer to is the fact that one galvanic system (vibrating air) has entered another system (consciousness). Likewise, the commonly made distinction between sound and light in reality is only a difference in the way an identical galvanic disturbance affects the ear and the eye, "as though the colors were *mute tones*, and tones, in turn, *speaking colors*."[29]

All this does not mean that Ritter was some sort of monist *avant la lettre* and that the soul for him was little more to him than a voltaic circuit. Quite to the contrary, like most late Enlightenment thinkers, the physicist insisted on a clear distinction between mind and matter. Galvanic disturbance may be the *condition* of consciousness, because it interrupts the physical automatism of resonance, but the mind itself, or what he calls, using the Kantian term, *Geist*, is not affected by the galvanic action. Here he differs markedly from Schelling. Whereas Schelling saw man and nature conjoined in an all-encompassing *Weltseele* or World Soul, for Ritter, the unity of nature was more a question of force relations, or, as he put it, of a "physiological scheme."[30] Sensory perception was one of the areas in which this was most evident. Even though the effects of galvanism were such that "the same thing that produces colors in the eye, in the ear produces tones," the information that visual and auditory sensations transmit to the soul remain grounded in the identity of the objects to which they relate, and not solely in subjective experience. A tone may "call us forth," but we do not have to heed its call. Rather, such a tone prompts us to decide "whether we may serve it."[31] Unlike Louis Althusser's man in the street who, interpellated by a policeman, has no choice but to turn around and become a subject to himself as someone subjected, Ritter's "we" become subjects because they do have a choice.

From here it is but a small step to the aesthetics of "absolute" music and an entirely different concept of listening. And, indeed, several commentators have claimed Ritter as a pioneer of this aesthetics, someone whose ideas were colored as much by Herder's notion of the "inner ear" as they in turn inspired E. T. A. Hoffmann and possibly even Robert Schumann.[32] Writing about the relationship of music and language in Schumann's songs, Charles Rosen, for instance, asserts that the doctrine underlying the musical form of these songs was conceived in the Jena circle of Friedrich Schlegel and presented in the appendix to Ritter's *Fragmente aus dem Nachlasse eines jungen Physikers*, the text Benjamin rescued from oblivion in 1936. Rosen gives an extended quote from this appendix, and parts of his elegant translation bear repeating here:

> The existence and the activity of man is tone, language. Music is also language, general language, the first of mankind. The extant languages are individualizations of music — not individualized music but relating to music as the separate organs relate to the organic whole. Music decomposes into languages. This is why each language can in addition serve music as its accompaniment; it is the representation of the particular in the general . . . it is to be remarked that his general language does not come from him [i.e. man]; but it is itself given with his consciousness, and to this degree comes forward itself. For only in expressing himself is man conscious.[33]

Rosen is right in suggesting that passages such as these associate music with consciousness as such. What is less clear is how this consciousness acquires the stability of an a priori, rather than being an effect of galvanic disturbance. Ritter's detailed reports on his galvanic ear experiments are highly instructive in this regard.

One experiment in particular appears to have triggered Ritter's concept of a new, aesthetic form of consciousness. Cutting the circuit between ear and finger, Ritter had observed, produced much the same pitches and, in attenuated form, the same sensation of shock as did the closing of the circuit. But the open circuit also had an additional effect. The head became *eingenommen*, "taken with" or "captivated" by the tone first heard upon closing the circuit. This sense of absorption or *Eingenommenseyn* of the head resembled more an "onward feeling" (*Fortfühlen*) than an "onward hearing" (*Forthören*).[34] As Ritter elaborates in a remarkable paragraph that is worth quoting in full,

> I know something that makes the point clear. It is an observation that I have often made while listening to a good song, and it is perhaps not unfamiliar to others. A tone that is sung exquisitely clearly and held for a long time is often conspicuous and audible to the external ear only as a tone for the first moment, then it ceases to be heard; but one continues most animatedly to feel and delight in it with all possible intimacy and magnitude; it is as if one were this tone oneself; its essence and our own are one, and utterly nothing of it remains external. The singer pauses; one is startled, feels himself forsaken by the beautiful company, only now does one know again that something must have been there for the ear, the imagination reflects, but reality offers nothing: in short, one has really heard nothing more — and yet more than ever. Each tone I thus perceived maintained its individuality in the sensation; but the external tone one might assume underpinning it, it is no longer. Yet such tones are rarely the ones through which the artist, almost unintentionally, achieves her ideal. As inferior as its origin may be, each tone, each chord, carries something similar with it, but the more it frees itself from what does not belong to what it shall be, the more it comes close to the ideal of its purity and the less it is present for the external, listening ear and the more for the inner, feeling ear. It ought to be clear what I mean when I say that every sound, as we commonly perceive it, is really a mix, in different proportions, of tone and sound (or noise); [this mix] approaches the pure tone, the tone par excellence, the more the less of the latter is contained in

the mix. Tones are no longer a matter of the external ear; one does not hear them as one hears any other thing; we ourselves are the string that, set into motion, perceives its own sound from inside to inside; perceives itself. By contrast, sound, noise, or whatever else one may call it, are a matter of the external ear; it alone one hears; one hears that it exists, but we barely enter into an intimate relationship with it; it passes as it arrived. Thus I am inclined to believe that a music ought to be possible that one does not hear in the ordinary sense of the word, but that one would savor for its own sake. We would be moved as by an enchanting play of our imagination; — it takes us through all the regions as it pleases and awakes in us everything, swaying in sadness and pleasure. [Such music] would extinguish itself as does the silent flame no longer in need of itself, but its memory would live on in us for the sake of lasting glorification. If ever such a thing were possible, the coming forebodings of it, surely, are the special privilege of vocal music.[35]

Many of the major motifs of the Jena circle are gathered here, including the famous assertion made by Ritter's mentor Herder that "music in us plays a clavichord that is our own innermost nature."[36] And Ritter even anticipates many of E. T. A. Hoffmann's later views, such as the privileging of not so "absolute" vocal music and the idea, often invoked by Schumann, of the *Nachklang*, or reverberation.

But beyond these more apparent parallels with German idealism and Romanticism, the most striking aspect of Ritter's merging of physiology and aesthetics is perhaps not his views about consciousness and self-reflexivity, but what Carl Schmitt, in his famous critique of Romantic ideology, has called "occasionalism."[37] When he wrote *Political Romanticism* after World War I, Schmitt's main concern was with what he took to be the threat that an "individualistically disintegrated society" posed to the authoritarian ideals embodied by defeated imperial Germany, with which he identified.[38] At the heart of Schmitt's critique was the claim that Novalis, Adam Müller, Schlegel, and, for that matter, Mozart had reduced the world to a mere *occasio*, a point of contact, a stimulus for the modern subject's imaginative powers. The Romantic relationship with the world was thus determined by purely aesthetic, formal criteria. In fact, the Romantic subject itself became an aesthetic object: unique, self-contained, and forever unfolding, like a novel. Yet what made this aesthetic stance so dangerous, Schmitt argued, was not the fact that the subject became an easy target for innumerable surrogate communities and ersatz religions, as an older generation of liberal critics such as Heinrich Heine had charged. Quite to the contrary, Romanticism was dangerous because it privatized everything and rendered the subject unfit for collective action of any kind, least of all the kind of volkish agenda Schmitt increasingly drifted toward before he finally became one of the Nazi regime's most prominent intellectual exponents. As restlessly self-reflexive as the occasionalist may be, he or she accepts whatever is the case. Romantic art, as a result, forsakes the purpose of all great art, affirmative representation.

While Schmitt does not mention Ritter specifically, elements of the incriminated occasionalism are hard to miss in the passage quoted earlier. No doubt, in these sentences, the physicist denies sound a material reality of its own, its true essence becoming that of his imagination instead. But we would ignore the full import of Ritter's occasionalism if we simply saw in it an unproblematic shift from hearing as a passive event to an "active expression," as Rosen seems to imply. The agonizing hearing experiments, rather, brought to light a more conflicted type of subject, one whose autonomy is incomplete and always in doubt. Such a subject does not take in a sound as much as the subject is taken, *eingenommen*, by it. Through "onward feeling," the subject may be enlarging its sphere of imagination to untold dimensions, but it remains a partial subject nonetheless. Forever hovering at the point of contact between the finite world of the senses and the Absolute, yet being at home in neither, the subject is first and foremost marked by absence.

It is in this form, as pure fiction, that the subject takes on aesthetic qualities, not unlike Schmitt's occasionalists. Ritter's persistent and deliberate intermingling of his own identity with the method guiding his experiments within a broader strategy of narrative self-fashioning is a case in point. Toying with the idea of publishing a selection of his most important scholarly writings, Ritter insisted that these were not simply a collection of papers, but "a kind of literary autobiography, of interest perhaps to anyone who wants or has to educate himself with the aim of becoming a physicist and experimenter."[39] The history of Ritter's experiments was thus not meant only to record the progressive accumulation of positive knowledge outside the subject. In many ways, that history constituted the aesthetic self in the first place. Self-experimentation, in other words, was just another form of autobiography.

Another illustration of the occasionalist blurring of the boundaries between aesthetic self-fashioning, empirical method, and scientific discourse is Ritter's frequent use of erotic metaphors in describing his electric self-experiments. These metaphors focus attention on the body of the scientist in ways that would have been inconceivable (if not downright scandalous) in earlier forms of scientific inquiry—and that would become anathema to emerging positivist ideology again soon thereafter. Ritter's framing of the electrocution of his extremities and of what he called his "froggy apparatuses" as amorous encounters stages the body as the site of intensely personal experiences of pleasure and pain, mastery and subjugation. But in so doing, Ritter also altered the epistemological status of nature generally as an object of knowledge. Occupying forever shifting positions as either laboratory device, metaphor for nature, or vessel for the experimenter's soul, the body came to metonymically stand in for a world that had become mere incitement or an elastic point for the absolute I's creative imagination—or, to use Novalis's formula, a mere beginning for a novel.

Finally, Ritter's self-experiments also turned aesthetics into the sole basis for truth making by offering up the experimenter's private experience to public arbitration. Well aware that "everything is too subjective for me to expect anyone to take it as true at first glance" and fearing that his readers, reluctant to perform similar experiments on themselves, might take his descriptions for mere fabrications, Ritter invoked the organicist and aesthetic premises of *Naturphilosophie*. Because in the realm of truth "everything is equally large and its signification infinite," only a chosen few would recognize in the "dead letter" of his experiments the "lively accord of the harmony" of the whole that had been there from the beginning.[40]

Much was at stake, then, in Ritter's "galvanization" of the ears. That is why the close connection in Ritter's hearing experiments between the ideology of "absolute" music and occasionalism cannot be addressed within the framework of a history of ideas or by attributing the origins of "absolute" music to a particular literary episode in the history of German Romanticism.[41] Least of all is this connection, as Mark Evan Bonds has suggested, the result of an eradication of the body.[42] By merging art and science, body and narrative self-constitution into a higher kind of enterprise, Ritter does the opposite. He squarely posits the physical ear at the center of the history of modern subjectivity.

Organ Space and the Expansion of the Audible

In 1827, after years of debilitating self-experiments à la Ritter, the renowned physiologist Johannes Müller (1801–1858), author of *Handbuch der Physiologie des Menschen*, one of the nineteenth-century's most respected compendiums of physiology, suffered a nervous breakdown.[43] Having begun to feel small jolts in his fingers, Müller was convinced that before long not only would his spinal cord be affected by the mysterious phenomenon, but that paraplegia and death would soon follow thereafter. The diagnosis was clear. Being endowed with a "rich imagination," Müller suffered from what his physician von Walther called a "peculiar kind of hypochondria" common among young scholars at the beginning of a successful literary career.[44]

Müller's "rich imagination" has often been brought into relation with his early writings on vision, most notably with *Über die
phantastischen Gesichtserscheinungen* (On Imaginary Apparitions)
of 1826.[45] And, indeed, the emphasis on vision and its cross connections with Müller's personal case history does seem to dovetail
with the often tacit correlation undergirding current scholarship
between the conventional image of the Romantic era as an age
of vision and the impact of *Naturphilosophie* on Müller's thinking. Contrary to the long-held assumption that Müller's voluminous output can be divided into a Romantic phase lasting until
the publication of the *Handbuch* (1833–1840) and an "objective"
phase ending with his death in 1858, there is evidence suggesting
that Müller never renounced some of *Naturphilosophie*'s fundamental tenets. Thus, not only did he hold on to the Romantics'
self-reflexive stance that later generations of scientists found so
abhorrent, *pace* Kant, he especially stuck to the belief that despite
the sense organs' subjectivism, our perception does produce signs
that ultimately refer to the objective world and thus make it fully
knowable.[46]

It is ironic that the current image of an enduring Romantic
legacy and hence of a heavily laden theory of the subject in Müller's work has not led to the parallel inquiry into the physiologist's
persistent preoccupation with the ear, after all the most "Romantic" of the senses. Why, one wonders, for instance, has Müller's
suggestive remark that "subjective tones" are frequent in cases of
"sympathy with other diseased organs" such as in hypochondria
escaped scholars' attention?[47] Why has the literature on Müller
and the Romantic physiology of the senses passed over in silence
such works as *Aussicht zur Physiologie des Gehörsinnes* (Preview
of the Physiology of the Sense of Hearing) and the section "Of
Hearing" in the second volume of the *Handbuch*? And what about
those rare instances such as Jonathan Sterne's account of the role
of nineteenth-century otology and physiology in the "cultural
origins of sound reproduction," where Müller's work on the ear
is dealt with in the terms of eighteenth-century sensualism?[48]

Sterne's overall argument rests on the idea that modern sound reproduction vitally depends on a prior education and separation of the ear from the other senses. And because he sees in Müller the pioneer of an "entirely functional and mechanical theory of hearing" who conceived of the ear as an "apparatus," he also sees Müller's theory of hearing as eminently suited as a model for modern devices of sound reproduction.[49]

Sterne's analogy is open to doubt, though, for Müller's theory of hearing was explicitly antimechanist and therefore Romantic to the core. Drawing on the research of François Magendie (1783–1855) and Jean-Marc Gaspard Itard (1775–1838) and with the help of equipment he designed himself, Müller had found that in air-water transfers, movements retain a maximum of their intensity even when such movements are transmitted by a membrane such as the membrane of the ear's round window. This holds true even of membranes that are connected to a solid part, such as the membrane of the oval window, which is attached to the foot plate of the stapes. Inside the cochlea, Müller argued, the intensity is maintained because the spaces between the fibers of the acoustic nerve share with the labyrinthine fluid the same overall liquid composition.[50] Furthermore, given the fact that the cochlear nerve fibers are concentrated in the smallest amount of space possible while at the same time being spread over a "considerable" surface, the fibers receive the wave pulses "nearly simultaneously," thus ensuring a maximum degree of compression and rarefaction throughout the entire organ. At the same time, the connection of the cochlea to the surrounding walls of the labyrinth adapt it to the perception of the sound waves transmitted by the bones of the head.[51]

The latter part of Müller's argument, incidentally, draws on the work of Ernst Heinrich Weber (1795–1878), a renowned anatomist and physiologist who had proposed his own highly idiosyncratic resonance theory of hearing. The purpose of the cochlea, Weber believed, is to perceive and amplify, in the manner of the sounding board of a clavichord, primarily those sound waves that are transmitted through the cranial bones.[52] But Weber was also the coauthor, together with his younger brother Wilhelm Eduard Weber (1804–1891) of *Wellenlehre* (Theory of Waves), the first major scientific study of water and sound waves, published in 1825.[53] It is this work, in particular, that formed the basis of Müller's experiments on the air-water transfers mentioned above.

Wave motion and resonance pervade the entire ear, then. There is resonance inside the meatus, there is resonance inside the tympanic cavity, and there is resonance between the cranial bones and the labyrinth. But none of this meant that Müller was an adherent of Duverney's embryonic theory of selective resonance. Contrary to the latter's concept of pitch location occurring either at the base of the cochlea (low pitches) and or at the apex (high pitches), Müller saw the ability to distinguish between different pitches as being spread out over the entire length of the lamina spiralis and as a function solely of the frequency of wave impulses. Needless to say, all this was a radical departure from the harpsichord metaphor of the eighteenth century. And so it is perhaps more than mere coincidence that the list of books Müller recommends for further reading in the *Handbuch* includes Claude-Nicolas Le Cat's *Traité des sens*, a work that, it will be recalled, was highly critical of the string metaphor.[54]

By far the most fascinating indication of Müller's deep interest in hearing, however, comes from a seemingly minor biographical detail mentioned by Müller's student Emile Du Bois-Reymond in his funeral speech delivered at Müller's death in 1858. Speaking only several years after the discovery of the organ of Corti in 1851, but also well before the publication of Hermann von Helmholtz's seminal *Die Lehre von den Tonempfindungen als physiologische Grundlage für die Theorie der Musik* (On the Sensations of Tone as the Physiological Basis for the Theory of Music) in 1863, the disciple here laments what he calls the "hopelessly dark nature of the object."[55] But Du Bois-Reymond also mentions one detail that casts Müller's role as torch bearer of the modern physiology of hearing in a radically different light: His teacher evidently had a musical ear. This gift, Du Bois-Reymond goes on to state, quite apart from Müller's uncanny ability to move his inner ear muscles in such a way that bystanders were able to hear the ossicles of the vestibule move, "naturally" destined him to penetrate the secrets of the sense of hearing, much like Müller's research on vision had been facilitated by his "rich inner sense."[56] The founder of the modern physiology of hearing inspired by music *après tout*? To unpack the truly far-reaching implications of Du Bois-Reymond's remark and those of music's privileged role in Müller's brush with "hypochondria," we first need to examine what is probably Müller's most powerful discovery, the law of specific sense energies.

In its first elaboration, published in 1826 in *Zur vergleichenden Physiologie des Gesichtssinnes des Menschen und der Thiere* (On the Comparative Physiology of the Visual Sense of Humans and in Animals), the law of specific sense energies stated that "individual nerves of the senses" have "a special sensibility to certain impressions by which they are supposed to be rendered conductors of certain qualities of bodies, and not of others."[57] This meant that a stimulus is not the source of an idea itself, but merely the occasion for the sense organ to produce the sensation peculiar *to itself*. In the same manner as the retina forms the field of vision, dark in a state of rest, bright in a state of affection, the auditory nerve constitutes the field of audition, "silent in its state of rest, sounding in its state of unrest."[58] In short, what becomes audible is not necessarily sound, but the specific reaction of the auditory nerve to whatever stimulus it is affected by, whether this be a slap on the ear, an internal cause such as an infection of the auditory nerve—or a sound. Or as Müller put it more floridly, "the nervous system here illuminates itself, there sounds itself, here feels itself, there again smells and tastes itself."[59]

Ironically, the larger implications of Müller's ingenious idea for the theory of hearing remained unrecognized for almost half a century, not least because of Müller's own failure to specify them further. Contrary to the pledge made in 1826 to extend the argument he had set forth in his work on vision to the realm of auditory perception, Müller in *Zur vergleichenden Physiologie des Gesichtssinnes* offered little more than a laundry list of phenomena illustrating the operation of specific sense energies in the ear.[60] From electricity (here Müller refers to Ritter's experiments) and sonorous vibration, to narcotics or stimulation of the blood, to the example of a tuning fork that causes a tickling sensation in the nerve of touch but to the ear gives the impression of sound, Müller says much about causes, but nothing about how specific tonal sensations of pitch, for instance, ensue from them. And so it is perhaps even more surprising that the same grand vagueness that informed Müller's law of specific sense energies also paved the way, almost half a century later, for Helmholtz's assertion — central to his own resonance theory — that the "qualitative difference of pitch and quality of tone is reduced to a difference in the fibers of the nerve receiving the sensation, and for each individual fiber of the nerve there remains only the quantitative differences in the amount of excitement."[61]

If, however, the scientific merits of the law of specific sense energies were apparently lost on Müller's contemporaries, the tremendous philosophical significance of the axiom was not. As Jan Purkinje, for instance, astutely remarked, the main thrust of Müller's work was to reinvent the natural sciences along the lines of an "empiricism of the subjective element" (*Empirie des Subjectiven*).[62] From as early as 1819, the Czech scientist had been instrumental in displacing mechanist models of visual perception, and it is mainly for his formative role as a cofounder of the school of subjective physiology that he is remembered today. What is perhaps less known is the fact that over his long and distinguished career, Purkinje also evinced a strong interest in how such empiricism of the subjective element might manifest itself in what he called "subjective phenomena of hearing." Here he was primarily referring to the hotly debated phenomenon of the so-called Tartini tones or the relationship between vertigo and the electrocution of the ears.[63] (First described by the eighteenth-century Italian violinist Guiseppe Tartini, the Tartini tones are the "combination" tones often heard when two tones are sounded together and whose frequency is the difference of the two primary notes.) These and other phenomena became the subject of extensive self-experiments similar to the ones carried out by Ritter and Müller and eventually gave rise to the concept of a "topology of the senses." Seeing or hearing, according to this "topology," literally consists in mapping subjective experiences such as the Tartini tones or double vision onto the object world. This is why, Purkinje argued, subjective, interior space "is the basis and the element of the representation of every objective, external space.... The tendency of the visual sense for objectification, or its power of projection, is so resolutely active that even those sensations and ideas that are not recognized as having a subjective cause are always understood as objective ones."[64]

Whether as "visual field" (*Sehfeld*) or "visual space" (*Sehraum*) filled with "eye music" (*Augenmusik*), visual perception, clearly, appeared to be a process of doubling in which a visual impression, as Müller put it, "can be conceived as a forward displacement of the entire visual field of the retina."[65] In much the same way, listening for Purkinje consisted of "in sounding" (*Einlauten*), of placing oneself into an auditory space filled with "after sounds" (*Nachgelaute*).[66] In short, more than a century before Freud famously declared "psyche is extended, knows nothing of it" Romantic physiology had defined seeing and listening as the unconscious projection of the senses into a virtually unlimited space.[67]

To a younger generation of physiologists (and, indeed, to virtually all of Western thought), such hypostatization of the researcher's subjectivity was of course highly suspect. In fact, it was downright redolent of mental illness, of hypochondria. It was Müller's "self-absorbed listening into his sense organs, their doubling, as it were," that had lead to his collapse in 1827, Emil Du Bois-Reymond wrote.[68] Worse, such self-absorption was embedded in a general climate favoring the "overgrowing of science with aesthetics." Of course, while Du Bois-Reymond's attempt to pathologize Müller's theory of projection casts men such as Ritter, Müller, and Fechner as tragic heroes who risked their lives for the sake of science and truth and whose extremism was eventually overcome by a more modern, objective (not to say more "healthy") way of doing science, the Romantic legacy in Müller's theoretical outlook and scientific practice consisted less in irrational self-destruction than in laying the groundwork for a "rational" and rigorously modern project.

Müller's goal was to capture "Man" in his entirety. Having no part in Enlightenment science's collapsing of the human and the inhuman in the image of the *homme machine*, self-experimenters such as Purkinje were attracted to the Müllerian axiom precisely because of the desire to cleanse the imagination of whatever lingering pathological connotations it had carried for centuries. By granting the experience of hearing Tartini tones an unfamiliar ordinariness, Purkinje hoped to redeem such experience as the "natural part given to our immediate experience" and to anchor it in what he called an "organic subjectivity."[69] In this view, the subject was to find its true essence not (or not exclusively) through self-reflexivity inside an a priori space, as defined by Kant, but as part of a finite organism, in the "real sensory sphere of the nervous system."[70]

Despite its Romantic origins, the fusion of nature and consciousness, sensory impression and self-consciousness in an "organic subjectivity" proved to be an extremely enduring concept throughout the nineteenth century. Take, for instance, the odd metaphorical juxtaposition of peril and maternity in Du Bois-Reymond's homage to the "reborn" Müller—that is, the Müller of the "objective-physiological-anatomical" period after the crisis of 1827. What are we to make of Du Bois-Reymond's thinly veiled admiration for the "phantastically brooding nature of the youth who had once ventured into the depths of the world of the senses, to the mothers of our knowledge?"[71] Why is the image of the mother, having gained renewed salience during mid-century, invoked here in relation to illness and the senses?[72] And what connection, if indeed there was one, exists between illness and Müller's and Purkinje's conception of sensory perception as projection? The answer to these questions, I believe, must ultimately come from cultural analysis, from a definition of Müller's alleged hypochondria in broader, cultural terms.

The image that came to be attached to hypochondria during the early nineteenth century and that attributed a heightened sensory awareness to purely pathological causes is difficult to sustain if we are to understand the role of the ear or, for that matter, any kind of sensory practice during this critical period. The semantic scope of "hypochondria" may therefore have to be broadened so as to encompass a larger set of meanings, including both pathological and "normal" operations of the perceiving subject. Indeed, hypochondria and its relation to the senses might more fruitfully be conceptualized as entailing an amplification of not just one's sense of bodily malfunctioning, but of a person's sensory sphere more generally and of everything else along with it: meaning, subjectivity, language, and thought.

The concept of projection is key here. As Jutta Müller-Tamm has convincingly shown, Müller was one of the first in a long line of thinkers, from Hermann Lotze to Hermann von Helmholtz to Sigmund Freud, who used the metaphor of projection to reorganize the troubled relationship between subject and object, psyche and physis, along closely monitored discursive lines.[73] The *Handbuch*, she argues, is the locus classicus of such projection theories. Its point of departure is the hiatus that had begun to open up at the end of the eighteenth century between the content of a signal and the sender of that signal, lending credence to emergent physiological theories that stressed the nonanalogous, arbitrary character of perception. Projection, Müller-Tamm concludes, closes the conceptually and empirically unbridgeable gap between idea and experience.

But there is also another dimension to the link between projection and hypochondria. Discussing the artwork of the French novelist Victor Hugo, art historian Georges Didi-Huberman is struck by what he calls the paradox of hypochondriac excess.[74]

In a series of dreamlike Indian-ink sketches accompanying his novel *Les travailleurs de la mer* (1866), Hugo had juxtaposed a giant letter "H" (as in *Homme* or "Hugo") onto the cliffs of Dover. It is through this anthropomorphic overflowing of the imagination, Didi-Huberman writes, that Hugo brings about a peculiar dispersion of what is visible, a complex set of ironies entangling vision, the visible and the invisible. For instance, the more that the boundaries of the object world appear to dissolve under the painter's hypersensitive gaze, the more his own self loses its substance. Conversely, once our organs shake off their traditional role as the soul's handmaiden, they gain control over us, balloon to enormous proportions that threaten to engulf us. It is then that the eyes become hyperbolic organs that turn every external object into an extension of their own activity. The immeasurable expansion of the subject's sensory scope endows the objects with a significance that transcends their immediate use, in turn allowing them to take on some of the functions formerly assigned to the organs themselves. And so on, ad infinitum: The expansion of meaning leads to the disappearance of the sign; the expansion of thought ends up in the vanishing of the cogitating ego.

The parallels between the dissolution of the visible in Hugo's eye space and the widening and ultimate collapsing of the boundaries between the subjectively heard (such as the Tartini tones) and the world of external acoustic stimuli as the material reference for audition proper in Müller's law of sense energies and Purkinje's "topology of the senses" are of course patent here. Both explode the homogeneous, acoustic space as the listening subject's Other and both enlarge the space of the "phantastical" by erasing the distinction between the imagination and the materiality of the auditory nerve. But unlike Hugo, Müller recoils from the threat the law of sensory energies poses to the subject's integrity, as his views on music reveal. In contrast to many of his contemporaries who openly embraced what they saw as the ears' unique ability to give away the hidden, inaudible secret of our inner selves by subjecting, much like those suffering from hypochondria, even the smallest detail to intense scrutiny and interpretation, Müller sought to press music into the service of a more stabilizing project. In the final paragraph of *Zur vergleichenden Physiologie des Gesichtssinnes*, he writes:

> The passions relate to each other through affinity [*Verwandtschaft*] or animosity [*Feindschaft*], as Spinoza has correctly shown in the fourth and fifth volume of his Ethics, of which, however, the psychology of our times has taken little notice. The consonances and dissonances of tones stand in a similar relationship. It is thus that out of the sensory energies there emerges the symbolism of all of our changing moods and most secret doings inside our passionate being. Music, in its becoming and assuaging, symbolizes the movement of our soul due to the combination and sequence of harmonic energies of the sense of hearing. It is unique in this respect among the arts, because every other art represents not so much the becoming and assuaging in the most subtle stirrings, relationships, transitions of the emotions, than the result, the outcome of this process, as it may be grasped in words and signs. Music would ignore its vocation if it depicted the actions resulting from the passions and the free will. There is also a kind of music that does not so much aim at accompanying the movements of the soul through the sensory energies as to make us aware, in a playful way, of the entire spectrum of the ear's sensuousness in tones. Yet this is only the first, youthful consciousness of our sensuousness in art [*das erste jugendliche Bewußtsein unserer Sinnlichkeit in der Kunst*]. From here, art branches out into two directions: as symbolism of the waxing and waning in nature and of the creative and destructive natural forces in instrumental music; as symbolism of the transitions in the movements of the soul in *vocal music*.[75]

There is much here that resists ready analysis. What is one to understand by the awkward phrase "youthful consciousness of our sensuousness in art?" How does the symbolism of our changing moods emerge from the sensory energies of the auditory nerve? But there are also several more familiar motifs that Müller clearly adopted from the aesthetics of "absolute" music, such as music's antimimetic, "organic" nature or music's unique status among the arts. The most striking aspect of this paragraph, however, is the reference to Baruch Spinoza. The seventeenth-century philosopher figures prominently in several of Müller's works, including the *Handbuch*, and as Michael Hagner has shown, was an important factor in Müller's early project of fusing physiology and philosophy.[76] According to Hagner, Müller drew on Spinoza's philosophy in two distinct ways. The first consisted in applying Spinoza's rigorous analytical method of deducing a potentially endless range of psychological phenomena from a basic set of psychophysical premises about the study of physiology. More important for our purposes is the way in which Müller invokes Spinoza's authority as one of the key ethical thinkers of the modern era. Here Hagner portrays Müller's work as split between two conflicting demands: that of integrating reason into an equilibrium of forces, on the one hand, and the desire to foreground the scientist as a genius commanding an extraordinary degree of inventiveness and imagination, on the other. Although Müller failed to resolve the tensions between these two demands, he concurred with Spinoza in positing that ethical behavior could result only from an equilibrium or, as he preferred to call it, from "life's harmonious movement" (*harmonische Lebensbewegung*).[77]

What Hagner does not mention (yet what the passage quoted clearly indicates) is the fact that within this broader ethical framework, Müller assigns a special role to musical listening. While the ethical component proper of Müller's inflection of Spinoza's thought is easily recognizable in phrases such as "actions resulting from the passions and the free will," the impact of aesthetics on Müller's project of a "useful" physiology requires a more careful unpacking of the above paragraph.

On a superficial reading, the reference to Spinoza and the analogy between music and the passions that underpin Müller's argument would appear to be a crossover between seventeenth-century *Affektenlehre* and eighteenth-century *Gefühlsästhetik*. Yet

Müller immediately undermines this impression by shifting the focus from music as mimetic representation to the organ of hearing and its "harmonic energies." It is tempting, of course, to read the latter term as being coterminous with the idea of "absolute" music, as though Müller saw harmonies as somehow propelling themselves forward by dint of some inherent, autonomous force or Schopenhauerian "word will." But Müller specifically speaks of the harmonic energies of the ear, not of musical harmonies. And so what the phrase alludes to, I believe, is the law of specific sense energies.

This is perhaps most evident in the paragraphs preceding the above quotation. There, Müller widens the largely visual premise of this law by linking the origin of our sense of musical harmony to the idea of the auditory nerve as a quasi-autonomous agent. Harmony, in Müller's view, cannot be derived mechanically from the series of overtones, but must be understood as ensuing from what he calls "fantastic auditory sensation" (*phantastische Gehörempfindung*), that is, subjective tones such as the Tartini tones.[78] In short, "the cause of musical harmony resides physiologically in the organ [of hearing], just as the cause of color harmony lies in the eye."[79]

If, then, according to this theory, music's ability to influence the passions is limited, how does the ear achieve its ethical mission of reining in the passions when its natural predisposition toward the "fantastic" appears to suggest otherwise? How can listening become the basis for ethics? Here the companion essay to *Zur vergleichenden Physiologie des Gesichtssinnes, Ueber die phantastischen Gesichtserscheinungen*, offers some important clues. In this work, Müller had famously devoted the last chapter to a comparison between the imagination as deployed by the poet and the imagination as the basis for the scientist's work. Both, he said, work along similar lines. The "fantasy" of the artist and the "intuitive perception of the natural scientist" (*anschauender Sinn des Naturforschers*) reproduce, each in its own way, the metamorphosis of forms pertaining to all living beings. For example, the ideal human form

that the ancient Greeks attained in the arts through an "unconscious, deep intuition of nature," in a modern scientist such as
the Dutch phrenologist Peter Camper (1722–1789), is simply the
outcome of measurements.[80] But both forms of imagination are
also crucially "determined" by ideas.[81] For instance, Goethe's
kaleidoscopic visions enabled him to discover the metamorphosis
of plants. But by remaining within the "sphere of the concept of
form produced by the idea," the poet's unruly imagination was
able to transcend what otherwise would have remained a mere
"example for the highest freedom in the sensuous life."[82]

Müller's vindication of the auditory imagination is thus both
embedded in and kept in check by a set of broader, ethical concerns. But the significance of this ethical dimension for Müller's
argument does not derive from a literal application of Spinoza's rather dated theory of affects to the realm of contemporary
musical listening. Rather, Müller conceives of the relationship
between "fantasy" and reason along thoroughly modern lines.
Ethical conduct, he suggests, results from the combination of two
key concepts: balance (*Gleichgewicht*) and expansion (*Steigerung*):
"Only where imagination and the rule of reason expand in equal
measure does life's harmonious movement endure."[83]

The concept of expansion is of particular interest here, indexing a far more dissonant aspect of modern aurality than is suggested by such master tropes of Romantic self-reference as dupli-
cation, multiplication, and transfiguration. As the law of specific
sense energies liberates "subjective phenomena of hearing" from
the stigma of moral aberration or psychological deficiency, the
ego embarks on an ambiguous process of aural self-formation.
While its demiurgic potency may be soaring to unprecedented
heights, the subject also forfeits its newfound autonomy. With the
proverbial figment of the imagination having become rationalized
as a mere objectification of innate sense energies, it is neutralized.
No longer the wings on which the subject ascends toward the
Absolute, the imagination throws the subject back onto itself in a
never-ending, self-referential loop.

This is where music gains particular salience for Müller's ethics. Music shares the logic of expansion, keeping imagination and reason in balance. From youthful, sensuous beginnings, it "branches out" like a plant, naturally progressing toward ever higher levels of maturity and perfection. In this way, music history's upward thrust mimics as it also becomes a prime vehicle for the broader Romantic project of replacing the finite divine cosmos with a world forever in the making. But music, more importantly, perhaps, also works at a metaphorical level by filling the void created by the disenchanted concept of "specific sense energies." Music, Müller seems to be arguing in a vein reminiscent of Ritter's *Feuerschrift*, is indissolubly bound up with language. But unlike Ritter, whose reflections on the relationship between music and language, ever since their rediscovery by Benjamin, have been interpreted as being indicative of a messianic concept of a pure language, Müller stresses more the conventional aspect of musical meaning. He no longer sees such meaning as being rooted in an innate correlation between signifier and signified, like Ritter, but in the hazier region delineated by the auditory nerve and its specific sensory energies. It is here, at the endpoint of the nerve, that the subject risks straying into uncertain territory, but it is also from here that our inner secrets and passions emerge into the more reassuring realm of the knowable. It is in the physiology of the inner ear, where the waves of the labyrinthine water meet the auditory nerve, that Müller reanchors the hypochondriac, demiurgic subject in what he calls "symbolism." And so, contrary to the assertion that music's unique position among the arts is due to its antimimetic qualities, it is precisely the denial of "absolute" music's freedom from representation that allows Müller to mobilize the ears for the broader ethical project of harnessing the passions in "vital harmonious movement."

CHAPTER SIX

The Labyrinth of Reason:
Hermann von Helmholtz's
Physiological Acoustics
and the Loss of Certainty

It was Galen of Pergamon, personal physician to the Roman emperor Marcus Aurelius, who first compared the inner ear to a labyrinth.[1] Of Greek descent, Galen was no doubt aware of the myth of Theseus and the Minotaur, and he may even have been familiar with the tangled association of the labyrinth with Dionysus and the ear. But perhaps the inward spiraling structure he found in dogs and monkeys—Roman law prohibited the dissection of humans—also reminded him of the sense of danger, loss, and even fear labyrinths are said to have evoked since their reputed origin on the island of Crete. We call the inner ear a "labyrinth" to this day. And even though modern medical science views the inner ear in an altogether different light, marveling at the organ's artistry and, in an almost complete reversal of the Galenic tradition, even equating the labyrinth with knowledge and accuracy, and even though Western labyrinth lore rarely invokes the ear directly, there are two areas related to the ear in which the labyrinth metaphor not only figures more prominently, but also retains some of the anguish that might have inspired Galen's original designation.[2]

In music, for instance, mazes have been an important part of the medieval imagination such as in *L'homme armé* masses, where the "armored man" represents a Christian version of Theseus. But in modern times, too, the image of the labyrinth is often invoked to signify such things as complex harmonic relationships as, for instance, in Denis Diderot's *Leçons de clavecin* (Harpsichord

Lessons).[3] The second area is of course reason. From Descartes' fear of error and Leibniz's continuum to Nietzsche's Dionysus and Ariadne cult, Georges Bataille's concept of the "insufficient" individual, and Michel Serres' "philosophy of mingled bodies," modern philosophy has invoked the labyrinth in various ways: to picture the meandering pathways and blind alleys of the mind, to capture the trial-and-error nature of thought, to fathom the inscrutable ways of memory and the unconscious, or, most importantly perhaps, to think about subjecthood and the senses in ways that challenge the split between cognition and experience and the unilinearity of classical thought.[4]

Of course, these linkages are not in the least accidental, and if on the following pages I add yet another twist to the maze, it is to trace further some of the intricate pathways mutually entwining reason and the labyrinth of the inner ear in a work universally considered to be one of the pinnacles of nineteenth-century bourgeois rationality and the "Bible" of resonance theories of hearing to boot: Hermann von Helmholtz's *Die Lehre von den Tonempfindungen als physiologische Grundlage für die Theorie der Musik* (On the Sensations of Tone as a Physiological Basis for the Theory of Music).[5] First published in 1863, *Die Lehre von den Tonempfindungen* is no doubt a work of stunning theoretical audacity, breathtaking erudition, and exceptional rhetorical force. As such, it ranks, as Helmholtz's contemporary Lord Kelvin was quick to observe, as the "Principia of the perception of sound."[6]

Yet, strangely enough, even though *Die Lehre von den Tonempfindungen* features in numerous encyclopedias, biographies, and other publications of general interest, in present-day scholarship, it is something of a bête noire. Contrary to the work's keen reception during the nineteenth century, present-day scholars tend to give Helmholtz's magnum opus a rather wide berth.[7] For instance, musicologists, perpetuating the views of those nineteenth-century critics who decried the alleged reductionism of Helmholtz's physiological acoustics, for the most part ignore the work entirely.[8] Historians of science, meanwhile, have pursued a slightly different approach. Some have seen in *Die Lehre von den Tonempfindungen* a prime example of Helmholtz's status as a highly visible *Bildungsbürger*, or culture bearer, and an eloquent testimony to his belief in the "civilizing" role of art.[9] Yet others, while acknowledging the book's rich empirical content, consider it to be a mere footnote to its author's broader philosophical claims, a somehow minor example of what has been called the neo-Kantian "rehabilitation of philosophy"—that is, the shift underway in mid-nineteenth-century German philosophy toward a new understanding of knowledge by way of a physiological modification of or, as Helmholtz saw it, a return to, the premises of Kantian idealism.[10]

There can be no doubt that the bulk of Helmholtz's epistemological reflections is to be found in his work on vision, in texts such as *Die neueren Fortschritte in der Theorie des Sehens* (The Recent Progress of the Theory of Vision), published in 1868, the magisterial *Handbuch der physiologischen Optik* (Handbook of Physiological Optics), or the essay "Die Thatsachen in der Wahrnehmung" (The Facts in Perception) of 1878. At the same time, Helmholtz frequently and from early on in his career used hearing and music to elaborate key aspects of his theory of knowledge, such as his famous sign theory. In fact, *Die Lehre von den Tonempfindungen* might even be read as a turning point in the larger course of Helmholtz's thought from an empiricist concept of scientific reasoning anchored in the distinction between subjective forms of perception and objective concepts to the gradual erosion of absolute certainty. While this shift is generally assumed to have occurred in the late 1870s, after the publication of *Die Lehre von den Tonempfindungen*, during Helmholtz's lifetime, the work not only saw four at times substantially revised editions, it was also "sandwiched" between a whole cluster of essays on acoustic topics written both before and after 1863.[11] Careful analysis of the structure and conceptual toolkit of these texts highlights the profound implication of Helmholtz's physiological acoustics in the so-called neo-Kantian revival, just as it reveals the contradictions haunting the project of giving "new content and relevance" to the theory of knowledge.[12] From the division of physiology into physics, physiology, and psychology, to the revived Leibnizian concept of "apperception," to new coinages such as "melodic affinity," the transition from discredited *Naturphilosophie* and Hegelian dialectics toward an empirically grounded and pragmatically oriented concept of truth making brought in its train numerous quandaries and slippages.

And so, beyond all the scientific pathos, cultural complacency, and blind trust in the progress of humanity pervading Helmholtz's oeuvre as a whole, *Die Lehre von den Tonempfindungen* needs to be rediscovered as a major document of the mounting crisis of modern rationality and aurality during the second half of the nineteenth century. Much less than being taken as the foundation charter of present-day psychoacoustics, the work must be read backward, as it were, as the belated heir to a tradition that sought, in denial of its own claims to enlightenment and reason, to deduce the interior from the exterior. *Die Lehre von den Tonempfindungen* can be read as the attempt to come to terms with the growing sense of distance between interior and exterior not by denying it, but by reversing the direction of the physiognomic access—that is, from the inside to the outside. Helmholtz's key insight that our sense of consonance and dissonance, even though externally determined by the physiology of the ear, is fundamentally an internal affair echoes Georg Christoph Lichtenberg's early criticism of Johann Lavater's physiognomy. It is difficult to say, the eighteenth-century thinker wrote, how we get to the concept "outside of us," since "what we sense is mere modification of ourselves and thus in us."[13] That is why it makes more sense to refer to the outside as a *praeter nos* instead of an *extra nos*. Helmholtz's entire theory of hearing, one might argue accordingly, is just such a theory of the outside as *praeter nos*, precisely because it assumes an acoustic world that exists parallel to our inner world, but that otherwise remains as inaccessible and hermetically closed as our inner self. Yet far from securing the concept of an a priori, unitary, self-possessed ego, this parallelism diminishes rather than enhances the subject's autonomy. Listening, for Helmholtz, one might say, is the product of processes of auto-affection with no certain outcome.

And so is thought. To be sure, the notion that science and inductive reasoning may ultimately prove incapable of superseding the truth claims of the elementary processes of perception hardly ruffles any feathers in today's intellectual climate. But such agnosticism is hardly a recent invention. Contrary to Ernst Cassirer's assertion that Helmholtz's balancing act between physiology and psychology, determinism and freedom, had established a "new and unique bond between empirical science and philosophy," Helmholtz's physiological acoustics played a major role in weakening such a "bond" by replacing reason as the sole means of achieving certainty with a more fragile partnership between science and aesthetics.[14] The significance of *Die Lehre von den Tonempfindungen* lies in the fact that the interdependence of auditory resonance and rational choice expounded in the work prefigures the parallels between scientific and artistic induction Helmholtz invoked during his mature period, at a time when philosophy's hegemony as maker of truth had all but vanished. Its place is taken by music to which now falls, as it had done for Perrault, Le Cat, and Müller, a task of far greater import: the task of stabilizing the modern subject split in the middle between the conflicting demands of physis and psyche, matter and mind. But in contrast to the earlier theorists of aurality for whom musical listening had extraordinary transformative potential, Helmholtz's physiological theory of music settles for a more modest agenda. Instead of "modern liberty," "enlightenment," or "vital harmonious movement," Helmholtz's goal is to make our sojourn in the labyrinth more comfortable. The ears, it turns out, are crucial partners in this endeavor.

The Dilemma of Cochlear Resonance

In many ways, the theory of cochlear resonance is the weakest part of *Die Lehre von den Tonempfindungen*. From the "Retrospect"

of the first edition through to the fourth edition of 1877, Helmholtz never left his readers in the slightest doubt as to the nature
of the analogy between the "small elastic parts" connected to the
end of every fiber of the auditory nerve and the strings of a piano.
Unlike the theory of consonance, which was based on the observation of facts, he stressed, the only advantage of his description
of cochlear mechanics was that it gathered "under one aspect all
the various acoustic phenomena with which we are concerned
and of explaining all of them by giving a clear, intelligible, and
evident explanation."[15] In other words, the description was but a
"hypothesis," one "that we must not cease to consider as such,"
or, as the preface to the third edition states, that may even "be
entirely dispensed with."[16]

The fact that after several decades of preoccupation with sensory perception and after only seven years of intense debate
over his new "theory of music," Helmholtz seems to have grown
increasingly comfortable with renouncing the theory of resonance as marginal to the "right path" on which he believed he had
set out in his book should give us pause. Why did Helmholtz seem
to be willing to sacrifice of his "theory of music" the one part
that bore the closest relationship to "sensations," thus calling into
doubt the notion, as one commentator calls it, that his approach
to the study of hearing was the result of his ability to lend plau-
sibility to a weak hypothesis by connecting it to "a complex yet
unified structure" of mathematical, theoretical, and experimental
elements?[17] Of course, the fact that the theory of resonance did
not strike Helmholtz as being of capital importance (much less as
being of rhetorical use) might well reflect the scientist's empiricist credo that unless proven wrong, all knowledge is provisional
and that "the natural philosopher is never bound to construct
systems about everything he knows and does not know."[18] Yet in
contrast to his routine condemnations of what he called "metaphysical proclivities," Helmholtz persistently upheld the idea that
science without some sort of philosophical guidance is blind. In
much the same way that anatomy is inconceivable without the

222

insight, "any vibrating motion of the air in the entrance to the ear, corresponding to a musical tone may be always and for each case only in a specific way represented as the sum of a certain number of vibrations corresponding to the partials of this musical tone."[21]

But how can we be sure that what has been proven mathematically also occurs in nature — that the ear actually decomposes a sound into what we would today call simple harmonic motions? After all, there is nothing in Fourier's analysis to suggest that it is little more than a mathematical fiction, "permissible for facilitating calculation, but not necessarily having any corresponding actual meaning in things themselves." Thus, while it may well be convenient to consider the number 12 as the sum of 8 + 4, in another case, it may be more advantageous to consider 12 as the sum of 7 + 5.[22] And so, to demonstrate whether the analysis of sounds into partials actually occurs outside the mathematical realm, Helmholtz turned to the phenomenon of sympathetic resonance. With the help of Chladni's sound figures, a membrane-covered bottle, and the strings of a piano, he provided compelling visual evidence that partials are constituent of all musical tones. The most effective and also aurally perceptible method, however, involved a device now commonly known as the Helmholtz resonator: a hollow metal or glass sphere with two openings, one of which (A in Helmholtz's original drawing reproduced in figure 6.1) is held against a piano string or some other such instrument while the other (B in figure 6.1) is inserted into the ear canal. When properly tuned to one of the partials of the musical sound being sounded — that is, when built with appropriate materials and according to the right measurements — the resonator would make even the faintest partials audible. In other words, partials are not mere figments of the imagination or deficiencies of the ear, as generations of musicians and listeners had been wont to believe: "The theoretical view that first led mathematicians to this method of analyzing compound vibrations is founded in the nature of the thing itself."[23]

Still, what certainty is there that the ear is actually perceiving along similar lines, according to natural laws and unassisted by auxiliary devices such as the resonator? Again, with unmatched adroitness at weaving a number of ideas previously only loosely related into a stringent line of argument, Helmholtz here drew on the findings of Georg Simon Ohm, a physicist who in 1843, almost two decades after having achieved fame through the discovery of the law of resistance in electric circuits, had published a paper in which he formulated a lesser-known law, now commonly referred to as Ohm's acoustic or "other" law. Proving to be of enormous consequence to the emerging field of physiological acoustics, this law essentially confirms that Fourier's theorem also applies to the ear. The auditory system, according to Ohm's argument, is a Fourier analyzer, in that it is capable of decomposing any sound into its constituent partials. Ohm's claims became the subject of intense debate with the physicist August Seebeck that we will review further below.[24] For now, suffice it to say that Helmholtz reaffirmed Ohm's findings, seeing it as empirically proven that the "sensation of a sound [Klang] is compounded out of the sensations of several simple partials [Töne]."[25] And, he added, rather than the relative phase of such partials, what is essential to the quality of a musical sound is their number and strength.[26]

The application of Johannes Müller's doctrine of specific sense energies, finally, is another demonstration of Helmholtz's knack for combining established, isolated facts into a complex theory. As we have seen in the previous chapter, Müller's concern was to trace the nature of specific sensations to the nerve producing them and in so doing to locate the criteria for our ability to differentiate between sensations in the differences between the nerves, not differences between the perceived objects themselves. A sound is sound not because it is produced by vibrating air or some other such "sound source," Müller reasoned, but because the auditory nerve is affected. It did not occur to him that the doctrine of specific sense energies might also lend new urgency to Duverney's resonance theory by arguing that it applies not only to the nerve in toto, but to each and every individual nerve ending. It is here that Helmholtz, even while politely suggesting that all he had done was to take "a step similar to that taken in a wider field by Johannes Müller," took his mentor's theory to a new level.[27] Expanding upon Müller's work on the distribution of the nerves in the labyrinth (and, to be sure, in contrast to the latter's notion that the sole purpose of this distribution is to compensate for the reduced effectiveness of wave transmission through the round window), Helmholtz limited the scope of the specific sense energies to individual nerve fibers, assigning the perception of each single pitch to only one fiber.

Key to this concept was a remarkable discovery that revolutionized the physiology of hearing. In 1851, a young Italian anatomist by the name of Marchese Alfonso Corti, with the help of new microscopes and improved histological procedures, had found that the basilar membrane of mammals is lined by a peculiar structure consisting of what to him looked like teeth and that he consequently called "teeth of the second range" (the structures discovered in 1830 by Emil Huschke being "teeth of the first range").[28] These rods of Corti, as they are now called, are exceedingly delicate pillars that protrude into the cochlear duct and that are attached to the inner and outer rows of hair cells. In the somewhat flattened illustration that Corti appended to his article "Recherches sur l'organe de l'ouïe des mammifères" (figure 6.2), much of this filigrane structure is not readily visible, and few subsequent researchers (including Helmholtz himself) have actually incorporated Corti's drawing into their accounts.

Helmholtz was not the first scientist to take note of Corti's discovery, however. (In fact, it is even doubtful whether he had read Corti's article, much less had seen Corti's structures himself.) The significance of the marchese's work was earlier recognized by researchers such as Albert von Kölliker (who was himself a student of Müller and Rudolf Virchow and in whose laboratory in Würzburg Corti had made his seminal findings), Friedrich M. Claudius, and, most notably, Otto Deiters. Between 1852 and 1860, these men added important details to Corti's initial results, many of which Helmholtz duly incorporated into later

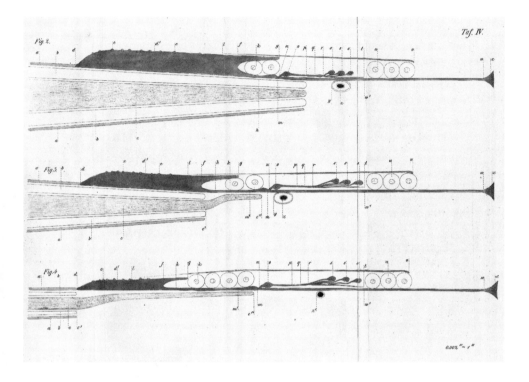

Figure 6.2. Marchese Alfonso Corti, "Recherches sur l'organe de l'ouïe des mammifères," fig. 4. Corti's drawings of the organ now named after him, are noteworthy less for accuracy of detail (although they are the first of the inner and outer hair cells) than for their abstract depiction of physiological function.

editions of *Die Lehre von den Tonempfindungen*, and which together with these authors' drawings are now fixtures in the scientific nomenclature of the inner ear, such as the all-important Deiters cells carrying the outer hair cells (figures 6.3 and 6.4).

Tracking the intricacies of the human anatomy, even when they are as miniscule and fragile as the organ of Corti, is one thing; understanding their function is quite another. It was virtually impossible during Corti's and Helmholtz's time to observe a live human ear in action—it still is. And so it comes as no surprise that the rapid advance of cochlear anatomy made possible by Corti's work did not find an equivalent in the physiology of these same structures. Progress in this area was much more slow moving and the findings highly conjectural, at best, often even contradicting eighteenth-century theories of sympathetic resonance. Prior to Corti's discoveries, for instance, Carl Gustav Lincke, whose numerous writings were in high demand during the 1830s, probably echoed the views of many Romantic otologists when he decried Duverney's and Le Cat's theories as being "grounded in weak reasons."[29] Because "the distinction of different objects is a purely psychic process and thus not to be looked for in any single part of a sense organ," he reasoned, the cochlea could not be considered as "an organ of specific pitches."[30] Instead, he argued, echoing Müller's views, that the cochlea provides to the acoustic nerve the greatest possible surface in the smallest space, thus amplifying the energy received by the labyrinthine fluid. Even Corti himself ventured only the flimsiest of hypotheses as to the function of the "teeth": They act "like drumsticks on a drum," he wrote.[31] And two years after the publication of Corti's findings, Emil Harleß, author of the article "Hören" (Listening) in Rudolph Wagner's widely read *Handwörterbuch der Physiologie mit Rücksicht auf physiologische Pathologie* (Handbook of Physiology with Reference to Physiological Pathology), was still at pains expanding the Italian's discovery into a more far-reaching theory of hearing. Granted, Harleß wrote, Müller's argument that the function of the finer parts of the cochlea is to enlarge the surface covered

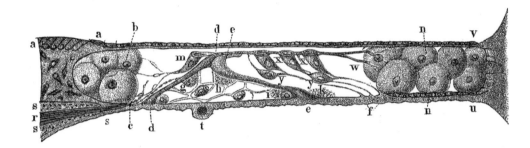

Figure 6.3. Hermann von Helmholtz, "Organ of Corti," *Die Lehre von den Tonempfind-ungen*, fig. 43. This cross section of the organ of Corti appears in the first edition of *Die Lehre von den Tonempfindungen*, but not in the third to fifth editions, where it is replaced by drawings from Otto Deiters's article "Untersuchungen über die Lamina spira-lis membranacea," published in 1860. The key components of interest are the following: *cu* (basilar membrane), *av* (tectorial membrane, called Corti's membrane by Helmholtz), *dd* (Corti's arches of the first range), and *ee* (Corti's arches of the second range).

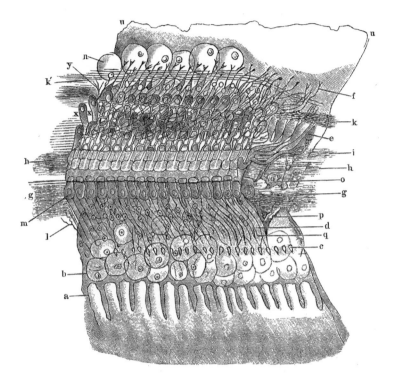

Figure 6.4. Hermann von Helmholtz, "Organ of Corti," *Die Lehre von den Tonempfindungen*, fig. 44. This drawing shows the organ of Corti as seen from above. The labeling is the same as in fig. 6.3 and like the previous figure it too is from Deiters's article "Untersuchungen über die Lamina spiralis membranacea." Note that the tectorial membrane has been omitted so as not to obscure the arches.

by the acoustic nerve was in need of revision. But to assume a linkage, in the manner of Duverney's resonance theory, between the "wonderful details" discovered by Corti (and, he hastened to add, by himself, independent of the marchese) and pitch perception clearly was a step in the wrong direction.[32] By 1858, Müller's student and Helmholtz's close friend Carl Ludwig was striking a similarly skeptical note. Lamenting the dearth of "sound hypotheses," he could bring himself only to the point of entertaining the possibility that "each sound wave that hits the spiral membrane must cause these delicate and easily movable corpuscles [of the organ of Corti] to move in accordance with their position and attachment and thus in turn excite the nerve fibers."[33]

One easily appreciates the boldness of Helmholtz's move. Not only was he the first scientist who introduced Corti's work to a wider audience, he was also the first who exploited it for an ambitious theory of resonance. First outlined in 1857 in a popular lecture "Ueber die physiologischen Ursachen der musikalischen Harmonie" (On the Physiological Causes of Harmony in Music) and subsequently expanded and modified in *Die Lehre von den Tonempfindungen*, the essence of Helmholtz's argument can be summarized as follows.[34] Unlike Corti's inner rods, which rest on the fibrous edge of the limbus, where the basilar membrane is anchored, and which are thus less suited for sympathetic movement, the outer rods—whose number Helmholtz estimated at 3,000—are under tension and are attached to the movable part of the basilar membrane. In addition, these outer rods vary in length, with those at the apex being somewhat longer than those at the base. The number of rods, in combination with the variation in tension and length and, of course, the degree of independence from the basilar membrane, are the key prerequisites for sympathetic resonance. In Helmholtz's classic nerve-piano analogy:

> The Marchese Corti discovered some very remarkable formations in the middle section [of the cochlea]. Innumerable plates, microscopically small, and arranged orderly side by side, like the keys of a piano,

these formations are connected at one end with the fibers of the auditory nerve, and at the other end with the stretched membrane.

...Now if we further venture to conjecture—it is at present only a conjecture, but after careful consideration of the physical performance of the ear, I am led to think it very probable—that every such appendage is tuned to a certain tone like the strings of a piano, then you see according to the example of the piano that only when that tone is sounded the corresponding structure may vibrate, and the corresponding nerve fiber experiences a sensation, and that, hence, the presence of each single such tone in the midst of a confusion of tones must always be indicated by the corresponding sensation.

Experience then shows us that the ear is capable of analyzing composite waves of air into their elementary components.[35]

In this early incarnation of the theory of cochlear resonance, Helmholtz's understanding of Corti's organ reveals a number of lacunae. There is, first of all, Helmholtz's use of the term "small plates" (*Plättchen*), suggesting that he may not have actually seen the structures that Corti had clearly referred to as "teeth." Also, which among the components of Corti's organ would best function as resonators? As subsequent research by Victor Hensen, Max Schultze, and Carl Hasse had shown, it was highly improbable that the arches of Corti themselves could be capable of the required sympathetic resonance. Not only does their length not vary sufficiently over the entire length of the basilar membrane so as to provide the resonant characteristics required for the entire range of human audition, the auditory nerve fibers also do not end on the arches, but on the hair cells. And, finally, although birds are known for their keen sense of pitch, they lack the arches altogether.

Helmholtz was extremely candid about the shortcomings of his findings, and consequently, some of the most extensive revisions he undertook in subsequent editions of *Die Lehre von den Tonempfindungen* are the ones in Chapter 6 that deal with the anatomy of the cochlea. Thus, in addition to incorporating new plates by Hensen, Jacob Henle, and Ernst Reissner, Helmholtz adopted, without further corroboration, Hensen's view that it is the transverse fibers of the basilar membrane that serve as resonators and that, unlike Corti's rods, these fibers show a progressive variation in length. He also laid to rest the notion that a clear distinction could be made between the perception of pitch in the bony labyrinth and that of noises in the cilia of the ampullae of the membranous labyrinth. Other amendments, finally, concerned the number of resonators. Assuming that the total number of resonators ought to be at least as large as all the pitches that a human ear is capable of distinguishing—which Ernst Weber earlier had put at about 64 per semitone in practiced musicians—then there would have to be 400 rods to each octave—far more than the 3,000 rods Helmholtz had allowed.

To recapitulate, resonance is an objective fact of nature that can be demonstrated on the strings of a piano, among other things. But it is also a subjective phenomenon that can be experienced with the help of the resonator. Yet no matter how often Helmholtz revised the anatomical part of his theory, the role of the inner ear in the sensation of partials remained elusive throughout, compelling the scientist to restate his original acknowledgment that "we cannot precisely ascertain what parts of the ear actually vibrate sympathetically with individual tones" in all subsequent editions of *Die Lehre von den Tonempfindungen*.[36] But the real point of interest in all this is not Helmholtz's candor in acknowledging the superiority of other researchers' findings. Neither is it his uncertainty about the exact identity of the resonators. Rather, it is what repercussions the hypothetical nature of cochlear resonance had on the considerable conceptual effort he invested in reconciling this principle with the broader thrust of his "theory of music" and his theory of knowledge all told. A closer look at the differences between the first, third, and fourth editions of *Die Lehre von den Tonempfindungen* is helpful here, revealing a series of major discrepancies.

"A theater of possibilities": Partials, Leibniz, and Apperception

What if we took Helmholtz at his word and dispensed with the theory of cochlear resonance? What if the ear does not do a Fourier analysis, at least not only mechanically? The Ohm-Seebeck dispute might provide some helpful clues here in the sense that Helmholtz's decision to side with Ohm was crucial in shaping his emerging neo-Kantian epistemology and in reframing the centuries-old romance of reason and resonance. Revisiting Helmholtz's summary of this dispute, one cannot but be struck by how the extended discussion in *Die Lehre von den Tonempfindungen* following the section on Ohm's law (as well as its revision in the fourth edition), instead of reconceptualizing the reason-resonance binary by placing it on a new, empirically sounder footing, actually opens up a veritable Pandora's box and in doing so undermines the unitary consciousness of the Kantian ego. Heavily laden with metaphysical speculation, these ruminations testify to the intensity of Helmholtz's epistemological ambitions and to how much of this broader endeavor was predicated on his long-standing interest in the intersections between psychology and acoustics antedating both *Die Lehre von den Tonempfindungen* and his work in physiological optics. But above all, Helmholtz's handling of the Ohm-Seebeck dispute speaks to the profound ambiguity inherent in the synthesis of philosophy and science and to how this synthesis ended up not generating more knowledge and certainty, but led ever deeper into the labyrinth.

The rudiments of the distinction between the physical and the psychological dimension of what Helmholtz called compound tones can be traced to 1856, only four years after he is believed to have embarked on the study of physiological acoustics and at a time when his broader epistemological views were about to take more definite shape.[37] In a long paper entitled "Ueber Combinations Töne" (On Combination Tones), the scientist proposed to resolve the Ohm-Seebeck dispute by distinguishing between what he called "the auditory nerve's sensation and the psychic activity."[38] The difference between the two could be summarized in a series of simple propositions. First, a sound (*Klang*), though seemingly a simple sensation of one pitch, in reality consists of several partials (*Ton*) of different pitches that can be heard by directing our attention to them or by using Helmholtz's resonators. Conversely, it follows that the fusion (*Verschmelzung*) of such partials into a single sound is not brought about by the activity of the auditory nerve, but rather by "psychic activity."[39] Second, the differences in the pitch and timbre of different sounds are a function of the relative strength of their constituent partials, the pitch of the sound being equal to the pitch of the fundamental and its timbre originating in the different amplitude of their partials. Third, like every form of perception, hearing is a matter of acquired behavior. We always hear the specific sounds of a musical instrument or voice as being composed of the same partials, and it is on the basis of this experience that we consider a certain sound to be "the sufficient sensory sign for the presence of a specific sounding body, and as such of interest."[40] That is to say, fourth, our perception of compound sounds requires no reflection, any more than we are always conscious of the fact that every time we see an object, it is really two different retinal images of both eyes with which we are dealing. As we will see later on, this ability to perceive compound sounds without reflection has significant ramifications for the status of both the subject and the objective world in Helmholtz's account of the relationship between artistic intuition and scientific knowledge.

The first edition of *Die Lehre von den Tonempfindungen* for the most part retains the framework of the argument expounded in 1856. Here, Helmholtz upholds the distinction between the sensation (*Empfindung*) of the partials by the ear and their synthesis (*Zusammenfassung*) into a sound (*Klang*) in an act of perception (*Wahrnehmung*).[41] Again, as in the paper of 1856, a partial tone heard in isolation is said to be nothing but a sensation that has no equivalent in a particular sounding body. Only when we hear a certain sound and infer that it is that of a violin can we speak of perception. In other words, perception is not based on conscious awareness and knowledge of the external world, but on a largely unconscious act. Consequently, the analysis of a sound into its constituent partials is of interest only to the scientist, whereas in everyday use, such a conscious analysis not only would be of no practical value, but also would be "extremely disturbing."[42] But Helmholtz also adds an important nuance to the "psychic activity" assumed to be driving the transition from sensation to sound in the early paper. "We call those impressions on our senses sensations," he elaborates, "of which we become conscious only as bodily states (especially those of our nervous apparatus)." Perceptions, by contrast, are "those out of which we form the representation [*Vorstellung*] of external objects."[43]

By the time the fourth edition of *Die Lehre von den Tonempfind-ungen* came out in 1877, little of this line of reasoning remained. In one of the book's most far-reaching revisions, the author inserted several paragraphs entitled "Scheidung der Obertöne" (Distinguishing between Partials) in which he famously intro-duced a new distinction, borrowed from Leibniz, between two modes of perception: *percipiren* and *appercepiren*, or basic perceiv-ing and conscious perceiving.[44] Roughly, Helmholtz's modified line of argument goes as follows. Humans are generally able to differentiate analytically between several different sensations occurring simultaneously. We are aware of what we hear, see, and feel, and we know that it is pressure we are feeling in our big toe and heat in our finger. In fact, our inner sense—the elusive faculty that tells us *that* we are hearing, smelling, or tasting—is not a given faculty, but the result of the prior knowledge that sensations that occur simultaneously can be told apart.[45]

Partials are a more "unusual" case. We become conscious of a sound, Helmholtz continues, when a sensation manifests itself only in our representation (*Vorstellung*) of external objects and thereby helps determine their nature. For instance, when a violin is being played, the prior experience of having heard the sound of a violin tells us that the sound is being produced on that instrument, but it does not tell us to what part of our sensation we owe this knowledge, to the fundamental or a combination of partials. This form of *percipiren* or basic perception, Helmholtz says, corresponds to a lower degree of consciousness. As such, it must be strictly distinguished from the second and higher form of perception, *appercipiren*, or conscious perception, in which we recognize a sensation as only one part of the total sum of sensations present at a given moment, such as when we hear a partial with the help of a Helmholtz resonator. Translated back into the terms of the Ohm-Seebeck debate, Helmholtz in the fourth edition of *Die Lehre von den Tonempfindungen* not only seems to argue that auditory perception entails more than the mechanism of Fourier analysis, but he also sharpens the conscious-unconscious divide. In 1856 and in the first three editions of *Die Lehre von den Tonempfindungen*, the synthesis of partials into a sound is still said to be an unconscious, "psychic" act called "perception," while partials, in turn, are taken to be simple sensations that can be obtained, paradoxically, by attentive listening. From the fourth edition on, the physical disappears from the earlier conflation of sensation and the conscious, only to be replaced by a "higher" and, as Helmholtz clearly believed, more distinct, conscious form of what Leibniz had called apperception.

What prompted this shift toward a sharper distinction between the "psychic" factor and consciousness? What had happened in the intervening fourteen years after the book's first appearance? After all, Helmholtz scholarship tells us that in 1871, as he moved from Heidelberg to Berlin to assume the chair in physics, Helmholtz became "indifferent to physiology and was only really interested in mathematical physics."[46] While it is true that no major publications from Helmholtz's pen on physiology are recorded after 1871, the period immediately before and after the supposedly sharp shift toward physics did witness an intense preoccupation with the psychological aspects of sensory perception. But this abiding interest in visual and auditory perception was not restricted to Leibnizian metaphysics and problems of attention. It also entailed, ironically, a peculiar blend of empirical research and metaphysics.

Between 1867 and 1877, while overseeing two new editions of *Die Lehre von den Tonempfindungen*, Helmholtz published four articles on sensory perception—three on the ear and one on the eye. Among the former, the extended article "Die Mechanik der Gehörknöchelchen und des Trommelfells" (The Mechanism of the Ossicles of the Ear and the Membrana Tympani), published in 1869 and subsequently incorporated into the third and fourth editions of *Die Lehre von den Tonempfindungen*, stands out. Here, Helmholtz offered what appears to be one of the most sophisticated accounts of the mechanics of the ossicles and the tympanum available at the time.[47] The ossicles, thus the physiologist's central assertion, essentially "transform a motion of great amplitude and little force, such as impinges on the eardrum, into a motion of small amplitude and great force, as is to be communicated to the fluid of the labyrinth."[48] In modern terms, the ossicles function as a transformer that matches the impedance of the medium (primarily air) through which sound waves travel in the outer and middle ear to the impedance of the fluid in the inner ear, in the process preserving more than 60 percent of the initial energy reaching the eardrum. If there were no ossicles, the difference between the acoustic impedance of air and water (which is around 3750 times that of air) would be too great and, as a consequence, much of the energy reaching the tympanic cavity would be reflected, instead of transmitted to the inner ear.

Helmholtz arrived at this conclusion by way of several important anatomical findings concerning the lever mechanism of the ossicles and, above all, via the argument that the transmission of energy through the ossicles is independent of frequency. To put it again in present-day terms, if the area of the eardrum is about 17 times that of the stapes footplate, then the pressure at the eardrum is converted to a 17-times-larger pressure at the entrance to the cochlea.

$$\frac{\text{pressure at cochlea}}{\text{pressure at eardrum}} = \frac{\text{area of eardrum}}{\text{area of stapes}} = 17$$

Likewise, since the incus is 1.2 times longer than the malleus, the relationship between the force at the eardrum and at the cochlea is 1.2.

$$\frac{\text{force at cochlea}}{\text{force at eardrum}} = \frac{\text{length of incus}}{\text{length of malleus}} = 1.2$$

Hence, the interaction of the eardrum and the ossicles (P_C/P_T, where / expresses the combination of the pressure of both mechanisms, not a ratio) enhances the pressure at the cochlea (P_C) over that of the eardrum (P_T) by a factor of a little over 20:

$$P_C/P_T = 17 \times 1.2 = 20.4$$

Helmholtz ostensibly wrote the study on the ossicles in response to a review of the first edition of *Die Lehre von den Tonempfindungen* by the eminent mathematician Bernhard Riemann and because concurrent work on the *Handbuch der physiologischen Optik* had prevented him from delving into a more detailed examination of the middle ear. While it is true that in the first edition the discussion of the ossicles takes up less than three pages — as opposed to eight in the third — the question is what this enlarged scope meant for Helmholtz's turn toward psychology and aesthetics. What are the linkages between the new theory of middle-ear mechanics and the section on Leibniz? Even though Helmholtz abstains from epistemological speculation in the article (and in the corresponding section in the third and subsequent editions of *Die Lehre von den Tonempfindungen*), it might be argued that the concept of the middle ear as an impedance-matching device undermined the physiological even further by, paradoxically, strengthening it. That is to say, in contrast to eighteenth-century otologists and music theorists, who either considered the ossicles to be part of a chain of neutral transmitters of pitch ratios perceived as such or, alternatively, focused their attention on the proportions of the semicircular canals, Helmholtz denied that the ossicles play a physiological role in the perception of pitch precisely by limiting their function to that of matching impedance. On the other hand, the peculiar articulation between malleus and incus — the fact that the "teeth" of the two ossicles may "click" during an outward motion of the handle of the malleus — might cause within the ear itself the formation of partials for simple loud tones and thereby ground the theory of functional harmony and musical aesthetics all told in "subjective" processes, independent of external alterations in the quality of tone.[49] And so, even if one grants that the hypothesis of transformer action was what Leo Koenigsberger extolled as a "model of the most delicate dissection, of the most ingenious physical methods, and of the profoundest mathematical analysis," it is open to question whether the scientific value of the idea of middle-ear resonance ensuing from this exemplary work might be less the outcome of objective deliberation than of the unstable nature of resonance in the first place.[50]

There is further proof of this vacillation between objective mechanics and subjective psychology in a short piece that Helmholtz wrote in 1871, shortly after the third edition of *Die Lehre von den Tonempfindungen*.[51] Here, the scientist elaborated on the experiments that his assistant Nikolai Baxt had carried out under the title "Ueber die Zeit, welche nötig ist, damit ein Gesichtseindruck zum Bewusstsein kommt," (On the Time Necessary for a Visual Impression to Come into Consciousness) in which Baxt showed how a stimulus can fail to be masked by a second stimulus coming after it. Depending on the duration of the interval, the intensity of the second stimulus, and other factors, Baxt argued, it is possible for the perception of the first stimulus to become conscious on purely physiological grounds. Hence, Helmholtz concluded, "what we term the voluntary direction of attention is a change in our nervous system that is independent of the motions of the external, moveable parts of the body," a change "whereby the excited state of certain fibers reaches consciousness."[52]

These experiments were not the only factors prompting the revisions of 1870 and 1877. Further evidence suggests that they were also due to a heavy dose of criticism that *Die Lehre von den Tonempfindungen* had received at the hands of some of the era's most ardent proponents of the neo-Kantian turn. One of these critics was Hermann Ulrici (1806–1884). A professor of philosophy at Halle, Ulrici shared the views of those neo-Kantian scholars who advocated an "idealist worldview on the basis of scientific findings," devoting a major portion of his *Leib und Seele* (Body and Soul, 1866, revised in 1874) to a subtle critique of Helmholtz' work.[53] The ear, he argued there in a teleological vein, is designed to further mankind's intellectual and ethic development because, in contrast to the eye, the sheer variety and quantity of language sounds processed by the organ's intricate inner structure by far exceeds what is necessary for naked survival.[54] What is interesting about this argument is that it put Ulrici in a position to modify Helmholtz's early concept of the discomfort that the conscious analysis of partials would cause in everyday perception by stripping this concept of its purely utilitarian dimension. "Attentive perception," he claimed, is about something "higher," something going beyond attention's role as a mere stimulus shield. Through it, "we are able to grasp, to throw into relief, and to memorize all that is of key importance."[55] Ultimately, it is this "psychological value" of the ear that distinguishes humans from beasts, which, with the exception of mammals, for the most part lack the cochlea.

Ulrici's analysis contrasts with that of Georg Elias Müller (1850–1934), a student of Lotze and, along with Carl Stumpf and Helmholtz's one-time assistant Wilhelm Wundt, an early pioneer of experimental psychology. In 1873, Müller had graduated from Göttingen University with a dissertation on sensory attention, *Zur Theorie der sinnlichen Aufmerksamkeit* (On the Theory of

Sensory Attention), in which he questioned Ulrici's and Helmholtz's concept of attention as a conscious "psychic activity."[56] He was especially critical of the notion that the soul could be readily split into two incommensurable domains, the domain of unconscious perception and the domain of conscious presentation. Trickier still, even if one granted that the latter could be as sharply distinguished from the purely physiological domain as Helmholtz claimed, how would the soul cross the threshold from unconscious perception to consciousness, from inattention to attention? On what basis is the soul able to switch from one moment to the next, from the perception of the compound sound or *Klang* to that of the partials, when in fact, the external source itself has remained the same? The solution, Müller suggested, could lie only in some kind of physical process in the brain whereby some partials existing prior to any "psychic" intervention would be suppressed in favor of others that were of greater importance to the perception of a musical tone.

Helmholtz gives no indication as to whether the revisions he undertook in the fourth edition of *Die Lehre von den Tonempfindungen* were in fact the result of Ulrici's and Müller's critiques (although Müller, in the first part of his dissertation, also engaged Ulrici's work at length and the passage that was replaced by the one introducing the Leibnizian terminology turns out to be the one Müller had singled out for censure). And so the question remains: Why Leibniz? Why, of all people, the author of the *Monadology*? And perhaps even more striking, why the inventor of the very preestablished harmony against which Helmholtz had railed so often?[57]

As it happens, Leibniz had been a major influence on Helmholtz's intellectual formation from the outset. The seventeenth-century philosopher's concept of the continuum had been crucial for the young scientist's seminal article "Ueber die Erhaltung der Kraft"(On the Conservation of Force) of 1847 and would again become important toward the end of Helmholtz's career in the context of his work on the principle of least action.[58] It is small wonder, of course, that an up-and-coming empirical scientist intent on challenging Romantic notions of *vis viva*, or life force, would turn to the mechanist physics of Newton or Leibniz for inspiration. Just as unsurprising, Leibniz's spirit also hung over Helmholtz's first steps as a physiologist. In his inaugural lecture of 1852, the newly appointed professor of physiology echoed one of the seventeenth-century philosopher's best-known illustrations of the *petites perceptions* and their role in his theory of consciousness—the passage, that is, in Leibniz's *Nouveaux essais sur l'entendement humain* (New Essays on Human Understanding) in which our perception of the sound of the sea is said to be composed of the sounds of each single wave we hear without being aware of doing so.[59] Likewise, it is a sure sign of Helmholtz's thorough acquaintance with Leibniz's works when, many pages before Leibniz's name and the conceptual pair perception/apperception are brought into play, he suggests that it is incumbent on the ear to decompose a "given aggregate [*Aggregat*] of sensations" into its elementary components.[60] Who would not be immediately reminded here of Leibniz's definition of the *petites perceptions* as that *je ne sais quoi*, "those flavours, those images of sensible qualities, vivid in the aggregate but confused as to the parts?"[61]

Still, none of this tells us why Helmholtz invoked Leibniz as part of his broader strategy of supplanting physiology with psychology—or, for that matter, resonance with reason—in later editions of *Die Lehre von den Tonempfindungen*. Part of the difficulty of explaining this shift lies in the protracted conceptual history of the term "apperception" and the wildly diverging interpretations to which it has become subject ever since the author of the *Nouveaux essais* incorporated it into the lexicon of modern philosophy. Leibniz himself seemed frequently to vacillate between apperception as a form of reflection of the mind on itself (*réflexion de l'esprit*), as self-consciousness (*conscience*), and, most importantly, as a kind of inner sense, a reflexive awareness of perception before and beyond all conscious thought. It is this latter meaning that Daniel Heller-Roazen explores in *The*

Inner Touch: Archaeology of a Sensation. Leibniz, he suggests, filled thousands of pages in pursuit of one goal—to "penetrate into that most resilient and opaque of philosophical objects, which, in his day, was still something of a novelty: consciousness."[62] But what exactly are the hallmarks of consciousness? Do my thoughts, for instance, always require the accompanying consciousness that I am thinking, as the Cartesians held? Or can thought occur without my being simultaneously aware of it? And, most importantly, if it could be shown that the Cartesians were simply wrong in assuming that thinking and consciousness are strictly correlative, how could something like self-identity be maintained?

In truth, terms such as "thought" tend to reflect an obsession peculiar to Descartes, John Locke, and their disciples; Leibniz preferred to speak of "perception" instead. And although the German thinker agreed with Descartes (contra Locke) that the soul "perceives" without interruption, even during one's sleep, he echoed Claude Perrault—whom he knew well and admired—in seeing such "perceptions" as being of two kinds: conscious acts of a cogitating mind and perceptions that are too "confused" for the soul to remember them distinctly: in other words, the *petites perceptions*. To add insult to injury, not only can the mind that perceives the *petites perceptions* do so without being aware of its perceiving, the relationship between both types of perception is one of degree, not substance. Much as nature makes no leaps, the author of the *Nouveaux essais* declares, proudly pointing to what he considered to be one of his "great maxims," perception is continuous. Just as in the extended, spatial realm there is a continuum in which every movement ensues from a previous lesser one without interruption, beginning, or end, as in a labyrinth, noticeable perceptions "arise by degrees from ones which are too minute to be noticed."[63] And only once these uninterrupted, unnoticed sensations have crossed a certain threshold can we speak of apperception. Only then do we perceive and, at the same time, do we perceive that we do so. Apperception, in other words, is the perception of perceiving.

Leibniz's invention marks a sharp departure from Cartesianism, implying nothing short of the idea that consciousness exists on a level with sensation. By introducing the dual concepts of *petites perceptions* and apperception, the polymath had restored the intimate relationship between reason and resonance that the Cartesians, ignoring Descartes' own intermittent wink at resonance, had spent much time and energy denigrating. Even more significantly, with this new way of thinking, the author of the *Nouveaux essais* had not only found what he claimed to be a way out of the dual labyrinths of human freedom and the continuum—labyrinths where, as he put it, "our reason very often goes astray"—he had also ventured far into the future.[64] He was aware, centuries before Freud, Heidegger, and Deleuze, of the fact that the difference between perception and apperception is one of degrees and that not everything that exists in our minds automatically belongs to the realm of consciousness.

The question is, was Helmholtz aware of this intimacy of reason and resonance? Did his appeal to Leibniz signal the possibility of a greater degree of multiplicity and instability being admitted into the concept of consciousness? Is the mind, as William James put it a few years later in a stunningly elegant review of Ulrici's and Helmholtz's work, really a "theater of simultaneous possibilities?"[65] Or were Helmholtz's revisions simply part of his continuing conversation with the seventeenth-century philosopher after all and, in that sense, just another instance of his abiding mechanist worldview? There is little evidence to support either notion. Helmholtz shows every sign of following a philosophical tradition in which the audacity of Leibniz's original concept had quickly faded, to acquire the more conventional connotation of "thought" and "self-consciousness" in thinkers from Kant and Hegel to Johann Friedrich Herbart and Wilhelm Wundt.[66] One can thus only concur with those commentators who see the author of *Die Lehre von den Tonempfindungen* as steeped in German idealism and for whom mind "as *ego* lies under an imperative to construct an image of reality in accordance with the a priori principle of causality, through the use of the will and through reflection on the imperfect data supplied by the senses."[67]

But this position was not limited to the first editions only, as R. Steven Turner maintains. Even in the fourth edition, Helmholtz remained unconvinced by Müller's attempt to ridicule the notion that a sound played on a violin is no less a fused sensation for one who has never heard such an instrument as for someone who concludes from prior experience that it is a violin he or she is hearing. To be sure, the scientist had excised a long passage from page 101 of the first edition in which he had described our perception of the sound of a violin as resulting from unconscious inference. And instead of the flurry of words such as "purpose," "interest," and "everyday use" deployed in the first three editions, in the fourth edition, such "pragmatist" terminology is scaled down to just two words, "practice" (*Uebung*) and "to teach" (*lehren*). But ultimately, Helmholtz's commitment to a concept of mind as self-consciousness outlasted even the fourth edition. As such, it not only remained firmly anchored in the broader neo-Kantian movement toward restoring to apperception the idea of a theory of learning.[68] Helmholtz was convinced, perhaps rightly so, that both the "dissolution [*Auflösung*] of the concept of intuition [*Anschauung*] into the elementary processes of thought," which he claimed to be "the most essential progress of recent times," and the new experimental psychology pioneered by, among others, his own assistant, Wilhelm Wundt, were compatible with Kantian idealism.[69] Even though it may consist of discrete, even sharply distinguished "grades" of perception, consciousness for Helmholtz balances all these potentially conflicting components and thus ultimately assures its own integrity.

In the end, then, the crux may not be with Helmholtz's failure to distinguish between the physiological and the psychological, but rather the manner in which he sought to escape the labyrinth into which the dualism of physiology and psychology had led him in the first place. And even as the outcome was far from certain, guiding him in this endeavor was an Ariadne's thread that had been his throughout: the fusion of scientific reason and aesthetics, concepts and intuition in the work of Johann Wolfgang von Goethe.

"Through the labyrinth of mind"

When Hermann von Helmholtz was born in 1821, Goethe was still alive—a larger-than-life figure whose influence was felt in all spheres of German public life. But even after Goethe's death in 1832, the poet's work continued to shape the views and beliefs of a wide spectrum of writers, artists, musicians—and scientists. Thus, Helmholtz not only paid frequent homage to Goethe's abiding impact, in two major essays and countless quotations throughout his writings he also invoked the poet's work more specifically to demonstrate the affinities and dissimilarities between the arts and the sciences, such as these lines culled from Goethe's "An den Mond" (To the Moon):

> That which man had never known,
> Or had not thought out,
> Through the labyrinth of mind
> Wanders in the night.[70]

The verse appears, almost three decades after the publication of *Die Lehre von den Tonempfindungen*, in an "autobiographical sketch" in which Helmholtz, now at age seventy, reflected back on his life and career. There, he mused about the role of inspiration and mental flashes in scientific research, only to reassure the audience a paragraph later of his preference for those fields in which he did not have to rely on such "lucky accidents and ideas."[71] As it happens, however, there follows after this passage a paragraph in which Helmholtz talks about his lifelong project of a new theory of knowledge (*Erkenntnistheorie*) and the place within it of what he considered to be the "principal result" of his life's labors—the notion that "the impressions of the senses are only signs for the constitution of the external world."[72] He was referring to one of the cornerstones of his epistemology, first presented in 1852 in his inaugural lecture "The Nature of Human

Sense Perceptions."[73] Although this "sign theory," as it became known, was to undergo major modifications over the course of the next decades, it is doubtful whether the *Erkenntnistheorie* of which it was meant to be the centerpiece ever crystallized into what Helmholtz's first biographer, Leo Koenigsberger, described as a "consistent system of philosophy."[74] Or, rather, did the parallels drawn in his "sketch" between cognition as a form of decoding and cognition as a dark, unconscious wandering have more in common with Goethe's "labyrinth of mind" than one might suspect? Of what did Helmholtz's purported "system of philosophy" consist, and what, if there indeed were any, were its trouble spots? Above all, what is the relationship of his *Erkenntnistheorie* to the ear?

There were several sources of Helmholtz's sign theory. While most of these sources were centrally concerned with the relationship between sensation and knowledge, two at least can be traced to his early training, especially his first encounters in his parental home with Kantian idealism and, several years later, Johannes Müller's doctrine of specific sense energies.[75] The axiom that not all is light that appears to us as light to Helmholtz constituted the "fulfillment of Kant's theoretical concept of the nature of human reason," because it was derived from the empirically proven fact that no qualitative resemblance existed between the cause of a sensation and the sensation itself. But if sensations can be caused from the outside, as well as from the inside, Helmholtz wondered, how can the sense organs supply us with reliable information about the external world? How do we know that a sound is the result of air waves set in motion by an outside object—such as a violin string—and not of a blow on the head or an inflammation of the auditory nerve?

Here Helmholtz appears to have happened upon the "local sign" (*Lokalzeichen*), a term introduced by Hermann Lotze in his wildly popular *Medicinische Psychologie oder Physiologie der Seele* (Medical Psychology or Physiology of the Soul) published just months prior to Helmholtz's lecture.[76] Sensations, Helmholtz claimed, echoing Lotze, are not imagelike reflections of reality, but merely signs that bear no resemblance to the objects themselves.

> Sensations of light and color are only symbols for relations of reality [*Verhältnisse der Wirklichkeit*]. They have as much and as little connection or relation with it as the name of a person or the letters of his name have to do with the person himself. They inform us by the sameness or difference of their appearance whether we are dealing with the same or with different objects and properties of reality.... Beyond this, they accomplish nothing. As to the real nature of the external phenomena to which we refer them, we learn nothing, as little as we know of a person from his name.[77]

But Helmholtz also departed significantly from the views of either Müller or Lotze, both of whom understood local signs in nativist terms — that is, as originating or being innate in the anatomical mechanism of the sense organ itself. The newly appointed professor of physiology instead had set his sights on a question of far greater epistemological significance. How is it that we do in fact escape from the world of the sensations of our nervous system into the world of real things? he wondered. We do not do so directly, as the phrase "relations of reality" implies. The little phrase is noteworthy because it contains in a nutshell the future direction of the scientist's theory of knowledge was to take as it evolved from the firm belief in the production of certainty through inductive reasoning and logical concepts to a dwindling trust in the infallibility of scientific reason and the concomitant acceptance of aesthetic modes of induction as equal partners in the search for truth. That is to say, while Helmholtz in 1852 unflinchingly reiterated the Kantian doctrine that, as he phrased it, idea and thing "belong to two entirely different worlds," conceiving of sensations as symbols of "relations of reality" pointed into an altogether different direction. The goal of scientific knowledge was no longer the classical *adaequatio intellectus et rei*, the correspondence between intellect and object, but what

Lorraine Daston and Peter Galison call "structural objectivity."[78] From now on, truth and objectivity would reside only in enduring time sequences of cause and effect, in relationships whose sole "truth content" is the unchanging, exceptionless character of the relationship itself. Signification, accordingly, is not about the singular object itself, but only about "a relationship to a second object (including our sense organs)."[79]

Of course, this causal relationship between sensory object and sensation cannot itself be experienced. It is given a priori and thus, *pace* Kant's doctrine of the a priori of space and time, the only transcendental law.[80] Consequently, there also could not be any proof of the truth of the acquired knowledge other than its practical consequences. Because our representations of things are nothing but naturally given signs, Helmholtz wrote, it is pointless to establish the veracity of our ideas on the basis of their likeness with things. All we can do is to learn to use these signs in order to regulate our movements and actions "so as to bring about the desired result."[81] Sensing individuals, one might say, then, behave like the experimenting scientist in his laboratory. By bringing their sense organs in various relations to the objects, such individuals, in a process that begins in earliest youth and continues all through life without interruption, learn to judge positively the causes of their sensations.[82]

Inference (*Schluss*), or to use Helmholtz's later preferred term, induction (*Induktion*), is the chief mental operation in this process of learning. Helmholtz identified two types of induction, and between the 1850s and 1870s his views on the precise nature of these types underwent a "complete turnabout."[83] The first type was what Helmholtz called "logical induction." The product of "great perseverance" and the "iron labor" of reasoning, logical induction ultimately aims at the formulation of what he variously glossed as "sharply defined general propositions" or "perfected form of logical conclusion."[84] The second type of induction Helmholtz called "artistic inference." Unlike the first type, to which it could never be perfectly assimilated, artistic inference plays a most important role in human life, he believed, because its realm is the senses, specifically the tactile sense.[85] Contrary to the widespread notion that Helmholtz's doctrine of unconscious inference was primarily elaborated (and is therefore also best illustrated) in the context of his work on vision, the scientist frequently and from early on invoked haptic metaphors to talk about artistic inference. Thus, tactile perception precedes the visual representation of space, as the example of blind-born individuals who regain their eyesight and who cannot immediately visually orient themselves demonstrates.[86] In fact, as Helmholtz put it in a lecture entitled "Ueber das Sehen des Menschen" (On the Vision of Man), even though we may think we are seeing, we really are only "eye jugglers" (*Jongleurs mit den Augen*).[87]

In the broad brushstrokes in which they are given here, the sign theory and its companion, the theory of induction, might appear as a seamlessly integrated whole. In reality, however, their elaboration occurred over a considerable period of time, creating numerous difficulties that threatened the "philosophical" status of Helmholtz's theory of knowledge all told. The first troubles began to appear on the horizon by 1855 in the above-mentioned lecture "Ueber das Sehen des Menschen."[88] By that time, Helmholtz had already begun his work in physiological acoustics, and terms such as "thought without consciousness," "unconscious reasonableness" (*unbewusste Vernunftmässigkeit*) and "sensory reason" (*sinnliche Verständlichkeit*) begin to dot his writings with increasing frequency.[89] The 1855 lecture would blur the distinction between sensation and consciousness, reason and resonance, even further by expanding the dualistic model of the sensory process introduced in the inaugural lecture of 1852 to a more complex, "tripartite" model in which the sensory process is divided into physical, physiological, and psychological parts and in which a key difference exists between sensation (*Empfindung*) and perception (*Wahrnehmung*).

It is clear that under these circumstances, perception cannot itself become the object of empirically established natural laws.

No longer tied solely to the materiality of the nerves, perception remains a purely subjective phenomenon rooted in the elusive "psychic" constitution of the individual. And yet, because it is impractical to deny the fact that our perceptions, beyond being owed to the free will, are fundamentally contingent on the impact of external objects, it follows that prior to any knowledge of the external world, the likelihood of such a causal nexus between the exterior and interior has to be posited. The causal relationship is thus a practical imperative, "needed for us to recognize at all that there are objects around us between which there may exist a relationship of cause and effect."[90] There may exist. Clearly, Helmholtz here departs significantly from Kant in supplanting the latter's concept of all natural phenomena as necessarily having preceding causes with what Gregor Schiemann calls a "noumenal causality:"[91] Causal relationships are not only given a priori, but their only raison d'être is the postulation of a world of external objects.[92]

Ultimately, it is this hybrid concept of causality that also undermines the sign theory and the concept of logical induction all told. And more ominously, perhaps, it also led to the wholesale dissolution of the boundaries between logical induction and artistic induction. For instance, as early as the 1860s, while completing work on *Die Lehre von den Tonempfindungen* and the *Handbuch der physiologischen Optik*, the polymath had begun allowing for the possibility that logical induction might not be the sole privilege of the sciences. Instead, the scientist's conscious and careful inferences are seen as mere replicas at a higher level of the basic and, to be sure, more rapid inductive process occurring in sensation without conscious reflection.[93] Another two decades later, in "Die Thatsachen in der Wahrnehmung," possibly Helmholtz's most substantial articulation of his theory of knowledge, this acceptance of a greater similarity between objective knowledge and subjective perception hardened to the settled conviction that lawlike statements about the external world, although true in principle, derive their claims only from their being "signs of something."[94]

By 1892, finally, it all came full circle. More than half a century after the death of his lifelong idol Goethe (and two years
before his own passing), it is again art to which the scientist
turns in his quest for answers to "the highest questions concerning the relationship of reason to reality." In a lecture called
"Goethe's Vorahnungen kommender naturwissenschaftlicher
Ideen," (Goethe's Presentiments of Coming Scientific Ideas), he
invokes such decidedly unscientific terms as "divination" and
Witz to adumbrate the profound parallels between the scientist's
hard conceptual labor and the artist's effortless, spontaneous
imagination.[95] *Witz* — which Helmholtz understood in its contemporaneous meaning of "inspiration" — and scientific method
are rooted in experience and are thus akin to thought. But at the
same time, they share an element of creativity, thus grounding
the production of knowledge in a higher compatibility between
induction and intuition, the part and the whole. Where scientific
induction generates new knowledge from the already known,
Witz produces novel insights by the sudden perception of the
totality. And so, much as Goethe had "intuited" the vertebral
structure of the human skull by chancing on a crumbling sheep's
skull in the Lido in Venice, Helmholtz admits to have found the
law of the constancy of energy by reflecting, just as casually, on
what he calls the "general character of life processes."[96]

Current scholarship has mixed feelings about the older Helmholtz's rapprochement between science and aesthetics. While
some scholars dismiss the scientist's poetic vein, as downright
"simplistic," others emphasize the historically contingent, "neo-
Romantic" nature of Helmholtz's marriage of realism and idealism and its role in mediating the competing idealist and material-
ist worldviews.[97] As important as these assessments undoubtedly
are for situating Helmholtz's *Erkenntnistheorie* within the broader
context of nineteenth-century culture, more pertinent for the
task at hand is the question how the shift toward aesthetics might
compel us to read *Die Lehre von den Tonempfindungen* in a new
light. What are the consequences of this shift for the marriage

of reason and resonance? What is the specific form of modern aurality that is being instituted or reflected by Helmholtz's later concept of certainty and objective truth?

To answer these questions (and in part also as a way of leading into a detailed discussion of Helmholtz's musical aesthetics in the final section of this chapter), it is helpful to take a closer look at two intertwined ideas, *Schluss* (conclusion or inference) and *Begriff* (concept). Although the former tends to encompass a fairly wide range of meanings (conclusion and inference being just two of the more common ones), and although Helmholtz later avoided the term in its more specific form of unconscious inference (*unbewusster Schluss*), both terms infuse his entire body of work often in ambiguous ways. On the one hand, traditionally regarded as the ultimate product of reason, concept and inference for Helmholz often assume a more operative role, doing reason's work by encapsulating reality at its most abstract level. On the other hand, concepts every so often also have a more mundane function, one that complicates the superficial analogy between concept and reason. For instance, although our ability to form concepts depends on the a priori causality of things, there is no ultimate proof of their truth other than their practicability. All concepts arrived at through inductive reasoning thus rest on trust—on the confidence that a previously observed law of nature will also hold true in all future cases that have not yet come under scrutiny. Without this universal trust, every particular instance would become untenable. Or, as Helmholtz advised his audience, quoting from Goethe's *Faust*: "Trust the inadequate and act on it; then it will become a fact."[98]

To complicate things even further, Helmholtz did not always see it as the scientist's only or even most important task to predict the future. Again, the ambiguity of the term *Schluss* captures some of this hesitant stance. While the sense of closure encoded in *Schluss* might be seen as undercutting Helmholtz' belief in the open-ended nature of knowledge, the scientist was actually quite indifferent toward the positivist principle of *savoir pour prévoir*, at times advocating a more contemplative ideal of truth going beyond the sole criterion of the technical mastery of nature.[99] "Intellectual satisfaction we obtain only from a connection of the whole."[100]

The concept of "intellectual satisfaction" being gained from the disinterested contemplation of a seamlessly integrated theoretical edifice is particularly striking because it reveals an aesthetic dimension of the empiricist's ideal of "pragmatic" truth. The delight in formal closure contrasts markedly with what Ernst Cassirer, Helmholtz's most loyal twentieth-century adherent, took as the radical novelty of Helmholtz's idea of the scientific concept.[101] Helmholtz's sign theory, Cassirer argued, did not mean that Helmholtz had relinquished science's claims to absolute truth. Quite the contrary: For Helmholtz, the sign theory was only a specific variant of the general theory of scientific knowledge. As such, it was emblematic of a broader shift from an older epistemology based on concepts whose referent is the finite substance of things or the thing in itself, and which Cassirer calls Substanzbegriff, to a more modern one in which a concept serves to designate the functions through which objects relate to other objects, and which he thus appropriately calls Funktionsbegriff.[102] Put differently, while substance concepts might be said to produce absolute objects, function concepts grasp reality as an essentially unfinished web of relationships whose logic exists independently of the objects to which the signs refer. To Cassirer, it is this idea that was at the core of Helmholtz's modernity, and not the empirical rigor nor the relativity of scientific knowledge implicit in the sign theory.

But the relationship between the aesthetic dimension and the referential aspect of Helmholtz's idea of conceptuality is not necessarily one of opposition only. Nor does this aesthetic dimension exclude eo ipso the imperative of certainty so central to Cassirer's Funktionsbegriff. This will perhaps become clearer by examining one of the core elements of Helmholtz's physiological acoustics: the elimination of disturbance by the intervention of concepts.

As we have seen, Helmholtz frequently glossed the ear's innate capability for perceiving compound sounds without any need to reflect on them by using an analogy with the systematic repression of disturbing optical phenomena such as the retinal blind spot or the double image.[103] The analysis of a compound sound into its partials, he argued "if we were conscious of it, would be not only unhelpful, but also extremely disturbing."[104] Hearing is repression.

And so are concepts. Just as the ear's Fourier analysis facilitates unconscious inference concepts reduce, if not eliminate disturbance by excluding everything that is not "of interest."[105] Just as the trust in unconscious inferences releases us from having to start over every time a new sensation hits us, concepts perform the same task that Helmholtz assigned to the natural sciences all told. They seek to make humans more and more independent of the constraints of the outside world encroaching upon them.[106] To use Hans Blumenberg's term, concepts are a form of *actio per distans*, action at a distance, keeping at a minimum the harm that might be caused by direct contact with the overwhelming multiplicity and intensity of things.[107] Much as the hunter sets his traps in accordance with the presumed shape, size, and behavior of the expected prey, on pain of being overwhelmed by its object, the concept cannot afford not to get a firm grip on reality.

Concepts are thus not the culmination of reason, but a consequence of fear. In fact, one might even go so far as to argue that this is the unspoken rationale behind Helmholtz's return to Goethe. The pragmatic dimension of Helmholtz's sign theory, even where it posits the concept's ultimate measure of success to be transcending naked survival, is the reason why scientific concepts might ultimately prove incapable of falling in with reason's demands for absolute truth and end up in the very labyrinth they were meant to lead out of in the first place. For all of Helmholtz's rhetorical bravura in distinguishing aesthetic induction from scientific concepts, as *actio per distans*, the latter are akin to art in the sense that concepts (including Cassirer's function concepts) forfeit the richness and messiness of their objects for certainty and hermetic perfection.[108] Works of art (especially those of the nineteenth century), likewise, do not tolerate any stains, rusty nails, or dents. Just as the society from which they emanate derives its legitimacy from the unthinking, trouble-free operation of the whole, the bourgeois likes his music to be spotless. Great works of art, Helmholtz claims accordingly, "bring before us characters and moods with such a lifelikeness, with such a wealth of individual traits and such an overwhelming conviction of truth, that they almost seem to be more real than the reality itself, because all disturbing influences are eliminated."[109]

As the title of Blumenberg's major work, *Höhlenausgänge* (Cave Exits), suggests, concepts as a form of *actio per distans* are the hallmark of a world of caves, both in the real sense of the caves inhabited by our prehistoric ancestors and in the larger, metaphorical sense of any type of enclosed space, from the modern nation-state to psychoanalysis's unconscious. And it is in the latter sense that one might read Helmholtz's drifting toward the kind of closure underpinning the affinity between scientific concepts and aesthetic induction as being squarely situated in the context of the nineteenth century. Here, the scientist's own prolific output on visual art offers valuable clues as to potential dangers inherent in the convergence of scientific concepts and works of art as being "more real than the reality itself."

As several scholars have pointed out, Helmholtz's obsession with order, harmony, and equilibrium was owed to a slightly obsolete aesthetics that was more in keeping with the "classicism" of Goethe and Beethoven than with the contemporaneous Romantic aesthetics of excess and formal rupture. As such, it rested on the "simplistic" notion that art's role is not to copy nature, but to search for universal truth by idealizing nature.[110] Aesthetic judgment, accordingly, for Helmholtz, consisted in a "reconciliation" between intellectual comprehension and imagination.[111] Alternately, Helmholtz's sign theory and views on painting have been shown as having emerged in parallel with a set of collective experiences and a common ideological imperative that one might describe as "realism."[112] Social, political, and economic reform in the wake of the failed Revolution of 1848 was one of the areas in which this realism became pertinent, primarily by way of a shift away from the idealism of the Romantic generation toward an emphasis on the practicalities of life and on material interests.

There is a grain of truth in these interpretations, no doubt. Yet the fact that Helmholtz frequently traced the aesthetic ideals of tonal and color harmony to the physiology of the ear and eye is not sufficiently explained by situating his aesthetics solely within the philosophical lineage stretching from Kant to Fichte and Herbart or by aligning it with realist painters such as Adolph Menzel. To grasp the profoundly conflicted nature of the mature Helmholtz's combined epistemology of conceptual reasoning and aesthetic induction, it is also necessary to turn to everyday culture, especially to what is undoubtedly the most sophisticated form of the labyrinth ever and the most popular form of entertainment by far during the nineteenth century: the panorama.

This was a circular structure whose walls were lined by a canvas on which was offered an unbroken vista of a city, battlefield, ancient ruins, or Alpine landscape. To view the panorama, the spectators entered through a tunnel that led them to an elevated platform in the middle of the structure.[113] In his *Panorama of the Nineteenth Century*, published at the same time that Walter Benjamin was at work on his *Arcades Project* on nineteenth-century Paris, Dolf Sternberger repeatedly invoked Helmholtz to describe the intermingling of the era's pathos of progress and reason with illusion and phantasmagoria.[114] The scientist's essay "Optisches über Malerei" (The Relation of Optics to Painting), Sternberger suggests, must be read against the backdrop of the panorama.[115] Much as the painted circular canvas of the panorama encircles the beholder standing on the platform in a total, illuminated space, the eye is its own "consonant sphere that is gentle toward the crasser outer world, an invisible cavern, as it were, which man takes along everywhere."[116]

But it is not only that illusion becomes an everyday occurrence, because "transfigurement had become cheap, for people had learned how to get it on their own."[117] In a deeper sense, the illusion afforded by the panorama can be said to happen for its own sake, or, better still, for the sake of the act of viewing. The true modernity of Helmholtz's sign theory, one might say accordingly, consists in a new meaning of illusion as a means for self-affection. Far from opening the floodgates to uncertainty about the outside world, the panorama of the eye and the hermetic perfection of the scientific concept merely take the edge off the psychological disparity that Helmholtz's contemporaries increasingly felt between the "empty," soulless object world and their subjective experience. But in so doing, the convergence of logical and artistic induction may end up dispensing with both—object and subject. In shifting the emphasis from the object to the subject of perception, it is finally the intensity of the experience itself that takes center stage. Whether as "intellectual satisfaction" or as "vividness of the viewing" (*Lebendigkeit der Anschauung*), such intensity encloses both subject and object in a magic circle.[118]

Which brings us, at long last, back to where we started, to music and the ear.

Elective Affinities

The third and final part of *Die Lehre von den Tonempfindungen* bears a strange heading: "Die Verwandtschaft der Klänge" (The Affinity of Sounds). It is an odd heading because, as Helmholtz explains, unlike the first two parts, which deal with physical necessity, this part of his book is about aesthetics, taste, and choice. After all, when modern individuals (or, at any rate, Western individuals) think of affinity, it is their families and the constraints that kinship relations impose on them that they associate, not freedom. We do not choose our parents, siblings, or uncles. We are born into structures that, although constructed socially, carry a sense of biological necessity and inevitability. So how does Helmholtz's subheading square with his famous assertion that "the modern system [of tonality] was developed not from natural necessity, but from a freely chosen principle of style?" And what about his striking statement in the preface to the third edition that the essential basis of music is melody and that harmony's role, in Western European music of the last three centuries, anyway, was merely to strengthen "melodic affinities"(*melodische Verwandtschaften*)?[119] And, above all, what kind of listening subject is being envisaged to inhabit the ambiguous space between necessity and freedom, science and aesthetics, reason and resonance, suggested by Helmholtz's choice of words?

Ever the self-styled neutral observer and reporter of facts, the author of *Die Lehre von den Tonempfindungen* largely shied away from such questions, alluring as he otherwise admitted the various "affections of the soul" (*Seelenstimmungen*) to be.[120] Nonetheless, reading between the lines of the work's third part, one cannot avoid the impression that despite (or perhaps, precisely because of) the scientist's bias toward a work-centered musical aesthetics, he tacitly assumed the existence of some kind of normative listening subject. And so, in borrowing for my own reflections on Helmholtz's aesthetics the title of a novel by his patron saint Goethe, I wish to capture some of the ambiguity of this hypothetical aurality—to trace the tensions between the mutually restraining areas of choice and necessity, nature and culture, and to show how the predicaments that haunt Helmholtz's project of mediating between them within the framework of liberal, historicist thought implicate his aurality in the larger labyrinth of nineteenth-century culture.

Central to this discussion is Helmholtz's theory of melodic affinities. Underpinning the entire third part of *Die Lehre von den Tonempfindungen*, this theory posits that listeners, despite the unconscious synthesis of partials into composite sounds, intuitively "feel" the presence of such partials. Since some sounds are more likely to have one or more partials in common than others, one can assume there to be different degrees of affinity between different sounds. Helmholtz distinguishes two such degrees: Sounds with two of the same partials are "related in the first degree" (*verwandt im ersten Grade*), and those that are both related in the first degree and share the same third partial are "related in the second degree."[121] While the first degree of affinity may be easily demonstrated in a melodic interval, say, of a major third (C4–E4 in figure 6.5), in a major second things are more complex. Thus, while in the former C4 and E4 clearly have C5 and G5 as the same partials, in the latter case, the common partials are too high and therefore too weak to be "felt" as being related. To get around this problem, Helmholtz dug deep into the history of music theory. Suppose, he argued, invoking Rameau, a "silent" G3 a fourth below the C4 and a fifth below the D4 were inserted in the transition between the two tones. Would such a phantom tone not establish a connection "if not for the corporeal ear, then at least for memory?" (figure 6.5).[122]

Of course, the crux of this elaborate procedure—not to mention an even more impractical, if theoretically elegant, derivation from the cycle of fifths—was that the G3 could never become the object of immediate perception, but had to be conjured up from the memory of prior sensory experiences of the fifth or fourth. And if this were not enough, historical and national differences of taste might further limit the ability or inclination to cultivate a feeling for such affinity in the first place. And last but not least, since the perception of overtones largely determines the timbre, the feeling for affinity would be greatly impeded by, say, the sound of a flute or soft organ stops, both poor in partials. When hearing melodic intervals such as thirds and sixths played on such instruments, a listener would of necessity have to draw on memory, not on sensation.[123]

In light of these complications, it comes as no surprise that the theory of melodic affinities met with a somewhat mixed reception. While musicologist Hugo Riemann would soon seize on it in an effort to bolster his own brand of a theory of musical listening based in "musical logic," others were more skeptical.[124] Helmholtz's colleague Gustav Fechner, for instance, in

Figure 6.5. "Tonal Affinities." The example (in scientific notation) shows Helmholtz's derivation of the tonal affinities in a major second via Rameau's "silent" tone.

two lengthy letters written in 1869, wondered how the ear is able to recognize the melodic affinities just as clearly in tones of rods, plates, and bells—that is, instruments with virtually no partials, even inharmonic ones—as in string instruments and the human voice.[125] Predictably, the author of *Die Lehre von den Tonempfindungen* responded by adding to the third editions the same mix of physiological and psychological explanation that had shaped his work on the ossicles published in the same year. As he had shown there, due to the ingenious articulation of the hammer and the anvil, partials are even audible "when powerful, objectively simple tones are sounded."[126] Yet although the mechanism of the ossicles made memory redundant, our perception of melodic affinities even in instruments devoid of rich partials might entail some form of recognition after all, as the example of the stereoscope, a contraption creating the illusion of a single three-dimensional image invented by Charles Wheatstone in the late 1830s, showed. The difference between a melody played on a glass harmonica (an instrument with almost no partials) and one played on a piano (which is rich in partials) is "somewhat of the same kind as that between viewing a single photograph of a landscape and seeing two corresponding photographs of it through a stereoscope," Helmholtz argued. While the first enables the viewer, by means of his memory, to form a conception of the relative distances in the scenery depicted, the stereoscopic fusion of the two pictures produces the real impression those distances would have themselves yielded in the naked eyes, which in the case of a single photograph would have to be furnished by memory. So it is with melodies executed in simple tones, he concluded: "We can recognize the melodies when we have heard them otherwise performed."[127]

But while the concept of melodic affinity ultimately failed to stand up to scrutiny as the basis for a scientific theory of melodic perception, and while Helmholtz, as a result of this failure, struggled to instantiate the rational listener physiologically, affinity did play a significant role in another, seemingly unrelated area—music history. To Helmholtz, an inquiry into the history of music was tantamount to tracing the progressive development of tonal systems peoples and nations had crafted by bringing rational choices to bear on the material possibilities afforded by tonal affinities. Having surveyed an enormous range of musical scales, from ancient Greece and the classical Arabic and Persian world all the way to "modern" European and even contemporary Scottish folk music, his method of deriving these scales from tones of the closest affinity was akin to, in his terms, the "rediscovery" of the "natural path of derivation" that the ancient Greeks, Arabs, Persians and "modern" Europeans had themselves "pursued consistently."[128]

Helmholtz had not been alone in this endeavor. Even though the idea of affinity as the basis for melodic perception was novel, the term "affinity" itself looked back on an illustrious ancestry. As Benjamin Steege has shown, the idea of affinity had long been part of music theory, dating back to at least the eleventh-century music theorist Guido of Arezzo's doctrine of *affinitas* between particular tones and the modes associated with them. And while echoes of this ancient theory reverberate as late as the eighteenth century in Johann Mattheson's notion of the affinity of keys, by the first half of the nineteenth century, the term came to be understood in a predominantly Romantic sense as an organic relationship between people and things. Steege mentions several musicological works that may have stood as godfathers to Helmholtz's concept in this regard, those of Carl von Winterfeld on Giovanni Gabrieli, Raphael Georg Kiesewetter on Arabic music, and Eduard Hanslick's classic *On the Beautiful in Music* being the most frequently cited.[129] To this list one might add Johannes Müller, who, as we have seen in the previous chapter, as early as 1826 had argued that consonances and dissonances relate to each other through "affinity or animosity" and that these are the forces driving the plantlike formation of musical genres.

For all these writers, then, it was a given that music is living matter. More than that, they held that like all "life," music had evolved through various historical stages, germinating from primitive beginnings and gradually striving toward ever greater perfection. Western functional harmony, for instance, had literally "grown" out of the increasing awareness of tonal affinities and thus represented the highest stage of development. Yet even though these Romantic authors subscribed to a teleological notion of history, music's organic development did not preclude human agency and rational choice wholesale. In fact, the primacy of such choices was the crucial distinctive mark of music's preeminent role on the world-historical stage. As Helmholtz put it in his famous statement at the beginning of the third part of *Die Lehre von den Tonempfindungen*: "The system of scales, modes, and their harmonic tissues does not rest on unchanging natural laws, but is rather the consequence of aesthetic principles that are, and will continue to be, subject to change with the progressive development of humanity."[130]

In the original text, Helmholtz's proposition is set in italics, no doubt because its author was convinced that, even decades after its demise, remnants of Romantic *Naturphilosophie* and organicist aesthetics were still preventing his new approach from being "sufficiently present to the minds of contemporary music theorists and historians."[131] The persistence of Romantic concepts might also be the reason why in the following paragraphs, Helmholtz goes to great lengths to expand on the paradox that these "principles" are nonetheless encumbered by the laws of nature. In a vein reminiscent of Claude Perrault, he turns to architecture to argue for the contingency of beauty. Although the most consistent, mightiest, and most impressive of architectural forms had been created in the Gothic style, Helmholtz writes, "no one would easily think of asserting that the pointed arch is the naturally given original form of all architectural beauty and must be introduced everywhere." But as little as the diatonic major scale, accordingly, can be regarded as a natural product, it is still the "necessary consequence, conditioned by the *nature* of things," of the aesthetic choices made.[132]

But it was not only music theorists and historians who were troubled by the apparent contradictions in Helmholtz's concept of music history as the simultaneous unfolding of freedom and force. Hermann Lotze, for instance, found fault with the "art-conscious scientist's" casual intermingling of aesthetic choice, reason, and history. In his *Geschichte der Ästhetik in Deutschland* (History of Aesthetics in Germany) published in 1868, Lotze not only took Helmholtz to task for the "inadequacy" of the physiological method, suggesting that it is not the nerves that experience aesthetic feelings as signs of external forces, but the soul, he also objected to the scientist's overly optimistic views about future change.[133] "In music as in all arts the scope for further developmental stages narrows in accordance with the advance already made toward the rich and full expression of beauty," he wrote.[134] For Lotze, in other words, the history of music was not an open-ended trajectory, as it appeared to be for Helmholtz. Music's development was of a more restrained kind. Its ultimate destination was not freedom but redemption.

This position stemmed from a profoundly melancholic strain in Lotze's philosophy of history, as Walter Benjamin shrewdly observed in the famous "Convolute N" of his *Arcades Project*.[135] In

calls "the ambiguity of Helmholtz's liberal historiography."[140] As is well known, the Viennese critic had famously claimed that "musical elements relate to one another through secret connections and elective affinities, based upon natural laws." These elective affinities, Hanslick elaborates, live "instinctively" in every cultivated ear that senses the "organic and reasonable" quality of a collection of tones.[141] While Steege sees major differences between Hanslick's and Helmholtz's concepts of aesthetic freedom, it is clear that the latter also shared with Hanslick the notion that the rationale for tonal affinities lies beyond the purview of consciousness. Thus, where the music theorist denied tonal *Wahlverwandtschaften* to be accessible to "scientific consciousness," his scientific colleague saw both the composer and the listener as being oblivious to the lawlike *Verwandtschaften* binding them.[142]

And so, Steege concludes, Helmholtz's *Verwandtschaft* retains some of the double-faced character of the very term "elective affinity" he so scrupulously avoided. If choice in Helmholtz's aesthetic thought is "fundamentally interstitial, subsisting *between* the prior constraints of *Verwandtschaft* and their subsequent determinations, then the actualization of tonality, which Helmholtz wished to validate as a 'freely chosen principle of style,' also sits astride such a doubled notion of choice." In other words, while we cannot autonomously choose the tonal relationships, any more than we can choose our relatives, Helmholtz's liberal composing and listening subjects find themselves situated "in the hiatus between the unconscious sense of affinity and the impulse to actualize that affinity (in a tuning system, scalar structure, or composition)."[143]

This position, Steege goes on to suggest, resonates strongly with the views of John Stuart Mill, an icon of nineteenth-century liberal-humanist thought who was held in high esteem by Helmholtz ever since he had invoked the British philosopher's ideas in his lecture of 1862 on the relationship of the sciences with the wider academy. Freedom, for Mill, entailed a distinction between the means and ends of one's actions. Thus, while we may be able to determine which means we put to what end, the outcome of our actions may not always be of our own choosing. Despite these limitations, however, volition and causation are compatible as part of a broader concept of liberty, the relationship between art to science being just one, albeit telling example of how the a priori definition of an end as "morally" desirable constitutes an act of freedom. Art, Mill wrote toward the end of his *Logic of the Moral Sciences*, invoking the relationship between a legislator and a judge, "proposes to itself an end to be attained, defines the end, and hands it over to the science." And while science investigates the conditions that must be met to produce the desired result and formulates these into a theorem, it is art that converts the theorem into a rule.[144]

There is good reason to accept Steege's verdict that Helmholtz's "liberal impulse" and appropriation of Mill are based on (or may perhaps even have been one of the driving motors behind) a compromise between, on the one hand, a desire to maintain a modicum of individual agency in a society increasingly dominated by a ruthless ideology of instrumental rationality and, on the other hand, the seemingly neutral truth claims of the natural sciences that vested that ideology with credibility in the first place. And in this sense, one might well regard Helmholtz's self-professed status as an "amateur," proclaimed at the end of *Die Lehre von den Tonempfindungen*, as an expression of false modesty. The work was every bit as symptomatic of the drift toward complacency in the German Reich as the subject of Helmholtz's "freely chosen stylistic principles" was an integral ingredient of the Wilhelminian pathos of Fatherland and progress. But to see in this celebration of the middle ground what Steege calls an "emancipatory potential" is also to ignore the profoundly inward-turning, cavernlike character of Helmholtz's aural imagination.[145] To be sure, Helmholtz's normative listening subject, literally and physically, hears only what it wants to hear, ignoring "disturbance." Yet at the same time, this "panoramic" aural posture negates its own possibility of freedom. Contrary to Helmholtz's assertion elsewhere that it "strives to acquaint us with reality, with psychological truths," art truly comes into its own only when mimetic conformity to nature is traded for an increase in beauty during "more important moments," such as when music is added to the text of the drama or *lied*.[146] That is to say, music is a mere form enveloping an otherwise given content grounded in mimetic likeness and rationally mastered by semiosis. Or as Sternberger, writing about Helmholtz's friend Richard Wagner and his jubilee essay of 1870 on Beethoven poignantly puts it, such music becomes mere "illumination," submerging in glowing light the remnants of reality in the stories pieced together by the living. History, in other words, is "artificially illuminated by flashes of genius when the final little stars of hope, freedom, enlightenment, humanity, and world peace had turned blind and cold."[147]

Helmholtz's theory of rationally chosen aesthetic principles, it seems, leads him back to where he started, to necessity, to resonance. In many ways, Helmholtz's listeners, even while they claim their rationality to be consonant with the mechanism of the auditory ossicles, the stapes, and the hair cells, are no closer to the *fundamentum inconcussum veritatis* than is Descartes' cogito or than Kant's transcendental subject is to the *noumenon*. At the same time it would be a mistake to attribute this return to the "material ear" solely to a failure of Helmholtz's project of modernizing Kantian idealism by reconciling the physics of sensation with transcendental epistemology. The recognition of the intricate and irreducible complementarity of reason and resonance, even as it foreshadows the loss of absolute certainty and, more ominously perhaps, the often invoked death of the subject, might also be seen as having a more salutary effect. The convergence of the mind and the ear does not necessarily make us better, more complete beings. Nor will this vindication of the ear, its acceptance as an equal partner in the project we call "self," provide us with an alternative to the badly worn, if not broken Ariadne's thread of reason that Helmholtz intuited. But the consciously resonating, aurally reasoning self that he envisioned, at the very least, does remind us of our insufficiency as dwellers of the labyrinth.

CHAPTER SEVEN

Rhythm and Clues:

Time and the Acoustic Unconscious,

ca. 1900

Richard Strauss's opera *Salome*, which premiered in 1906, begins and ends with dissonance: a brief clarinet motif slithering along an oddly disjointed scale when the curtain rises and a din of howling horns and shrieking woodwinds as the curtain falls, moments after Herod orders Salome killed. In between, an unnerving, volatile kind of music, a hellish noise, heralds the dawn of a new, clamorous century of war, chaos, and uncertainty.

This is roughly how the classical music critic of the *New York Times*, Alex Ross, begins *The Rest is Noise: Listening to the Twentieth Century*, a highly popular account of the twentieth-century musical avant-garde published in 2007.[1] And, indeed, dissonance and noise feature prominently in many works written during the formative period of modernism around the turn of the twentieth century—that is, other than *Salome*, works such as Arnold Schoenberg's piano pieces op. 11 (1907), or Franz Schreker's opera *Der ferne Klang* (The Distant Sound, 1912), to name but two more prominent examples. But these works, and thus also the century they helped to define, might also be heard from a more unaccustomed angle. The breathless succession of irregular meters in Herod's soliloquy, the abruptness of Schoenberg's op. 11, the juxtaposition of rapidly changing moods, sonorities and motifs in Schreker's opera—all are signs of a new concept of musical time emerging around 1900 and of a larger crisis at the heart of what Stephen Kern has called the "culture of time and place."[2] But this broader crisis of time consciousness was registered not only at the level of the consciously heard. The crisis of homogeneous time — the universal, absolute, and forward-moving time of New-ton, no less than Kant's a priori of time — occurred in a realm well below the threshold of the audible, in what one might call the "acoustic unconscious."

The term is modeled after the "optical unconscious," which Walter Benjamin uses in an evocative remark in his classic essay "The Work of Art in the Age of Its Technological Reproduc-ibility": "It is through the camera that we first discover the opti-cal unconscious, just as we discover the instinctual unconscious through psychoanalysis."[3] The "swooping and rising, disrupting and isolating, stretching or compressing" of the movie camera, acccording to Benjamin, would give access to a "space informed by the unconscious." With the "dynamite of the split second," the camera would accomplish a "deepening of apperception" in much the same way that Freud's analysis of everyday slip-ups had brought to light "things which had previously floated unnoticed on the broad stream of perception."[4]

Benjamin's fascination with the new technology and the almost magic access it promised to the unconscious was of course part of a much more ambitious project. Film, Benjamin held, was unique among the new forms of mass culture in that it had the potential for forging a new time consciousness and thus, ultimately, for ushering in a new society. Of course, few today share Benjamin's messianic fervor and confidence in technology as a key to "another nature" (current scholarship tends to stress the reverse notion that technology "inscribes" nature before it becomes recognized as Nature). Yet the idea that in addition to optical space, there might also be an acoustic one that is informed by the unconscious nonetheless has enormous relevance for the complex relationship between time and the ear during the forma-tive period of modernism around 1900. What, for instance, do the uncanny recurrences that modernism's subjects often expe-rienced and that prompted Freud's invention of the concept of the compulsion to repeat have in common with Herod's eerie soliloquy? Could the ear be the quintessential organ of time perception? From the work of early rhythm theorists such as Ernst Meumann, the differential psychology of William Stern, and the discourse of motor energy of economist and rhythm expert Karl Bücher to the more mainstream theory of empathy propounded by Theodor Lipps and on to musicologist Hugo Riemann's theory of rhythm, a diffuse assortment of little-known texts homed in on the ear in an effort both to exploit and to keep in check the explosive force with which the acoustic unconscious encroached upon turn-of-the-century subjects.

0.0014 Seconds

Western culture, Cathérine Clément writes, differs from that of the East (which is supposedly more open to the unexpected) in that it fears the hiatus, or, as she calls it, the syncope: "With us, every disconnection, every rupture that would take consciousness by surprise would threaten the idea of the subject."[5] While it is far from certain that fear of the "syncope" is indeed the exclusive property of the West, there is ample evidence of the fact that the sense of time is of fundamental importance to humans' sense of self — so important, in fact, that Freud himself considered a "vacillating rhythm" or *Zauderrhythmus* to be crucial for the proper interaction of consciousness and the unconscious.[6] Having tested a recently invented contraption called the *Wunderblock* or Mystic Writing Pad, the inventor of psychoanalysis saw the secret of our psychic apparatus in the way perception appeared to be subject to a "periodic" motion that wards off or at least slows down the "haste" of excessive excitations. In this way, Freud noted, the apparatus not only sustains the organism and enlarges the domain of the ego by allowing us to step back from the urge to respond to each and every stimulus, it also determines our concept of time.[7] Our entire time consciousness is based on the breaks that occur in the interplay between consciousness and the unconscious, or, to use the nomenclature Freud had introduced earlier in *The Interpretation of Dreams*, between a conscious system of perception

called *Pcpt.-Cs* and the unconscious *Ucs.* Just as the writing on the
paper covering the Mystic Writing Pad can be erased, the system
Pcpt.-Cs receives only fleeting sensory impressions. However,
much in the same way that lasting traces of these inscriptions are
preserved in the device's wax layer, the system *Ucs.* stores the
sensory impressions even after they have disappeared from *Pcpt.-
Cs*. Key to the preservation of the organism, then, is the ability
of *Ucs.* to dock to *Pcpt.-Cs* by means of rapid jolts or "cathectic
innervations" and to undock from it at periodic intervals, thereby
leaving *Pcpt.-Cs* temporarily inactive and impervious to over-
stimulation. In short, the constant toggling between *Ucs/Pcpt.*
and *Cs/Ucs* is the rhythmic formula of the ego.

The contrast between Clément's ego-threatening syncopes
and Freud's ego-preserving, wavering rhythms was symptomatic
of the decades before and after 1900. But this dividing line not
only traversed the entire spectrum of philosophical and scientific
discourse about the temporal patterning of subjectivity, in many
ways it also harked back to the late eighteenth century, especially
to the controversy sparked by Kant's attempt to define time,
along with space, as an intuitive form (*Anschauungsform*) that
exists a priori of any experience and that is thus not an object
itself of sensory perception. Those who, like Wilhelm Heinse,
rejected transcendental idealism and, as we have seen in Chapter
4, remained committed to the sensualist strand of enlightened
epistemology, greeted the loss of unitary consciousness symbolized by the experience of rushing waterfalls as liberation. Others,
such as Marcus Herz, troubled by the quickening pace of post-
revolutionary bourgeois society, sought comfort in Kant's dictum
and declared vertigo to be a mere subjective anomaly, rather than
a problem of epistemology.

Both positions were unattractive to the emerging psychophysiology of the early nineteenth century and the attempt to ground
the theory of consciousness in the empirical study of experience,
especially sensory perception. How do we perceive time? What
is musical rhythm? What does it actually mean when a sensation

strikes us sooner than we anticipated? Exactly how early is "too early?" And what does it all have to do with the ear anyway? These were the kind of questions that, along with a host of others concerning memory, olfaction, attention, emotion, locomotion, and even animal psychology, stood at the center of the larger and rapidly developing field of the neurophysiology and psychology of time.[8]

One of the pioneers of that field was Johann Friedrich Herbart. As early as 1824, the student of Fichte had attacked the Kantian a priori by arguing that time results from the perception of series of sensory stimuli. To represent something of a temporal nature, he argued (often invoking musical phenomena to argue his case), we need to recall prior conditions or events. In this way, things appear to us in a different light depending on whether we examine the series from its beginning or its end. Time, in other words, is a question of perspective, and although inherently subjective, the psychology of time — indeed psychology all told — is essentially a mechanics of representation.

Herbart's deft combination of metaphysical speculation and empirical observation eschewed the larger issue of the nature of the relationship between the interior representations of time and external events. In much the same way that Romantic scientists such as the early Johannes Müller believed external reality to be a projection of our inner world, "objective" time was seen as inner time. It was not until Hermann von Helmholtz's seminal experiments of 1850 that the interplay of sensory stimulation and perception came to be seen in a different light, as occurring across a divide between two radically disconnected, if parallel spheres.[9] Having determined that in a frog, electric shocks are registered in the gastrognemius muscle at an interval of 0.0014 to 0.0020 seconds, Helmholtz challenged classical dogma by concluding that sensation and perception do not occur simultaneously, but rather are separated by infinitesimal intervals determined by the velocity of nerve impulses and the duration required for muscular contraction, among other factors. In other words, body and mind do not simply operate *within* a given spatial and temporal matrix, they *are* that matrix. "External appearance," the young scientist wrote, "is just as necessarily a function of time as it is of space." Conversely, consciousness and the transmission of sensory stimuli do not share the same termporal axis. As the example of sound showed, the "transmission within the body is just as much something external to the mind as is the propagation of sound from its point of origin to the ear." And, he added, the fact that the time required for this transmission appears to be so infinitesimal is because the movements of the nerve substance are slower than the propagation of sound. We are "unable to perceive more quickly than our nervous system can act."[10]

Helmholtz' findings sparked a lively debate among some of the era's most prominent scholars.[11] And even as some of these scholars contested Helmholtz's neo-Kantian axiom that time is the only sphere in which there exists, if not a copylike correspondence between the temporal relationships of objects and the sequence of our sensations, at least a structural analogy between the sequential order of stimuli and sensations, the desire to maintain perceptual synthesis as the basis of the self-possessed seeing, hearing, and feeling individual weighed heavily on these thinkers' epistemological agendas. As the boundary between subject and object became more fluid, locating a part within consciousness capable of stabilizing this boundary took an unprecedented urgency. Inspired by Wilhelm Weber's landmark study on the location of spatial perception in the skin, in 1857, the otolaryngologist Johannes Nepomuk Czermak, for instance, conducted experiments to determine the existence of what he called a *Zeitsinn*, a sense by which we recognize time intervals.[12] By having test persons compare several time intervals (marked by two acoustic or optical signals) and by measuring the difference in their judgments, Czermak sought to ascertain a quasi-innate, standard psychological time unit by which the mind would accurately judge the duration of a given time interval. In this way, he hoped, it would be possible to specify the smallest Weber fraction at which such a time interval changes. (Having observed that it is easier to distinguish between a 1-pound and a 2-pound weight than between a 100-pound and a 101-pound weight, Weber in the early 1800s had concluded that the "just-noticeable difference" [ΔS] between two weights is proportional to the smaller weight [S], and hence the Weber fraction is $\Delta S/S$.) In reality, though, this "temporal indifference point," as Karl Vierordt eventually labeled the interval, putting its average duration at 0.755 seconds, varies considerably. As he and a host of subsequent researchers found, it depends as much on the subject's physical constitution and emotional state as it does on external circumstances, such as climate.

Interestingly, as the physiology of time perception expanded into a subdiscipline of its own, with scientific journals such as the renowned *Zeitschrift für die Physiologie der Sinnesorgane* increasingly devoting entire sections to the perception of time and space, the question arose: Which sense is the most reliable in determining the "just-noticeable difference"? Would an identical time interval be perceived by all senses equally, or is the ear better equipped to judge time intervals?

Not surprisingly, one of the first and most vocal advocates of the idea of the ear as the *Zeitsinn* proper was Ernst Mach. Musically gifted and a fervent proselytizer of Helmholtz's physiological acoustics, the Viennese physicist had evinced a keen interest in the ear from early on in his career. In several papers published between 1863 and 1872, Mach posited that the ear surpasses the other senses in the ability to determine time intervals correctly.[13] But Mach also went beyond his predecessors, claiming the existence of a rhythm sense that functions independently of any other sensation—independently of musical pitch, for instance. In contrast to Herbart's notion that time consciousness results from the willed reproduction of series of sensory stimuli such as an identical rhythmic pattern of different melodies, Mach argued that the perception of the rhythm of a melody occurs separately from the series of pitches. Tapping a certain rhythm of a Wagner leitmotif on a table automatically reproduces—in the minds of

277

trained musicians, at any rate — the melodic contour of that leit-motif. Hence, Mach concludes, prefiguring his later monism: To talk about time consciousness, one needs to go beyond the psychophysical parallelism of Weber and Fechner. Time is little more than the "representability" (*Darstellbarkeit*) of all phenomena — whether physical or psychic — by each other.[14]

By 1900, the physiological literature on the perception of time had run to thousands of pages, with studies on "reaction" and attention accounting for the bulk of the material published. How long does it take for a word such as "mountain" to trigger associations such as "valley?" one article in the journal *Archiv für die gesamte Psychologie* asked, for instance. How much time would elapse for the word "honor" to elicit "fatherland," or "state," or "Prussia?" another author in the same issue of *Archiv* wondered. And what effect, finally, did the intensity of a sound delimiting a time interval have on the sense of time?[15] Meanwhile, working along more speculative lines, the noted Russian physiologist (and teacher of Ivan Pavlov) Élie de Cyon suggested that the labyrinth not only enables us to orient ourselves in space, but because the cochlea is a calculus machine capable of Fourier analysis, the ear is also the quintessential sense of arithmetic and, hence, of time.[16]

The preoccupation with the (auditory) control of consciousness culminated in the work of Ernst Meumann, founder of the Psychology Department at the University of Hamburg and one of the pioneers of rhythm studies. In several articles and a seminal *Habilitationsschrift* entitled "Untersuchungen zur Psychologie und Aesthetik des Rhythmus" (Inquiries into the Psychology and Aesthetics of Rhythm), Meumann reframed the intertwining of auditory perception and temporal fragmentation in nonevolutionary, nonbiological terms.[17] Rhythm, thus the basic idea running through his works, is in large part the result of an intellectual act, rather than, as evolutionists such as Herbert Spencer had claimed, a biological necessity. Rhythm requires a conscious effort to allow the mind to be affected by sensory stimuli in the first place. In other words, it requires attention. By virtue of an

278

intrinsic physiological mechanism that enables the individual to recognize different time atoms and to recombine them into what Meumann's successor William Stern (of whom we will hear more further below) would call *Präsenzzeit* or "present time," the ego is able to reduce the risk of being undercut by unconscious mechanisms and, hence, to maintain an ordered time continuum. (This position, incidentally, also rubbed off on Meumann's aesthetic writings, in which he attempted to distance himself from the sensualist theories of his contemporaries by arguing for what he called the "specifically aesthetic" realm.)[18]

Yet regardless of these scholars' insistence on the ear's remarkable precision in mediating between external time and our internal sense of time, the thought that the same ear might also be the site of a more fundamental crisis hardly ever crossed these scholars' minds. To be sure, the ear is prone to numerous errors, but such errors ultimately were seen as validating the notion that auditory perception is a stabilizing element more than they challenged it. As the nineteenth century drew to a close, however, this confidence in the temporal basis of the self-possessed individual increasingly gave way to a more skeptical view in which such individuals' macronarratives about autonomy and integrity were seen as being undercut by the acoustic unconscious—by the minute shifts, imperceptible loops, and automatisms of modern listening: in short, by Clément's "syncopes." Several examples from the early twentieth-century history of sociology and psychology may illustrate this shift.

Uncanny Recurrences

One of the areas of modernist thought in which the threat of temporal disorder loomed perhaps the largest is the sociology of Georg Simmel, especially his persistent concern with what he called the "tempo of life." The locus classicus of this obsession is the section called "The Rhythm or Symmetry of the Contents of Life" in Simmel's chef d'oeuvre *The Philosophy of Money*.[19] In modern society, the sociologist argues there, what were once

clearly demarcated time periods are being leveled out by a growing artificiality of the patterns of everyday life. Electric light
eliminates the difference between day and night. Print obliterates
the natural alternation between periods of mental exertion and
rest by providing us with thoughts and stimulation at our whim.
Modern individualism and spontaneity thus lead to two mutually
exclusive styles of life. They free the individual from the need to
adjust his or her needs and deeds to an overarching periodicity,
but they also subject this individual to another, altogether more
disorienting and involuntary sort of rhythm. Modern, differentiated individuals, then, might be defined as individuals who have
traded the rhythmic regularity characteristic of traditional social
formations for a "continuous readiness for experience and action,
combined with a continually open ear for the autonomous life
of things in order to adjust to its opportunities and challenges as
they arise."[20]

The modern "tempo of life," then, prevents the subject from
crafting itself into a unified whole by violating a key human principle, rhythmic symmetry. Such symmetry, Simmel suggests, is
the first and most important means by which the mind stylizes,
governs, and assimilates the material of life, and as such, it provides stability to societies that privilege totality over its constituent parts. Whether as archaic empires, as absolute monarchies, or
as Tommaso Campanella's utopian Sun state, such symmetrically
and rhythmically structured societies do a double form of violence. First, they do violence to the subject, whose impulses and
needs are allowed to make themselves heard only when, by some
happy coincidence, they are in synchrony with the fixed scheme.
But they also contravene external reality, whose relationship to
us can be integrated into such a simple framework only by force.

Musical listening is no exception to this. While listening in
classical aesthetic theories of subject formation was said to occur
within a stable correlation between a spatially fixed subject and an
external stimulus, around 1900, such listening was being reconfigured along more unpredictable lines. But these shifting boundaries

not only blurred the conventional distinctions between subject and object, perception and cognition, more significantly, they also displaced the temporal basis of the relationship between the work of art and aesthetic experience as conscious sublimation in general. The idée fixe, the haunting melody that keeps coming back without any apparent reason—far from being mere clever artistic devices or symptoms of emerging mass culture, such uncanny moments of recurrence and repetition are at the heart of a more general shift in the subject's experience of musical time.

The tectonic shift was registered in the most obscure of texts, such as the work of Ernst Jentsch. A psychiatrist by trade, Jentsch was mainly interested in fits of shivering and mood swings—in other words, in involuntary mechanisms and "syncopes" disrupting the flow of conscious time.[21] Small wonder that listening to modern music, too, for him had more in common with compulsion than with cognition. Thus, in *Musik und Nerven* (Music and Nerves), a long-winded, labyrinthine work, Jentsch describes modern music as verging on the abnormal and the pathological.[22] Rambling over a wide range of topics, from the "natural history of tonal sensation," to the interconnections between human hearing and the animal world, to music's archaic roots, Jentsch confidently declared Wagnerian infinite melody to be the root cause of a whole string of disorders, from a "functional instability of the entire nervous system," to a "proclivity toward narcotics," to an "increased hunger for affect." He was of course hardly alone in this, Nietzsche and a host of other intellectuals likewise having suspected infinite melody of being little more than what the Viennese musicologist Richard Wallaschek called a "detailed stammering," a symptom of upset temporal coordinates.[23]

In a second text, entitled "On the Psychology of the Uncanny," Jentsch elaborated his fixation with spasms and mood swings into a broader theory of the uncanny. The sensation of the uncanny, he argued, is caused by the subject's intellectual uncertainty as to whether a perceived object is inanimate or a living being.[24] While such doubts typically afflict children, "imbeciles," and "primitives" who suddenly find themselves confronted with mysterious natural phenomena or complex machinery, in "civilized" man, the uncanny could be used to great (and supposedly less harmful) effect in art, provided such doubts were allowed to slip imperceptibly into one's consciousness. (As he had elaborated in *Musik und Nerven*, a musical example of such "safer" use of the uncanny, is a scene in the last act of Wagner's *Flying Dutchman* in which the invitation of Daland's sailors to join in the merrymaking elicits only a muted, otherworldly echo coming from inside the haunted vessel.)

To readers familiar with the psychology of the uncanny, Jentsch is of course no stranger. His theory of the uncanny enjoyed a brief, if contentious afterlife of its own, inspiring none other than Freud to a theory of the uncanny or *das Unheimliche* in his famous article of the same title.[25] The uncanny, Freud's argument runs, is not something foreign or new, as Jentsch had claimed. It is something that, even though it may return at unexpected moments, we know only too well. As the German word for "uncanny," *unheimlich*, suggests, the uncanny contains the idea of something being secret (*heimlich*) or "homely," something familiar that has become foreign to us only because it has been repressed, kept hidden from view. And so what the term *unheimliche* really refers to is *Wiederholungszwang*, the inner compulsion to repeat something.

In what is surely one of the most brilliant interpretations of Freud's text ever written, Hélène Cixous has pointed to the parallels between Freud's analysis and *das Unheimliche*.[26] More of a novel than a discourse on the science of psychology, she writes, the essay entangles the author and the object of his desire—to speak the truth about *das Unheimliche*—in a delirium that threads together *das Heimliche* and *das Unheimliche* in a way that is itself compulsive. For instance, in the same manner that Freud, using E. T. A. Hoffmann's short story *Der Sandmann* (The Sandman) as example, had argued that *das Unheimliche* was rooted in the child's fear of losing its eyes and, in the last instance, of being castrated, Freud's text castrates (cancels, eliminates, critiques)

Jentsch's essay. In other words, Freud's text repeats the same repressive logic that structures the experience of *das Unheimliche*. For the same reason, she goes on to argue, one has to query Freud's understanding of the parallel art form of fiction as liberating the poet from the need to check whether something is really dangerous. Fiction does not so much stand opposed to reality, she claims, as it is a double of the uncanny, a "vibration of reality," connected to reality by a link as ambiguous and compulsive as the one passing from the *heimlich* to the *unheimlich*.[27]

Cixous' reading of Freud's text might also be usefully applied to a theory of listening to time. What it explodes is the way Freud's and Jentsch's supposedly scientific style of reasoning about the role of the artist is predicated on the fantasy that the artist is able consciously to distance himself from the compulsion to repeat by an a priori notion of literature (or music) as fiction. But if fiction is a double of the uncanny, and hence another form of *Wiederholungszwang*, where does this leave the notion of the author as a stable subject as expounded by Jentsch and Freud? Or, mapping Cixous' critique on to the acoustic realm, what is listening other than the compulsion to repeat, laced with the same set of fear-provoking ambiguities as the relationship of the *unheimlich* to the *heimlich*? And, finally, how is it possible under such circumstances for listeners to speak of themselves as authentic, autonomous beings endowed with historical consciousness?

More than an issue of overwrought nerves, then, the simultaneously discontinuous and uncanny temporalities that so troubled Jentsch and Freud entangle our ears in what Henri Bergson called a "zone of indetermination" between perception and memory. The acoustic unconscious confronts our ears with a strange reversal of roles. In a series of slippages and doubles, subjects and works become embroiled with each other without one being able to claim sovereignty over the other. As music ceases to be a medium through which the listening individual constitutes itself as a substantive subject, the listener takes on the intermediary qualities of a medium.

Few texts, in the emerging field of the psychology of perception anyway, describe such a medial subject in more radical terms than *Über Psychologie der individuellen Differenzen* (On the Psychology of Individual Differences), published in 1900, the same year that saw the publication of Freud's *Interpretation of Dreams*.[28] Its author, William Stern, is remembered today mostly as a pioneer of child psychology and as the inventor of the "intelligence quotient," the IQ. But early in his career, after having studied under Hermann Ebbinghaus and after becoming Meumann's successor at the University of Hamburg, Stern's writing bordered more on the flamboyantly speculative. Concocting a heady brew of Kantianism, Romanticism, and probability calculus, Stern conceived of the individual in terms outside of intention and authorship and, it turns out, by shifting the emphasis toward rhythm, time, and sound as major parameters of the medial subject. In particular, Stern was taken with the attempts of Romantic theorists such as Herbart, Franz Hemsterhuis, and Friedrich Schleiermacher to grasp human consciousness in purely formal, quantitative terms.[29] Selfhood, Herbart had asserted, for example, vitally depends on a maximization of resources or an economy of speed and data. A person does not merely command to the fullest his or her powers of reasoning, as prescribed by German idealism. Such a person also can and indeed must maximize the number of ideas, thoughts, or representations while simultaneously reducing the amount of time needed to process them.

Stern's differential psychology took Herbart's optimization of the individual to the extreme. Discarding normative concepts of "Man" derived from aesthetic, anthropological, or metaphysical discourses, Stern defined the individual formally, that is, as a "synthesis of endlessly high complexity" or, even more soberingly, as a mere "point of intersection between an unlimited number of types."[30] The latter term is especially important to Stern's argument, because it enabled him to eschew a concept of the individual characteristic of an older genre of "general" psychology. According to this type of psychology, individual peculiarities are to be understood as variations on a more general theme called "psychic life." The differential psychologist, by contrast, instead of focusing on how general psychic traits manifest themselves in particular individuals, is after the combination and interdependence of the factors defining such specificity. In Stern's view, individuals do not so much assemble themselves from a stock of traits stored, as it were, in the warehouse of their psyche as much as they just happen—against all statistical odds. Because they emerge out of an intricate web of innumerable behaviors, utterances, and sensory perceptions, individual differences cannot be determined other than in inversely proportional terms: "The more compound the complex, the smaller the number of individuals to whom it applies."[31] The ego, in other words, is essentially unknowable. It is an approximation or "asymptote of science" at best—a likelihood, rather than a rule.[32]

So why, and particularly, how is the ear involved in all this? Quite simply because it is crucial in distinguishing between many of Stern's types, or, more surprisingly even, because Stern's auditory work was the starting point for the doctrine of types to begin with.[33] For instance, individuals can be classified according to the ways in which they tend to privilege certain sensory impressions over others and the ways in which out of these they form representations. Thus, there is a visual type whose entire psychological system is organized around vision and who therefore tends to dream in vivid images or memorizes colors, forms, and faces easily. The aural type, by contrast, oftentimes hears colors where the visual type only sees them. Likewise, auditory perception of a series of pitches changing at different speeds serves to differentiate between "objective types" and "subjective" types—so labeled because of their ability (or inability) to separate judgments about a certain sensory stimulus from other subjective factors. Thus, the subjective type "takes his time" before a difference in pitch strikes him as noteworthy, whereas the objective type tends to report a difference in sensation in accordance with the actual time intervals at which the pitch changed. At the next level up, that of representation, memory, and association, one can also distinguish between several types: motor types, visual types, and of course, aural types. Whereas the motor types tend to enact a word they imagine and the visual types see a printed word before their inner eye, aural types hear an inner voice speaking to them.

In practice, such types can of course never be neatly separated from each other, and characteristics of the aural type, for instance, frequently bleed into several other types, such as the "formal" type. The reason why the formal type focuses more on the temporal or spatial aspects of a sensation, rather than, like its counterpart, the "material" type, on color or timbre—and often overlaps with the aural type—is that both display a high degree of rhythmic sensitivity. Another complicating factor is that the interplay between the different types, which Stern refers to as the "complex," does not always form a harmonious whole. Thus, the relatively high number of auditory types does not match the comparatively low occurrence in real life of the so-called "sensory reaction type." This is a type that reacts to a sensory stimulus by focusing on the stimulus itself, rather than, on the ensuing muscular reflex, as the corresponding motor type does. And while the former's sensory reaction occurs faster than the muscular response, with the motor type, it is the other way around.

And so on. Any reading that takes Stern's myriad types and subtypes at their word is of course doomed to failure. The point about all these types and the numerous transitions between them is, quite simply, this: The longer the list of types and combinations of types, the more improbable the concrete individual corresponding to the "complex" becomes. Putting the whole conundrum in auditory terms, one might say that the more the various synesthetic, motor, and cognitive aspects of listening cut across different "types" and thus, in the complexity of their combination, establish a listener's credentials as an individual, the fewer listeners there are who can actually be considered individuals. Or, to put it yet another way, the more we know about a person's listening experience, the less we are likely to know about him or her as an individual and the more as a listener-medium, instead.

Stern was not the only scholar hoping to redeem the individual by typifying it. Eager to preserve what little had been left of the enlightened ego amid what sociologists called the "crowd," he and scholars such as Max Weber and Werner Sombart busied themselves with subsuming the endangered individual under "ideal types," such as "the Serb" or, more odiously "the Jew." Meanwhile, Simmel believed he had found a simple mathematical equation to grasp individuality. Speaking of the pace of life (or what Stern had called "tempo," an optimal value indexing a person's "vitality" that was to be established on the basis of her "natural" pace in basic operations such as speaking, singing, walking, or beating out a simple triple meter) he wrote: "The greater the differences between the content of our imagination at any one time—even with an equal number of conceptions—the more intensive are the experiences of life, and the greater is the span of life through which we have passed."[34] At the same time, such "intensity of life" is less a manifestation of the "qualitative individualism" that Simmel frequently attributed to the Romantic era—which he saw superbly realized in the figure of Goethe—than the stuff of probability calculus. Like Stern's asymptotic individual, Simmel's fully differentiated individual, too, is a mere mathematical function: "Regardless of the content of [a person's] individual features, the form of individuality inheres in every man and determines his worth according to the moment of rarity."[35]

Listening, Lying

Subjects around 1900—Jentsch's "intellectually uncertain" listener no less than differential psychology's "asymptotic" individual and Simmel's "rare" individual—are like Debussy's Mélisande on her deathbed: They no longer see what they see, smell what they smell, or, of course, hear what they hear. But least of all are they the self-reflexive Cartesian cogito or Kantian *Ich* they claim to be. Such subjects, one might say, assert their autonomy pre-cisely where it is missing most—in the act of listening to rhythms. They are, in the words of Hugo von Hoffmansthal, pathological liars, whose "words lie, feelings lie, and even self-consciousness lies."[36] But they are liars not in any moral sense, but because they continue asserting their autonomy as subjects even when their consciousness has fallen out of step with the rest of their bodies—when in fact, consciousness had become plain deception, a mas-querade hiding the automatisms and syncopes of the very body that physiology was meant to make transparent in the first place.

As Stefan Rieger has shown, under such conditions of reduced accountability, self-reflexivity can take the form only of radi-cal self-doubt. To counter the devastating effects of their own demise as egos, turn-of-the-century individuals found themselves in constant need of rehabilitation through self-authentication.[37] There are perhaps two partly overlapping methods of such self-authentication. The first is based on the media-technological a priori first theorized in Benjamin's parallel between the camera and microphone, on the one hand, and the probing eye and ear of the psychologist, on the other. In essence, this is a form of authentication that bypasses the level of consciously asserted individuality by extracting clues from the subject's more hidden and hence authentic layers. The second method of authenticat-ing the self differs from the first in terms of the space that the self-authenticating subject is meant to inhabit. In contrast to the camera, the microphone, or the multitude of devices scanning the individual's surface for clues about its interior truth, this form of self-authentication works in the opposite direction. It clues or keys the individual in, as it were. But it does so not by putting it in the know, than by helping the individual get its groove back, by rebalancing the realm of the inner "syncope" and by synchro-nizing the ego's *Zauderrhythmus* with other, purportedly more regular rhythmic orders.

William Stern's intellectual trajectory in the wake of his *Über Psychologie der individuellen Differenzen* is a good example of this trend toward a new, more even-paced cadence for subjectivity, even though his earlier twin interests in the physiology of time and auditory "types" of representation receded into the background in later years. Having retreated from the radical premise of his differential psychology as early as 1901, over the course of the next three decades, Stern pursued a more temperate agenda, one centered on what he called a theory of "critical personalism." Convinced that more was required to grasp "individuality" than differential psychology's blind dissection of the soul into types, he concentrated on two fields in which personal unity was to become immediately apparent: art and metaphysics. In both, he felt, "a connecting higher unity was at work." And so the bulk of Stern's later philosophical work—but particularly the massive *Person und Sache* (Person and Thing), begun in 1916—is thick with metaphysical speculation, with art remaining if not a central, a persistent concern throughout.[38] For instance, the artist, or more particularly, the musician, is seen as the incarnation of a higher form of "personality." In a time of rapidly disappearing worldviews (*Weltanschauungslosigkeit*), it is incumbent on the genius to access, like a seer, life's deeper essence and turn it into universal truth.

Stern's longing for reenchantment, meanwhile, was shared by Simmel. Seeking to grasp social relationships under purely formal aspects, the sociologist placed a great deal of emphasis on rhythmic synchronicity and symmetry. The unity and transparency that symmetrical forms of social organization impose on life's contingencies, Simmel claimed, turn one's life into a work of art in much the same way as the regularity and formal integration of the human soul are innate aesthetic qualities. "We do not *possess* that elemental quality as we do its aesthetic, moral, social, intellectual, eudaemonistic manifestations in practical life, but rather we *are* that quality."[39]

Finally, an aestheticism of a more frivolous kind permeates one of the most widely read works of its time, *Arbeit und Rhythmus* (Labor and Rhythm), by Karl Bücher.[40] The book was part

289

of a wider debate that had been raging for much of the last quarter of the nineteenth century over how to organize rationally
the labor power of the rapidly growing urban proletariat and
how to balance economic "development" with social justice. But
instead of moral exhortation, reform-minded economists such as
Bücher, Charles Féré, and Guillaume Ferrero hoped to achieve
this reorganization through a "productivist calculus of fatigue
and energy."[41] The specter of revolution, they argued, might be
spirited away by replacing unnatural work conditions with a supposedly more natural economy of bodily energy expenditure.
Rhythm was at the center of this project. A law of nature, a
principle of order, and an aesthetic rule — rhythm is the basis of
life, arising from the "organic essence of mankind."[42] But such
rhythm stands in stark contrast to factory work. The irregular
and unnatural pace of machine labor is no longer "music and
poetry," as it still was for the "savages" of Africa and Asia, and
instead of enticing workers to production, the absence of rhythm
kills the human instinct for industry. And so Bücher nostalgically
invoked a primordial utopia in which "technology and art reunite
in a higher rhythmic unity."[43]

Bücher was quite taken with the idea that a "national division of labor," as he euphemistically called capitalism, would
lead to "an advance towards higher and better forms of social
existence."[44] But what exactly a reorganized, rhythmically more
"organic" kind of labor might contribute to this "advance" was
ultimately less a question of Orientalist fantasies than of a decidedly modernist agenda, one that speaks to an altogether more
troubled, almost cynical relationship with the new forms of selfhood emerging at the turn of the century. Bücher knew of the
medial nature of the subject. He knew that it is not people that
process rhythms, but rhythms that process people. Yet despite
this, Bücher's plea for a reunion of art and technology did not
confine itself to advocating the economization of effort and the
humanization of industrial production. Echoing a host of other
theorists of energy and fatigue and, like these, turning his back on

humanity's utopian goal of a life free of pain, he actually turned alienated industrial labor into aesthetics, a beautiful play untarnished by power relationships and devoid of material interests.

Bücher's reformist fantasies resonate strongly with a little-noticed chapter in the history of musical aesthetics that has much to tell us about the intertwined fields of rhythm, listening, and subjectivity in the period between 1885 and 1914: the aesthetics of empathy or, as its (mostly German) proponents called it, *Einfühlungsästhetik*. The brainchild of Theodor Lipps (1851–1914), a student of Wilhelm Wundt who taught at universities in Bonn, Breslau, and finally Munich, where he replaced Carl Stumpf as head of the Psychology Department in 1894, the aesthetics of empathy had its roots in the writings of Gustav Fechner, Robert Vischer, and Johannes Volkelt. Like these, Lipps defined aesthetic pleasure as a form of animation (*Beseelung*) in which the subject lends a part of itself to the beheld work of art. In this act of imputing soul to an object, the subject traverses two stages of empathetic immersion: a basic or "practical" empathy operating in everyday life and a higher, sympathetic form of empathy that becomes the basis for the aesthetic experience.[45] Practical empathy, for instance, emerges when an expression of anger in another person impels us instinctively to reproduce the feeling of a previously experienced anger, thus creating an almost organic "articulation" or *Verwachsensein* between two objectified forms of anger and, by extension, between the persons that experience the feeling. Practical empathy, then, is essentially a form of borrowing and selves, accordingly, are mirrored selves, doppelgängers, or copies of each other: "'Other people,' psychologically speaking, are duplicates of my own self."[46]

The transition from this basic, everyday form of empathy to the higher type of empathy occurs when the objectified anger and the act of empathically projecting oneself into the other person blend seamlessly to form a unity in which the experience imposed from the outside triggers an activity of one's own. This experience of sympathetic fusion of "objectivity and activity," while it supposedly entails the possibility of freedom, for the most part does so only in theory, because in real life, such freedom is never pure, always conjuring up a looming "remainder" of "inner unfreedom and tangible coercion."[47]

This is where art comes in. Art, Lipps believed, not only holds the potential for a higher, more complete form of empathy, a sympathetic bond between a listener and a work of art, it also shields the individual from the ever-looming "danger of inner unfreedom." In other words, art must dissolve the "remainder" and in this way enable the subject to reach a maximum of pleasure and self-realization, or what Lipps calls the "greatness of my being an ideal I, heightened in itself."[48]

It has been suggested that the articulation of art and body in the theory of empathy owes its origin to a "drive towards an objective presentation of facts" inherent in modern industrial society or, in broader epistemological terms, to an anti-idealist, antimetaphysical thrust.[49] Nothing could be further from the truth. At issue in Lipps's work is not certainty about the object world so much as the growing skepticism, first articulated half a century earlier in Helmholtz's neo-Kantian physiology of sensation, that perception and reason may no longer be able to bridge the chasm separating subject and object. In short, at stake is, as it was for Stern and Simmel, the dilemma of the syncope and how to turn rhythmic disjuncture into periodicity and symmetry.

So how does one listen empathetically? Lipps's writings are laced with acoustic metaphors. Tapping into a rich field of Romantic imagery, Lipps variously glosses sympathetic empathy as echo, resonance, vibration, or simply "cosounding." But a particular burden falls on rhythm. Lipps considers rhythm to be at the base of even the most elementary musical forms. From a C-major chord to a melody to a larger musical work, music is a system of "tonal rhythms" (*Tonrhythmen*) or "microrhythms." First outlined in his *Psychologische Studien* (Psychological Studies) of 1885 and further elaborated in 1905, Lipps's theory of "microrhythm" is essentially a modernized version of the seventeenth-century coincidence theory of consonance we encountered in Chapters 1 and 2.[50] Benedetti, Galileo Galilei, Descartes, and Mersenne, it will be recalled, had all defined consonance as ensuing from the more or less frequent coincidence of "pulses" of vibrating air. Thus, an octave was deemed the most consonant interval, because every second pulse of the higher tone coincides with every pulse of the lower tone. Accordingly, in a fifth, every third pulse of the higher pitch coincides with every second pulse of the lower pitch, and so on. Lipps, in a sense, takes this temporal aspect of consonance down to the level of unconsciously perceived mico-rhythmic relationships. In the terms of the earlier example of the octave, two tones with a frequency of 100 and 200 cycles per second, respectively, although sounding simultaneously, relate to each other rhythmically. Not only is each tone the result of a suc-cession of a certain number of vibrations per second, the relation-ship between these two pitches is one of time, as well, because both share a "fundamental rhythm" (*Grundrhythmus*) of 100 cycles per second.[51] But while the same "fundamental rhythm" also determines the fifth (200 and 300 cycles per second), in a disso-nant interval such as between 200 and 250 cycles per second, the fundamental rhythm is 50. And while the latter may of course be said to be the "fundamental rhythm" for all three intervals, it is so only "potentially."[52] The feeling of consonance as such results only from the actual coincidence of "tone-excitations": "In this union, each tone-excitation 'fixes' in the other, as it were, the common rhythm, emphasizes it, makes it, in a word, the actual fundamental rhythm. This fundamental rhythm then appears dif-ferentiated one way in one tone, another way in another."[53]

Lipps's theory of microrhythm is less scurrilous than it may seem. For one thing, it engages Helmholtz's concept of beats as the basis for the perception of dissonance. Second, Lipps's theory might be considered a precursor to the current concept of peri-odicity pitch or missing fundamentals — that is, the phenomenon whereby the brain produces the illusion of a fundamental in a series of upper partials where in reality no such fundamental exists. Third and most importantly for our purposes, Lipps conceives of tonal microrhythms as a form of resonance by which physical vibrations unconsciously "sound over" (hinüberklingen) into the soul and there produce the sensation of tones. However, instead of venturing further into the physiology of the inner ear's time processing, toward the end of his tract, in the section "The Theory of Melody," Lipps retreats from the potentially far-reaching implications of his theory by connecting the resonant dimension of "tonal rhythm" with his broader metaphysics of auditory empathy. In a lengthy critique of the theory of melody advanced by the pioneer of melodic gestalt perception, Max Friedrich Meyer (1873–1967), Lipps argues that variations in just intonation (pure harmonic intervals without any beats) and hence impossibly complex "fundamental rhythms" are necessary preconditions of aesthetic pleasure. They are expressions of the "life" we project into the "characterless" forms of perfect circles, lines, or consonances by empathy, by "coming out of" ourselves.[54] And even though such lifelike deviations violate the norm, the forms themselves are presupposed qua norm, lending the listener rhythmic stability and framing the subject in a narrative with a beginning and an end. "The I that feels itself empathetically in the tones is not an imaginary one, but a really felt I that in the successively emerging tonal totality experiences an integrated, inner story."[55]

Of course, Lipps's comforting Einfühlungsästhetik stands in marked contrast to the jagged rhythms actually emanating from turn-of-the-century Europe's orchestra pits, concert halls, and nightclubs. And so the invention of "fundamental rhythms" as the foundation of a new synthesis of personhood speaks powerfully to the profound narcissistic insult experienced by Lipps's generation. At the same time, it points to the conservative, nineteenth-century roots of the attempt to overcome the offense. One of these roots lies in social Romanticism: In an age of sharpening class divisions, all the talk about empathy and sympathy quite plainly smacks of social glue. In this respect, it is also noteworthy that

Lipps's stress on harmony and pleasure stands in stark contrast to the eighteenth-century's celebration of pain as the basis of subject formation. Even elements of eighteenth-century *Gefühlsästhetik* are discernible in the ready association of melody with vocal intonation and emotion. By far the heaviest nineteenth-century ideological baggage, however, is Lipps's persistent formalism. As the early twentieth-century music theorist Paul Moos, arguing from the standpoint of a normative philosophy of art, clearly recognized, the theory of empathy leaves the formal givenness of the work untouched. Through the act of empathy, the subject merely "affixes" itself to the immutable, objective structure, thus surrendering the autonomy it had gained on purely formal grounds.[56]

Yet the theory of empathy also shares a number of more progressive features. For instance, implicit in the celebration of "inner rhythm" is an insight that would later became central to psychoanalysis: the notion that the source of displeasure—the hideous, dissonant, and disjointed—might not reside outside our bodies, but inside, in the disarticulations of the soul. Likewise, the notion that aesthetic pleasure resides at the heart of a form of knowledge that, in the words of Simmel, "interprets the world according to our inner reactions, and as an inner world proper," also is a thoroughly modern one.[57] And finally, for all its hidden formalism and willingness to sacrifice authorship to totality, the theory of empathy also reinstates the right of the copy. Lipps's aesthetic psychologism proved remarkably resistant to any lingering old-European derision of art as mere appearance.

"Luxuriating in the infinitesimal"

No inquiry into the world of rhythm in the period between 1885 and 1914 can avoid evoking the work of Hugo Riemann, Europe's leading music theorist at the turn of the twentieth century and author of the most developed theory of musical rhythm of the time. Yet it is hard to reconcile the hegemony of Riemann's thought with the broader argument I have pursued in this chapter, that of rhythm being at the core of the modern crisis of listening.

295

For clearly, when it comes to the defenders of post-Wagnerian musical modernism, the name Hugo Riemann is not one that comes to mind. His sprawling oeuvre hardly if ever considers music written after Liszt and Wagner, and by the time Riemann broke ranks with his student Max Reger in 1907, he had forever severed his connections to the emergent musical avant-garde.

Yet Riemann's lifelong work on rhythm—framed by the seminal *Musikalische Dynamik und Agogik* (Musical Dynamics and Agogic Accents, 1884) and the no less ground-breaking *System der musikalischen Rhythmik und Metrik* (System of Musical Rhythm and Meter, 1903)—clearly exhibits some of the features of early twentieth-century modernism. Nobody sensed this more acutely than Nietzsche, possibly Riemann's sharpest critic. Riemann's views on rhythm, the philosopher alleged, were the sign of *décadence*, his preferred moniker for the inexorable march of modern society into the abyss. In two lengthy letters to the pianist, music theorist, and Riemann acolyte Carl Fuchs, Nietzsche spelled out the broader symptoms of this decay. There was, for instance, the "growing attention to the singular gesture of affect." Then there were "the histrionic art of shaping the moment as convincingly as possible" and the fact that "the part triumphed over the whole, phrase over melody, and the moment over time (and also *tempo*)." All these were signs of dissolution, "proof that life had withdrawn from the whole and is *luxuriating* in the infinitesimal."[58]

So it was with Riemann's famous *Phrasierungslehre* (Theory of Phrasing), the core of his work on rhythm. Although the idea behind the profusion of caesurae, crosses, and other signs with which Riemann and Fuchs had freighted their editions of the common repertoire (the so-called *Phrasierungsausgaben*), was to redeem the dignity of the single phrase from the iron rule of measure and meter, to Nietzsche's ears, the performance style that was meant to emerge from these "phrase markings" had an altogether more garish ring. Far from rescuing music's newfound "living" substance from the shackles of meter, these markings were actually the symptoms of decline. And instead of acting like some sort of glue preventing musical form from unraveling, all they revealed was the growing inability "to bridge *big* areas of relations rhythmically."[59]

The result was a change of perspective in music, a different kind of "optics": "The more the eye is focused on the single *rhythmic* form ('phrase'), the more myopic it becomes with regard to the broad, long, big forms.... This is happening everywhere, *not only* in the surfeit of rhythmical life in the infinitesimal—also our capacity for enjoyment is restricting itself more and more to the tender, *small*, sublime things...as a result of which one only creates such things."[60]

"Luxuriating" was more than a question of compositional practice then. It reflected a broader shift in perception and in the bodily basis of pleasure all told, not just in the act of looking and listening. What is more, it was also a relatively recent phenomenon that bore the traces of the reification of social relations in the fully developed capitalist world more broadly. To grasp the essential modernity of this reconfiguration—and, as Nietzsche sensed, objectification—of aural pleasure in Riemann's work on rhythm, it is useful to cast our net a little wider and trace Riemann's project of a "reform of the theory of rhythm" to Germany's intellectual and cultural landscape during the second half of the nineteenth century.[61]

Like many scholars of his generation, Riemann subscribed to what he called a "bottom-to-top" aesthetics. The phrase stemmed from Fechner's wildly popular writings on art and encapsulated the notion that at the heart of the aesthetic experience stands not ideas, as Kant and Hegel had taught, but sensation. To understand what a person sees or hears, one had to begin with that person's body. One had to take measure of his or her sensations of color, heat, and sound and, ultimately, register the feelings of pleasure or pain these have evoked. By attending to the bodily basis of ideas of beauty, by grounding aesthetic theory in the physiology of perception, Fechner's and Riemann's teacher Hermann Lotze hoped to turn aesthetics from a normative theory into an empirical science.

Riemann wholeheartedly subscribed to such ideas, convinced that before long scientific methods would bestow on musical aesthetics the status of an exact science. At the same time, he remained beholden to a tradition in which music represented the pinnacle of ideality, maintaining the closest relationship among the arts with the metaphysical realm. From early on in his career, Riemann had become attached to the idea of a "musical logic," as he called the quintessentially immaterial, purely music-immanent category shaping the aesthetic experience. In contrast to musical listening as a passive digestion of objective acoustic inputs advocated, or so he believed, by Helmholtz, Riemann stressed what he took to be the more active component of musical listening, arguing that it could be illuminated only psychologically, "from the nature of the perceiving mind."[62] As the core principle of a self-styled "natural science of music," "musical logic" thus found itself charged with providing the conceptual bracket within which a synthesis of inductive empirical science and deductive formal reasoning might be achieved.

From the outset, then, Riemann's work was marked by the unresolved conflict between music as an affair of the mind and music as a bodily matter. But while the former linkage simply tied the idea of a "musical logic" back to idealist and even rationalist thought, the music-body nexus rested on an entirely different theoretical foundation. This foundation may be less obvious than Riemann's professed debt to Rameau and Fichte, but it is not therefore any less normative. Thus, in addition to reinforcing music theory's status as a theory of transcendentally based representations of tones (*Tonvorstellungen*), rather than of bodily perceptions of pitch relations or sensations of tone (*Tonempfindungen*), as Helmholtz had called it, Riemann also enlarged this theory's scope so as to account for another, less easily discernible type of truth—an embodied truth, one might call it. It was not only that the aesthetic experience was seen as obeying a certain mental "logic" that lent it authenticity. The body that forms the enabling condition and repository of such an experience was

298

increasingly being conceptualized in normative terms. Such a body gained its truth as part of a field that, in Foucault's words, "is determined by the opposition between the normal and the pathological."[63]

The scientific paradigm defining this field during the nineteenth century was physiology, and the normal body constituted its secret logos. However, this normality was anything but a truth to be excavated from the bodily depths. It was first and foremost the product of various regimes (and technologies) of visibility and audibility, regimes whose own rules determined the outcome. The normal, healthy, functioning body is known to us through what we know of things external to it, such as other normal, functioning systems, scientific instruments, or systems of measurement.[64] The measure of normality was thus derived not from any holistic image, meaning, or idea of an entity called "Man" that is governed by intentionality, memory, or consciousness. Rather, normality was coming to be defined in terms of the quantifiable, individual performance (or lack of such performance) of each and every one of the body's constituent parts. After centuries during which it had been but the outer covering of an elusive interior called the soul, the space of the normal body now was a more dispersed type of space. Legs and knees, to name but one example, now occupied a more indistinct position on a continuum that stretched from the differential equations to which the Weber brothers had reduced the human walking apparatus in 1836, at one end, to a rather more pitiful construct or, to use Emil Du Bois-Reymond's inimitable expression, the "drunken town musician," at the other.[65] In other words, what counted as normal under such conditions was the outcome of the cultural and technological standards imposed by industrial society. It was the mirror image of the instrumental rationality that reduces everything—bodies, language, and sense organs—to mere isolated functions.

One understands what Nietzsche's aphorism about the proclivity toward the small "thing" hints at: why the only kind of listening experience available is a listening conforming to physiology's parameters of normality. The "decadent" or abnormal was less a deficiency than an error built into the system called "body" itself, one possibility among many in the grand scheme of life. Or as Nietzsche elsewhere put it, the value of all morbid states is "that they show us under a magnifying glass certain states that are normal—but not easily visible when normal."[66]

Two early texts by Riemann might help us understand the impact this sort of normative logic had on the study of rhythm: his dissertation, submitted in 1873 and later published under the title *Wie hören wir Musik?* (How Do We Listen to Music?) and the aforementioned *Musikalische Dynamik und Agogik*. Inspired by pianist Hans von Bülow's spectacular Beethoven interpretations, Riemann in these works boldly stood classicist theories of musical rhythm on their head. Unlike earlier scholars such as Moritz Hauptmann and Rudolph Westphal, who had insisted on an abstract metric system as the a priori of all rhythmic phenomena, Riemann saw musical rhythm as functioning independently of any given poetic meter. Instead, he saw meter as closely intertwined with what he called the "concrete musical content" or, resurrecting a long-forgotten term, the motif. In other words, the time-honored difference between meter and rhythm as discrete levels of temporal organization to be filled with specific thematic content was replaced with a model in which rhythm itself was the content, figured as a series of motifs or singular expressive gestures. The proper purview of a theory of rhythm hence was the structure of motifs, whereas meter was demoted to a mere handmaiden responsible for organizing their sequencing. Thus freed from the domination of abstract meters, rhythm ceased to be the Cinderella of music theory and, along with harmony and melody, now constituted music's very essence.

Though no small feat, the emancipation of rhythm from meter and language—and thus, in a way, the motivic cell's rise as the pivot of music(ologic)al knowledge—also posed its own set of auditory problems, affecting listeners' actual ability to listen to such minute motivic structures. Comparing the visitor to the melody, one of its most prominent and technically advanced features, in reality is "a veritable polyp." It is a kind of "counterfeit" that lends an appearance of continuity to what is essentially little more than a series of melodic fragments, gestures, and formulas.[69] Yet surprisingly, there was no protection against this fraudulent hijacking of totality, no escape from music's complicity with the "physiological contradiction," as Nietzsche adumbrates the coexistence in modern bodies of "values, words, formulas, moralities of opposite descent."[70] No recourse was to be had in a return to presumably more wholesome forms. Rhythmic fragmentation was *the* modern condition. It was "the only track *which still exists.*"[71]

The subtlety of Nietzsche's antimodernism was apparently lost on Riemann. Emboldened, as he saw it, by Nietzsche's "word of redemption" (in *The Case of Wagner*, the philosopher had finally, if half-sardonically, come around to Riemann's view that the musical phrase is indeed the particular gesture of musical affect), he clung all the more stubbornly to the belief that the eight-bar period is the "normative fundamental principle," condemning any attempt to break free from this norm as just plain "monstrous."[72]

That characterization should give us pause. Might it suggest a set of deeper affinities between Riemann's conservative and Nietzsche's more overly progressive stance than is suggested by the alarmist rhetoric of *décadence*? Theodor W. Adorno has rightly identified Wagner's deployment of formal devices such as leitmotif and infinite melody as "phantasmagoria," a principle that permeates Wagner's entire aesthetic. No less seminal than the composer's other innovations (the darkened theater, the orchestra pit, among others), leitmotifs and infinite melody bear the imprint of the industrial mode of production and of the atomization it requires in the name of the totality. "It is not just the nullity of the individual that has such dire implications for the Wagnerian totality, but rather that the atom, the descriptive motif, must always put in an appearance for the sake of characterization, as if it were something, a claim it cannot always satisfy. In this way the themes and motivs join forces in a sort of pseudo-history."[73] Thus, totality reveals itself as mere illusion (*Schein*) — as contradiction raised to the level of the absolute.

Meanwhile, the singular is not any less problematic. Although the obsession with large-scale form shields the smallest unit from the petit-bourgeois listener's desire for property, its fragmented nature is nonetheless subservient to the larger whole. Since "the listener's memory is denied any small-scale musical unit to latch on to, this has the effect of harnessing him all the more inexorably within the total effect."[74]

Thus, the true monstrosity sensed by Riemann and Nietzsche does not reside in any isolated feature, such as the alleged disintegration into the atomic (which Nietzsche diagnosed with the help of ears that, according to Adorno, were still those of the Biedermeier). It is the phantasmagoric quid pro quo of small and large, the compulsion of late-bourgeois consciousness under which "the individual insists the more emphatically on his own importance, the more specious and impotent he has become in reality."[75] That is why Riemann's and Nietzsche's attacks on "modern" music's decadence ultimately run into a void. But it is also why Riemann's horror of modern musical deformity and Nietzsche's acceptance of the unavoidability of the small-scale form brought them even more firmly under the spell of this monstrously distorted subject-object relationship.

This is perhaps most glaringly illustrated in the way both authors invoke rhythm as the central category in the attempt at a new synthesis. Riemann's entire theory rests on the Romantic notion that art is just another form of nature and therefore, like nature, is subject to the same rhythms of becoming and vanishing. A motif, for instance, is an "element of movement" (*Bewegungselement*), an "organism endowed with a strange vital force."[76] Likewise, the agents thrusting the motifs forward on their form-shaping trajectory through time are those imputed by the listener to the rhythmic structure, not any properties inherent in the work as such. Yet by thus granting the ear a pivotal role, Riemann did not conceive of listening as a form of individuation.

Essentially occurring in accordance with music's foundation in the laws of nature, such listening for him reflected a more diffuse anthropocentrism prevalent in nineteenth-century science and culture. Like Wundt's pyschophysics Riemann's theory was one of two inner worlds, a physiological world of causalities and, parallel to it, a world of subjective experience. Though separate, both worlds were to be harmonized through the consciousness that only the autonomous subject possesses.

Nietzsche, too, considered rhythm to be at the heart of the reinvention of the individual. But unlike Riemann, he did not see such a rhythmic reconfiguration of the subject as a matter of consciousness, instead mocking the music theorist's "whole endeavor" as the thinly veiled attempt "to strengthen and recapture the total rhythmic sense." Having renounced the idea of an indivisible core of the subject and having advocated a notion of the individual as a contest of opposing forces, bodily drives, and sensory perceptions, the philosopher had become wary of attempts to define the self within the more conventional parameters of culture and language. The higher selfhood or Overman that he envisaged was one that (re)formed itself according to its own rhythms, and not to those of the "grammatical habit"—that is, words, logos, and reflection. It was a self that listened and danced more than it thought itself as an I.[77] Its pulses and rhythms did not originate in the brain, but from within the solitary space of Zarathustra's self-empowerment and self-configuration.

Delaying

In Ernst Mach's (unpublished) diaries, there is a little diagram of the interaction of the eyes and ears, the nerves and the brain (see figure 7.1). With its multiple neural pathways originating in the ear (*Ohr*) and eye (*Auge*) and thence looping through areas such as "concept" (*Begriff*) and "sonic image" (*Lautbild*), the diagram more than aptly illustrates Mach's monist belief that physics, physiology, and psychology are part of a single field of knowledge in which "reality" is but a conglomeration of "sensational

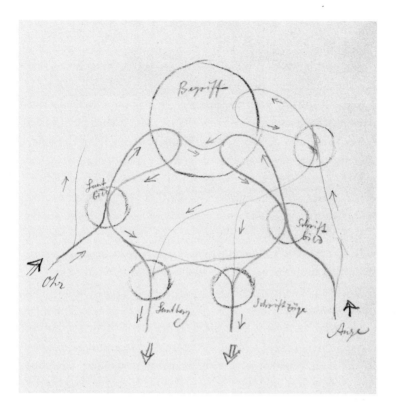

Figure 7.1. Ernst Mach, *Skizze "Sinnesempfindungen."* Archiv des DM, NL 174/486 (courtesy of Foto Deutsches Museum). Mach was one of the first theorists to embrace the musical component of Helmholtz's physiological acoustics. In later years, as he worked on his famous *The Analysis of Sensations* (1886), he returned to issues of auditory perception. The diagram Sinnesempfindungen (sensory perceptions) most likely stems from this period. It is published here for the first time.

elements" and the "mysterious entity" called ego, consequently, is "unsavable."[78]

The notion Mach is trying to advance in the diagram is that consciousness is not of a substantive nature, but a mere formal property resulting from disturbance. Just as an external force hindering the steady rotation of a chain or the even flow of water creates a moment of pause, consciousness arises from the delay caused in such movements and from the opportunity for the formation during such moments of lull of associations or group-ings of "elements"—in short, of forms. The peculiar point about this notion of consciousness is that Mach, on one level, seems to have been well aware of the fact that the "go slow" (or, for that matter, Freud's *Zauderrhythmus*) inherent in the network of neural detours depicted in his little diagram is vital for main-taining even the most minimal sense of reality and thus also for self-preservation.

But the drawing also conveys a deeper sense of the vacillation between the notion of consciousness as a stable foundation of the self and an infatuation with ego-dissolving immediacy and con-ceptless apperception. The diagram, one might say, represents the acoustic unconscious, and it thus also reflects a fascination with the ecstasy of the second, the rapture of pure sensation, and the syncope as the basis for a new vitality beyond the stodgy dualism of body and mind.[79]

1930. It was the deeply unsettling impact of radio and film (both of which had come into their own during the 1920s) on traditional patterns of perception that provided much of the critical impetus to the thinkers of the emerging Frankfurt School. The new mass media, Walter Benjamin, Siegfried Kracauer, and Theodor W. Adorno held, are anything but neutral transmitters functioning independently of the social constraints under which they operate. Nor do radio and film leave the human senses unaffected. As an integral part of the capitalist mode of production, media technology inscribes itself deep into the human sensorium, increasingly defining the subject in terms of its compatibility with the standards set by such technology. "The way in which human perception is organized—the medium in which it occurs—is conditioned not only by nature but by history," Benjamin wrote in 1936.[3] Key in this intermingling of cultural and sensorial transformation, of social history and natural history, and thus also at the heart of some of Benjamin's and Adorno's most influential contributions, was the problem of distraction. It is in film, Benjamin declared, for instance, that a reception that was increasingly becoming dominated by distraction or, as he called it, "reception in distraction," had found its *true training ground*.[4] Radio, Adorno meanwhile observed, was a key factor leading to what, in a famous article of 1938, he called the "regression of listening."[5]

The influence of Frankfurt School theory on the study of cinema, radio, the arts, and, more recently, of "auditory culture" has been pervasive, of course.[6] But the rise to prominence and almost total hegemony today of Benjamin's and especially Adorno's work has also obscured that of another critic of the modern conditioning of the ear as formidable as Adorno and Benjamin: Günther Anders. Philosopher no less than antinuclear activist and novelist, as well as moralist, Günther Anders (1902–1992) was considered during his lifetime to be one of the most influential thinkers of the twentieth century. Yet despite a modest renaissance of interest in his work in recent years and with the exception perhaps of the two-volume critique of (nuclear) technology *Die Antiquiertheit des Menschen* (The Obsoleteness of Man), many facets of Anders's enormously productive life now seem forgotten.[7] For instance, it is a little-known fact that apart from being the son of the psychologist William Stern, whom we met earlier, Anders had studied under such luminaries as Edmund Husserl and Martin Heidegger, collaborated with (and for a brief period, after she broke up with Heidegger, was even married to) Hannah Arendt, and inspired Jean-Paul Sartre to one of the core ideas of existential philosophy. But perhaps the least-known aspect of Anders's central position in twentieth-century intellectual life is as a philosopher of music and the author of *Philosophische Untersuchungen über musikalische Situationen* (Philosophical Inquiries into Musical Situations). Written between 1929 and 1930, *Philosophische Untersuchungen* remains to be discovered as the only significant counterproject to Adorno's critical theory of music between the two world wars and, beyond this, as the most compelling attempt at rethinking musical listening since Descartes.[8]

Of profound theoretical ambition and considerable length (over two hundred pages), *Philosophische Untersuchungen* has never been published, largely, it appears, because Adorno had recommended that the University of Frankfurt reject Anders's bid to submit the work as a *Habilitationsschrift*. The text's musicological basis was "slim," and its overall orientation was "ahistorical," the newly appointed *Privatdozent* argued. But above all it was what he took to be the intellectual affinity between *Philosophische Untersuchungen* and Heidegger's hugely successful *Sein und Zeit* (Being and Time, published the year before) that irked Adorno.[9]

The latter charge, especially, ought to be taken with a grain of salt. The parallels that Adorno perceived between Anders's text and Heidegger's prose are far less prominent than those between *Sein und Zeit* and Adorno's own early work, such as the essay "Schubert" that first appeared in 1928 and is considered as a milestone in the emergence of a new critical *écriture* pioneered by Walter Benjamin and Adorno.[10] On closer inspection, however, the essay's oft-noted singularity and boldness of composition

turn out to owe much more to Heidegger than did Anders's so-
called "ahistorical" orientation. For instance, apart from a host of
phrases such as "authentically ontological" or the untranslatable
seinsgewaltig, which Adorno replaced with seemingly less laden
terms such as "truly legitimate" or "command of the harmonic
principle" in the second edition of the essay in *Moments musicaux*,
one of the essential features of Adorno's essay is that its very
structure "reenacts what it recognizes in Schubert's music."[11]
Because Adorno believed to have found the secret of Schubert's
music in juxtaposition, repetition, and a deeply ingrained distrust
of Romantic organicism, much of the essay accordingly must be
read or, better perhaps, experienced performatively as a montage
of images and thought fragments without a center or frame. Much
the same can of course be said of *Sein und Zeit*. Heidegger's clunky
neologisms are not the private quirk of a man beholden to archaic
language. Rather, such coinages and the book's larger drift break
up the ordered subject-object relationship of classical metaphysics
by replicating the very jagged course that *Dasein* takes on its path
toward death.

Another major feature of Adorno's essay is the concept of
music as landscape. "Schubert" opens with a grandiose mountain
panorama in which Adorno likens the fissured scenery of peaks,
craters, and lava to the absence in Schubert's music of the "deceptive human totality."[12] Standing in stark contrast to hermeneutic
musicology's cozy world of trout, linden trees, and millwheels,
the bleak setting illustrates Adorno's use of the chthonic and
inorganic as a means of disrupting idealist notions of subjectivity
and intention. Again, much the same may be said of Heidegger's
work, such as his later readings of Hölderlin's poems, in which the
existentialist philosopher does not evince the slightest interest in
either the poet's subjective disposition or the structure and style
or other objective features of these poems. Rather, like Adorno,
his primary focus is on the imbrications of the subjective and
objective and especially on his own hearing of Hölderlin's verse
as a thinking of the "between" or "fiction" (*Dichtung*). And just as

the truth of Schubert's music does not reside in its relationship to the subjectivity of either the composer or the listener, Heidegger, too, sees the essence of *Dichtung* not in an intentional act, but in what he calls the *Stiftung*, or bequest of truth.

And finally, Adorno shares with Heidegger the sense of an irrevocably shattered subjective autonomy, as well as a disintegrating compositional unity in Schubert's and Hölderlin's works. Note, for example, the emphasis on death and decay. Far from being mere "themes" or objects to be represented, death is music's inner formal law, no less than Being's as it tends toward death.

Anders's *Philosophische Untersuchungen* differs fundamentally from either Adorno's or Heidegger's concerns. Unlike the former, it is not formal experiment or self-reflexivity, let alone empathy with music that he is after. And in contrast to the latter, Anders seems remarkably indifferent both to the work's formal qualities and to what Adorno liked to call its "truth content." Anders's project, I claim, constitutes nothing less than the end of the concept of the resonant ego. For centuries, scores of illuminati, savants, *philosophes*, and *Naturphilosophen* had taken resonance as more than just the physiological mechanism responsible for audition. Resonance was inextricably linked with presence — the presence of an idea, emotion, or object — and as such, it was key to a definition of reason as the key vehicle of modern self-fashioning. In fact, it was not the interplay of consciousness and aesthetic experience so fundamental to the nineteenth-century German philosophical tradition that defined the bourgeois subject, but reasonance, the strange coupling of reason and resonance that had enthralled even the most stubborn champions of the cogito, from Descartes to Nietzsche.

And so, when Anders embarked on his *Philosophische Untersuchungen* it was first and foremost the issue of reasonance that commanded his attention. It was a combination of the two questions that Hannah Arendt and Peter Sloterdijk would pose decades later that captivated him: Where are we when we think, and where are we when we listen to music? His answer, vaguely reminiscent of the philosophical schooling he had received in Freiburg, is perplexingly simple: When listening to music we are *out* of the world and *in* music.[13] Yet the plain elegance, or perhaps the sheer Romanticism of this hypothesis should not deceive us. As we will see below, the concept of listening as "being in music" takes the author of *Philosophische Untersuchungen* through a dense series of ruminations in which listening emerges as the key vehicle allowing Anders to dismantle the central position in modern Western thought of the Cartesian *fundamentum inconcussum*. And while he may well be said to have shared this approach with the Romantics, or with Heidegger, for that matter, Anders differs from Heinse, Ritter, Lipps, and Heidegger in combining, in a second step, the ontological, anti-Cartesian line of his argument with an equally powerful critique of resonance as the basis for the aesthetic experience and, indeed, for existence all told.

Eddies, Visionary Hearing, and the "Hear-Stripe"

Surveying the acoustic landscape of Germany between the two world wars, one cannot but wonder about the fact that the same period that saw the composition of Anders's *Philosophische Unter-suchungen*, the publication of Adorno's "Schubert," and Heidegger's *Sein und Zeit*—in other words, the years between 1928 and 1930—also coincides with the decline of resonance as the centerpiece of modern theories of hearing. It was in 1928 that the renowned *Physikalische Zeitschrift* published an article by a young communications expert named Georg von Békésy entitled "Zur Theorie des Hörens: Die Schwingungsform der Basilarmembran" (Toward the Theory of Hearing: The Pattern of Vibrations of the Basilar Membrane). Although barely twenty pages long, the article contained the first major critique of resonance-based theories of hearing as they had been in force since Joseph-Guignard Duverney and Hermann von Helmholtz.[14]

In essence, Békésy's theory of hearing is a "place" theory.[15] Like Helmholtz more than half a century earlier, Békésy presupposes the perception of pitch to be spatially distributed over the length of the basilar membrane. Yet in contrast to Helmholtz's theory, Békésy's was also a "nonresonance" or "wave theory," because the spatial distribution of pitches in the cochlea is said to be the result of a progressively moving wave of displacement on the basilar membrane, and not of the sympathetic resonance of hair cells. More to the point, the wavelike motion of the basilar membrane traveling from the lower end of the membrane — the end near the oval window — to its apex continually varies its amplitude along the way. The point at which this movement reaches a maximum thus depends on the wave frequency: Higher tones with shorter wavelengths reach their maximum in the basal part, low tones toward the apex. To be sure, this distribution of pitch location coincides with Helmholtz' findings, but it also differs from them because of the considerable variations in phase relations between the stapes and various cochlear structures, such as the tectorial membrane, the organ of Corti, and Reissner's membrane, all of which also vibrate. As Békésy found, while in low tones the structures located near the apex move in phase with the stapes, higher frequencies cause the phase of the apical structures to lag behind the stapes, thus casting doubt on Helmholtz's model of tuned resonators.

Even so, it remained unclear how pitch location could be specific enough if the source of the stimulation is not restricted to the crest of the wave, but is dispersed over the entire length of the wave. Here Békésy introduced two concepts: the restrictive action of what he called "eddies" and a "law of contrast." Eddies are vortexlike movements that occur in both scalae above and below the place where the amplitude of the travelling wave was at its maximum (figure 8.1). Békésy believed these eddies, which occur independently of various mechanical disturbances to the overall basilar structure, to be one of the factors restricting the impact of wave motion by exerting steady pressure on a smaller section of the membrane and hair cells nearby.

The law of contrast, for its part, increases the precision of pitch location even further. Just as a gradual increase in light

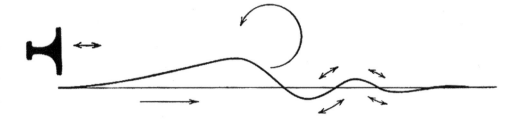

Figure 8.1. Georg von Békésy, "Eddies," *Zur Theorie des Hörens: Die Schwingungsform der Basilarmembran*, fig. 21.

intensity is experienced by the eye as two clearly separated stimuli, Békésy argued, our ability to differentiate between two tonal frequencies rests on the fact that the stimulation of the membrane reaches a peak at the crest of the wave. And even though adjacent sections of the membrane also are affected by the wave motion, compared with the maximum amplitude, the intensity of the corresponding sensation falls off sharply.[16]

Georg von Békésy did not share the broader philosophical and musical ambitions of a Perrault or Helmholtz, even though he was a consummate art collector who liked to ponder the similarities between Persian miniature painting, Renaissance woodcuts, and the role of hazard and fortune in scientific research.[17] But there can be no doubt that the dwindling authority of Helmholtzian resonance theory and the blow that Békésy's findings dealt to the trope of the resonant self were part of a broader cultural trend toward what Martin Jay has called the "denigration of vision" and a quest for a more privileged role for hearing in twentieth-century thought.[18]

The development of German philosophy after World War I may serve as an example of this trend. Prior to the war, the discipline had been in the throes of the sterile abstractions of neo-Kantian doctrine, but when the war was lost and the imperial regime collapsed, it was not only the "long" nineteenth century that came to a close. Gone, too, was its stockpile of metaphysical verities, worldviews, and truth games. Indeed, philosophy as a whole had fallen into crisis. Shrinking in horror from the massive mutilation a technology grounded in the ocular phantasm of Cartesian rationalism had inflicted on the subject, many intellectuals held that the way out of the crisis would crucially depend on regaining the intermingling of subject and object repressed in all post-Cartesian traditions. Drawing on the phenomenology of Edmund Husserl, thinkers as varied as Oswald Spengler, Helmuth Plessner, Ernst Bloch, and Martin Heidegger rediscovered our complex, sensory entanglement with the world and the tenuous position of the subject within it. A different kind of aural sensibility, or, as Bloch called it in his *Philosophie der Musik* (Essays on the Philosophy of Music) of 1918, a "visionary hearing" (*Hellhören*), became the pivot around which a new understanding of this subject was to form.[19]

It would be an understatement to think that Anders's early work was a mere reflection of this new preoccupation with the ear. Unlike other critics of modernity, such as Georg Simmel, who attributed the "alienation" of modern society to a combination of overcrowding, rising noise levels, and mass neurasthenia in Europe's exploding industrial centers, it was Anders who first linked the feeling of existential forlornness so widespread after World War I to a more fundamental form of disturbance: the loss of echo.[20] In an early essay on Rainer Maria Rilke's *Duineser Elegien* (Duino Elegies) coauthored with Hannah Arendt, Anders explored the linkages between this echolessness and the individual's dwindling capacity for self-reflection.[21] In Rilke's poems, the two authors argue, the hopeless situation of Man having lost the world manifests itself in a kind of "word compulsion without answer"—in a darkness and abruptness of style that forsakes any pretensions to form, intelligibility, and indeed to being heard at all.[22] All that is left to do for such poetry, Anders and Arendt go on to suggest, is to invoke a certain *Inständigkeit* or "urgency" of listening. Rilke conceived of such urgent listening as

a quasi-religious act, as a "being in hearing" that achieves fulfillment in itself as a mode of being and that, if it needs an object at
all, finds it in the "wafting between the ranks," in the gaps and
ruins left behind by the disappearing object world.[23]

Anders later distanced himself from this reading, blaming it
on what he called the "decidedly religious" position Arendt had
adopted in her dissertation on Augustine completed under Karl
Jaspers the year before.[24] And even though the conceptual lineage
linking Augustine to Arendt and Anders may seem far-fetched,
it is perfectly in keeping with the impact the Christian saint had
on the early Heidegger and the intellectual climate of the inter-
war generation generally. In fact, Augustine's famous dichotomy
between *cantus* (song) and *res quae canitur* (that about which you
sing) had been a major component of an argument Anders had
advanced several years earlier about what he called the phenomenology of hearkening.[25]

At the heart of this phenomenology is a critical reflection on
the mediation of the subject-object relationship through what
Anders calls "authentic listening." What would an authentic mode
of listening be like that is adequate to *The Art of the Fugue*, he
wonders. How does one listen to Debussy? Is an authentic listening experience possible at all? Questions like these, thus Anders's
hypothesis, cannot be negotiated on the basis of conventional
dichotomies such as between attentive and inattentive modes
of listening or, as Augustine's conceptual pair implies, between
music's sensory dimension and its ideational content. Instead, he
goes on to argue, there are two kinds of aural stance: a joining
in (*Mitmachen*) with the musical structure, on the one hand, and
a passive kind of listening or being with (*Mitsein*) the music, on
the other. The latter stance relates to its object by becoming itself
a state or condition and, as such, it does not so much grasp an
object as it is a "Zustand zum Gegenstand," a disposition toward
an object.[26] Even the most cursory analysis of the chord shifts in
the first couple of bars of the overture to Debussy's opera *Pel-
léas et Mélisande*, for instance, will (or, rather, should) reveal that

the hovering, almost stationary character of this music cannot be grasped from an active listening stance. Because here "the sense of unity in the object is itself the unity of a state," a listening that is more commensurate with Debussy's music is one that disavows the analytic Kantian subject.[27] By drifting in and out of various states of inactivity, such listening does not so much open up what it hears to the subject as it remains itself in a state of "openness" (*Aufgeschlossenheit*) or "inactive attention" (*zuständliche Aufmerksamkeit*).[28]

Another example of the growing emphasis on hearing during the period following World War I is a new attentiveness to the "listener" within the burgeoning field of musicology. Having long been neglected by musicology's twin fixations on authorial intent and Riemann's "musical logic," listening after 1918 came to be construed as the missing link in the musical experience, an experience whose integrity was increasingly coming under pressure from two interrelated sources. The first was the rise of mass-produced popular music. Perceived as a threat to the hegemony of the concert tradition and to a form of listening based in what the influential Viennese critic Eduard Hanslick had called "unflagging attendance and keenest vigilance," popular music was met with a mixture of outright derision, studied avoidance, and carefully crafted attempts to adapt elite aural sensibilities to the changed acoustic landscape by grounding them in "human nature."[29]

Representative of the latter trend, for instance, is a series of articles by Helmuth Plessner in which the founder of philosophical anthropology sought to provide alternatives to the prevailing dualism between formalism and hermeneutics by shifting the focus to musical listening as a time machine.[30] Rather than merely producing a mental image of a musical work, Plessner argued, listening mediates between the time of music and the time of consciousness. Of course, whether the temporal unity of such consciousness, let alone the metaphysical concept of consciousness itself, might have to be called in question remained outside of Plessner's purview.

Another example is Heinrich Besseler's inaugural lecture delivered in 1925 after having studied with Heidegger.[31] On the surface, Besseler's rationale in this text was to elaborate a typology of listening in which certain "phases" of listening corresponded to major stylistic periods, a topic he explored more fully in the late 1950s in *Das musikalische Hören der Neuzeit*.[32] At a deeper level, however, Besseler (who would eventually join the Nazi party) pursued a much more questionable agenda. Troubled by the disintegration of the classical canon and the "intrusion," as he called it, of the "new rhythms and sounds of the nigger jazz band," he searched for ways to stabilize the post–World War I subject traumatized by radical transformation and "relativism" by anchoring musical listening in new, purportedly more participatory forms of experience centered on, in Besseler's formulation, "associative" (*umgangsmäßig*) music or "use music."[33] Unlike the solo concert, which is predicated on a separation between the virtuoso performer and a passive, atomized audience, such use music is sustained by the rhythm of everyday life. It requires a listening stance hovering between practical, collective involvement and a "listening devotion" that draws the listener into the "free-floating world of the aesthetic."[34] In this way, Besseler hoped, musical listening might rise above the modern "dissension of art and *Dasein* and thus [contribute] to a more authentic life whose concentrated power might sustain music in everyday life."[35]

The second and most important source of the destabilization of bourgeois listening habits was the introduction of radio broadcasting in 1923. As will be evident from even the most cursory review of the contemporary literature, radio was understood as having enormous repercussions on how listeners were supposed to relate to the new technology and, above all, to themselves as part of new collectivities determined by class, race, gender, and national identity.[36] The initial experience of the new medium was a profoundly unsettling one, engendering a torrent of lament over radio's allegedly flagrant debasement of the classical canon and the degeneration of bourgeois listening etiquette following in its wake. Radio, "Mozart" in Hermann Hesse's *Steppenwolf* (1928) declares, for instance, "projects the most lovely music without regard into the most impossible places," stripping it of "sensuous beauty, spoils and scratches and beslimes it and yet cannot altogether destroy its spirit."[37]

"Mozart's" anxiety over the dislocation of music was shared by Anders, at least in part. In an article entitled "Spuk und Radio" (Spooks and Radio), published in 1930 in the music journal *Anbruch* (edited at the time by Adorno), Anders's concern is not with music's "spirit" or the supposed vilification of beauty, but with a series of uncanny effects produced by radio's ubiquity.[38] Music, Anders begins somewhat paradoxically, is essentially "spaceless"; it "is nowhere and everywhere it is heard." Yet this fundamental character is altered as soon as music is transmitted over the airwaves and "assumes a definite relation to space."[39] Thus, when one hears a piece of music being played over the radio, first in one room and then, after leaving the room, in another and yet another, the piece becomes "localized." Another aspect of radio's ubiquity is the shock that ensues from the doppelgängerlike "plurality of musics" that deny to the heard piece what Walter Benjamin would soon call "aura": the uniqueness of the *hic et nunc*. And, finally, radio's spookiness is heightened by the rivalry between each of these "musics" claiming to be the original piece. Hence, experiencing such music by fits and starts, as it were, provokes a drama of Promethean dimensions. In trying to mitigate the shock of technology playing cat and mouse with him, the listener can either ignore the voices coming from the screen or the radio or can seek to identify with such soulless, prosthetic tools and thus become inhuman himself.

Clearly, Anders here not only rises above the moral panic of Hesse's text, but casts aside the more mystic terms that had led him to interpret Rilke's *Duineser Elegien* as signs of an "existential" loss of echo. Instead, Anders shifts the emphasis from a lament over some ill-defined, all-out hearing loss to a different, more specific kind of danger. The threat looming over radio listeners, he seems to suggest, is the possibility of a complete loss of self.

Adorno would later subject Anders's piece to a benevolent, if incisive critique. In several texts dating from his brief tenure at the Princeton Radio Research Project, in which he expanded on his famous 1938 article "On the Fetish-Character in Music and the Regression of Listening," he takes issue with Anders's claim that music is essentially "spaceless" and is noticed in terms of space only when it becomes ubiquitous, when the same piece of music pours out of the window of different houses.[40] This, Adorno objects, would imply that radio in a private room is somehow devoid of space. But even though this assertion would be hard to maintain, might there be anything to the reverse notion that radio music in the bourgeois home has the character of "hereness? "[41] Drawing on Benjamin's famous essay "The Work of Art in the Age of Its Technological Reproducibility," which had appeared in 1936, Adorno refutes this myth so central to radio's impact. The haunting character of radio music, he argues, is not a consequence of different listening experiences somehow being existentially at odds with each other, but of an ideology that claims such music to be "here and now"—"which, at the same time, is disclaimed by technical reproduction."[42]

Furthermore, radio music always seems to be coming from a distant place. The spatial distance between the living room and the studio or the concert hall is never fully bridged, thus lending radio sound a "new and very specific space relation," removing music even further from the direct experience of the *hic et nunc*.[43] Radio music, Adorno went on to suggest, coining one of the most intriguing phrases in his analysis, is heard as though it came from a *Hörstreifen* or "hear-stripe." Its effect is that of a kind of acoustic celluloid onto which the music has been printed, like the images on a film strip.[44] Physiologically, this flattening of the aural experience into the two-dimensionality of an image may well have been owed to early radio's rudimentary technology, Adorno concedes. The narrow spectrum of overtones and the monaural depthlessness made music sound like an echo of something that has first been projected to a kind of acoustic rear-view mirror before it reaches the listener. But, Adorno concludes his pessimistic analysis, even as technology may improve over time and the initial "shock" diagnosed by Anders may subside, the hear-stripe nevertheless has a lasting psychological effect. Music, concert music no less than popular music, becomes reified, thus affecting the very autonomy that distinguishes music from the other arts.

Being in Music

So where are we when we hear? From Claude Perrault and Johann Wilhelm Ritter through to Johannes Müller, the answer has been an emphatic "We are with us." For the past three hundred years, resonance has figured as one of the key elements in modern concepts of personhood, equally foundational and just as troubled as modernity's other bastion, reason. Musical listening, too, during the same period, has been understood to be fundamentally about ourselves and how our sense of self is never given, rarely stable, and always subject to rational scrutiny. However transcendentally removed, visceral, or emotionally touching the content of a piece of music, for listeners from Claude-Nicolas Le Cat to Wilhelm Heinse to Roland Barthes, it is always this reasoning self that has been at the core of the listening experience. So what does it mean when Anders, in a blatant reversal of the idea of resonance, declares listening to be "being in music?" And why is Anders interested in musical "situations," rather than, like any self-respecting neo-Kantian or hermeneutic philosopher of music of his time, in music as the sensuous embodiment of an idea or meaning? Likewise, why is there such little attention being given to the "subject" behind the work?

The Heideggerian ring of the term "being in music" should not deceive us. While the author of *Sein und Zeit* undoubtedly stood godfather to many of Anders's coinages, the terminological debt cannot gloss over the fact that the main source for Anders's

Philosophische Untersuchungen lies elsewhere: in two highly original lectures given to the Kant Society in 1929 and published
several years later in French translations (by Emmanuel Levinas,
among others) on what he called "Man's a posteriori."[45] Man,
according to Anders's bleak premise, suffers from an ontological
defect. Unlike animals, which inhabit specific worlds exclusive
to their respective species, "Man" cannot call any particular
part of the world his.[46] More *dividuum* than *individuum*, his is an
"ontological difference," an a priori separation from the world.
But while this deficit, this lack of a specific relationship to the
world, is the only specificity distinguishing Man from other
beings, it is also the condition of his freedom. Lacking his own
ecological niche, Man is not only an artificial being capable of
creating his own world, he is also the only being that *must* create
a world because none is already at hand. And so Man is caught
in a dilemma, which Anders describes as "distanced inherence."
(*inhérence distancée*).[47] As natural beings, humans are quite obviously part of the world, but as unfixed (*unfestgestellte*) beings,
they are also excluded from the world. This is the reason why for
Anders freedom is not achieved, as in the classical subject theories
of German idealism, but endured.

There are several consequences of this "pathology of freedom." The first is what Anders calls the "shock of contingency"
(*choc du contingent*). I experience myself as someone, as a particular I. But because as an unfixed being I could also be any other
way, the particular I that I am is anything but inevitable: It is
contingent, and therefore I am shocked.[48] Another consequence
is that Man's entire relationship to the world, too, becomes a
mere aftereffect, an a posteriori. Because the only a priori is the
absence of any a priori, the forms in which Man creates the world
can only arise *après coup*, and not, as in Kant's categories of space
and time, a priori. What we call experience—and what to Kant
was possible only on the basis of the a priori of time and space—in
Anders's view is part of prior distanced inherence. Our exclusion
from the world is the reason why we need experience in the first

place, but the same experience also enables us to overcome the distance from the world. "The a posteriori is an a priori characteristic of Man; the element of posteriority inherent in the a posteriori experience is a priori included in the essence of Man."[49]

To illustrate the interbraiding of distance-induced freedom and distance-reducing experience, Anders chooses an example from the realm of visual perception, one to which he would return time and again in his critique of technology.[50] Vision, he claims, is a model of human experience sui generis, because it is through vision that we overcome distance without merging with the seen object. But at the same time, we may step back from the object and direct our attention to another object, thus ending up in the same situation of pathological freedom that started the cycle of distanced inherence in the first place.

The parallels with William Stern's concept of the individual as an "asymptote" of knowledge are of course palpable here. And so, too, do the two models of human self-fashioning that Anders identifies as responses to the shock of contingency recall his father's concept of representation types. The first of these models is the "nihilist."[51] Faced with his own randomness and unable to identify with himself, the nihilist is ashamed of himself. But to cope with this shame, the nihilist finds a compromise: If he cannot be part of the world, he at least wants to have it. In short, the nihilist is in constant pursuit of power. The second model is what Anders calls "historical Man."[52] Although he, too, is threatened with contingency, historical Man differs from the nihilist in that he mitigates the shock of contingency by maintaining a sense of continuity with his former self, the I of the previous day. Historical Man creates the illusion of a past by incorporating everything that happens to come his way into what he calls his "life." The most advanced philosophical models for this sort of identity formation, according to Anders, are Hegel's concept of history as the progression and coming to itself of Spirit and Marx's parallel notion of the history of class struggles leading to the disappearance of alienated labor. Yet unlike these teleologically oriented types of anthropology, which see history as the realization of Man's destiny as a free being, Anders' historical Man is caught in a paradox: He needs history precisely because there is no teleology. Likewise, social and cultural forms do not so much lead Man toward his true destiny as they provide respite from the pressures of self-identification.

Art is no exception to this. While neither of the two early texts addresses this question directly, Anders in the early 1940s outlined a "theory of needs" in which he insisted that, in contrast to animals, Man can never satisfy all his needs. His artificiality forces him to produce the means for satisfying these needs himself. Art is one such means, as artificial as Man himself.[53] In its final consequence, and as Max Horkheimer and Adorno were quick to point out, Anders's concept of art, like his antiteleological theory of historical Man generally, denies art any role in redeeming Man from the real situation of unfreedom into which he has placed himself under capitalism. And indeed, "cultural values," in Anders's view, are no more tools of class rule than art is a refuge for utopian ideas. Art is simply a compromise that is reached when competing factions under pressure from a higher authority need to accept each other's cultural traditions as "valuable." In short, "cultural value is neutralized power." (A few years later, after Auschwitz and Hiroshima had altered his career forever, the idea of art as a mere "need" born from Man's "passive freedom" and as removed from the struggles of daily life would prompt Anders to join Adorno in denouncing as a "fashion event" and as neutralizing the "unthinkable" works such as Arnold Schoenberg's *Survivor from Warsaw* or Luigi Nono's *Sul ponte di Hiroshima*, the latter being set to a poem from Anders's own pen, no less.[54])

As uncompromising as Anders's axiom of the pathology of freedom and the theory of needs are, *Philosophische Untersuchungen* strikes a much more conciliatory, even metaphysical note. Whereas in the Kant lectures the shock of contingency can be compensated for only through nihilism and history, and art and culture in turn become neutralized, in the unpublished *Habilita-tionsschrift*, Anders seems to grant music altogether more excep-tional powers. There is no mention of music being an a posteriori artifact or "need." In contrast to the claim put forward much later, in *Die Antiquiertheit des Menschen*, that every minute of music making and listening is a "piece of identity philosophy come true,"[55] Anders in 1929 saw listening in a more ambiguous light; as the ultimate release from the pathological condition of being detached from the world. But in contrast to historical Man's and the nihilst's search for refuge in identity, such aural release does not reinstate the subject as the condition and absolute origin of experience. The subject of Anders's musical situations, if it ever was one, simply falls away.

Accordingly, to grant music the status of an object of expe-rience by means of a formal analysis of musical works or by attending to the histories or motives of the subjects producing it, for Anders is utterly futile. Music's secret lies elsewhere, in a realm beyond objective knowledge and subjective choice, beyond music theory and music psychology. As such, it is accessible only through a form of gnosis, one that captures the simultaneity of being in the world and being in music as part of *one* existence, *as* one existence. "On the one hand, one lives in the world, in the medium of one's own historical life, understanding world and life comparatively . . . i.e. philosophizing; but on the other hand, one is also not in the world, but *in music*."

Hence, the only way to talk about this existence is in sentences beginning with "that": That in music,

> one falls out of the world; that one is somehow somewhere nonethe-less; that, even in this hiatus, one remains in the medium of time; that in face of the other reality, one's own (personal, historical) life becomes imaginary; that it becomes a mere interstice between the situations of being in music; that one no longer is oneself; that one is transformed; that one needs to return to oneself; that music says something in every note and yet — in the sense of a sentence — does

not say anything; that music seems to explain; that it nevertheless keeps silent about what it reveals, what reveals itself.[56]

Musical situations, then, differ fundamentally from the Augustinian dichotomy between song and "that about which you sing." Likewise, the philosophy that emerges from rather than speaks to or poses questions about such musical situations has to operate from outside the false binaries shaping modern musical aesthetics, such as the one between objective musical time and the subjective experience of such time between the work and its reception. A theory of musical situations, consequently, cannot but be a theory of listening as a fundamentally ahistorical experience. By this Anders does not mean that musical works do not exist as "pieces of world," in a specific time and place. They obviously do. But to understand our relationship to such concrete works in the terms of a subject-object relationship and to confuse this experience with the idea of being in music would neutralize the specific meaning of being in music. For how can that within which one lives become an object? Does not instead each work open up the "unlimited sound space in which the existence now lives, completely?"[57] Being in music, in other words, is conceivable only as an "enclave." To be in music means to catch up with one's existence by circumventing the a posteriori, as it were, that is, by avoiding "historical Man's" futile attempt at achieving self-identification by remembering the past as his own life.[58]

Although the situation of being in music is an extraterritorial one, then, it differs from similar situations, phases, periods, and deadlines (*Fristen*) that structure life and turn life into a historical medium — situations such as shock, play, sleep, or dreams. Shock, for instance, arrests the flow of life by calling into question the ordinary horizon of life. Play, in turn, is a kind of gap, albeit a positive one. Sleep, finally, is a hiatus in historical life, much like the regular repetition of (historical) day and (ahistorical) night is itself ahistorical. Of course, some similarities between these kinds of ahistorical time and being in music do exist. For instance, like play, the musical situation is a closed situation,

326

bounded by the gestalt character of its object. Yet the enclave of being in music differs from play and sleep because its time is that of music itself. And finally, unlike play, the musical situation does not position us in abstract spaces, just as music is not a Hanslick-ian play of sounding-moving forms. In short, the musical situation is both structure and process. It is *energeia*.[59]

The contrast between music's extraterritoriality and the oscillation of phases of waking and sleeping is a clear indication that Anders's philosophy of music has little in common with the aestheticism of Georg Simmel, as is sometimes maintained. True, like Simmel (and like the elder Stern), Anders deplores the growing gulf between a culture of things and a culture of humans, but he refuses to bridge this gulf with a "happy rhythm." In fact, the concept of the enclave explicitly excludes the possibility of art giving time to life. Rather like a parasite, being in music feeds off life's time, living a "ghostly side life" at the expense of the life that realizes itself in time.[60]

But if the ahistorical character of being in music does not resemble play, sleep, or dreaming, is being in music a condition or mood (*Stimmung*) that subjects may feel when they listen to music? In a passage reminiscent of his earlier article on the phenomenology of hearkening—and, again, echoing Heidegger—Anders rejects the notion of *Stimmung* being such a passive affective state, because the implied contrast between it and a more active listening stance is modeled on visual perception. Seeing is an "act" that confronts its object. Listening, by contrast, is a form of *Befindlichkeit*, a state situated somewhere between "act" and condition, between object-directedness and objectless disposition.[61]

Music, accordingly, is a transformative art. Because human existence, as Heidegger had taught, is both *gestimmt* and *umstimm-bar*, both attuned and tuned, music in Anders's opinion is a form of retuning or *Umstimmung*. It allows the listener to follow certain forms of movement or dispositions (*Gestimmtheiten*, in Heideggerian parlance), a process Anders calls *Mitvollzug* and that one might translate, for want of a better term, as "coperformance."

327

The notion of *Mitvollzug*, Anders is careful to point out, is distinct from a number of concepts that have dominated theories of art throughout the nineteenth century. (And despite a number of terminological parallels it differs as well, of course, from Heinrich Besseler's proto-fascist fascination with collectivities and "use music.") Thus, neither is the transformation made possible by being in music to be confused with Kant's notion of the aesthetic experience as an "as if," nor is *Mitvollzug* a metaphysical matter, as in Schopenhauer's objectification of the world will in four-part harmony. Anders's philosophy of music is first and foremost an *anthropology*, and thus its object is "Man" coping with pathological freedom by transforming himself into one of his own "dimensions."[62]

Not content with only setting himself apart from nineteenth-century idealist philosophy, however, Anders was especially keen also to distinguish the notion of *Mitvollzug* from some of the more current models of musical listening put forth by some of Kant's and Schopenhauer's twentieth-century heirs. Thus, he not only rejects the spatial and organicist metaphors of contemporary musicologists Ernst Kurth and Heinrich Schenker, but Max Scheler's concept of sympathy or *Mitschwingen* (resonance) as an essential part of the human condition likewise comes under scrutiny.[63] Although sympathy goes beyond distanced observation, Anders writes, it still remains separate from the suffering of the other. At best, it is a cosuffering of the other "as the other." In sum, as a being (*Seiendes*) of other forms of movement, Man in musical situations may well merge completely with these movements and hence, in analogy with Augustine's famous definition of music as *ars bene movendi*, the auditory *Mitvollzug* may be called an art of moving well. In the end, however, such *Mitvollzug* is as irreducibly solitary and nonresonant as is Nietzsche's dancing Zarathustra.

Having thus staked out the terrain for his discussion of listening as *Mitvollzug* and *Umstimmung*, Anders in the main part of *Philosophische Untersuchungen* proceeds to a more detailed analysis of three main types of *Umstimmung*: dissolution (*Auflösung*), release

(*Gelöstsein*), and separation (*Abgelöstheit*). To begin with dissolution, the endless sequences of Wagner's *Tristan und Isolde*, for instance, are pure "becoming," devoid of any telos. Consequently, in listening to *Tristan*, we are not so much redeemed (*erlöst*), like Wagner's ideal listener as — to use Nietzsche's term — "swimming," undone (*aufgelöst*).[64] We become this "becoming" and, thus transformed, we *are* the musical process and we are *in* the musical process at one and the same time. Neither mere subject nor simply the other of the *res quae canitur*, Man here becomes a medium.[65]

As for the second type of *Umstimmung*, Anders associates the concept of being released (*Gelöstsein*) with the interplay of tension and release in the music of the classical period, most notably the music of Mozart. Here, the voice figures as the epitome of a musical situation in which the world simply "falls away" and Man is released into the possibility of freedom. It is in this freedom that

> the voice or what it intones [*anstimmt*], represents its own, magic world. There is no longer any difference between the act and its world. Each time, this world is there as sung into existence, as it were, in *intuitus originarius*. But it also falls apart as soon as the act ends. And it is in its fragility that this world is not yet a "world," in the sense of a conditioning medium for actions. Neither is it an already separate world or is the voice only subjective and unreleased *Stimmung*. The musical situation of the voice is between both, it is *Gelöstheit*.[66]

Anders: a metaphysician *malgré lui*? A phonocentrist even, advocating what Derrida would famously call the "absolute proximity of voice and being, of voice and the meaning of being, of voice and the ideality?"[67] There can be little doubt that the passage, both in its rhetorical force and in the emphasis on intonation as an instantiation of freedom, demonstrates the "strange privilege of sound in idealization" and the production of the "concept and the self-presence of the subject" that Derrida found in Hegel, for instance.[68] And indeed, it is in Hegel's concept of music as the art of moving immediacy (*bewegte Unmittelbarkeit*) that

Anders finds a model for the kind of transformation he calls being released. In a lengthy digression on the "coordination of tone and subject" and taking Hegel's familiar definition of *Empfindung* (feeling) as the sphere of music proper as his point of departure, Anders sees in the vibration (*Schwingung*) or trembling (*Erzittern*) common to feeling and tone some sort of middle ground, a first negation of the separation of subject and object. Because in listening to music feeling is more than merely unspecific subjectivity, and musical tone for its part is no longer specific objectivity, *Umstimmung* cannot occur in the medium of physical sound, but only in sounding (*Ertönen*). It is not sounds that are an essential prerequisite for the representation of tones (*Tonvorstellung*), but sounding. Yet even though the object of listening is sounding, an additional condition must be met for such listening to be able to transcend its passive, visionlike character of observation. Only when it becomes what Anders in his 1927 article had called "hearkening" and that he now, after the appearance of *Sein und Zeit*, defined as a kind of Heideggerian *Horchen*, does the world of objects dissolve into a world of voices and does listening open itself up to these voices. The hearkening ear, Anders exclaims ecstatically, "does not know what to listen for."[69] It "does not aim at the tone that is there, but at the voice that comes."[70] Hearkening is a listening into silence, a "nondirectional readiness" that requires measures of getting rid of, turning off.[71]

This leaves us with Anders's third form of *Umstimmung*: *Abgelöstheit*, or co-objectification (*Mit-gegenständlich-werden*). The term "object" here is at first taken in its basic meaning as the structures, forms, and works in and through which "music" crystallizes: a fugue, a sonata, atonality, Beethoven's Fifth, and so on. But because the objectification making up Anders's third form of *Umstimmung* occurs in conjunction with these given objects, it is obviously more than a mere objectification of the subject in the sense of an unmediated expressive act, exteriorization, or utterance (*Äußerung*). As Anders explains, what is usually overlooked in the discussion of musical expression is the fact that in uttering, we already distance ourselves from our selves and that, hence, an utterance negates immediacy. Much the same occurs in musical listening, since here, the dialectic of objectification differs fundamentally from the "metaphysics of presence" inherent in the situation of Derrida's "hearing (understanding)-oneself-speak" in the sense that the subject here "catches up" with itself only ex post facto. Because a musical work can exist only in time, the subject merging with the object no longer constitutes an uttering *of* itself, but an *Ablösung* or separation *from* itself. Subjectivity, then, here differs not only from *Gelöstheit*, but also from *Auflösung* and resonance (*Mitschwingen*) — all of which dissolve not only the subject, but also the object character of the music itself.

An admirer of the musical avant-garde, Anders was of course acutely aware of the sharpening crisis of music and the inadequacy of listening models based on Kant's notion of disinterested pleasure. And yet it is a striking reading of Kant's "analytic of the sublime" and of the music of Arnold Schoenberg that enables him to detect a sinister element in auditory co-objectification.[72] On the one hand, Anders suggests, Kant's expanding imagination is the secular heir to Augustine's call for auditory participation in eternity as a means for closing the gap between Man and God. Take, for instance, the *cantus firmus* of Josquin des Pres' *L'homme armé*. In trying to grapple with its seeming timelessness, Kant might have said, the imagination seeks to follow the voice of reason calling for totality. Of course, as the poorer cousin of reason, the imagination is ultimately doomed to what Kant calls a "discovering failure" in its effort to progress toward the idea of eternity. Likewise, the subject is able to catch up with itself as a reasonable being only through "regression."[73] Yet despite all the ambiguity surrounding the work of the imagination, the images that Kant invokes in trying to accommodate the interplay between imagination and reason within the order of knowledge show that he thought of this process in predominantly resonant terms, as a form of vibration (*Erschütterung*) or "harmonious" oscillation.[74]

But there is also another, potentially more unsettling side to the process. In allowing its imagination to "progress" toward the totality of the idea, the subject also negates its own inescapable time-bound nature as a human being and as a listener. Schoenberg's "constructions," as Anders calls the music issuing from the composer's dodecaphonic period begun only a few years before, are the correlate of this negation.[75] Anders here anticipates Adorno's later criticism of twelve-tone rationality as a "self-opaque" and yet self-contained system, suggesting that, like Rilke's poems, these works are the products of an age in which the very idea of subjective expression as the sign of authorship and the attendant concept of a "for someone" or audience have all but vanished.[76] Having thus achieved total object status, Schoenberg's music is, literally, inhuman, mimicking the social system to which it objects. Faced with such echoless music, the promise of freedom embedded in the aesthetics of the sublime runs into a void. The expansion of the imagination reaches its limit, listening comes full circle. Centuries after Perrault invented the "animated" listener, ambiguously poised between excess and taste, not long after Enlightenment thinkers celebrated the self compulsively listening itself to happiness, and less than a hundred years after Romantically inclined scientists such as Jan Purkinje and Johannes Müller envisaged the subject as an "organic," yet infinitely self-transfiguring entity, avant-garde composers such as Schoenberg irreversibly harness the listener to the totality of the rationally organized work. Listening becomes *Gehorchen,* an act of obedience.

The End of Resonance?

Günther Anders, *pace* Heidegger biographer Rüdiger Safranski, never thought of himself as a Heideggerian.[77] In fact, as Thomas Macho has noted, the differences between Anders and the author of *Sein und Zeit* are so profound as to amount to a total opposition between a certain messianic streak in Anders's "negative theology" of music, on the one hand, and the anti-Christian, antisoteriological thrust of Heidegger's philosophy, on the other.[78] Once Heidegger had weaned himself from Catholicism and metaphysics, Macho writes, his work took an antiacoustic turn, renouncing both Christianity's moral imperative and its central organ, the ear. Heidegger did not want to listen any longer, and instead favored the Greek world of the eye, of numinous flashes and "clearings."

Both readings of the Anders-Heidegger relationship—and, indirectly, of the Adorno-Heidegger-Anders triangle—call for critical examination. Anders's terminological loans from *Sein und Zeit* do not amount to a mere application of Heidegger's existential ontology to music, nor is there any real affinity between Anders's pathos of *Umstimmung* and Walter Benjamin's messianic tendencies. But by the same token, it would also be a mistake to overlook the deeper convergences between Anders's musical thought and Heidegger's puzzling relationship with music and the ear.

Heidegger, for better or worse, never formulated a philosophy of music. Nor is he known to have evinced an interest in the problems of musical listening. With the exception of a handful of cryptic remarks on the music of Mozart, Schubert, Stravinsky, and Carl Orff, music does not have a well-defined place in his work.[79] But the philosopher did write prolifically on hearing and sound, and in consonance with his nemesis Descartes, much of this fascination with sound was nurtured by the magic of voices, poetry, and bells.[80] What wonder, then, that highly poetic and suggestive texts such as the famous analysis of Hölderlin's poem "Der Rhein" (The Rhine) or the childhood memories as altar boy and sexton described in *Vom Geheimnis des Glockenturms* (On the Secret of the Bell Tower) have proven irresistible to commentators attempting to reduce existential ontology to a critique of the ocular bias of Western metaphysics.[81] According to these commentators, Heidegger's rupture with the idealist tradition was possible in large part because he finally recognized the unofficial, acoustic version of the story of modern self-fashioning to be the real story of *Dasein*. In one bold stroke, Heidegger had reconfigured philosophy's relationship with its other in ways that defy the stability of Cartesian representation and instead involve resonance, oscillation, and vibration, in short: acoustics. What is more, the novel articulation of thinking and being that we owe to the author of *Sein und Zeit* is no longer determined by pragmatic use, asking in line with the philosophical tradition stretching from Descartes to Kant what one can do with truth once it has been found. It is, in the words of Heidegger's student Hans Jonas, the "suppressed side of 'hearing,'" which "gets a hearing after the long ascendancy of 'seeing' and the spell of objectification which it cast upon thought."[82]

Despite the ready recognition of existential ontology's aural bias, deciphering Heidegger's more hidden relationship with music and musical listening has proven to be altogether more challenging, as is evident in the small number (and frequently also the conceptual paucity) of studies devoted to the topic. Yet it is nevertheless possible, if only *ex negativo*, to uncover the hidden layers of Heidegger's musical thinking and their relationship to Anders's musical aesthetics. To do so, a detour via a somewhat enigmatic phrase in *Sein und Zeit* is required in which Heidegger claims that "hearing even constitutes the primary and authentic openness of Da-sein for its own most possibility of being, as in hearing the voice of the friend whom every Da-sein carries with it."[83]

In *The Politics of Friendship*, Jacques Derrida has devoted an entire chapter to Heidegger's enigmatic phrase and its cross connections with a plethora of remarks on the ear dotting Heidegger's oeuvre. It is in sentences such as this, Derrida argues, that a powerful sympathetic bond, a great entente, begins to take root at the very center of Being. For the first time in the history of modern thought, this amorous relationship ceases to be a problem requiring constant discursive monitoring and even containment. For the first time since Descartes, Perrault, Le Cat, Sömmerring, and Müller, hearing ceases to be a mere tool, gaining an unprecedented ontological primacy in its place. For the first time, philosophy's relationship to truth is not just defined by *philein*, but by what Derrida has called a "privileged metonymy" of ear and friend.[84] (In fact, as Heidegger would later argue, *philosophia* as such emerges only after the *homologein*, the original *symphonia* or *harmonia* with the logos, has been disrupted and *philosophia* becomes a form of eros, a search for totality, saturation, and fulfillment.)

This metonymy, in Derrida's rich analysis, is extremely multi-faceted in the sense that it designates the simultaneity and parallel existence of domains that in ordinary understanding are often thought of as extreme opposites, *philia* and *polemos*, above all, but also the near and the far, the inside and the outside, and agreement and dissent. Indeed, the metonymy of hearing and friend is so inextricable that *Dasein* can hear only to the extent that the possibility to be itself already requires some form of cobeing or *Mitsein*. That is why for Heidegger, the ear is not a sensory organ *with* which we hear, in the way that we use our hands to grasp an object. The physiological act or psychological phenomenon we call "listening" is only a consequence of the "existentially primary potentiality for hearing" that is embedded in the metonymy of ear and friend. Proof of this existential primacy of hearing is the fact that *Dasein* as a form of being in the world dwells on innerworldly things at hand, not sensations. "Initially," Heidegger says, we do not ever hear "noises and complexes of sound, but the creaking wagon, the motorcycle. We hear the column on the march, the north wind, the woodpecker tapping, the crackling fire."[85] In order to become an issue for *Dasein*, the jumble of aural sensations would first have to be formed. Only then would such sensations become a "springboard from which the subject jumps off finally to land in a 'world.'"[86] In short, *Dasein* as an essential form of understanding is initially together *with* what is understood. Hearing, consequently, necessitates a prior being with another *Dasein*, a belonging to (*Zugehören*).

After *Sein und Zeit*, Heidegger would not tire of exploring this "with," ever more bluntly revealing his disdain for the scientific study of the ear as a discourse *about* the ear, whether it is conceived as the basis or the object of such a discourse. What he would advocate instead is a discourse *of* the ear, one in which the ear itself becomes a "subject," as it were: an ear that "speaks and writes." This, I believe, is also the reason why Heidegger's "otophilology," as Derrida calls the unity of *philein* and *polemos* made possible by logos, accounts for Heidegger's failure to formulate a theory of musical listening going beyond the embarrassing platitudes usually ascribed to him. It is not disinterest in music per se (Heidegger actually owned a large record collection) that led him to claim that we will never hear a Bach fugue if we perceive only "what strikes the tympanum as sound waves."[87] Nor do we need to assume lack of technical expertise to be the reason behind Heidegger's famous statement made after having listened to a sonata by Schubert: "This we can't do with philosophy."[88] Rather, it is one of the biggest ironies of Heidegger's otophilology (at least as outlined in *Sein und Zeit*) that it is precisely the absolute centrality of hearing as presubjective and intermingled with its object that prevented Heidegger from defining the limit of philosophy and the beginning of music.

And so the clue to what music can and philosophy cannot do lies elsewhere, beyond *philein* and *Mitsein*. In what is probably one of Heidegger's most poignant statements on anxiety, written in 1929, we read:

> Anxiety makes manifest the nothing.
>
> We "hover" in anxiety. More precisely, anxiety leaves us hanging, because it induces the slipping away of beings as a whole. This implies that we ourselves — we humans who are in being — in the midst of beings slip away from ourselves. At bottom therefore it is not as though "you" or "I" feel uncanny; rather, it is this way for some "one." In the altogether unsettling experience [*Durchschütterung*] of this hovering where there is nothing to hold on to, pure Da-sein is all that is still there.[89]

The term *Durchschütterung* has a familiar ring. Anxiety itself, Heidegger seems to say, is concussion, oscillation: "its breath quivers perpetually through Dasein.'"[90] But why are neither the ear nor, for that matter, any sound mentioned? The reason for this, as Peter Sloterdijk has convincingly shown, is that *Dasein* as a form of autovibration works only when it has lost its primary capacity for sympathetic resonance or existential being able to hear, when it has suffered some kind of primal auditory defect.[91] When the Being (*Seiende*) disappears, and our panic reveals to us the presence of the nothing, what also disappears with the Being is, obviously, sound. Our panic is thus in reality a fear of the silence that surrounds us when *Dasein* is being "held out" into nothing. Silence is an inevitable part of *Dasein* when, oscillating and panic-stricken, it faces nothingness.

And so a sharp divide separates *Mitsein*, friendship, and resonance from the isolation and echolessness of pure *Dasein*.[92] Loss of love and hearing loss—both negate *Dasein*'s own possibility of being. Descartes most likely would have considered the autovibrating, panicked *Dasein* a hopelessly failed subject, because its percussive qualities prevent it from becoming a resonance-proof cogito and make it prone to such sensual excesses as music, among other irrationalities. By contrast, Heidegger may have found in the pure oscillation and resonance of our relationship to music precisely what existential ontology—defined as a kind of hearing prior to physiology, psychology, anthropology, and the subject—cannot fully accomplish. If Aristotelian *philosophia* for him is ultimately a search for the lost Heraclitian *hen panta*, the one and the many, and Schubert's sonata in turn touches a sphere beyond *philosophia*, would not the lost world of *homolegein*, of speaking the way the logos speaks, ultimately be the space of music? If we are to believe Peter Sloterdijk, Heidegger's moment of echolessness, beyond *Durchschütterung* and the sense of anxiety that accompanies it, is the birth hour proper of music. It is through music that the primal resonant space before our coming into the world, the acoustic uterus as it were, is regained.[93] In this analysis, then, Heidegger may well have understood music as a *musique retrouvée*, as the lost sympathetic bond and the memory of the cosmic silence of existence at the same time. And, *bien entendu*, to the question where we are when we listen to such a rediscovered music, he may have simply replied: in resonance.

There are several consequences of this for my reading of Anders's *Philosophische Untersuchungen* as heralding the end of the resonant ego. One of these is that while Heidegger and Anders equally seem to have conceived of music as some sort of sonar — and, accordingly, of works as echograms of what our constant hearkening into the silence of being held out into nothing might cast back — they differ sharply in the role they assign to musical listening and resonance. Being in music — or being in hearing, as Anders and Arendt had put it in their Rilke essay — are modes of being that seek fulfillment not so much in cavity resonance, as in Sloterdijk's or Heidegger's uterine theory of music, but in separation, in obstetrics. Despite the sympathetic connotations of *Mitvollzug*, Anders's musical situations are defined by the various stages of *Lösung* through which *Dasein* moves while being in music: The unraveling alluded to in terms such as dissolution (*Auflösung*), detachment (*Ablösung*) or being released (*Gelöstsein*) is that of cutting the umbilical cord. The *ars bene movendi* of musical situations is the art of coming into the world.

Another consequence of the differences between Heidegger's musical embryology and Anders's understanding of music as a kind of midwifery touches on two central categories of Heidegger's philosophy: time and its relationship to truth or "uncancealing." In *Sein und Zeit*, Heidegger had famously critiqued the traditional concept of truth as being based in *adaequatio intellectus et rei*, a correspondence between intellect and object. This "empty" assimilation between subject and object, in Heidegger's view, is merely a degenerated form of truth and as such obscures a more profound kind of truth, which he sees embodied in Aristotle's concept of *aletheia*, or, as Heidegger glosses it, *Unverborgenheit*, what is unconcealed. In central parts of his coming to grips with Heidegger, Anders latches on to the latter's rejection of the concept of *adaequatio*, arguing that the primal scene of truth

338

does not share the eruptive quality of Heidegger's light-infused moments of "shining forth" and "showing." The true significance of *adaequatio* resides in a deeper aspect of truth: in a pliant, reciprocal relationship between subject and object, similar to what happens when we "warm up" on a violin or get the feel of another person.[94] Or in a remark that reads like the downright reversal of the prenatal fantasy and that harkens back to Anders's theory of needs, truth is a form of incorporation:

> This—to have, consumption—is the primary image of presence; and the coincidence of the chased-after and the satisfying in incorporation and "assimilation" is the model of "*adaequatio*" that does not, *pace* H. [Heidegger], constitute a derivative mode of truth, but the archetype of the successful relationship between needful *Dasein* and the need-satisfying world. The starved person who, spooning up his soup, declares: "This is truth" does not speak in metaphors.... It is in this moment of presence...that time stops, for hours do not strike for a happy man; and if the phrase "the meaning of *Dasein*" is to have any meaning, it is not (as in H.) in *time*, but rather in *timelessness*.[95]

It is in passages such as this that we sense the kernel of Anders's critique of Heidegger. For Anders, truth does not emerge suddenly, in a moment of rupture, as it does for Heidegger. The resolution of our longing for timelessness, according to Anders, is not a question of ontology or of Heidegger's pseudohistorical phantasm, but of a well-lived life, of the successful handling of time in the satisfaction of our vital needs. If this reading is correct, Anders's theory of culture is less the product of his emancipation from Heidegger than its medium. And so, the ultimate lesson of Anders's anthropology of listening is perhaps the idea that it is in the plenitude of presence, in a realm beyond the threshold of sensory immediacy, but also well below the arrogance of reason, that musical situations put a stop to time.

Oscillation

How to finish? Can there be a conclusion to something as fluctuating as the long and troubled relationship between reason and resonance? Can there be a middle ground between the competing demands of physics and metaphysics, *cogito* and *cutio*, Hartley and Heinse, Le Cat and Lipps? For five centuries, the predominant force in Western epistemology has been fear—fear, that is, that body and mind might resist and even overcome the division that has been imposed on them in the name of knowledge and reason. But why, one might ask, do we continue to invest so much cultural capital in one single project: to avoid recognizing the fact that nothing can be divided into equal halves and that ambiguity and the absence of clear lines of demarcation, whether between sensation and thought, left and right, or inside and outside, is not a defect, but the very essence of human existence?

Perhaps there is no definite answer to this question, and the best way to end this book is not by way of a conclusion, but an oscillation—by nourishing the belief that to achieve something approaching synthesis, more is required than mere denial of the mind-body split. It sometimes takes going back and forth between extremes to escape the tyranny of the binary and to recognize that indeterminacy and the neither-nor are the secret of the unity between reason and resonance, knowing bodies and feeling minds. Virtually all of the thinkers, poets, musicians, and scientists who figured in the preceding pages shared this central insight. Seventeenth-century and eighteenth-century thinkers such as Montesquieu, David Hartley, and even Descartes and the later Kant knew that, left to its own devices, our mind lacks elasticity, becoming ever more confined in its own immutable, solitary sphere. Their Romantic counterparts—poets such as Wilhelm Heinse, scientists such as Johannes Ritter and Johannes Müller—in turn understood that our bodies, our ears, do not exist independently of the mind. They were able to show that what we hear, while certainly being a product of "galvanism" and "sense energies," does not merely depend on, much less than reflect, the object world. Rather, what we call "truth" or "reality" is a usable approximation that emerges not because of the strict separation of subject and object, fact and fiction, outside and inside, but from the neglect of these dichotomies.

Even during the late nineteenth and early twentieth centuries, as the pendulum swung ever more violently between denying the mind any autonomy of its own and nostalgically reclaiming reason's sovereignty over the body, theorists as varied as Hermann von Helmholtz, Georg Simmel, and Günther Anders never lost sight of the ear's often asymmetrical, yet always inextricable intimacy with reason.

The aurality that emerges from these examples and many others like them is, of course, profoundly at odds with current concepts of modernity. It is an aurality that does not bear out the tenet that modernity is, at root, a period dominated by vision, images, and distanced observation. But by the same token, it also casts doubt on the claim that modern individuals became rational subjects because over the past four centuries the eye has asserted itself as the dominant sense organ. Above all, the intertwined histories of the reasoning ear and the resonating mind complicate any substantive concept of the modern subject, in the most literal sense of the term "substance," as an entity whose relationship to the larger world can be described in terms of a base, center, or axis. As Michel Serres, the thinker of "mingled bodies," has persistently argued, knowledge does not so much place us in front of the world as it entangles us with it in folds and knots.[96] The error of modern epistemology is that, eager to declare such a distanced stance as the sine qua non of reason, it excluded these formations of complementarity as too complex to be known and named. And because complex formations exist only as capacity, "as a black memory, a middle between presence and absence, forgetting and memory," they are ill suited for founding the subject in modernity's either-or logic.[97]

Serres' argument may be given an acoustic inflection. Echoing the motto that opened this book, one might argue that thinking and hearing do not so much place the subject in a fixed position vis-à-vis the world as they entangle it in ever-changing relationships of tonal resonance. Just as the interaction between a chord played on a violin and the hair cells of the inner ear can yield anything from the most perfect harmony to the sharpest of discords (as, for instance, in Helmholtz's theory of beats), our cognitive relationship to the larger world, too, can be one of certainty and truth or one of error and delusion. But in neither case is there something like a point of stability or center. As in a vibrating string, the axis of the oscillations performed is the string at rest. Such a middle ground would be tantamount to silence. Resonance, by contrast, requires oscillation of both the mind and the ear. It summons us always to keep on percussing, discussing, percussing.

Notes

INTRODUCTION: THE STRING AND THE MIRROR

1. Denis Diderot, *Oeuvres* (Paris: Gallimard, 1951), p. 879. Here and throughout this book, unless otherwise noted, all translations are my own.

2. Richard Rorty, *Philosophy and the Mirror of Nature* (Princeton, NJ: Princeton University Press, 1979). For more on the mirror metaphor, see Benjamin Goldberg, *The Mirror and the Man* (Charlottesville: University of Virginia Press, 1985). On other ocular aspects of modernity, see Jonathan Crary, *Techniques of the Observer: On Vision and Modernity in the Nineteenth Century* (Cambridge, MA: The MIT Press, 1990) and David Levin (ed.), *Modernity and the Hegemony of Vision* (Berkeley: University of California Press, 1993). These authors are of course not alone in scrutinizing what one might call modernity's mirror stage, nor is the mimetic, unidirectional aspect of visual perception the only issue currently being debated in the field of visual studies. Equally noteworthy are the interactive, "echoic" qualities of the relationship between seeing and cognition explored in, among others, Jonathan Crary, *Suspensions of Perception: Attention, Spectacle, and Modern Culture* (Cambridge, MA: The MIT Press, 1999); and Barbara Maria Stafford, *Echo Objects: The Cognitive Life of Images* (Chicago: University of Chicago Press, 2007).

3. Diderot, *Oeuvres*, p. 879.

4. William James, *The Principles of Psychology*, 2 vols. (New York: Henry Holt and Company, 1890), vol. 1, p. 297.

5. Jacques Derrida, *Of Grammatology*, corrected ed., trans. Gayatri Chakravorty Spivak (Baltimore: Johns Hopkins University Press, 1998), p. 23.

6. Gary Tomlinson, *The Singing of the New World: Indigenous Voice in the Era of European Contact* (Cambridge: Cambridge University Press, 2007).

7. Derrida, *Of Grammatology*, p. 23.

8. *Ibid.*, p. 12.

9. Joseph-Guichard Duverney, *Traité de l'organe de l'ouïe* (Paris: Estienne Michallet, 1683). For an early English translation, see *A Treatise of the Organ of Hearing* (1737; New York: AMS Press, 1973). Hermann von Helmholtz, *On the Sensations of Tone as a Physiological Basis for the Theory of Music* (New York: Dover Publications, 1954).

10. Georg von Békésy, "Zur Theorie des Hörens: Die Schwingungsform der Basilarmembran," *Physikalische Zeitschrift* 29 (1928): pp. 793–810. An English version of this paper appeared in Georg von Békésy, *Experiments in Hearing*, ed. and trans. Ernest G. Wever (n.pl.: Acoustical Society of America, 1960), pp. 403–29.

11. Marshall McLuhan, *The Gutenberg Galaxy* (Toronto: University of Toronto Press, 1962); Walter J. Ong, *The Presence of the Word* (New Haven, CT: Yale University Press, 1967).

12. For a critique of the "great divide" theory, see Mark M. Smith, *Sensing the Past: Seeing, Hearing, Smelling, Tasting and Touching in History* (Berkeley: University of California Press, 2007), pp. 1–18; and David Howes, "Sensorial Anthropology," in David Howes (ed.), *The Varieties of Sensory Experience: A Sourcebook in the Anthropology of the Senses* (Toronto: University of Toronto Press, 1991), pp. 167–91.

13. Jonathan Sterne, *The Audible Past: Cultural Origins of Sound Reproduction* (Durham, NC: Duke University Press, 2002), p. 15.

14. *Ibid.*, p. 16.

15. W. J. T. Mitchell, *What Pictures Want: The Lives and Loves of Images* (Chicago: University of Chicago Press, 2005), pp. 336–56.

16. *Ibid.*, p. 345.

17. *Ibid.*

18. Hanns Eisler and Theodor W. Adorno, *Composing for the Films* (London: Athalone, 1994), p. 20.

19. Jessica Riskin, "The Defecating Duck, or, the Ambiguous Origins of Artificial Life," *Critical Inquiry* 29, no. 4 (Summer 2003): pp. 599–633.

20. In addition to the books already mentioned, the following is a (partial) list of some of the more noteworthy titles: Karin Bijsterveld, *Mechanical Sound: Technology, Culture, and Public Problems of Noise in the Twentieth Century*

(Cambridge, MA: The MIT Press, 2008); Michael Bull and Les Back (eds.), *The Auditory Culture Reader* (New York: Berg, 2004); Veit Erlmann (ed.), *Hearing Cultures: Essays on Sound, Listening and Modernity* (New York: Berg, 2004); Myles W. Jackson, *Harmonious Triads: Physicists, Musicians, and Instrument Makers in Nineteenth-Century Germany* (Cambridge, MA: The MIT Press, 2008); Douglas Kahn, *Noise, Water, Meat: A History of Sound in the Arts* (Cambridge, MA: The MIT Press, 1999); Leigh Eric Schmidt, *Hearing Things: Religion, Illusion, and the American Enlightenment* (Cambridge, MA: Harvard University Press, 2002); Bruce Smith, *The Acoustic World of Early Modern England: Attending to the O-Factor* (Chicago: University of Chicago Press, 1999); Mark M. Smith, *Listening to Nineteenth-Century America* (Chapel Hill: University of North Carolina Press, 2000).

21. There are many excellent books on the anatomy of the ear and the physiology of hearing. Anthony F. Jahn and Joseph Santos-Sacchi (eds.), *Physiology of the Ear*, 2nd ed. (San Diego, CA: Singular, 2001), collects essays treating many different aspects of the subject. Especially useful is the succinct historical account in the same volume by Joseph E. Hawkins, Jr., "Auditory Physiological History: A Surface View," pp. 1–28. A reliable and readable introductory treatise is Stanley S. Stevens et al., *Sound and Hearing*, rev. ed. (New York: Time, 1980). A well-illustrated chapter on the anatomy of the ear may be found in Don W. Fawcett, *A Textbook of Histology*, 12th ed. (Philadelphia: Saunders, 1994).

22. Bruno Latour, *Pandora's Hope: Essays on the Reality of Science Studies* (Cambridge, MA: Harvard University Press, 1999), p. 29.

23. Mitchell, *What Pictures Want*, p. 345.

24. Siegfried Zielinski, *Deep Time of the Media: Toward an Archaeology of Technical Hearing and Seeing* (Cambridge, MA: The MIT Press, 2006); Wolfgang Scherer, *Klavier-Spiele: Die Psychotechnik der Klaviere im 18. und 19. Jahrhundert* (Munich: Wilhelm Fink Verlag, 1989); Penelope Gouk, *Music, Science, and Natural Magic in Seventeenth-Century England* (New Haven: Yale University Press, 1999). For a remarkable study on the use of sound makers in pre-Columbian Mexico as tools of power, see Dorothy Hosler, *The Sounds and Colors of Power: The Metallurgical Technology of Ancient West Mexico* (Cambridge, MA: The MIT Press, 1994).

25. Sterne, *The Audible Past*, pp. 1–2.

26. Lorraine Daston, "The Moral Economy of Science," *Osiris* 10 (1995): pp. 2–24.

27. On attention more broadly, see Michael Hagner, "Toward a History of Attention in Culture and Science," *MLN* 118, no. 3 (2003): pp. 670–87.

28. Roland Barthes, "Listening," in *The Responsibility of Forms: Critical Essays on Music, Art, and Representation* (Berkeley: University of California Press, 1991), p. 259.

29. See Howard Eiland, "Reception in Distraction," *boundary 2* 30, no. 1 (2003): pp. 51–66.

30. See James Johnson, *Listening in Paris: A Cultural History* (Berkeley: University of California Press, 1996); Matthew Riley, *Musical Listening in the German Enlightenment: Attention, Wonder, and Astonishment* (Burlington, VT: Ashgate, 2004); William Weber, "Did People Listen in the Eighteenth Century?" *Early Music* 25, no. 4 (1997): pp. 678–92.

31. Crary, *Suspensions of Perception.*

32. *Ibid.*, p. 1.

33. Andrew Dell'Antonio (ed.), *Beyond Structural Listening?: Postmodern Modes of Hearing* (Berkeley: University of California Press, 2004).

34. Richard Taruskin, *Text and Act: Essays on Music and Performance* (New York: Oxford University Press, 1995).

35. Michel Foucault, "What is an Author?" in *Aesthetics, Method, and Epistemology*, ed. James D. Faubion, trans. Robert Hurley and others, *Essential Works of Foucault*, vol. 2 (New York: The New Press: 1994), p. 221.

36. There are, however, several historical surveys — often written by otologists themselves — that the reader may find useful, such as Georg von Békésy and Walter Rosenblith, "The Early History of Hearing," *Journal of the Acoustical Society of America* 20, no. 6 (1948): pp. 727–48; Ernest Glen Wever, *Theory of Hearing* (New York: Dover Publications, 1949); P. J. Kostelijk, *Theories of Hearing* (Leiden: Universitaire Pers Leiden, 1950); Douglas Guthrie, "The History of Otology," *Journal of Laryngology and Otology* 55, no. 11 (November 1940): pp. 473–94; and the gold standard of all histories, Adam Politzer's massive *Geschichte der Ohrenheilkunde* (1907; Hildesheim: Georg Olms, 1967). An abbreviated, English translation of volume 1 of this work is available as Adam Politzer, *History of Otology*, trans. Stanley Milsetin, Collice Portnoff, and Antje Coleman (Phoenix, AZ: Columella Press, 1981).

37. Lorraine Daston and Peter Galison, *Objectivity* (New York: Zone Books, 2007); Mary Poovey, *History of the Modern Fact: Problems of Knowledge in the Sciences of Wealth and Society* (Chicago: University of Chicago Press, 1998); Jackson, *Harmonious Triads*; Gouk, *Music, Science, and Natural Magic*.

38. Gouk, *Music, Science, and Natural Magic*, p. 273; Jackson, *Harmonious Triads*, pp. 13–44, 45–74.

CHAPTER ONE: THE GREAT ENTENTE

1. Martin Jay, *Downcast Eyes: The Denigration of Vision in Twentieth-Century French Thought* (Berkeley: University of California Press, 1993), p. 70.

2. René Descartes, *Discourse on Method and Meditations on First Philosophy*, ed. David Weissman, trans Elizabeth S. Haldane and G. R. T. Ross (New Haven, CT: Yale University Press 1996), pp. 62, 63–64, 70.

3. For more on the etymology of *concutere*, see *Thesaurus Linguae Latinae* (Leipzig: BSB B. G. Teubner Verlagsgesellschaft, 1988), vol. 4, fasc. 1, pp. 118–21. For *percutere*, see *ibid.*, vol. 10/1, fasc. 8, pp. 1234–50.

4. An excellent overview of seventeenth-century vibration theories is offered in Sigalia Dostrovsky, "Early Vibration Theory: Physics and Music in the Seventeenth Century," *Archive for History of Exact Sciences* 14, no. 3 (1975): pp. 169–218. Also Clifford Truesdell, "The Rational Mechanics of Flexible or Elastic Bodies 1638–1788," in *Leonhard Euleri Opera Omnia: Series Secunda* (Basel: Birkhäuser, 1960), vol. 11, pp. 15–37; and Alistair Crombie, "The Modelling of the Senses," in *Styles of Scientific Thinking in the European Tradition: The History of Argument and Explanation Especially in the Mathematical and Biomedical Sciences and Arts* (London: Duckworth, 1995), vol. 2, pp. 1106–87.

5. The definitive account of Ficino's views of music and hearing is Gary Tomlinson, *Music in Renaissance Magic: Toward a Historiography of Others* (Chicago: University of Chicago Press, 1993).

6. Martinus Schoockius, *De Natura Soni, & Echus, in Lusus Imaginis Iocosæ sive Echus a Variis Poetis, variis Linguis & numeris exculti* (Ultrajecti: Ex Officina Aegidii Roman, Acad. Typog., 1638). For more on the debate see Johannes A. van Ruler, *The Crisis of Causality: Voetius and Descartes on God, Nature and Change* (Leiden: E. J. Brill, 1995).

7. Schoockius, *De Natura Soni*, p. 8.

8. *Ibid.*, p. 9.

9. René Descartes, *The World and Other Writings*, trans. and ed. Stephen Gaukroger (Cambridge: Cambridge University Press: 1998), p. 5.

10. Anon., *Musica Enchiriadis and Scolica Enchiriadis*, trans. Raymond Erickson (New Haven, CT: Yale University Press, 1995), p. 65.

11. Girolamo Fracastoro, *Hieronymi Fracastorii Veron: Liber I de sympathia & antiphatia rerum, de contagione & contagiosis morbis, & eorum curatione libri tres* (Lugduni: Apud Guielmum Gazelum, 1550), p. 37. Quoted in Crombie, *Styles of Scientific Thinking in the European Tradition*, p. 786.

12. Hendrik Floris Cohen, *Quantifying Music: The Science of Music at the First Stage of the Scientific Revolution, 1580–1650* (Dordrecht: D. Reidel Publishing Company, 1984).

13. Galileo Galilei, *Two New Sciences: Including Centers of Gravity and Force of Percussion*, trans. with a new introduction and notes by Stillman Drake, 2nd ed. (Toronto: Wall & Thompson, 1989), pp. 104–108.

14. Descartes, *Meditations*, pp. 63–64.

15. René Descartes, *Compendium musicae*, in Charles Adam and Paul Tannery (eds.), *Oeuvres de Descartes*, 13 vols. (Paris: Librairie Philosophique J. Vrin, 1973–1978), vol. 10, pp. 89–141. For a modern English translation, see René Descartes, *Compendium of Music*, trans. Walter Robert (Rome: American Institute of Musicology, 1961). In what follows, I am using (with minor modifications) the latter translation, referring to the corresponding pages and lines in the original Latin text from the *Oeuvres de Descartes*, vol. 10 (abbreviated as AT, page/line) in parenthesis.

16. Paolo Gozza, "A Renaissance Mathematics: The Music of Descartes," in Paolo Gozza (ed.), *Number to Sound: The Musical Way to the Scientific Revolution* (Dordrecht: Kluwer, 2000), p. 164.

17. Adrien Baillet, *La vie de M. Descartes* (Paris: Daniel Horthemels, 1691), p. 47.

18. Patrice Bailhache, *Une histoire de l'acoustique musicale* (Paris: CNRS–Éditions, 2001), p. 67.

19. Brigitte van Wymeersch, *Descartes et l'évolution de l'esthétique musicale* (Sprimont, Belgium: Mardaga, 1999), p. 101.

20. Descartes, *Compendium of Music*, p. 53 (AT, 141/8).

21. Stephen Gaukroger, who considers the *Compendium* to be otherwise "conventional," points out the "clarity of representation from the very start"

with which the philosopher argues for an arithmetic division. Stephen Gauk-roger, *Descartes: An Intellectual Biography* (Oxford: Clarendon Press, 1995), pp. 73 and 76.

22. Descartes, *Compendium of Music*, p. 21 (AT, 102/29).

23. *Ibid.*, p. 16 (AT, 97/7-13).

24. *Ibid.*, p. 17 (AT, 98/2-4).

25. *Ibid.*, p.18 (AT, 98/13).

26. *Ibid.*, p. 18 (AT, 99/9).

27. *Ibid.* p. 21 (AT, 103/5).

28. *Ibid.*, p. 20 (AT, 102/19-20).

29. Jairo Moreno, *Musical Representations, Subjects, and Objects: The Construction of Musical Thought in Zarlino, Descartes, Rameau, and Weber* (Bloomington: Indiana University Press, 2004), pp. 50-84.

30. Descartes, *Compendium of Music*, p. 14 (AT, 93/19-94/10).

31. Michel Foucault, *The Order of Things: An Archaeology of the Human Sciences* (New York: Vintage Books, 1994), p. 45.

32. Michel Foucault, *History of Madness*, ed. Jean Khalfa, trans. Jonathan Murphy and Jean Khalfa (London: Routledge, 2006), p. 45.

33. Jacques Derrida, "Cogito and the History of Madness," in *Writing and Difference*, trans. Alan Bass (London: Routledge and Kegan Paul, 1978), pp. 31-63.

34. *Ibid.*, p. 50.

35. *Ibid.*, p. 55.

36. *Ibid.*, p. 63.

37. Descartes, *Compendium of Music*, p. 11 (AT, 90/6-7).

38. *Ibid.*, pp. 52-55 (AT, 140/24-141/2).

39. *Ibid.*, p. 90 (AT, 90, n. a). Moreno, likewise, sees these remarks as evidence of a "cognitive ambivalence" in the philosopher's early work. Moreno, *Musical Representations, Subjects, and Objects*, p. 83.

40. Gozza, "A Renaissance Mathematics," pp. 159-60. Gozza does, however, have important things to say about Descartes' parallel quest for an agreement between pleasure and what he calls the "movement of life."

41. Jacques Derrida, *The Ear of the Other: Otobiography, Transference, Translation*, ed. Christie McDonald, trans. Peggy Kamuf (Lincoln: University of Nebraska Press, 1985). On Derrida and Gadamer, see Diane p. Michelfelder

and Richard E. Palmer (eds.), *Dialogue and Deconstruction: The Gadamer-Derrida Encounter* (New York: State University of New York Press, 1989); Jacques Derrida, *Glas*, trans. John p. Leavy, Jr. and Richard Rand (Lincoln: University of Nebraska Press, 1986). Jacques Derrida, "Tympan," *Margins of Philosophy*, trans. Alan Bass (Chicago: University of Chicago Press, 1982), pp. ix–xxix.

42. *Ibid.*, p. x.

43. *Ibid.*, p. xix.

44. On the relationship between macrocosm and the body, see Leonard Barkan, *Nature's Work of Art: The Human Body as Image of the World* (New Haven: Yale University Press, 1975).

45. For a useful summary of Galen's views on hearing, see Rudolph E. Siegel, *Galen on Sense Perception* (Basel: S. Karger, 1970), pp. 127–39.

46. Roger French, *Dissection and Vivisection in the European Renaissance* (Aldershot, UK: Ashgate, 1999).

47. These are but some of the key questions at the heart of a number of recent works on anatomy and dissection such as Katherine Park, *Secrets of Women: Gender, Generation, and the Origins of Human Dissection* (New York: Zone Books, 2006); Andrea Carlino, *Books of the Body: Anatomical Ritual and Renaissance Learning* (Chicago: University of Chicago Press, 2000); and Andrew Cunningham, *The Anatomical Renaissance: The Resurrection of the Anatomical Projects of the Ancients* (Brookfield, VT: Scolar Press, 1997).

48. Caroline Walker Bynum, *Fragmentation and Redemption: Essays on Gender and the Human Body in Medieval Religion* (New York: Zone Books, 1992), p. 290.

49. *Ibid.*, pp. 280 and 285.

50. Victoria Nelson, *The Secret Life of Puppets* (Cambridge, MA: Harvard University Press, 2001).

51. K. B. Roberts and J. D. W. Tomlinson, *The Fabric of the Body: European Traditions of Anatomical Illustration* (Oxford: Clarendon Press, 1992).

52. Nancy J. Vickers, "Members Only: Marot's Anatomical Blazons," in Carla Mazzio and David Hillmann (eds.), *The Body in Parts: Fantasies of Corporeality in Early Modern Europe* (New York: Routledge, 1997), pp. 3–22.

53. Francis Barker, *The Tremulous Private Body: Essays on Subjection* (Ann Arbor: University of Michigan Press, 1995), p. 87.

54. Foucault, *The Order of Things*, p. 66.

55. Giulio Casseri, *De vocis auditusque organis historia anatomica* (Ferrara: V. Baldino, 1600–1601).

56. Foucault, *The Order of Things*, p. 66.

57. Foucault, *The Order of Things*, p. 63.

58. Volcher Coiter, "De auditus instrumento," *Externarvm et interarvm principalivm hvmani corporis partivm tabvlae* (Nuremberg: Theodorici Gerlatzeni, 1573), pp. 89–105.

59. For more details on these pioneers see Adam Politzer, *History of Otology*, trans. Stanley Milsetin, Collice Portnoff, and Antje Coleman (Phoenix, AZ: Columella Press, 1981), pp. 43–72.

60. Quoted from Alistair C. Crombie, "The Study of the Senses in Renaissance Science," in *Science, Optics and Music in Medieval and Early Modern Thought* (London-Ronceverte: Hambledon Press, 1990), p. 386.

61. Gaspard Bauhin, *Institutiones Anatomicae Corporis Virilis et Muliebris Historiam exhibentes* ([Lyons]: Apud Joannem le Preux, 1604). Also known to Descartes may have been Bauhin's *Theatrum anatomicum novis figures aenis illustratum* (Frankfurt am Main: M. Becker, 1605).

62. René Descartes, "Anatomica Quaedam ex Mto Cartesii," in Adam and Tannery (eds.), *Oeuvres de Descartes*, vol. 11, p. 581.

63. René Descartes, *Treatise of Man*, trans. Thomas Steele Hall (Cambridge, MA: Harvard University Press, 1972), pp. 45–46.

64. Bauhin, *Theatrum anatomicum*, caput LVII, pp. 835–39.

65. Hans-Jörg Rheinberger, *Toward A History Of Epistemic Things: Synthesizing Proteins in the Test Tube* (Stanford: Stanford University Press, 1997).

66. Descartes, *Discourse on Method and Meditations on First Philosophy*, p. 60.

67. Descartes, *Treatise of Man*, p. 47.

68. Heinrich Besseler, *Das musikalische Hören der Neuzeit* (Berlin: Akademie-Verlag, 1959), pp. 30 and 41.

69. *Ibid.*

70. "Cognitive ambivalence" is Jairo Moreno's phrase for Descartes' early thought. See Moreno, *Musical Representations*, p. 83. The expression "aesthetic rationalism" is from Timothy Reiss, *Knowledge, Discovery and Imagination in Early Modern Europe: The Rise of Aesthetic Rationalism* (Cambridge: Cambridge University Press, 1997), p. 200.

CHAPTER TWO: POINT OF AUDITION

1. Antoine Picon, "The Freestanding Column in Eighteenth-Century Religious Architecture," in Lorraine Daston (ed.), *Things That Talk: Object Lessons from Art and Science* (New York: Zone Books, 2004), p. 75.

2. The best account by far of Claude Perrault's life and work is Antoine Picon, *Claude Perrault, 1613–1688, ou la curiosité d'un classique* (Paris: Picard Editeur, 1988). An older, but still useful portrait is Wolfgang Herrmann, *The Theory of Claude Perrault* (London: A. Zwemmer, 1973). For a modern English translation of the ordonnance essay, see Claude Perrault, *Ordonnance for the Five Kinds of Columns after the Methods of the Ancients*, trans. Indra Kagis McEwen (Santa Monica, CA: Getty Center for the History of Art and the Humanities, 1993). For more on the Perrault family, see André Hallays, *Les Perrault* (Paris: Librairie Académie Perrin, 1926). On Perrault's zoological work, see Anita Guerrini, "The 'Virtual Menagerie': The *Histoire des animaux* Project," *configurations* 14, nos. 1–2 (2006), pp. 29–42. The best discussion of Perrault's role in the architecture of the Louvre is Michael Petzet, *Claude Perrault und die Architektur des Sonnenkönigs* (Munich: Deutscher Kunstverlag München Berlin, 2000).

3. Claude Perrault, *Essais de physique; ou, Receuil de plusieurs traitez touchant les choses naturelles*, 4 vols. (Paris: Jean Baptiste Coignard, 1680). I am translating *bruit* as "sound," because Perrault intended the concept to encompass more than just noise. A reprint of parts of *Du bruit* appeared as Claude Perrault, *Du bruit et de la musique des anciens: Préface de François Lesure* (Geneva: Éditions Minkoff, 2003). This edition is based on the Leiden edition of Perrault's *Oeuvres diverses de physique et de mécanique*, volume 2 (1721) and, regrettably, omits the third part on the anatomy of the ear. In what follows, I am quoting from the first edition of the *Essais de physique* throughout.

4. Exceptions to this neglect are, among others, Alistair C. Crombie, *Styles of Scientific Thinking in the European Tradition: The History of Argument and Explanation Especially in the Mathematical and Biomedical Sciences and Arts*, 3 vols. (London: Gerald Duckworth & Company, 1995), vol. 2, pp. 1158–63; and André Charrak, *Raison et perception: Fonder l'harmonie au XVIIIe siècle* (Paris: Librairie philosophique J. Vrin, 2001), pp. 230–59.

5. Stephen Jay Gould, *The Hedgehog, the Fox, and the Magister's Pox* (New York: Knopf, 2003), p. 81. The Perrault brothers are eulogized on pp. 75–81.

6. *Ibid.*, p. 22.

7. Richard Taruskin, *The Oxford History of Western Music: The Earliest Notations to the Sixteenth Century*, 6 vols. (Oxford: Oxford University Press, 2005), vol. 1, p. 797.

8. Gary Tomlinson, *Metaphysical Song: An Essay on Opera* (Princeton, NJ: Princeton University Press, 1999), pp. 40–61.

9. *Ibid.*, p. 48.

10. Georgia Cowart, *The Triumph of Pleasure: Louis XIV and the Politics of Spectacle* (Chicago: University of Chicago Press, 2009).

11. *Ibid.*, p. 162.

12. *Ibid.*, p. 172.

13. Joseph-Guichard Duverney, *Traité de l'organe de l'ouïe* (Paris: Estienne Michallet, 1683). For a reprint of the English translation of 1737, see *A Treatise of the Organ of Hearing* (1737; New York: AMS Press, 1973).

14. Duverney, *Traité de l'organe de l'ouïe*, pp. 96–98.

15. *Ibid.*, pp. 203–206.

16. Perrault, *Essais de physique*, vol. 1, p. 162.

17. Perrault, *Essais de physique* vol. 2, pp. 333–34.

18. *Ibid.*, pp. 217–18.

19. *Ibid.*, p. 219.

20. *Ibid.*, pp. 248–49.

21. *Ibid.*, p. 251.

22. *Ibid.*, pp. 265–66.

23. *Ibid.*, p. 284. For a more detailed discussion of the ups and downs of Cartesian mechanism in the second half of the seventeenth century, see Jacques Roger, *The Life Sciences in Eighteenth-Century French Thought* (Stanford, CA: Stanford University Press, 1997), pp. 133–204.

24. Perrault, *Essais de physique*, vol. 2, p. 312.

25. *Ibid.*, p. 313.

26. *Ibid.*, p. 331.

27. Reprinted as Claude Perrault, "Préface manuscrite du Traité de la musique de Claude Perrault (Bibl. Nat. manuscr. fr. 25,350)," in Claude Perrault, *Du bruit et de la musique des anciens*, pp. 576–91.

28. While it is true that Claude Perrault played a prominent, albeit often overlooked part in the dispute, he was not alone in his defense of Lully's

innovations. Charles Perrault soon joined the fray with the brief, if ultimately more influential tract, *Critique de l'opéra*, followed by Pierre Perrault's rejoinder *Critique des deux tragédies*, written in response to a sharp rebuttal of the opera penned by Racine. The texts in question are available in two collections: William Brooks, Buford Norman, and Jeanne Morgan Zarucchi (eds.), *Alceste, suivi de La Querelle d'Alceste: Anciens et Modernes avant 1680* (Paris: Droz, 1994); and François Lesure (ed.), *Textes sur Lully et l'opéra français* (Geneva: Editions Minkoff, 1987).

29. Perrault, "Préface manuscrite," p. 577.

30. *Ibid.*, pp. 586–87.

31. Cowart, *The Triumph of Pleasure*, p. 121.

32. On the parallels between early modern spectacle and postmodern aesthetics, see, for instance, Angela Ndalianis, *Neo-Baroque Aesthetics and Contemporary Entertainment* (Cambridge, MA: The MIT Press, 2004).

33. Jean-François Marmontel, "Opéra," *Oeuvres complètes*, 19 vols. (Paris: Verdière, 1818–20), vol. 14, p. 409.

34. Catherine Kintzler, *Théâtre et opéra à l'âge classique: Une familière étrangeté* (Paris: Fayard, 2004), pp. 10–11.

35. *Ibid.*, p. 11.

36. Catherine Kintzler, *Poétique de l'opéra français de Corneille à Rousseau* (1991; Paris: Minerve, 2006), pp. 301–302.

37. *Ibid.*, pp. 303–305.

38. *Ibid.*, pp. 303–308.

39. Jean-Philippe Rameau, *Génération harmonique, ou traité de musique théorique et pratique* (1737), in Jean-Philippe Rameau, *Complete Theoretical Writings*, ed. Erwin R. Jacobi (n.p.: American Institute of Musicology, 1968).

40. Jean-Jacques Dortous de Mairan, "Sur la propagation du son dans les différens tons qui le modifient," in *Histoire de l'Académie royale des sciences avec les mémoires de mathématique et de physique pour la même année tirés des registres de cette académie—Année 1737*, pp. 1–58. The *corps sonore* and its discovery by Rameau are expertly discussed in Thomas Christensen, *Rameau and Musical Thought in the Musical Enlightenment* (Cambridge: Cambridge University Press, 1993), pp. 133–68.

41. Rameau, *Génération harmonique*, p. 15. Rameau refers his readers,

incorrectly, only to the "Mémoires de l'Académie des Sciences de l'année 1720. pag. 11," which does not contain any of Mairan's work.

42. On identification in early eighteenth-century opera see Downing A. Thomas, *Aesthetics of Opera in the Ancien Régime, 1647–1785* (Cambridge: Cambridge University Press, 2002), pp. 201–64. On "exteriorizing" identification, see Kaja Silverman, *Male Subjectivity at the Margins* (New York: Routledge, 1992), p. 264; Max Scheler, *Wesen und Formen der Sympathie* (Bonn: F. Cohen, 1923).

43. Christine Buci-Glucksmann, *La folie du voir: Une esthétique du virtuel* (Paris: Galilée, 2002).

44. *Ibid.*, p. 112.

45. *Ibid.*, p. 93.

46. Gilles Deleuze, *The Fold: Leibniz and the Baroque* (Minneapolis: University of Minnesota Press, 1993), pp. 132–37.

47. *Ibid.*, p. 136.

48. *Ibid.* pp. 19–20.

49. *Ibid.*, p. 22. For a fascinating discussion of "point of view" in "Baroque" art see Mieke Bal, *Quoting Caravaggio: Contemporary Art, Preposterous History* (Chicago: University of Chicago Press, 1999), pp. 1–44.

50. Rick Altman (ed.), *Sound Theory/Sound Practice* (New York: Routledge, 1992).

51. *Ibid.*, p. 60.

52. *Ibid.*, pp. 60–61.

53. Robert Estienne, *Dictionaire francoislatin contenant les motz et manieres de parler francois, tournez en latin* (Paris: R. Estienne, 1549); Antoine Furetière, *Dictionnaire universel* (Amsterdam: Reinier Leers, 1690).

54. Linda Phyllis Austern, "'For, Love's a Good Musician': Performance, Audition, and Erotic Disorders in Early Modern Europe," *Musical Quarterly* 82, nos. 3–4 (1998): p. 622.

55. Kate van Orden, "An Erotic Metaphysics of Hearing in Early Modern France," *Musical Quarterly* 82, nos. 3–4 (1998): p. 682.

56. "The Ticklish Subject" is of course the title of Slavoj Žižek's reflections on the subject of German idealism. See Slavoj Žižek, *The Ticklish Subject: The Absent Centre of Political Ontology* (London: Verso, 2000).

57. Descartes to Marin Mersenne, October 1631, in Charles Adam and Paul

Tannery (eds.), *Oeuvres de Descartes*, 13 vols. (Paris: Librairie Philosophique J. Vrin, 1969), vol. 1, p. 224.

58. Descartes to Marin Mersenne, March 4, 1630, *ibid.*, p. 126.

59. Descartes to Marin Mersenne, October 1631, p. 223.

60. On the "coincidence theory" of consonance, see H. Floris Cohen, *Quantifying Music: The Science of Music at the First Stage of the Scientific Revolution, 1580–1650* (Dordrecht: D. Reidel Publishing Company, 1984), pp. 90–96.

61. J. Reiss (ed.), "Jo. Bapt. Benedictus, De intervallis musicis," *Zeitschrift für Musikwissenschaft* 7 (1924–25): pp. 13–25.

62. *Ibid.*, p. 20.

63. Galileo Galilei, *Two New Sciences: Including Centers of Gravity and Force of Percussion*, 2nd ed., trans. with a new introduction and notes by Stillman Drake (Toronto: Wall & Thompson, 1989), p. 104.

64. *Ibid.*, p. 107.

65. For these see Cohen, *Quantifying Music*, pp. 97–204.

66. Marin Mersenne, *Questions inouyes ou recreation des scavans* (1634; Paris: Fayard, 1985), pp. 17–18.

67. René Descartes, *Treatise of Man*, trans. Thomas Steele Hall (Cambridge, MA: Harvard University Press, 1972), p. 47.

68. *Ibid.*, pp. 47–48.

69. René Descartes, *Les passions de l'âme*, § 94, in: René Descartes, *Oeuvres et lettres* (Paris: Gallimard, 1953), p. 740.

70. *Ibid.*, §147, p. 766.

71. For a fuller discussion of the ethical component of *chatouillement*, see also Alexandre Matheron, "Psychologie et politique: Descartes et la noblesse du chatouillement," in *Anthropologie et politique au XVIIe siècle (études sur Spinoza)* (Paris: Vrin, 1986), pp. 29–48.

72. Perrault, *Essais de physique*, vol. 1, p. 353.

73. Claude Perrault, *Les dix livres d'architecture de Vitruve* (1673; Paris: Bibliothèque de l'Image, 1995).

74. René Ouvrard, *Architecture harmonique, ou Application de la doctrine des Proportions de la Musique à l'Architecture* (Paris: R. J. B. de La Caille, 1679); François Blondel, *Cours d'architecture* (Paris: Lambert Roulland, 1675), pp. 756–60.

75. Perrault, *Ordonnance*, p. 48.

76. *Ibid.*, p. 49.

77. *Ibid.*, p. 52.

78. *Ibid.*, p. 54.

79. *Ibid.*, p. 160.

80. Perrault, *Essais de physique*, vol. 2, p. 388.

81. *Ibid.*, p. 390.

CHAPTER THREE: GOOD VIBES

1. Anon. [Claude-Nicolas Le Cat], *Discours qui a remporté le prix à l'Académie de Dijon, en l'année 1750: sur cette question proposée par la même Académie; si le rétablissement des sciences & des arts a contribué a épurer les moeurs. Nouvelle édition, accompagnée de la réfutation de ce discours, par les apostilles critiques de l'un des académiciens examinateurs, qui a refusé de donner son suffrage à cette pièce* (London: Edouard Kelmarneck, 1751). For a modern English translation of this text, see Jean-Jacques Rousseau, *Discourse on the Sciences and Arts (First Discourse)* (Hanover, NH: University Press of New England, 1992), pp. 130–74.

2. [Le Cat], *Discours qui a remporté le prix à l'Académie de Dijon*, p. 7; Rousseau, *Discourse on the Sciences and Arts*, p. 135.

3. [Le Cat], *Discours qui a remporté le prix à l'Académie de Dijon*, pp. 35–36; Rousseau, *Discourse on the Sciences and Arts*, p. 151.

4. Voltaire to Le Cat, March 26, 1765, in Theodore Besterman (ed.), *Voltaire's Correspondence* (Geneva: Institut et Musée Voltaire, 1965), vol. 105, p. 237.

5. Claude-Nicolas Le Cat, *Traité de la couleur de la peau humaine en général & de celle des nègres en particulier: et de la métamorphose d'une de ces couleurs en l'autre, soit de naissance, soit accidentellement: ouvrage divisé en trois parties* (Amsterdam, 1765), p. 7. The work is discussed at some length in George S. Rousseau, "Le Cat and the Physiology of Negroes," *Enlightenment Crossings: Pre- and Post-Modern Discourses Anthropological* (Manchester, UK: Manchester University Press, 1991), pp. 26–40.

6. Denis Ballière de Laisement, *Eloge de Monsieur Le Cat, ecuyer, docteur en medecine, chirurgien en chef de l'Hotel-Dieu de Rouen* (Rouen: Laurent Dumesnil, 1769), p. 75. For more biographical detail on Le Cat, see M. Bayle, *Encyclopédie des sciences médicales*, Sixième Division, Biographie médicale, II (Paris: Bureau de l'Encyclopédie, 1841), pp. 294–99.

7. Claude-Nicolas Le Cat, *Traité des sens* (Amsterdam: Wetstein, 1744)

and *La théorie de l'ouie: supplément a cet article du Traité des sens: ouvrage qui a remporté le prix triple proposé pour 1757 par l'Académie de Toulouse* (Paris: Vallat-La-Chapelle, 1768); also in Le Cat, *Oeuvres physiologiques*, 3 vols. (Paris: Vallat-La-Chapelle, 1767–68), vol. 2.

8. Adam Politzer, *Geschichte der Ohrenheilkunde* (1907; Hildesheim: Georg Olms, 1967), p. 279.

9. On these debates see, among others, Thomas Christensen, "Music Theory as Scientific Propaganda: The Case of D'Alembert's *Elémens de Musique*," *Journal of the History of Ideas* 50, no. 3 (1989): pp. 409–27; Thomas Christensen, *Rameau and Musical Thought in the Musical Enlightenment* (Cambridge: Cambridge University Press, 1993), esp. pp. 209–90.

10. The standard works on sensibility are Anne C. Vila, *Enlightenment and Pathology: Sensibility in the Literature and Medicine of Eighteenth-Century France* (Baltimore: Johns Hopkins University Press, 1998); and Jessica Riskin, *Science in the Age of Sensibility: The Sentimental Empiricists of the French Enlightenment* (Chicago: University of Chicago Press, 2002).

11. For useful accounts of vitalism and the Montpellier school, see Elizabeth A. Williams, *The Physical and the Moral: Anthropology, Physiology, and Philosophical Medicine in France, 1750–1850* (Cambridge: University Press, 1994), and Roselyne Rey, *Naissance et développement du vitalisme en France de la deuxième moitié du XVIIIe siècle à la fin du Premier Empire* (Oxford: Voltaire Foundation, 2000).

12. Théophile de Bordeu, *Recherches sur l'histoire de la médicine* (Paris: G. Masson, 1882), p. 250.

13. Riskin, *Science in the Age of Sensibility*, p. 5. In fact, the very frontispiece to Le Cat's *La Théorie de louie* (figure 3.1) leaves the reader in no doubt as to this intimacy of reason with resonance. The engraving depicts the author (in the lower left corner) as he surveys a scene populated with a swarm of putti busying themselves with an array of ear ossicles, acoustic instruments, and an organ. Occupying the center of the image, however, is a female figure who, with a lyre in one hand and a stave of radiating light in the other, sits astride a huge, cochlea-shaped mound: Music and Reason united and, literally, supported by the ear!

14. Chevalier de Jaucourt, in Denis Diderot and Jean le Rond d'Alembert (eds.), *Encyclopédie, ou Dictionnaire raisonné des sciences, des arts et des métiers*

(Paris, 1765), s.v. "Sympathie (Physiolog.)," vol. 15, p. 736.

15. Frédéric-Melchior Grimm, *Correspondance littéraire*, 16 vols. (Paris: Garnier Frères, 1877), vol. 10, p. 416.

16. On this shift in aural sensibilities see James H. Johnson, *Listening in Paris: A Cultural History* (Berkeley: University of California Press, 1995); and Christopher Gärtner, "Remuer l'âme or plaire à l'oreille? Music, Emotions and the Mind-Body Problem in French Writings of the later 18th Century," in Penelope Gouk and Helen Hills (eds.), *Representing Emotions: New Connections in the Histories of Art, Music and Medicine* (London: Ashgate, 2005), pp. 173–88.

17. Barbara M. Stafford, *Artful Science: Enlightenment Entertainment and the Eclipse of Visual Education* (Cambridge, MA: The MIT Press, 1994). For more on the *moi* in eighteenth-century France, see Jan Goldstein, "Mutations of the Self in Old Regime and Postrevolutionary France: From *Ame* to *Moi* to *Le Moi*," in Lorraine Daston (ed.), *Biographies of Scientific Objects* (Chicago: University of Chicago Press, 2000), pp. 86–116.

18. Claude-Adrien Helvétius, "Le Bonheur," *Oeuvres complètes d'Helvétius* (Paris: p. Didot l'Aîné, 1795), p. 106.

19. Fritz Breithaupt, "Goethe and the Ego," *Goethe Yearbook* 11 (2002), p. 81.

20. For more on this metaphor see Françoise Dion-Sigoda, "L'homme-clavecin: évolution d'une image," in Jean-Louis Jam (ed.), *Ecclectisme et cohérence des Lumières: Mélanges offerts à Jean Ehrad* (Paris: Nizet, 1992), pp. 221–28.

21. Cartaud de la Vilate, *Essai historique et philosophique sur le goût* (1736; Geneva: Slatkine, 1970), p. 280.

22. Abbé Jacquin, *De la santé: Ouvrage utile à tout le monde.* 2nd edition (Paris: Durand, 1763), p. 347.

23. Charles de Secondat, Baron de Montesquieu, "An Essay on Causes Affecting Minds and Characters," in *The Spirit of Laws* (Berkeley: University of California Press, 1977), pp. 421–22.

24. Charles Bonnet, *Essai de psychologie* (1755; Hildesheim: Georg Olms 1978), p. 13.

25. Julien Offray de la Mettrie, *L'homme-machine* (1748; Paris: Denoël/Gonthier, 1981), p. 29.

26. François Couperin, *L'art de toucher le clavecin* (Leipzig: Breitkopf & Härtel, 1933), p. 14.

27. For more on the harpsichord metaphor in Diderot's work, see Jacques Chouillet, *Diderot: Poète de l'energie* (Paris: Presses Universitaires de France, 1984), pp. 245–78; and Herbert Dieckmann, *Studien zur europäischen Aufklärung* (Munich: Wilhelm Fink, 1974), pp. 155–202.

28. Albrecht von Haller, *Tagebuch der medicinischen Litteratur der Jahre 1745 bis 1774*, 3 vols. (Hildesheim: Georg Olms, 1974), vol. 1, p. 87.

29. Claude-Nicolas Le Cat, "Du fluide animal," in *Oeuvres physiologiques* (Paris: Vallat-La-Chapelle, 1767–68), vol. 1, p. 115; and "La Sympathie, les pressentimens," *ibid.*, p. 232.

30. Le Cat, *Traité de l'existence, de la nature et des propriétés du fluide des nerfs* (Berlin, 1765), pp. 19–20. The violonists Le Cat refers to are Jean-Joseph de Mondonville (1711–1772) and Pierre Gaviniés (1728?–1800), a professor of violin at the Paris Conservatoire who, according to the nineteenth-century musicologist François-Joseph Fétis, moved audiences to tears.

31. Claude-Nicolas Le Cat, "Physiologie des sensations et des passions," in *Oeuvres physiologiques*, vol. 1, p. 37.

32. Le Cat, "Du fluide animal," p. 184.

33. *Ibid.*, p. xv.

34. Le Cat, "Physiologie des sensations et des passions," p. 30.

35. Ernst Cassirer, *The Philosophy of the Enlightenment* (Princeton, NJ: Princeton University Press, 1951), p. 45.

36. Le Cat, *Traité des sens*, pp. 281–82.

37. For more on *gradation*, see Erich Kleinschmidt, *Die Entdeckung der Intensität: Geschichte einer Denkfigur im 18. Jahrhundert* (Göttingen: Wallstein, 2004).

38. Le Cat, *La théorie de l'ouie*, p. 183.

39. For more on Rameau's "mechanization of harmonic movement," see Thomas Christensen, *Rameau and Musical Thought in the Enlightenment* (Cambridge: Cambridge University Press, 1993), pp. 107–109.

40. Le Cat, *La théorie de l'ouie*, pp. 194–95 and 195–96.

41. *Ibid.*, p. 197.

42. *Ibid.*, p. 200.

43. Denis Diderot and Jean le Rond d'Alembert (eds.), *Encyclopédie, ou Dictionnaire raisonné des sciences, des arts et des métiers* (Paris, 1755), s.v. "Ébranler," vol. 5, p. 215.

44. Jean Astruc, *Dissertation sur l'origine des maladies épidémiques et principalement sur l'origine de la peste* (Montpellier: Jean Martel, 1721); John Arbuthnot, *Essai des effets de l'air, sur le corps-humain* (Paris: Jacques Barois, fils, 1742).

45. For a useful account of the interconnections between meteorology and the Enlightenment in the British context, see Jan Golinski, *British Weather and the Climate of the Enlightenment* (Chicago: University of Chicago Press, 2007). For a richly evocative literary treatment of the era's obsession with smell, see Patrick Suskind, *Perfume: The Story of a Murderer* (New York: Vintage, 2001).

46. Abbé Dubos, *Réflexions critiques sur la poësie et sur la peinture* (1719; Paris: P.-J. Mariette, 1733).

47. Surprisingly, discussions of eighteenth-century musical aesthetics or anthologies of core texts never mention Dubos' belief in the atmospheric determinants of art. An exception is Belinda Cannone, *Philosophies de la musique (1752–1780)* (Paris: Aux Amateurs de Livres, 1990), pp. 128–32.

48. Abbé Dubos, *Réflexions critiques*, pp. 148 and 289.

49. Montesquieu, *The Spirit of Laws*, p. 294.

50. François Boissier de Sauvages, *Dissertation ou l'on recherche comment l'air, suivant ses différentes qualités, agit sur le corps humain* (1753), pp. 25–26. On Sauvages, see also Julian Martin, "Sauvages' Nosology: Medical Enlightenment in Montpellier," in Andrew Cunningham and Roger French (eds.), *The Medical Enlightenment of the Eighteenth Century* (Cambridge: Cambridge University Press, 1990), pp. 111–37, and Michel Foucault, *The Birth of the Clinic: An Archaeology of Medical Perception* (New York: Vintage Books, 1994), p. 4.

51. Sauvages, *Dissertation ou l'on recherche*, pp. 26–27.

52. Jean Laurent de Béthizy de Mézières, *Effets de l'air sur le corps humain, considéré dans le son; ou Discours sur la nature du chant* (Amsterdam and Paris: Lambert and Duchesne, 1760), p. 9. For a discussion of de Mézières' views on French *opéra comique*, see Downing A. Thomas, *Aesthetics of Opera in the Ancien Régime: 1647–1785* (Cambridge: Cambridge University Press, 2002), pp. 223–26.

53. Joseph-Louis Roger, *Traité des effets de la musique sur le corps humain* (Paris: Brunot, 1803); Charles Lorry, *De melancholia et morbis melancholicis*, 2 vols. (Paris: Guillelmum Cavelier, 1765), vol. 1, pp. 148 and 168; vol. 2, pp. 105–18 and 274.

54. Quoted in Thomas L. Henkins, *Jean d'Alembert: Science and the Enlightenment* (New York: Gordon & Breach, 1970), p. 81 n.2.

55. Quoted in Jean Ehrard, *L'idée de nature en France dans la première moitié du XVIIIe siècle* (1963; Paris: Albin Michel, 1994), p. 731.

56. David Hartley, *Observations on Man, His Frame, His Duty, and His Expectations* (Gainesville, FL: Scholars' Facsimiles and Reprints, 1966). For the French edition see David Hartley, *Explication physique des sens, des idees, et des mouvemens, tant volontaires qu'involontaires, traduite de l'anglois, par M. l'abbe Jurain* (Reims: Delaistre-Godet, 1755).

57. *Ibid*, pp. 11 and 22.

58. *Ibid.*, pp. 83–84.

59. *Ibid.*, p. 84.

60. *Ibid.*, p. 426.

61. On the role of optical technology and Enlightenment entertainment in the emergence of what she calls "high-order thinking," see Barbara Maria Stafford, *Artful Science: Enlightenment Entertainment and the Eclipse of Visual Education* (Cambridge, MA: The MIT Press, 1994). The parallel argument for hearing was first made by Leigh Eric Schmidt in *Hearing Things: Religion, Illusion, and the American Enlightenment* (Cambridge, MA: Harvard University Press, 2000), a book that provided much of the initial inspiration for the present attempt.

62. The literature on tarantism published in France alone is vast. See, for instance, *Dictionnaire portatif de santé*. 4th ed. (Paris: Vincent, 1765), p. 507; Jean-Fr. Lavoisien, *Dictionnaire portatif de médecine* (Paris: Theophile Barrois, 1793), pp. 564–66; Noel Chomel and J. Marret, *Dictionnaire oeconomique*, 4 vols. (Commercy: Henry Thomas & Compagnie, 1741), vol. 2, p. 287.

63. Penelope Gouk, "Introduction," *Musical Healing in Cultural Contexts* (Aldershot, UK: Ashgate, 2000), p. 9.

64. My account is based in part on the excellent analysis in Alain Cernuschi, *Penser la musique dans l'Encyclopédie: Étude sur les enjeux de la musicographie des Lumières et sur ses liens avec l'encyclopédisme* (Geneva: Honoré Champion, 2000), pp. 167–220.

65. Denis Diderot, in Diderot and d'Alembert (eds.), *Encyclopédie*, s.v. "Ame," vol. 1, p. 343.

66. On *organisation*, see Rey, *Naissance et développement du vitalisme en France*, pp. 123–84.

67. Diderot, s.v. "Ame," p. 343.

68. D. J. [Chevalier de Jaucourt], in Diderot and d'Alembert (eds.), *Encyclo-pédie*, s.v. "Tarentule ou Tarantule," vol. 15, pp. 905–8. For Geoffroy's report, see Etienne-François Geoffroy, "Diverses observations de physique générale," *Histoire de l'Académie royale des Sciences: Année MDCCII* (Amsterdam, 1737), pp. 20–24. Jaucourt also mentions the work of Johann Jakob Scheuchzer and criticizes Giorgio Baglivi's views on tarantism expounded in his *Practice of Physick* (1704). Other works that come in for censure are Richard Mead's work on poison (*A Mechanical Account of Poisons*, London, 1702) and the more obscure treatise *De Ictu tarantulae & Vi musices in ejus Curatione, Conjecturae physico-medicae*, by Hermann Grube (Frankfurt, 1679).

69. Pierre Desault, *Dissertation sur les maladies vénériennes: Avec deux dis-sertations, l'une sur la rage, l'autre sur la phtisie* (Bordeaux: Pierre Calamy, 1733), p. 314.

70. Foucault, *The Birth of the Clinic*, p. 15. Across the English Channel, many of these French texts probably circulated widely among the educated elite, but relatively few works were written in the English language itself. Notable excep-tions are Richard Browne and Richard Brocklesby, both discussed in Penelope Gouk, "Raising Spirits and Restoring Souls: Early Modern Medical Explana-tions for Music's Effects," in Veit Erlmann (ed.), *Hearing Cultures: Essays on Sound, Listening and Modernity* (Oxford: Berg, 2004), pp. 87–106.

71. *Nouveau dictionnaire universel et raisonné de médecine, de chirurgie et de l'art véterinaire* (Paris: Hérissant le fils, 1772), p. 457.

72. Philippe Hecquet, *De la digestion et des maladies de l'estomac* (Paris: François Fournier, 1712), p. 212. Even as late as 1802, the renowned physi-cian Pierre-Jean-Georges Cabanis, in his *Rapports du physique et du morale de l'homme*, claimed that the effect of auditory stimulation on "living nature" is by "more immediate action." This, he argued, is especially the case when the music is simple, its phrases short and easy to grasp. And, he insists, all this does not involve the thinking organ and occurs solely in the "sympathetic domain." Jean-Georges Cabanis, *Rapports du physique et du morale de l'homme* (1802, Paris: Charpentier, 1843), p. 476. Foucault, *The Birth of the Clinic*, pp. 3–21.

73. *Ibid.*, p. 15.

74. *Ibid.*, pp. 15–16.

75. Anon., in Diderot and d'Alembert (eds.), *Encyclopédie*, s.v. "Phrénésie," vol. 4, pp. 530–31.

76. D [Denis Diderot], in Diderot and d'Alembert (eds.), *Encyclopédie*, s.v. "Délire," vol. 12, p. 785.

77. Foucault, *The Birth of the Clinic*, p. 16.

78. See Jean Starobinski, *Histoire du traitement de la mélancholie des origines à 1900* (Basle: J. R. Geigy S. A., 1960).

79. John Moore, *Of Religious Melancholy* (London: William Rogers, 1692), p. 21.

80. Voltaire, *Candide and Other Writings* (New York: Modern Library, 1984), p. 186.

81. Le Cat, *Traité des sens*, pp. 68–69.

82. Abbé Dubos, *Réflexions critiques*, p. 29.

83. André-François Boureau-Deslandes, *L'art de ne point s'ennuyer* (Paris: E. Ganneau, 1715), "Préface," p. viii.

84. Abbé Dubos, *Réflexions critiques*, p. 448.

85. Catherine Kintzler, *Poétique de l'opéra français, de Corneille à Rousseau* (Paris: Minerve, 1991).

86. *Ibid.*, p. 240.

87. Thomas, *Aesthetics of Opera in the Ancien Régime*, pp. 154–75.

88. *Ibid.*, p. 169.

89. Jean-Jacques Menuret de Chambaud, in Diderot and d'Alembert (eds.), *Encyclopédie*, s.v. "Manie," "Mélancolie," and "Musique, effet de la" (Paris, 1765), vol. 10, pp. 31–34, 307–11, 903–909.

CHAPTER FOUR: WATER, SEX, NOISE

1. Wilhelm Heinse to Friedrich Heinrich Jacobi, August 29, 1780, in Wilhelm Heinse, *Sämmtliche Werke*, 10 vols. (Leipzig: Insel-Verlag, 1902–25), vol. 10, pp. 33–34. For the sake of poignancy, my quotation is culled from different sections of the letter, leaving out the usual marks of omission.

2. Samuel Thomas Sömmerring, *Über das Organ der Seele* (1796; Amsterdam: E. J. Bonset, 1966), pp. 48–49.

3. In addition to anatomical works, Sömmering's output also included texts on the dangers of corsets (*Über die Schädlichkeit der Schnürbrüste* [1788]) and the cruelty of the guillotine (*Sur le supplice de la guillotine* [1795]). Toward the end of his life, Sömmerring invented the prototype of what was to become the telegraph.

4. For an example from Papua New Guinea, see Steven Feld, "'Flow like a Waterfall': The Metaphors of Kaloli Musical Theory," *Yearbook for Traditional Music* 13 (1981), pp. 22–47.

4. Sömmerring, *Organ der Seele*, p. 42.

6. *Ibid.*, p. 43.

7. *Ibid.*, p. 45.

8. Ernst Florens Chladni, *Entdeckungen über die Theorie des Klangs* (Leipzig: Weidmanns, Erben und Reich, 1787).

9. For more on Chladni, see Myles W. Jackson, *Harmonious Triads: Physicists, Musicians, and Instrument Makers in Nineteenth-Century Germany* (Cambridge, MA: The MIT Press, 2006), pp. 13–44.

10. Sömmerring, *Organ der Seele*, p. 46.

11. Samuel Thomas Sömmerring, *Abbildungen des menschlichen Hoerorganes* (1806), in *Werke*, 20 vols., ed. Gunter Mann, Jost Benedum and Werner Friedrich Kümmel (Stuttgart: Gustav Fischer, 1990), vol. 7.

12. Sömmerring, *Organ der Seele*, pp. 48–50.

13. Goethe to Sömmerring, August 28, 1796, in Manfred Wenzel (ed.), *Goethe und Sömmerring, Briefwechsel 1784–1828*, Sömmerring-Forschungen 5 (Stuttgart: Gustav Fischer, 1988), pp. 105–107.

14. Sömmerring, *Organ der Seele*, p. 86.

15. *Ibid.*, p. 85.

16. Novalis, *Werke, Tagbebücher und Briefe Friedrich von Hardenbergs*, 3 vols., ed. Hans-Joachim Mähl and Richard Samuel (Munich: Carl Hanser, 1978–1987), vol. 1, p. 228, 656. For more on the reception of Sömmerring among German literati, see Friedrich Strack, "Sömmerings Seelenorgan und die deutschen Dichter," in Christoph Jamme and Otto Pöggeler (eds.), *"Frankfurt aber ist der Nabel dieser Erde": Das Schicksal einer Generation der Goethezeit* (Stuttgart: Klett-Cotta, 1983), pp. 185–205.

17. Franz von Baader, *Beyträge zur Elementar-Physiologie* (Hamburg: E. Bohn, 1797). Quoted from *Sämmtliche Werke*, 16 vols. (Leipzig: Herrmann Bethmann, 1852), vol. 3, p. 226.

18. Friedrich Hölderlin, "Sömmerrings Seelenorgan und die Deutschen," *Sämtliche Werke*, 8 vols. (Stuttgart: J. G. Cottasche Buchhandlung Nachfolger, 1946), vol. 1, p. 227.

19. Barbara Naumann, *"Musikalisches Ideen-Instrument": Das Musikalische in*

Poetik und Sprachtheorie der Frühromantik (Stuttgart: J. B. Metzler, 1990), p. 4; Sylvie Le Moël, *Le corps et le vêtement: Écrire et penser la musique au siècle des Lumières. Wilhelm Heinse (1746–1803)* (Paris: Honoré Champion, 1996), p. 408.

20. I am basing this passage on Robert J. Richards, *The Romantic Conception of Life: Science and Philosophy in the Age of Goethe* (Chicago: University of Chicago Press, 2002).

21. Wilhelm Heinse, *Die Aufzeichnungen Frankfurter Nachlass*, 5 vols. (Munich: Carl Hanser, 2003), vol. 1, p. 1100.

22. Heinse, *Sämmtliche Werke*, vol. 8, pt. 1, pp. 287–88 and 518.

23. *Ibid.*, p. 94.

24. Heinse, *Sämmtliche Werke*, vol. 4, p. 306.

25. Ernest Jones, "The Madonna's Conception through the Ear," *Essays in Applied Psycho-analysis*, 2 vols. (New York: International Universities Press, 1964), vol. 2, pp. 266–357.

26. Johann F. Reichardt, "Neue deutsche Werke," *Deutschland*, 4 vols. (Nendeln: Kraus Reprint, 1971), vol. 1, pt. 1, p. 128. For Goethe's famous epigram about Heinse's novel mixing word music with "doggish love," see Johann Wolfgang Goethe, *Goethe's Werke*, 17 vols. in 10 (Berlin: G. Grote'sche Verlagsbuchhandlung, 1873), vol. 4, p. 107.

27. Heinse, *Sämmtliche Werke*, vol. 7, p. 198.

28. Christine Lubkoll, *Mythos Musik: Poetische Entwürfe des Musikalischen in der Literatur um 1800* (Freiburg: Rombach, 1995), pp. 111–17.

29. Heinse, *Sämmtliche Werke*, vol. 5, p. 118.

30. Heinse, *Die Aufzeichnungen*, vol. 2, p. 291.

31. *Ibid.*, p. 310; Heinse, *Sämmtliche Werke*, vol. 7, p. 22.

32. *Ibid.*, p. 56.

33. Heinse, *Sämmtliche Werke*, vol. 4, p. 106.

34. Johann Wolfgang Goethe, *Tagebücher* (Historisch-kritische Ausgabe im Auftrag der Stiftung Weimarer Klassik), 10 vols., ed. Jochen Golz, with Wolfgang Albrecht, Andreas Döhler, and Edith Zehm (Stuttgart: J. B. Metzler, 1998) vol. 1, pt. 1, p. 6.

35. Johann Mattheson, *Critica musica*, 2 vols. (Hamburg, 1722–25), vol. 1, pp. 103–104.

36. Johann George Sulzer, *Allgemeine Theorie der Schönen Künste: In einzeln, nach alphabetischer Ordnung der Kunstwörter auf einander folgenden, Artikeln*

abgehandelt, 4 vols. (Leipzig: M. G. Weidmanns Erben und Reich, 1774), vol. 2, pp. 755–56.

37. Christian Friedrich Michaelis, *Ueber den Geist der Tonkunst* (Chemnitz: Gudrun Schröder Verlag, 1997), p. 160. Ironically, Michaelis did not believe his views to differ from those of either Heinse or Herder. In a short article of 1804, he quotes extensively from Herder's *Kalligone* and Heinse's *Hildegard von Hohenthal*.

38. Michel Serres, *The Parasite* (Baltimore: Johns Hopkins University Press, 1982).

39. Heinse, *Die Aufzeichnungen*, vol. 2, p. 700 and 562; Heinse, *Sämmtliche Werke*, vol. 8, pt. 3, p. 213.

40. Heinse, *Sämmtliche Werke*, vol. 3, pt. 2, p. 379.

41. Heinse, *Die Aufzeichnungen*, vol. 2, p. 500.

42. Heinse, *Sämmtliche Werke*, vol. 5, p. 302.

43. *Ibid.*, p. 341.

44. *Ibid.*, pp. 75–76.

45. Wolfgang Amadeus Mozart, *Briefe und Aufzeichnungen*, 8 vols. (Kassel: Bärenreiter, 1962–2005), vol. 2, p. 358.

46. Walter Serauky, *Die musikalische Nachahmungsästhetik im Zeitraum von 1700–1850* (Emsdetten: Lechte, 1929), p. 241. Similar assessments are made by Ruth Müller, *Erzählte Töne: Studien zur Musikästhetik im späten 18. Jahrhundert*, Beihefte zum Archiv für Musikwissenschaft 30 (Stuttgart: Franz Steiner Verlag Wiesbaden, 1989), and Rita Terras, *Wilhelm Heinses Ästhetik* (Munich: Wilhelm Fink, 1972), pp. 109–36.

47. Werner Keil, "Heinses Beitrag zur romantischen Musikästhetik," in Gert Theile (ed.), *Das Mass des Bacchanten: Wilhelm Heinses Über-Lebenskunst* (Munich: Wilhelm Fink, 1998), pp. 139–58.

48. On Schenker's organicism and the attendant feminization of music, see Lawrence Kramer, *Classical Music and Postmodern Knowledge* (Berkeley: University of California Press, 1995), p. 44.

49. Heinse, *Die Aufzeichnungen*, vol. 2, p. 445.

50. *Ibid.*, pp. 445–46.

51. Martin Seel, *Aesthetics of Appearing* (Stanford, CA: Stanford University Press, 2005), pp. 139–58.

52. Heinse, *Sämmtliche Werke*, vol. 8, pt. 2, p. 175.

53. Marcus Herz, *Versuch über den Schwindel*, 2nd, enlarged ed. (Berlin: Vossische Buchhandlung, 1791,), p. 211.

54. *Ibid.*, p. 55.

55. *Ibid.*, pp. 91–92.

56. *Ibid.*, pp. 57–58.

57. Heinse, *Sämmtliche Werke*, vol. 4, p. 237.

58. Denis Dodart, "Mémoire sur les causes de la voix de l'homme & de ses différens tons," in *Mémoires de mathématique et de physique de l'Académie royale des sciences (1700)*, pp. 244–93; Antoine Ferrein, "De la formation de la voix de l'homme," in *Mémoires de l'Académie royale des sciences (1741)*, pp. 409–32.

59. Heinse, *Die Aufzeichnungen*, vol. 2, pp. 533–39.

60. Wolfgang von Kempelen, *Mechanismus der menschlichen Sprache nebst der Beschreibung seiner sprechenden Maschine* (1791; Stuttgart–Bad Cannstatt: Friedrich Frommann Verlag, 1970).

61. Quoted in Joachim Gessinger, *Auge und Ohr: Studien zur Erforschung der Sprache am Menschen, 1700–1850* (Berlin: de Gruyter, 1994), p. 598. See also pp. 586–601 of Gessinger's book for an extended discussion of von Kempelen's machine.

62. Von Kempelen, *Mechanismus der menschlichen Sprache*, pp. 17–18.

63. I owe this analysis to Gessinger, *Auge und Ohr*, p. 598.

64. Kant to Sömmerring, August 10, 1795, in Gunter Mann and Franz Dumont (eds.), *Soemmerring und die Gelehrten der Goethezeit*, Sömmerring Forschungen 1 (Stuttgart: Fischer, 1985), p. 33.

65. John Cuthbertson, *Beschreibung einer Elektrisirmaschine und einigen damit von J. R. Deimann und A. Paets von Troostwyck angestelten Versuchen* (Leipzig: Kummer, 1790).

66. Anon., "Schreiben des Herrn Paets von Trostwyk und Deimann an Herrn de la Méthérie, über die Zerlegung des Wassers in brennbare und Lebensluft durch den elektrischen Funken," *Journal der Physik* 2, no. 130 (1790), pp. 130–41.

67. Immanuel Kant, *Kritik der Urteilskraft*, § 13 (Hamburg: Felix Meiner, 1924), p. 62. Most English editions render *Reize*, incorrectly, as "charms."

68. Friedrich Schlegel, *Die Entwicklung der Philosophie in zwölf Büchern*, in *Kritische Friedrich-Schlegel-Ausgabe*, ed. Ernst Behler (Paderborn, Germany: Ferdinand Schöningh, 1958), vol. 12, p. 346.

69. August Wilhelm Schlegel, *Vorlesungen über schöne Literatur und Kunst (1801–1802). Erster Teil: Die Kunstlehre*, in *Kritische Ausgabe der Vorlesungen, Vol. 1: Vorlesungen über Ästhetik I (1798–1803)*, ed. Ernst Behler (Paderborn, Germany: Schöningh, 1989), p. 375.

CHAPTER FIVE: HEARING ONESELF HEAR

1. Walter Benjamin, "German Men and Women: A Sequence of Letters," in *Walter Benjamin: Selected Writings, Volume 3, 1935–1938*, ed. Howard Eiland and Michael W, Jennings, (Cambridge, MA: Harvard University Press, 2002), pp. 167–235.

2. Walter Benjamin, *The Origin of German Tragic Drama*, trans. John Osbourne (London: NLB, 1977).

3. *Ibid.*, pp. 213–15.

4. *Ibid.*, p. 213.

5. *Ibid.*, pp. 210–11.

6. *Ibid.*, p. 214.

7. Walter Benjamin, "The Concept of Criticism in German Romanticism," in *Walter Benjamin: Selected Writings, Volume 1, 1913–1926*, ed. Marcus Bullock and Michael W. Jennings, trans. David Lachterman, Howard Eiland, and Ian Balfour (Cambridge: Harvard University Press, 1996), pp. 116–200.

8. Some representative examples include the following: John Daverio, *Nineteenth-Century Music and the German Romantic Ideology* (New York: Schirmer Books, 1993); Ulrich Tadday, *Das schöne Unendliche: Ästhetik, Kritik, Geschichte der romantischen Musikanschauung* (Stuttgart: Metzler, 2002); Berthold Hoeckner, *Programming the Absolute: Nineteenth-Century German Music and the Hermeneutics of the Moment* (Princeton, NJ: Princeton University Press, 2002); Anthony Newcomb, "Schumann and Late Eighteenth-Century Narrative Strategies," *19th-Century Music* 11, no. 2 (1987): pp. 164–74; and Michael p. Steinberg, *Listening to Reason: Culture, Subjectivity, and Nineteenth-Century Music* (Princeton, NJ: Princeton University Press, 2004). For a different take on Benjamin's role for music criticism, see Eli Friedlander, "On the Musical Gathering of Echoes of the Voice: Walter Benjamin on Opera and the Trauerspiel," *Opera Quarterly* 21, no. 4 (2005): pp. 631–46.

9. Roland Barthes, "Loving Schumann," in *The Responsibility of Forms: Critical Essays on Music, Art and Representation*, trans. Richard Howard (Berkeley:

University of California Press, 1991), pp. 293–98.

10. Slavoj Žižek, "Robert Schumann: The Romantic Anti-Humanist," in *The Plague of Fantasies* (London: Verso, 1997), pp. 192–212.

11. Ernst Florens Chladni, *Entdeckungen über die Theorie des Klangs* (Leipzig: Weidmanns, Erben und Reich, 1787).

12. Antonio Scarpa, *Anatomicae disquisitiones de auditu et olfactu* (Ticino: Typog. p. Galeatus, 1789); *De structura fenestrae rotundae auris et de tympano secundario, anatomicae observationes* (Modena: Apud Soc. typog., 1772).

13. Ernst Florens Friedrich Chladni, *Die Akustik* (1802; Hildesheim: Olms, 2004), pp. 284–88.

14. See, in this regard, Ulrike Kranefeld, *Der nachschaffende Hörer: Rezeptionsästhetische Studien zur Musik Robert Schumanns* (Stuttgart: Metzler, 2000); Bettine Menke, "'However one calls into the forest...': Echoes of Translation," in Beatrice Hansen and Andrew Benjamin (eds.), *Walter Benjamin and Romanticism* (New York: Continuum, 2002), pp. 83–97; and Katherine Bergeron, "The Echo, the Cry, the Death of Lovers," *19th-Century Music* 18, no. 2 (1994): pp. 136–51.

15. Johann Wilhelm Ritter, *Beweis, dass ein beständiger Galvanismus den Lebensprocess in dem Thierreich begleite: Nebst neuen Versuchen und Bemerkungen über den Galvanismus* (Weimar: Im Verlage des Industrie-Comptoirs, 1798).

16. Quoted in Rüdiger Safranski, *Romantik: Eine deutsche Affäre* (Munich: Hanser, 2007), p. 85.

17. Friedrich Schelling, *Einleitung zu seinem Entwurf eines Systems der Naturphilosophie* (Jena: Christian Ernst Gabler, 1799), in *Sämmtliche Werke*, 14 vols. (Stuttgart: J. G. Cotta'scher Verlag, 1856–1861), vol. 3, p. 320.

18. Johann Wilhelm Ritter, "Beweis, daß die Galvanische Actio auch in der Anorganischen Natur Möglich und wirklich sey," in *Beyträge zur nähern Kenntnis des Galvanismus und der Resultate seiner Untersuchung*, 2 vols. (Jena: Frommann, 1800–1805), vol. 1, p. 283.

19. Ritter to Carl Friedrich Ernst Frommann, January 9, 1802, in Klaus Richter (ed.), *Der Physiker des Romantikerkreises: Johann Wilhelm Ritter in seinen Briefen an den Verleger Carl Friedrich Ernst Frommann* (Weimar: Hermann Böhlaus Nachfolger, 1988), p. 123; Ritter, "Nachricht von der Fortsetzung seiner Versuche mit Volta's Galvanischer Batterie," *Physisch-Chemische Abhandlungen in chronologischer Folge*, 3 vols. (Leipzig: C. H. Reclam, 1806), vol. 2,

p. 293; and "Versuche über den Einfluß des Galvanismus auf das Zeugungsor-
gan," in *Beyträge zur näheren Kenntnis des Galvanismus und der Resultate seiner
Untersuchung*, vol. 2, p. 83.

20. Ritter, *Beweis, dass ein beständiger Galvanismus*, pp. 98–99.

21. Johann Wilhelm Ritter, "Neue Versuche und Bemerkungen über die
Wirkungen des Galvanismus der Voltaischen Batterie auf das Gehörorgan."
The article was first published in *Beyträge zur nähern Kenntniss des Galvanismus
und der Resultate seiner Untersuchung*, vol. 2, and later reprinted in *Physisch-
Chemische Abhandlungen in chronologischer Folge*, vol. 2, pp. 108–25.

22. Johann Wilhelm Ritter to Hans Christian Ørsted, March 31, 1809, in
M. C. Harding (ed.), *Correspondance de H. C. Örsted avec divers savants*, 2 vols.
(Copenhagen: H. Aschehough & Co., 1920), vol. 2, p. 224; Johann Wilhelm
Ritter, *Fragmente eines jungen Physikers*, pp. 227–28.

23. Hans Christian Ørsted, "Experiments on Acoustic Figures," in *Selected
Scientific Works of Hans Christian Ørsted*, ed. and trans. Karen Jelved, Andrew D.
Jackson, and Ole Knudsen (Princeton, NJ: Princeton University Press, 1998),
pp. 264–80. On Ørsted's musical aesthetics, see Dan Charly Christensen,
"Ørsted's Concept Of Force & Theory Of Music," in Robert M. Brain, Robert
S. Cohen, Ole Knudsen (eds.), *Hans Christian Ørsted and the Romantic Legacy in
Science: Ideas, Disciplines, Practices*, Boston Studies in the Philosophy of Science,
vol. 241, (Dordrecht: Springer, 2007), pp. 115–33.

24. Ørsted, "Experiments on Acoustic Figures," p. 279.

25. *Ibid.*, p. 280.

26. Hans Christian Ørsted, "A Letter from Mr. Ørsted, Professor of Philosophy in Copenhagen, to Professor Pictet on Acoustic Vibrations, May 26,
1785," in *Selected Scientific Works*, p. 184.

27. Novalis, *Werke: Tagebücher und Briefe Friedrich von Hardenbergs*, ed.
Hans-Joachim Mähl and Richard Samuel, 3 vols. (Munich: Hanser, 1978–1987),
vol. 2, p. 816.

28. Ritter, *Beweis, dass ein beständiger Galvanismus*, p. 164.

29. Ritter, *Beyträge zur nähern Kenntnis des Galvanismus*, vol. 2, pts. 3–4,
p. 167; Ritter, "Neue Versuche und Bemerkungen über die Wirkungen des
Galvanismus der Voltaischen Batterie auf das Gehörorgan," in *Physisch-
Chemische Abhandlungen*, vol. 2, p. 124.

30. Johann Wilhelm Ritter, *Fragmente aus dem Nachlasse eines jungen*

Physikers: Ein Taschenbuch für Freunde der Natur, ed. Steffen Dietzsch and Birgit Dietzsch (1810; Hanau: Müller & Kiepenheuer, 1984), p. 184, no. 420.

31. Ritter, *Fragmente aus dem Nachlasse eines jungen Physikers*, p. 234.

32. See, for instance, Daniel Chua, *Absolute Music and the Construction of Meaning* (Cambridge: Cambridge University Press, 1999), pp. 174 and 196. Also Thomas Strässle, "'Das Hören ist ein Sehen von und durch innen': Johann Wilhelm Ritter and the Aesthetics of Music," in Siobhán Donovan and Robin Elliott (eds.), *Music and Literature in German Romanticism* (Rochester, NY: Camden House, 2004), pp. 27–41.

33. Charles Rosen, *The Romantic Generation* (Cambridge, MA: Harvard University Press, 1995), p. 59.

34. Ritter, "Neue Versuche und Bemerkungen über die Wirkungen des Galvanismus der Voltaischen Batterie auf das Gehörorgan," p. 119.

35. *Ibid.*, pp. 120–21.

36. Johann Gottfried Herder, *Kalligone*, in *Werke*, 10 vols. (Frankfurt am Main: Deutscher Klassiker Verlag, 1998), vol. 8, p. 703.

37. Carl Schmitt, *Political Romanticism* (Cambridge, MA: The MIT Press, 1986).

38. *Ibid.*, p. 20.

39. Johann Wilhelm Ritter to Hans Christian Ørsted, February 2, 1806, in Ørsted, *Correspondance*, vol. 2, p. 147.

40. Ritter, "Neue Versuche und Bemerkungen über die Wirkungen des Galvanismus der Voltaischen Batterie auf das Gehörorgan," pp. 109–11. For more on Ritter's self-experiments, see Stuart Strickland, "The Ideology of Self-Knowledge and the Practice of Self-Experimentation," *Eighteenth-Century Studies* 31, no. 4 (1998): pp. 453–71.

41. Novalis, *Werke*, vol. 3, p. 425.

42. Mark Evan Bonds, *Music as Thought: Listening to the Symphony in the Age of Beethoven* (Princeton, NJ: Princeton University Press, 2006), p. 50.

43. Johannes Müller, *Handbuch der Physiologie des Menschen*. The bibliography of the *Handbuch* is notoriously complex. For reasons of accessibility, I am relying on the edition of 1840, available on-line at http://vlp.mpiwg-berlin. mpg.de/library/data/lit17252 (last accessed August 27, 2009). Readers who prefer an English translation are referred to the heavily edited and not always reliable *Elements of Physiology*, trans. William Baly (Philadelphia: Lea and

Blanchard, 1843).

44. Emil Du Bois-Reymond, "Gedächtnisrede auf Johannes Müller," *Reden*, 2 vols. (Leipzig: Veit, 1912), vol. 1, pp. 157 and 297 n. 37.

45. Johannes Müller, *Ueber die phantastischen Gesichtserscheinungen* (1826; Munich: Werner Fritsch, 1967).

46. On all this, see Michael Hagner and Bettina Wahrig-Schmidt (eds.), *Johannes Müller und die Philosophie* (Berlin: Akademie Verlag, 1992), especially Frederick Gregory, "Hat Müller die Naturphilosophie wirklich aufgegeben?" pp. 143–54.

47. Johannes Müller, *Zur vergleichenden Physiologie des Gesichtssinnes des Menschen und der Thiere* (Leipzig: Cnobloch, 1826), p. 453.

48. Jonathan Sterne, *The Audible Past: Cultural Origins of Sound Reproduction* (Durham, NC: Duke University Press, 2003), pp. 60–62.

49. *Ibid.*, p. 62.

50. Müller, *Handbuch*, vol. 2, p. 460.

51. *Ibid.*, p. 466.

52. Ernst Heinrich Weber, *De aure et auditu hominis et animalium* (Leipzig, 1820).

53. Ernst Heinrich Weber and Wilhelm Eduard Weber, *Wellenlehre auf Experimente gegründet, oder, Über die Wellen tropfbarer Flüssigkeiten mit Anwendung auf die Schall- und Lichtwellen* (Leipzig: Gerhard Fleischer, 1825).

54. *Ibid.*, p. 479.

55. Du Bois-Reymond, "Gedächtnisrede auf Johannes Müller," p. 198. Müller himself in 1825 had deplored the "wholly unfertile ground" that had prevented him from completing his otological studies. Müller, *Zur vergleichenden Physiologie*, p. xxiv.

56. Du Bois-Reymond, "Gedächtnisrede auf Johannes Müller," p. 198.

57. Müller, *Zur vergleichenden Physiologie*, p. xxiv.

58. Müller, *Handbuch*, p. 350; *Über die phantastischen Gesichtserscheinungen*, p. 453.

59. Müller, *Zur vergleichenden Physiologie*, p. 50.

60. *Ibid.*, p. xxiv.

61. Hermann von Helmholtz, *On the Sensations of Tone*, trans. Alexander J. Ellis (New York, Dover Publications, 1954), p. 148.

62. Jan Purkinje, "Zur vergleichenden Physiologie des Gesichtssinnes des

Menschen und der Thiere, etc. Von Dr. Johannes Müller," in *Opera omnia*, 13 vols. (Prague: Society of Czech Physicians, 1913–1985), vol. 5, p. 28.

63. Jan Purkinje, "Untersuchungen über den Tartinischen dritten Ton," in *Opera omnia*, vol. 2, p. 59. See also Wilhelm Weber, "Ueber die Tartinischen Töne," *Annalen der Physik und Chemie* 15, New Series (1829): pp. 216–22. On the debate about combination tones more broadly, see V. Carlton Maley, *The Theory of Beats and Combination Tones 1700–1863* (New York: Garland Publishing, 1990).

64. Jan Purkinje, "Die Topologie der Sinne im Allgemeinen, nebst einem Beispiel eigenthümlicher Empfindungen der Rückenhaut bei Gebrauche des Regenbades," in *Opera omnia*, vol. 3, p. 79–80.

65. Jan Purkinje, "Beiträge zur Kenntnis des Sehens in subjectiver Hinsicht," in *Opera omnia*, vol. 5, p. 51.

66. Jan Purkinje, "Einbildungskraft," in *Opera omnia*, vol. 2, pp. 194–95.

67. Sigmund Freud, "Findings, Ideas, Problems," in *The Standard Edition of the Complete Psychological Works of Sigmund Freud*, ed. James Strachey (London: Hogarth Press, 1953–1974), vol. 23, p. 300.

68. Du Bois-Reymond, "Gedächtnisrede auf Johannes Müller," p. 156.

69. Purkinje, "Zur vergleichenden Physiologie des Gesichtssinnes," p. 30.

70. Purkinje, "Untersuchungen über den Tartinischen dritten Ton," p. 59.

71. Du Bois-Reymond, "Gedächtnisrede auf Johannes Müller," p. 158.

72. For the idolization of motherhood and its role in the emergence of cultural modernism of the late nineteenth and early twentieth centuries, see Christine Kanz, *Maternale Moderne: Männliche Gebärphantasien zwischen Kultur und Wissenschaft (1890–1933)* (Munich: W. Fink, 2009).

73. Jutta Müller-Tamm, *Abstraktion als Einfühlung: Zur Denkfigur der Projektion in Psychophysiologie, Kulturtheorie, Ästhetik und Literatur der frühen Moderne* (Freiburg: Rombach, 2005), p. 101.

74. Georges Didi-Huberman, "L'immanence figurale: Hypocondrie et morphologie selon Victor Hugo," *Cahiers du Musée National d'Art Moderne* 85 (2003): pp. 90–120.

75. Müller, *Zur vergleichenden Physiologie*, pp. 461–62.

76. See, in particular, Müller, *Handbuch*, vol. 2, pp. 513–52. Michael Hagner, "Sinnlichkeit und Sittlichkeit: Spinozas 'grenzenlose Uneigennützigkeit' und Johannes Müllers Entwurf einer Sinnesphysiologie," in Hagner and

Wahrig-Schmidt, *Johannes Müller und die Philosophie*, pp. 29–44.

77. Müller, *Ueber die phantastischen Gesichtserscheinungen*, p. 88.

78. Müller, *Zur vergleichenden Physiologie*, p. 454.

79. *Ibid.*, p. 458.

80. Müller, *Ueber die phantastischen Gesichtserscheinungen*, p. 105.

81. *Ibid.*, p. 104.

82. *Ibid.*, p. 28.

83. *Ibid.*, p. 88.

CHAPTER SIX: THE LABRYINTH OF REASON

1. Galen, *De usu partium*, 8.6, in Galen, *On the Usefulness of the Parts of the Body*, trans. Margaret Tallmadge May, 2 vols. (Ithaca, NY: Cornell University Press, 1968), vol. 1, p. 404; Adam Politzer, *Geschichte der Ohrenheilkunde*, 2 vols. (1907; Hildesheim: Georg Olms, 1967), vol. 1, p. 27.

2. By 1880, the interest in the metaphorology of the ear had faded completely, so much so that Joseph Hyrtl called it "an innocent diversion in the tiresome description of the organs of smell and hearing." See Joseph Hyrtl, *Onomatologia anatomica: Geschichte und Kritik der anatomischen Sprache der Gegenwart* (Vienna: W. Braumüller, 1880), p. 287. Also Louise Vinge, *The Five Senses: Studies in a Literary Tradition*, Acta Regiae Societatis Humaniorum Litterarum Lundensis 72 (Lund, Sweden: Publications of the Royal Society of Letters at Lund, 1975).

3. On music's association with labyrinths, see Pierre Saint-Amand, *Diderot: Le labyrinthe de la relation* (Paris: Librairie Philosophique J. Vrin, 1984), pp. 101–10; and Craig Wright, *The Maze and the Warrior: Symbols in Architecture, Theology, and Music* (Cambridge, MA: Harvard University Press, 2001).

4. For more on the history of labyrinths see Penelope Reed Doob, *The Idea of the Labyrinth from Classical Antiquity through the Middle Ages* (Ithaca, NY: Cornell University Press, 1990). On the labyrinth in philosophy, see Hans Blumenberg, *Höhlenausgänge* (Frankfurt am Main: Suhrkamp, 1996), pp. 465–90; on Descartes' fear of labyrinths, see G. Nador, "Métaphors de chemins et de labyrinths chez Descartes," *Revue Philosophique de la France et de l'Etranger* 152 (1962): pp. 37–51. Also Douwe Draaisma, *Metaphors of Memory: A History of Ideas about the Mind* (Cambridge; Cambridge University Press, 2000), pp. 68–102. On Georges Bataille, see Benjamin Noys, *Georges Bataille: A Critical*

Introduction (London: Pluto Press, 2000), pp. 14–17; and Georges Bataille, "The Labyrinth," *Visions of Excess: Selected Writings 1927–1939* (Minneapolis: University of Minnesota Press, 1985), pp. 171–77. Also see Michel Serres, *The Five Senses* (London: Continuum, 2009).

5. Hermann von Helmholtz, *Die Lehre von den Tonempfindungen als physiologische Grundlage für die Theorie der Musik* (Braunschweig: Friedrich Vieweg und Sohn, 1865). Throughout this chapter, this edition will be referred to as *LT 1*. Subsequent editions will be referred to as follows: the second edition (1865) *LT 2*; the third, revised edition (1870) *LT 3*; the fourth, revised edition (1877) *LT 4*. Occasional reference will also be made, under the abbreviation *ST*, to the second English edition, translated from the fourth German edition by Alexander Ellis as *On the Sensations of Tone as a Physiological Basis for the Theory of Music* (New York: Dover Publications, 1954). Most translations of Helmholtz's other works are outmoded. Even the essays in a more recent collection edited by David Cahan, *Hermann von Helmholtz, Science and Culture: Popular and Philosophical Essays* (Chicago: University of Chicago Press, 1995) are reproduced unchanged from the much older English editions of 1873 and 1881 of *Popular Lectures on Scientific Subjects*, 2 vols. (New York: D. Appleton and Company, 1873 and 1881). Therefore all translations are my own, but whenever possible the reader will be referred to Cahan's translation of the passages quoted.

6. Quoted from Leo Koenigsberger, *Hermann von Helmholtz* (Oxford: Clarendon Press, 1906), p. iii.

7. See, however, Stephan Vogel, "Sensations of Tone, Perception of Sound, and Empiricism: Helmholtz's Physiological Acoustics," in David Cahan (ed.), *Hermann von Helmholtz and the Foundations of Nineteenth-Century Science* (Berkeley: University of California Press, 1993), pp. 259–90; Elfrieda Hiebert and Erwin Hiebert, "Musical Thought and Practice: Links to Helmholtz's Tonempfindungen," in Lorenz Krüger (ed.), *Universalgenie Helmholtz: Rückblick nach 100 Jahren* (Berlin: Akademie Verlag, 1994), pp. 295–314; Youn Kim, "Theories of Musical Hearing 1863–1931: Helmholtz, Stumpf, Riemann, and Kurth in Historical Context," Ph.D. diss., Columbia University, 2003. For the most recent and probably also best account, see Benjamin Steege, "Material Ears: Helmholtz, Attention, and Modern Aurality," Ph.D. diss., Harvard University, 2007.

8. See, however, Leon Botstein, "Music and Its Public: Habits of Listening

and the Crisis of Musical Modernism in Vienna, 1870–1914," Ph.D. diss., Harvard University, 1985.

9. David Cahan, "Helmholtz and the Civilizing Power of Science," in David Cahan (ed.), *Hermann von Helmholtz and the Foundations of Nineteenth-Century Science*, pp. 559–601.

10. Herbert Schnädelbach, *Philosophy in Germany 1831–1933* (Cambridge: Cambridge University Press, 1984), p. 103.

11. Gregor Schiemann, *Hermann von Helmholtz's Mechanism: The Loss of Certainty* ([Dordrecht]: Springer, 2009), pp. 160–61. Among the more noteworthy of Helmholtz's acoustic works published before and immediately after *Die Lehre von den Tonempfindungen* are the following: "Ueber Combinationstöne," *Annalen der Physik und Chemie* 99, no. 12 (1856): pp. 497–540; "Ueber musikalische Temperatur," *Annalen der Physik und Chemie* 113 (1861): pp. 87–90; *Die Mechanik der Gehörknöchelchen und des Trommelfells* (Bonn: Max Cohen & Sohn, 1869).

12. Ernst Cassirer, *The Problem of Knowledge: Philosophy, Science, and History since Hegel* (New Haven, CT: Yale University Press, 1950), p. 4.

13. Georg Christoph Lichtenberg, *Schriften und Briefe*, ed. Wolfgang Promies vol. 2, *Sudelbücher II* (Munich: Carl Hanser, 1971), p. 284. I owe the reference to Lichtenberg and the early inspiration to some of the ideas explored in this chapter generally to Hans Blumenberg's extraordinary *Höhlenausgänge*. Blumenberg's thoughts on Lichtenberg's critique of physiognomy appear on pp. 666–68.

14. Cassirer, *The Problem of Knowledge*, p. 4. Gregor Schiemann in turn, in his otherwise excellent discussion of Helmholtz's theory of knowledge, has little to say about *Die Lehre von den Tonempfindungen* other than that it is an expression of its author's "halved mechanism" and the "doubt about someday being able to exhaustively explain the phenomena of life by the mechanical structure of matter." Schiemann, *Hermann von Helmholtz's Mechanism*, p. 142.

15. *LT* 1, p. 355. See also pp. 198, 343, and *ST*, p. 151.

16. *LT* 3, p. ix; *ST*, p. vii.

17. Vogel, "Sensations of Tone, Perception of Sound, and Empiricism," p. 260.

18. *LT* 3, p. ix; *ST*, p. vii.

19. Hermann von Helmholtz, "Das Denken in der Medizin," *Vorträge und*

Reden, 4th ed., 2 vols. (Braunschweig: Vieweg, 1896), vol. 2 (hereafter *VR* 2), p. 189; Cahan (ed.), *Hermann von Helmholtz, Science and Culture*, p. 325.

20. *LT* 1, pp. 237–62; *ST*, pp. 159–73. The literature on beats is vast, but for a good summary, see V. Carlton Maley, *The Theory of Beats and Combination Tones, 1700–1863* (New York: Garland Publishing, 1990).

21. *LT* 1, p. 56; *ST*, p. 34.

22. *Ibid.*

23. *LT* 1, p. 72; *ST*, p. 42.

24. For more details see R. Steven Turner, "The Ohm-Seebeck Dispute, Hermann von Helmholtz, and the Origins of Physiological Acoustics," *British Journal for the History of Science* 10, no. 1 (1977): pp. 1–24.

25. *LT* 1, p. 97; *ST*, p. 56. Helmholtz's terms are notoriously difficult to translate. Thus, although the correct English equivalent for *Ton* would be "tone," in order to distinguish better between a musical tone and its partials (and to avoid confusion with the current meaning of "tone" as a simple sinusoid or sine wave), I will refer to *Ton* as "partial." Likewise, while *Klang* is frequently rendered as "tone" in older English translations, here I use "sound" instead.

26. *LT* 1, p. 195; *ST*, p. 127.

27. *LT* 1, p. 220; *ST*, p. 148.

28. Le Marquis Alphonse [Marchese Alfonso] Corti, "Recherches sur l'organe de l'ouïe des mammifères," *Zeitschrift für wissenschaftliche Zoologie*, 3 (1851): pp. 109–69. For an excellent overview of research immediately before and after Corti's discovery (complete with reproductions of key illustrations), see Jochen Schacht and Joseph E. Hawkins, "Sketches of Otohistory. Part 4: A Cell by Any Other Name: Cochlear Eponyms," *Audiology & Neuro-Otology* 9, no. 6 (2004): pp. 317–27.

29. Carl Gustav Lincke, *Das Gehörorgan in anatomischer, physiologischer und pathologisch-anatomischer Hinsicht* (Leipzig: Verlag der J. C. Hinrichsschen Buchhandlung, 1837), p. 525.

30. *Ibid.*, p. 528.

31. Corti, "Recherches sur l'organe de l'ouïe des mammifères," p. 163.

32. Emil Harleß, in Rudolph Wagner (ed.), *Handwörterbuch der Physiologie mit Rücksicht auf physiologische Pathologie* (Braunschweig: Fr. Vieweg und Sohn, 1853), s.v. "Hören," vol.4, p. 440. See also Rudolf Hermann Lotze, *Medicinische*

Psychologie oder Physiologie der Seele (Leipzig: Weidmann'sche Buchhandlung, 1852), p. 342.

33. Carl Ludwig, *Lehrbuch der Physiologie des Menschen*, 2nd ed., 2 vols. (Leipzig and Heidelberg: C. F. Winter'sche Buchhandlung, 1858–61), vol. 1, p. 370.

34. Hermann von Helmholtz, "Ueber die physiologischen Ursachen der musikalischen Harmonie," in *Vorträge und Reden*, 4th ed., 2 vols. (Braunschweig: Vieweg, 1896), vol. 1 (hereafter *VR* 1), pp. 119–56; Cahan (ed.), *Hermann von Helmholtz, Science and Culture*, pp. 46–75.

35. Helmholtz, "Ueber die physiologischen Ursachen der musikalischen Harmonie," in *VR* 1, p. 139–40; Cahan (ed.), *Hermann von Helmholtz, Science and Culture*, pp. 60–61.

36. *LT* 1, p. 218; *ST*, p.145.

37. Henry Margenau gives 1852 as the beginning of Helmholtz's interest in acoustics. See *ST*, "Introduction."

38. Helmholtz, "Ueber Combinationstöne," p. 525.

39. *Ibid.*, p. 527.

40. *Ibid.*, p. 526.

41. *LT* 1, p. 101.

42. *Ibid.*

43. *Ibid.*

44. *LT* 4, pp. 106–111. Alexander Ellis renders both terms, somewhat misleading, as to perceive "synthetically" and "analytically," respectively (*ST*, p. 62). Kim translates them as "mere perception" and "more active apperception" (88).

45. *LT* 4, p. 106.

46. Koenigsberger, *Hermann von Helmholtz*, p. 280.

47. Helmholtz, *Die Mechanik der Gehörknöchelchen und des Trommelfells*. For an English translation, see *The Mechanism of the Ossicles of the Ear and the Membrana Tympani*, trans. Albert H. Buck and Normand Smith (New York: William Wood & Co., 1873).

48. *LT* 3, p. 206; *ST*, p. 134.

49. *Ibid.*, p. vii.

50. Koenigsberger, *Hermann von Helmholtz*, p. 247.

51. Hermann von Helmholtz, "Ueber die Zeit, welche nötig ist, damit ein

Gesichtseindruck zum Bewusstsein kommt, Resultate einer von Herrn N. Baxt im Heidelberger Laboratorium ausgeführten Untersuchung," in *Wissenschaftliche Abhandlungen von Hermann Helmholtz*, 3 vols. (Leipzig: Johann Ambrosius Barth, 1882–1895), vol.2, pp. 947–52. For a modern English translation of Baxt's article see *Psychological Research* 44, no. 1 (1982): pp. 1–12.

52. Helmholtz, "Ueber die Zeit," p. 952.

53. Hermann Ulrici, *Leib und Seele: Grundzüge einer Physiologie des Menschen* (Leipzig: T.D. Weigel, 1874), p. v.

54. *Ibid.*, p. 284.

55. *Ibid.*, p. 289.

56. Georg Elias Müller, *Zur Theorie der sinnlichen Aufmerksamkeit* (Leipzig: A. Edelmann, 1873).

57. For instance in Hermann von Helmholtz, *Handbuch der physiologischen Optik* (Leipzig: Leopold Voss, 1867), p. 447; Hermann von Helmholtz, *Helmholtz's Treatise on Physiological Optics, Vol. 3: The Perceptions of Vision*, trans. James P. C. Southall ([Rochester, NY]: The Optical Society of America, 1925), p. 24.

58. For more on the early Helmholtz's relationship to Leibniz, see Fabio Bevilacqua, "Helmholtz's *Ueber die Erhaltung der Kraft*: The Emergence of a Theoretical Physicist," in Cahan (ed.), *Hermann von Helmholtz and the Foundations of Nineteenth-Century Science*, pp. 291–333. On Leibniz's role in Helmholtz's late period see Harmut Hecht, "Actio, Quantité d'action und Wirkung: Helmholtz' Rezeption dynamischer Grundbegriffe," in Krüger (ed.), *Universalgenie Helmholtz*, pp. 107–23.

59. Hermann von Helmholtz, "Ueber die Natur der menschlichen Sinnesempfindungen," in *Wissenschaftliche Abhandlungen*, vol. 2, p. 601.

60. *LT* 4, p. 106. The phrase also recurs on p. 109.

61. Gottfried Wilhelm Leibniz, *New Essays On Human Understanding*, trans and ed. Peter Remnant and Jonathan Bennett (Cambridge: Cambridge University Press, 1981), pp. 54–55.

62. Daniel Heller-Roazen, *The Inner Touch: Archaeology of a Sensation* (New York: Zone Books, 2007), pp. 190–91.

63. Leibniz, *New Essays*, p. 57.

64. Gottfried Wilhelm Leibniz, *Theodicy: Essays on the Goodness of God, the Freedom on Man and the Origin of Evil*, trans. E.M. Huggard (La Salle, IL: Open

Court, 1985), p. 53.

65. William James, "Are We Automata?" *Mind* 4, no. 12 (1879): p. 13.

66. See W. Janke, in Joachim Ritter (ed.), *Historisches Wörterbuch der Philosophie*, 13 vols. (Basel: Schwabe, 1971), s.v. "Apperzeption," vol. 1, pp. 448–56.

67. R. Steven Turner, "Helmholtz, Sensory Physiology, and the Disciplinary Development of German Psychology," in William R. Woodward and Mitchell G. Ash (eds.), *The Problematic Science: Psychology in Nineteenth-Century Thought* (New York: Praeger, 1982), p. 158.

68. Klaus Christian Köhnke, *The Rise of Neo-Kantianism: German Academic Philosophy between Idealism and Positivism*, trans. R. J. Hollingdale (Cambridge: Cambridge University Press, 1991), p. 233.

69. Hermann von Helmholtz, " Die Thatsachen in der Wahrnehmung," in *VR* 2, p. 244; Cahan (ed.) *Hermann von Helmholtz, Science and Culture*, p. 364.

70. Hermann von Helmholtz, "Erinnerungen," in *VR* 1, p. 15; Cahan (ed.), *Hermann von Helmholtz, Science and Culture*, p. 388.

71. *Ibid.*; Cahan (ed.), *Hermann von Helmholtz, Science and Culture*, p. 389. Elsewhere, Helmholtz speaks of the "labyrinth of conflicting opinions," Helmholtz, *Helmholtz's Treatise on Physiological Optics, Vol. 3*, p. 19; the "Icarus flight of speculation," "Ueber das Verhältniss der Naturwissenschaften zur Gesammtheit der Wissenschaften. Akademische Festrede," in *VR* 1, p. 165; and the "maze of erudition," *ibid.*, p. 168.

72. Helmholtz, "Erinnerungen," p. 17; Cahan (ed.), *Hermann von Helmholtz, Science and Culture*, p. 390.

73. Hermann von Helmholtz, "Ueber die Natur der menschlichen Sinnesempfindungen," in *Wissenschaftliche Abhandlungen*, vol. 2, pp. 591–609.

74. Koenigsberger, *Hermann von Helmholtz*, p. 207.

75. Helmholtz, *Helmholtz's Treatise on Physiological Optics, Vol. 3*, p. 20.

76. Lotze, *Medicinische Psychologie oder Physiologie der Seele*, p. 331. But Johannes Müller had earlier claimed that representation (*Vorstellung*) is related to sensation (*Empfindung*) "rather like the sign for a thing." Johannes Müller, *Handbuch der Physiologie des Menschen für Vorlesungen*, 2 vols. (Coblenz: Verlag von J. Hölscher, 1837–1840), vol. 2, p. 526. For a discussion of Lotze's notion of "local sign" in the context of spatial perception, see Gary Hatfield, *The Natural and the Normative: Theories of Spatial Perception from Kant to Helmholtz* (Cambridge, MA: The MIT Press, 1990), pp. 158–64.

77. Helmholtz, "Ueber die Natur der menschlichen Sinnesempfindungen," in *Wissenschaftliche Abhandlungen*, vol. 2, p. 608.

78. Lorraine Daston and Peter Galison, *Objectivity* (New York: Zone Books, 2007), pp. 253–307.

79. Helmholtz, *Handbuch der physiologischen Optik*, vol. 3, p. 444; *Helmholtz's Treatise on Physiological Optics, Vol. 3*, p. 21.

80. Helmholtz, "Thatsachen in der Wahrnehmung," pp. 243–44. Cahan (ed.), *Hermann von Helmholtz, Science and Culture*, p. 363.

81. Helmholtz, *Helmholtz's Treatise on Physiological Optics, Vol. 3*, p. 19.

82. *Ibid.*, p. 31.

83. Gary Hatfield, "Helmholtz and Classicism: The Science of Aesthetics and the Aesthetics of Science," in Cahan (ed.), *Hermann von Helmholtz and the Foundations of Nineteenth-Century Science*, p. 546.

84. Helmholtz, "Ueber das Verhältniss," pp. 178 and 171; Cahan (ed.), *Hermann von Helmholtz, Science and Culture*, pp. 90 and 85.

85. *Ibid.*, p. 175; Cahan (ed.), *Hermann von Helmholtz, Science and Culture*, p. 88.

86. Helmholtz, "Thatsachen in der Wahrnehmung," p. 234; Cahan (ed.), *Hermann von Helmholtz, Science and Culture*, p. 356.

87. Hermann von Helmholtz, "Ueber das Sehen des Menschen," in *VR* 1, p. 114.

88. *Ibid.* This contrasts with the view that the changes in Helmholtz's thought originated in the late 1860s. See, for instance, Olivier Darrigol, "Helmholtz's Electrodynamics and the Comprehensibility of Nature," in Krüger (ed.), *Universalgenie Helmholtz*, pp. 216–44; and Michael Heidelberger, "Force, Law, and Experiment: The Evolution of Helmholtz's Philosophy of Science," in Cahan (ed.), *Hermann von Helmholtz and the Foundations of Nineteenth-Century Science*, pp. 461–97.

89. The phrase "thought without consciousness" appears in Helmholtz, "Ueber das Sehen des Menschen," p. 111. For the second term, see Hermann von Helmholtz, "Ueber die physiologischen Ursachen der musikalischen Harmonie," in *VR* 1, p. 154. Cahan translates this as the "principle of artistic beauty in its unconscious conformity to law." Cahan (ed.), *Hermann von Helmholtz, Science and Culture*, p. 74. The third term, finally, is from Hermann von Helmholtz, "Die neueren Fortschritte in der Theorie des Sehens," in *VR* 1,

p. 361, and "The Recent Progress of the Theory of Vision," in Cahan (ed.), *Hermann von Helmholtz, Science and Culture*, p. 200, where Cahan translates the phrase as "Sensible Intelligibility."

90. Helmholtz, "Ueber das Sehen des Menschen," p. 116.

91. Schiemann, *Hermann von Helmholtz's Mechanism*, p. 126.

92. Helmholtz, "Ueber das Sehen des Menschen," p. 116.

93. Helmholtz, *Handbuch der physiologischen Optik*, p. 448.

94. Helmholtz, "Thatsachen in der Wahrnehmung," p. 223; Cahan (ed.), *Hermann von Helmholtz, Science and Culture*, p. 348.

95. Hermann von Helmholtz, "Goethe's Vorahnungen kommender naturwissenschaftlicher Ideen," in *VR* 2, pp. 335–62; Cahan (ed.), *Hermann von Helmholtz, Science and Culture*, pp. 393–412.

96. Helmholtz, "Goethe's Vorahnungen kommender naturwissenschaftlicher Ideen," pp. 348 and 361; Cahan (ed.), *Hermann von Helmholtz, Science and Culture*, pp. 401, 411.

97. Hatfield, "Helmholtz and Classicism," p. 558; Schiemann, *Hermann von Helmholtz's Mechanism*, p. 247.

98. Helmholtz, "Thatsachen in der Wahrnehmung," p. 244; Cahan (ed.), *Hermann von Helmholtz, Science and Culture*, p. 363.

99. Ernst Cassirer, *Determinism and Indeterminism in Modern Physics* (New Haven, CT: Yale University Press, 1956), pp. 63–64.

100. Hermann von Helmholtz, "Ueber die Erhaltung der Kraft," in *VR* 1, p. 191; Cahan (ed.) *Hermann von Helmholtz, Science and Culture*, p. 97.

101. Ernst Cassirer, *Substanzbegriff und Funktionsbegriff: Untersuchungen über die Grundfragen der Erkenntniskritik* (1910; Darmstadt: Wissenschaftliche Buchgesellschaft, 1969).

102. *Ibid.*, p. 404.

103. Helmholtz, "Ueber Combinationstöne," p. 526.

104. *LT* 1, p. 101.

105. Helmholtz, "Ueber Combinationstöne," p. 526.

106. Helmholtz, "Ueber das Verhältniss," in *VR* 1, p. 183; Cahan (ed.) *Hermann von Helmholtz, Science and Culture*, p. 94.

107. Hans Blumenberg, *Theorie der Unbegrifflichkeit* (Frankfurt am Main: Suhrkamp, 2007), p. 10.

108. Blumenberg, *Theorie der Unbegrifflichkeit*, p. 11; also Blumenberg,

Höhlenausgänge, p. 37.

109. Helmholtz, "Ueber das Verhältniss," in *VR* 1, p. 192; Cahan (ed.) *Hermann von Helmholtz, Science and Culture*, p. 85.

110. Hatfield, "Helmholtz and Classicism," p. 558.

111. *Ibid.*, p. 524.

112. Timothy Lenoir, *Instituting Science: The Cultural Production of Scientific Disciplines* (Stanford, CA: Stanford University Press, 1997), p. 135.

113. For more on the panorama, see Stephan Oettermann's classic study *The Panorama: History of a Mass Medium* (New York: Zone Books, 1997).

114. Dolf Sternberger, *Panorama of the Nineteenth Century*, trans. Joachim Neugroschel (1938; New York: Urizen Books, 1977).

115. Hermann von Helmholtz, "Optisches über Malerei," in *VR* 2, pp. 93–136; Cahan (ed.) *Hermann von Helmholtz, Science and Culture*, pp. 279–308.

116. Sternberger, *Panorama of the Nineteenth Century*, p. 172.

117. *Ibid.*, p. 174.

118. Helmholtz, "Optisches über Malerei," p. 127; Cahan (ed.) *Hermann von Helmholtz, Science and Culture*, p. 302.

119. *LT* 3, pp. ix–x; *ST*, p. vii.

120. *LT* 1, p. 560.

121. *LT* 1, pp. 423–24.

122. *LT* 1, p. 456.

123. *LT* 1, p. 424.

124. For more on the impact of Helmholtz on Riemann, see Michael Kevin Mooney, "The 'Table of Relations' and Music Psychology in Hugo Riemann's Harmonic Theory," Ph.D. diss., Columbia University, 1996; and Chien-Chang Yang, "Music as Knowledge: Hugo Riemann's Theory of Musical Listening and the Foundation of German *Musikwissenschaft*," Ph.D. diss., University of Chicago, 2002.

125. Fechner's comments were part of a series of letters he exchanged with Helmholtz in 1869. See Herbert Hörz (ed.), *Physiologie und Kultur in der zweiten Hälfte des 19. Jahrhunderts: Briefe an Hermann von Helmholtz* (Marburg: Basilisken Presse 1994), pp. 417–25. For an extended discussion of the correspondence with Fechner and Helmholtz's analogy with the stereoscope, see Steege, "Material Ears," pp. 164–72.

126. *LT* 3, p. 452; *ST*, p. 289.

127. *LT* 3, pp. 452–53.

128. *LT* 1, p. 451.

129. Steege, "Material Ears," pp. 182–89.

130. *LT* 1, p. 358.

131. *Ibid.*

132. *LT* 1, p. 361.

133. Hermann Lotze, *Geschichte der Ästhetik in Deutschland* (Munich: J. G. Cotta'sche Buchhandlung, 1868), p. 280, 282.

134. *Ibid.*, p. 463.

135. Walter Benjamin, *The Arcades Project*, trans. Howard Eiland and Kevin McLaughlin (Cambridge, MA: Harvard University Press, 1999), pp. 478–81.

136. Hermann Lotze, *Mikrokosmus: Ideen zur Naturgeschichte und Geschichte der Menschheit*, 3 vols. (Leipzig: S. Hirzel, 1856–1864) vol. 3, p. 28. I am quoting from the English edition, *Microcosmus: An Essay Concerning Man and His Relation to the World*, 4th ed., trans. Elizabeth Hamilton and E. E. Constance Jones (New York: Scribner & Welford, 1890) p. 151.

137. *Mikrokosmus*, p. 52; *Microcosmus*, p. 174.

138. Benjamin, *The Arcades Project*, p. 479.

139. *LT* 3, p. 370; *ST*, p. 235.

140. Steege, "Material Ears," p. 210.

141. Eduard Hanslick, *Vom Musikalisch-Schönen* (Leipzig: Rudolph Weigel, 1858), p. 41.

142. Steege, "Material Ears," p. 205.

143. *Ibid.*, pp. 201–11.

144. John Stuart Mill, *The Logic of the Moral Sciences* (Chicago: Open Court, 1988), pp. 135–36.

145. Steege, "Material Ears," p. 223.

146. Quoted in Koenigsberger, *Hermann von Helmholtz*, p. 173. Helmholtz, "Goethe's Vorahnungen kommender naturwissenschaftlicher Ideen," in *VR* 2, p. 345; Cahan (ed.) *Hermann von Helmholtz, Science and Culture*, p. 399.

147. Sternberger, *Panorama of the Nineteenth Century*, p. 180.

CHAPTER SEVEN: RHYTHM AND CLUES

1. Alex Ross, *The Rest is Noise: Listening to the Twentieth Century* (New York,

Farrar, Straus and Giroux, 2007), pp. 4–8.

2. Stephen Kern, *The Culture of Time and Space 1880–1918* (Cambridge, MA: Harvard University Press, 1983).

3. Walter Benjamin, "The Work of Art in the Age of Its Technological Reproducibility: Third Version," trans. Harry Zohn and Edmund Jephcott, in *Walter Benjamin: Selected Writings, Volume 4, 1938–1940*, ed. Howard Eiland and Michael W. Jennings (Cambridge, MA: Harvard University Press, 2003), p. 266.

4. *Ibid.*, pp. 265–66.

5. Cathérine Clément, *Syncope: The Philosophy of Rapture* (Minneapolis: University of Minnesota Press, 1994), p. 51.

6. Sigmund Freud, "Beyond the Pleasure Principle," in *The Standard Edition of the Complete Psychological Works of Sigmund Freud*, ed. James Strachey (London: Hogarth Press, 1953–1974), vol. 18, p. 41.

7. Sigmund Freud, "A Note Upon the 'Mystic Writing-Pad,'" in *The Standard Edition of the Complete Psychological Works of Sigmund Freud*, vol. 19, pp. 226–32.

8. For a brief overview of the early history of the psychophysiology of time see Claude Debru, "Time, from Psychology to Neurophysiology: A Historical View," *Comptes Rendus Biologies* 329, nos. 5–6 (May–June 2006): pp. 330–39.

9. Hermann von Helmholtz, "Ueber die Methoden, kleinste Zeittheile zu messen, und ihre Anwendung für physiologische Zwecke," in *Wissenschaftliche Abhandlungen von Hermann Helmholtz*, 3 vols. (Leipzig: Johann Ambrosius Barth, 1882–1895), vol. 2, pp. 862–80.

10. Leo Koenigsberger, *Hermann von Helmholtz* (1902; Bristol, UK: Thoemmes Press, 2001), vol. 1, pp. 122–24.

11. For a more detailed account of these debates, see Henning Schmidgen, "Of Frogs and Men: The Origins of Psychophysiological Time Experiments," *Endeavour* 26, no. 4 (2002): pp. 142–48; and "Sound, Writing, and the Speed of Thought: Physiological Time Experiments in Utrecht, 1860–1870," in Henning Schmidgen (ed.), *Experimental Arcades: The Materiality of Time Relations in Life Sciences, Art, and Technology (1830–1930)* (Berlin: Max Planck Institut für Wissenschaftsgeschichte, 2003), pp. 25–44; and "Time and Noise: The Stable Surroundings of Reaction Experiments, 1860–1890," *Studies in History and Philosophy of Biological and Biomedical Sciences* 34 (2003): pp. 237–75.

12. Johann Czermak, "Ideen zu einer Lehre vom Zeitsinn," *Sitzungsberichte der Kaiserlichen Akademie* 24 (1857): pp. 231–36.

13. Ernst Mach, "Zur Theorie des Gehörorgans," in *Sitzungsberichte der kaiserlichen Akademie der Wissenschaften, mathematisch-naturwissenschaftliche Classe* 48 (1863): pp. 283–300; "Untersuchungen über den Zeitsinn des Ohres," *Sitzungsberichte der kaiserlichen Akademie der Wissenschaften, mathematisch-naturwissenschaftliche Classe* 51, 2. Abtheilung (1865): pp. 133–50; Ernst Mach and Johannes Kessel, "Versuche aber die Akkomodation des Ohres," *Sitzungsberichte der kaiserlichen Akademie der Wissenschaften, mathematisch-naturwissenschaftliche Classe* 111, no. 66 (1872): pp. 337–43.

14. Mach, "Untersuchungen über den Zeitsinn des Ohres," p. 150.

15. Ernst Meumann, "Über Assoziationsexperimente mit Beeinflussung der Reproduktionszeit," *Archiv für die gesamte Psychologie* 9 (1907): pp. 117–50; Henry J. Watt, "Über den Einfluss der Geschwindigkeit der Aufeinanderfolge von Reizen auf Wortreaktionen," *ibid.*, pp. 151–80; Vittorio Benussi, "Zur experimentellen Analyse des Zeitvergleichs," *ibid.*, pp. 366–449. For a comprehensive summary of the whole debate from a contemporary perspective, see Johannes Quandt, "Literaturbericht: Das Problem des Zeitbewußtseins," *Archiv für die gesamte Psychologie* 8 (1906): pp. 143–89.

16. Élie de Cyon, *Das Ohrlabyrinth als Organ der mathematischen Sinne für Raum und Zeit* (Berlin: Julius Springer, 1908).

17. Ernst Meumann, "Untersuchungen zur Psychologie und Ästhetik des Rhythmus," *Philosophische Studien* 2 (1894): pp. 249–322 and 393–430.

18. Ernst Meumann, *System der Ästhetik* (Leipzig: Quelle & Meyer, 1914).

19. Georg Simmel, *The Philosophy of Money*, trans. Tom Bottomore and David Frisby. 2nd enl. ed. (New York: Routledge, 1990), pp. 485–503. Interestingly, before he turned to philosophy and sociology, Simmel had envisioned a career as a musicologist. His inaugural dissertation was "Psychologische und ethnologische Studien über Musik." See Georg Simmel, *Gesamtausgabe* (Frankfurt am Main: Suhrkamp, 1989), vol. 1, pp. 45–90.

20. Georg Simmel, *Soziologie: Untersuchungen über die Formen der Vergesellschaftung*, in *Gesamtausgabe*, vol. 11, pp. 689–90.

21. Ernst Jentsch, *Über Zitterbewegungen und deren Simulation* (Bonn: Universitäts-Buchdruckerei von Carl Georgi, 1893); and *Die Laune: Eine ärztlich-psychologische Studie* (Wiesbaden: J. F. Bergmann, 1902).

22. Ernst Jentsch, *Musik und Nerven*, 2 vols. (Wiesbaden: J. F. Bergmann, 1904–1911).

23. Richard Wallaschek, *Psychologie und Pathologie der Vorstellung* (Leipzig: J. A. Barth, 1905), p. 138.

24. Ernst Jentsch, "On the Psychology of the Uncanny" (1906), *Angelaki* 2, no. 1 (1996): pp. 7–16.

25. Sigmund Freud, "The 'Uncanny,'" in *The Standard Edition of the Complete Psychological Works of Sigmund Freud*, vol. 17, pp. 217–56.

26. Hélène Cixous, "Fiction and Its Phantoms: A Reading of Freud's *Das Unheimliche*," *New Literary History* 7, no. 3 (1976): pp. 525–48.

27. Cixous, "Fiction and Its Phantoms," p. 546.

28. William Stern, *Über Psychologie der individuellen Differenzen: Ideen zu einer "Differentiellen Psychologie"* (Leipzig: J. A. Barth, 1900).

29. Johannes Herbart, "Psychologische Untersuchung über die Stärke einer gegebenen Vorstellung als Function ihrer Dauer betrachtet," in *Sämtliche Werke in chronologischer Reihenfolge*, ed. Karl Kehrbach and Otto Flügel, 19 vols. (1887–1912; Aalen: Scientia Verlag 1964), vol. 3, pp. 121–45.

30. Stern, *Über Psychologie der individuellen Differenzen*, p. 14.

31. *Ibid.*, p. 14.

32. *Ibid.*, p. 15.

33. See Stern's study in three parts on the perception of pitch changes, "Die Wahrnehmung von Tonveränderungen," all published in *Zeitschrift für Psychologie und Physiologie der Sinnesorgane*, pt. 1, 11 (1896): pp. 1–30; pt. 2, 21 (1899): pp. 360–87; pt. 3, 22 (1900): pp. 1–12. Also William Stern, *Psychologie der Veränderungsauffassung* (Breslau: Preuss und Jünger, 1898) and "Ein Beitrag zur differentiellen Psychologie des Urtheilens," *Zeitschrift für Psychologie und Physiologie der Sinnesorgane*, 22 (1900): pp. 13–22.

34. Simmel, *The Philosophy of Money*, p. 498. Stern's reflections on tempo appear in "Das Tempo des Seelenlebens," *Zeitschrift für Pädagogische Psychologie* 1 (1899): pp. 369–70.

35. Georg Simmel, "Über sociale Differenzierung," in *Gesamtausgabe*, vol. 2, p. 183.

36. Hugo von Hofmannsthal, *Reden und Aufsätze I*, in *Gesammelte Werke*, ed. Herbert Steiner, 10 vols. (Frankfurt am Main: Fischer Taschenbuch, 1979–1980), vol. 9, p. 95.

37. Stefan Rieger, *Die Individualität der Medien: Eine Geschichte der Wissenschaften vom Menschen* (Frankfurt am Main: Suhrkamp, 2000).

38. Wilhelm Stern, *Vorgedanken zur Weltanschauung (Niedergeschrieben im Jahre 1901)* (Leipzig: J. A. Barth, 1915).

39. Simmel, *The Philosophy of Money*, p. 493.

40. Karl Bücher, *Arbeit und Rhythmus*, 4th ed. (1896; Leipzig: B. G. Teubner, 1909).

41. Anson Rabinbach, *The Human Motor: Energy, Fatigue, and the Origins of Modernity* (Berkeley: University of California Press, 1992).

42. Bücher, *Arbeit und Rhythmus*, p. 358.

43. *Ibid.*, p. 383.

44. Karl Bücher, *Industrial Evolution* (New York: Henry Holt & Co., 1904), pp. 385–86.

45. Theodor Lipps, "Aesthetische Einfühlung," *Zeitschrift für Psychologie und Physiologie der Sinnesorgane* 23 (1900): pp. 415–50.

46. *Ibid.*, p. 418.

47. *Ibid.*, p. 424.

48. *Ibid.*, p. 432.

49. Bojan Bujić, *Music in European Thought 1851–1912* (Cambridge: Cambridge University Press, 1988), p. 275; and Georg Braungart, *Leibhafter Sinn: Der andere Diskurs der Moderne* (Tübingen: Niemeyer, 1995), p. 222.

50. Theodor Lipps, *Psychologische Studien*, 2nd ed. (Leipzig: Verlag der Dürr'schen Buchhandlung, 1905), pp. 115–230. For an English translation, see Theodor Lipps, *Consonance and Dissonance in Music*, trans. William Thomson (San Marino, CA: Everett Books, 1995).

51. Lipps, *Consonance and Dissonance*, p. 122.

52. *Ibid.*

53. *Ibid.*

54. *Ibid.*, pp. 124–25.

55. Theodor Lipps, *Ästhetik* (Hamburg: Leopold Voss, 1903), p. 481. On rhythm, see especially pp. 406–24.

56. Paul Moos, *Die deutsche Ästhetik der Gegenwart* (Berlin: Schuster & Loeffler, 1919), p. 469.

57. Georg Simmel, "Rodins Plastik und die Geistesrichtung der Gegenwart," in *Gesamtausgabe*, vol. 7, pp. 92–100; and "Michelangelo: Ein Kapitel zur

Metaphysik der Kultur," in *Gesamtausgabe*, vol. 12, pp. 111–36.

58. Friedrich Nietzsche to Carl Fuchs, August 26, 1888, in *Selected Letters of Friedrich Nietzsche*, ed. and trans. Christopher Middleton (Chicago: University of Chicago Press, 1969), p. 307.

59. *Ibid.*

60. *Ibid.*

61. Hugo Riemann, *Wie hören wir Musik?: Grundlinien der Musik-Ästhetik* (Berlin: Max Hesses Verlag), p. 46.

62. Hugo Riemann, *Die Natur der Harmonik*, Sammlung musikalischer Vorträge, no. 40 (Leipzig: Breitkopf & Härtel, 1882), p. 186. On Riemann's reception of Helmholtz, see Youn Kim, "Theories of Musical Hearing 1863–1931: Helmholtz, Stumpf, Riemann, and Kurth in Historical Context," Ph.D. diss. Columbia University, 2003; and Chien-Chang Yang, "Music as Knowledge: Hugo Riemann's Theory of Musical Listening and the Foundation of German Musikwissenschaft," Ph.D. diss., University of Chicago, 2002.

63. Michel Foucault, *The Birth of the Clinic: An Archaeology of Medical Perception*, trans. A. M. Sheridan Smith (New York: Pantheon Books, 1973), p. 36.

64. See Rieger, *Die Individualität der Medien*.

65. The Weber brothers' work on walking is discussed in Friedrich Kittler, "Man as a Drunken Town-musician," trans. Jocelyn Holland, *MLN* 118, no. 3 (2003): pp. 637–52. Du Bois-Reymond's phrase also appears there. See Wilhelm Weber and Eduard Weber, *The Mechanics of the Human Walking Apparatus*, trans. R. Furlong (Berlin: Springer Verlag, 1992).

66. Friedrich Nietzsche, *The Will to Power*, book 1, § 47, trans. Walter Kaufmann and R. J. Hollingdale, ed. Walter Kaufmann (New York: Random House, 1967), p. 29.

67. Hugo Riemann, *Wie hören wir Musik?*, p. 44.

68. *Ibid.*, p. 45.

69. Friedrich Nietzsche, *The Case of Wagner*, §1, in *The Complete Works of Friedrich Nietzsche*, ed. Oscar Levy, 18 vols. (Edinburgh: T. N. Foulis, 1909), vol. 8, p. 2.

70. *Ibid.*, "Epilogue."

71. Friedrich Nietzsche to Carl Fuchs, August 26, 1888, in *Selected Letters*, p. 307.

72. Hugo Riemann, *Systematische Modulationslehre* (Hamburg: J. F. Richter,

1887), p. 2.

73. Theodor W. Adorno, *In Search of Wagner*, trans. Rodney Livingstone (London: Verso, 1991), p. 50.

74. *Ibid.*, p. 54.

75. *Ibid.*, p. 50.

76. Riemann, *Musikalische Dynamik und Agogik*, p. 11.

77. For more on Nietzsche as a pioneer of twentieth-century rhythm and dance cults, see Inge Baxmann, *Mythos: Gemeinschaft: Körper- und Tanzkulturen in der Moderne* (Munich: Wilhelm Fink, 2000); and Kimerer L. LaMothe, *Nietzsche's Dancers* (New York: Palgrave Macmillan, 2006).

78. Ernst Mach, *Contributions to the Analysis of the Sensations*, trans. C. M. Williams (Chicago: Open Court, 1897), pp. 23 and 20 n.1.

79. Manfred Sommer, *Evidenz im Augenblick: Eine Phänomenologie der reinen Empfindung* (Frankfurt am Main: Suhrkamp, 1987).

CHAPTER EIGHT: ECHOLESS

1. Hannah Arendt, *The Life of the Mind, Volume 1: Thinking* (New York: Harcourt Brace Jovanovich, 1977), p. 185.

2. Peter Sloterdijk, "Wo sind wir, wenn wir Musik hören?" in *Weltfremdheit* (Frankfurt am Main: Suhrkamp, 1993), pp. 294–331.

3. Walter Benjamin, "The Work of Art in the Age of Its Technological Reproducibility: Third Version," trans. Harry Zohn and Edmund Jephcott, in *Walter Benjamin: Selected Writings, Volume 4, 1938–1940*, ed. Howard Eiland and Michael W. Jennings (Cambridge, MA: Harvard University Press, 2003), p. 255.

4. *Ibid.*, p. 269. Emphasis in the original.

5. Theodor W. Adorno, "On the Fetish-Character in Music and the Regression of Listening" (1938), in *Essays on Music*, selected, with introduction, commentary, and notes by Richard Leppert (Berkeley: University of California Press, 2002), pp. 288–317.

6. See, for instance, Michael Bull, *Sound Moves: iPod Culture and Urban Experience* (New York: Routledge, 2007); and Andrew Dell'Antonio (ed.), *Beyond Structural Listening?: Postmodern Modes of Hearing* (Berkeley: University of California Press, 2004).

7. Günther Anders, *Die Antiquiertheit des Menschen*, 2 vols. (Munich: C. H.

Beck, 1987). Anders adopted the *nom de plume* Anders in the early 1930s. Consequently, only works written before that period will be quoted under their author's original family name, Stern.

8. Günther Stern [Anders], *Philosophische Untersuchungen zu musikalischen Situationen*, typescript, Österreichisches Literaturarchiv der Österreichischen Nationalbibliothek, Vienna. Nachlass Günther Anders. ÖLA 237/04. Henceforth *PU*.

9. Theodor W. Adorno, letter to Günther Anders, October 31, 1963. Typescript. Briefwechsel Günther Anders–T. W. Adorno, Nachlass Günther Anders, ÖLA 237/04, Österreichisches Literaturarchiv der Österreichischen Nationalbibliothek, Vienna. Anders would later defer to Adorno's musical proficiency, and Adorno, in turn, would deplore how the growing distance between the two men obscured the "truly deep convergences" in their thinking. For more details on this episode, see Elisabeth Young-Bruehl, *Hannah Arendt: For Love of the World* (New Haven, CT: Yale University Press, 1982), pp. 78–81. Also Konrad Paul Liessmann, "'Hot Potatoes': Zum Briefwechsel zwischen Günther Anders und Theodor W. Adorno," *Zeitschrift für kritische Theorie* 6 (1998): pp. 29–38.

10. Theodor W. Adorno, "Schubert," in *Gesammelte Schriften*, ed. Rolf Tiedemann (Frankfurt am Main: Suhrkamp, 1970), vol. 17, pp. 18–33. For an English translation see *19th-Century Music* 29, no. 1 (2005): pp. 7–14.

11. Richard Leppert, "On Reading Adorno Hearing Schubert," *19th-Century Music* 29, no. 1 (2005): pp. 56–63.

12. Adorno, "Schubert," *19th-Century Music* 29, no. 1 (2005): p. 7.

13. *PU*, p. 6.

14. Georg von Békésy, "Zur Theorie des Hörens: Die Schwingungsform der Basilarmembran," *Physikalische Zeitschrift* 29 (1928): pp. 793–810. For an English translation, see Georg von Békésy, *Experiments in Hearing*, trans. and ed. Ernest G. Wever (New York, McGraw-Hill, 1960), pp. 403–29.

15. Ernest G. Wever, *Theory of Hearing* (New York: Dover Publications, 1949). My summary of Békésy's theory is based on Wever's book.

16. Von Békésy was not the first to challenge Helmholtz's resonance theory. From as early as 1886, a number of scientists had been experimenting with alternative theories in which the ear's capacity for pitch analysis was shifted to the brain, for instance, in William Rutherford's "telephone" theory. Still others

assigned a key role to areas of concentration or "bulges" in the wave motion of the cochlear fluid in determining pitch perception. For a fuller discussion of these theories, see Chapter 7 and Wever, *Theory of Hearing*, pp. 43–96.

17. Von Békésy, *Experiments in Hearing*, pp. 3–10.

18. Martin Jay, *Downcast Eyes: The Denigration of Vision in Twentieth-Century French Thought* (Berkeley: University of California Press, 1993).

19. Ernst Bloch, *Essays on the Philosophy of Music* (Cambridge: Cambridge University Press, 1985), p. 138.

20. Urban noise has recently begun to attract a great deal of attention. See, for instance, Karin Bijsterveld, *Mechanical Sound: Technology, Culture, and Public Problems of Noise in the Twentieth Century* (Cambridge, MA: The MIT Press, 2008); Michael Cowan, "Imagining Modernity through the Ear," *Arcadia* 41 (2006): pp. 124–46.

21. Hannah Arendt and Günther Stern [Anders], "Rilkes 'Duineser Elegien'," in Ulrich Fülleborn and Manfred Engel (eds.), *Materialien zu Rilkes "Duineser Elegien,"* 3 vols. (Frankfurt am Main: Suhrkamp, 1982), vol. 2, pp. 45–65.

22. *Ibid.*, p. 45.

23. *Ibid.*, p. 48.

24. *Ibid.*, p. 45.

25. Günther Stern [Anders], "Zur Phänomenologie des Zuhörens," *Zeitschrift für Musikwissenschaft* 9 (1927): pp. 610–19.

26. *Ibid.*, p. 618.

27. *Ibid.*, p. 616.

28. *Ibid.*, p. 619. There is a striking parallel here between the way Anders defines "authentic" listening to Debussy and a recent "experiment" in which musicologist Elisabeth Le Guin listened to Debussy's song "Soupire" by bearing in mind one of the composer's famous apodictic statements: "When one really listens to music...one hears at once what should be heard." See Elisabeth Le Guin, "One Bar in Eight: Debussy and the Death of Description," in Dell'Antonio (ed.), *Beyond Structural Listening?* pp. 233–51.

29. Eduard Hanslick, *On the Musically Beautiful*, trans. Geoffrey Payzant (Indianapolis, IN: Hackett, 1986), p. 57.

30. Helmuth Plessner, "Hören und Vernehmen," *Melos* 4, no. 6 (1925): pp. 285–90; "Zur Phänomenologie der Musik," in *Gesammelte Schriften*, ed.

Günter Dux, Odo Marquard und Elisabeth Stroker, 10 vols. (Frankfurt am Main: Suhrkamp, 1980–1985), vol. 7, pp. 59–66.

31. The lecture was published as "Grundfragen des musikalischen Hörens," *Jahrbuch der Musikbibliothek für 1925* (1926): pp. 35–52.

32. Heinrich Besseler, *Das musikalische Hören der Neuzeit* (Berlin: Akademie-Verlag, 1959).

33. Besseler, "Grundfragen des musikalischen Hörens," p. 38.

34. *Ibid.*, pp. 51–52.

35. *Ibid.*, p. 46.

36. See, for instance, Brian Currid, *A National Acoustics: Music and Mass Publicity in Weimar and Nazi Germany* (Minneapolis: University of Minnesota Press, 1996).

37. Hermann Hesse, *Steppenwolf* (New York: Bentham Books, 1969), pp. 242–43.

38. Günther Stern [Anders], "Spuk und Radio," *Anbruch* 12, no. 2 (1930): pp. 65–66.

39. *Ibid.*, p. 65.

40. Theodor W. Adorno, *Nachgelassene Schriften, Abteilung I: Fragment gebliebene Schriften — Band 3 Current of Music: Elements of a Radio Theory*, ed. Robert Hullot-Kentor (Frankfurt am Main: Suhrkamp, 2006). The critique of Anders's theory of radio (who is referred to under his parental name, Stern) appears in two versions: a long version written in somewhat halting English (pp. 128–45) and a more polished, but shorter version (pp. 546–54). See also Adorno, "On the Fetish-Character in Music and the Regression of Listening (1938)."

41. Adorno, *Current of Music*, p. 546.

42. *Ibid.*, p. 143.

43. *Ibid.*, p. 138.

44. Adorno, *Current of Music*, pp. 173–82.

45. Günther Stern [Anders], "Une interprétation de l'a posteriori," *Recherches philosophiques* 4 (1934): pp. 65–80; and Günther Stern [Anders], "Pathologie de la liberté," *Recherches philosophiques* 6 (1936): pp. 22–54.

46. The parallels between this concept and Georges Bataille's "principle of insufficiency," formulated in 1935–36 while Anders was living in Paris, are striking. See Georges Bataille, "The Labyrinth," *Visions of Excess: Selected*

Writings, 1927–1939 (Minneapolis: University of Minnesota Press, 1985), pp. 171–77.

47. Stern, "Une interprétation de l'a posteriori," p. 69.

48. Stern, "Pathologie de la liberté," p. 24.

49. Stern, "Une interprétation de l'a posteriori," p. 71.

50. See, for instance, Günther Anders-Stern [Anders], "The Acoustic Stereoscope," *Philosophy and Phenomenological Research* 10, no. 2 (1949): pp. 238–43.

51. Stern, "Pathologie de la liberté," pp. 23–24.

52. *Ibid.*, pp. 40–51.

53. Anders outlined his "theory of needs" in a discussion in Los Angeles involving, among other German émigrés, Max Horkheimer, Theodor W. Adorno, Bertolt Brecht, and Hanns Eisler. See Max Horkheimer, "Günther Anders, Thesen über 'Bedürfnisse,' 'Kultur,' 'Kulturbedürfnis,' 'Kulturwerte,' 'Werte,'" in *Gesammelte Schriften*, 19 vols., ed. Alfred Schmidt and Gunzelin Schmid Noerr (Frankfurt am Main: Fischer Taschenbuch Verlag, 1985), vol. 12, pp. 579–86.

54. Günther Anders, *Ketzereien* (Munich: Beck, 1996), p. 69; Theodor W. Adorno, "Commitment," in *Notes to Literature,* 2 vols., ed. Rolf Tiedemann, trans. Sherry Weber Nicholsen (New York: Columbia University Press, 1992), vol. 2, p. 88.

55. Anders, *Antiquiertheit des Menschen*, vol. 1, p. 314.

56. *PU*, p. 6.

57. *Ibid.*, p. 34.

58. *Ibid.*, p. 36.

59. *Ibid.*, p. 48.

60. *Ibid.*, p. 51.

61. *Ibid.*, p. 68.

62. *Ibid.*, p. 87.

63. Max Scheler, *Wesen und Formen der Sympathie* (Bonn: F. Cohen, 1923).

64. *PU*, p. 80.

65. *Ibid.*, p. 93.

66. *Ibid.*, p. 102.

67. Jacques Derrida, *Of Grammatology*, corrected ed., trans. Gayatri Chakravorty Spivak (Baltimore: Johns Hopkins University Press 1998), p. 12.

68. *Ibid.*

69. *PU*, p. 147.

70. *Ibid.*, p. 143.

71. *Ibid.*, p. 147.

72. *Ibid.*, pp. 170–84.

73. Immanuel Kant, *Critique of the Power of Judgment*, trans. Paul Guyer and Eric Matthews (Cambridge: Cambridge University Press, 2000), p. 142.

74. *Ibid.*, p. 141.

75. *PU*, p. 177.

76. Theodor W. Adorno, *Philosophy of New Music*, ed. and trans. Robert Hullot-Kentor (Minneapolis: University of Minnesota Press, 2006), p. 53.

77. Rüdiger Safranski, *Martin Heidegger: Between Good and Evil* (Cambridge, MA: Harvard University Press, 1998), p. 168.

78. Thomas H. Macho, "Die Kunst der Verwandlung: Notizen zur frühen Musikphilosophie von Günther Anders," in Konrad Paul Liessmann (ed.), *Günther Anders kontrovers* (Munich: C. H. Beck, 1992), pp. 89–102 and 304–305.

79. For details on Heidegger's views on these composers, see Heinrich Wiegand Petzet, *Encounters and Dialogues with Martin Heidegger, 1929–1976* (Chicago: University of Chicago Press, 1993). On Stravinsky, see Martin Heidegger, "Über Igor Strawinsky," *Aus der Erfahrung des Denkens*, in *Gesamtausgabe* (Frankfurt am Main: Klostermann, 1975), vol. 13, p. 181.

80. Heidegger shares this fascination with Derrida. See Jacques Derrida, *Glas*, trans. John p. Leavy, Jr. and Richard Rand (Lincoln, University of Nebraska Press, 1986).

81. Martin Heidegger, *Hölderlins Hymnen "Germanien" und "Der Rhein"* (Frankfurt am Main: Klostermann, 1980); "Das Geheimnis des Glockenturms," *Aus der Erfahrung des Denkens*, in *Gesamtausgabe*, vol. 13, pp. 63–66.

82. Hans Jonas, *The Phenomenon of Life: Toward a Philosophical Biology* (Chicago: University of Chicago Press, 1982), p. 240. In a similar vein, see David Michael Levin, *The Listening Self: Personal Growth, Social Change and the Closure of Metaphysics* (London: Routledge, 1989).

83. Martin Heidegger, *Being and Time: A Translation of Sein und Zeit*, trans. Joan Stambaugh (Albany: State University of New York Press, 1996), p. 153.

84. Jacques Derrida, "Heidegger's Ear: Philopolemology (Geschlecht IV)," in *The Politics of Friendship*, trans. George Collins (London: Verso, 1997), p. 164.

85. Heidegger, *Being and Time*, p. 163.

86. *Ibid.*, p. 153.

87. Martin Heidegger, *The Principle of Reason*, trans. Reginald Lilly (Bloomington: Indiana University Press, 1991), p. 47.

88. Quoted in Safranski, *Martin Heidegger*, p. 333.

89. Martin Heidegger, "What is Metaphysics?" in *Pathmarks*, ed. William McNeill (Cambridge; Cambridge University Press, 1998), pp. 88–89.

90. *Ibid.*, p. 93.

91. Sloterdijk, *Weltfremdheit*, pp. 323–24.

92. In the original French text of "Heidegger's Ear," Derrida speaks of *résonance* (resonance) between the voice of the friend and *Dasein*. See Jacques Derrida, *Politiques de l'amitié suivi de l'oreille de Heidegger* (Paris: Galilée, 1994), p. 387.

93. Sloterdijk, *Weltfremdheit*, pp. 322–25.

94. Günther Anders, *Über Heidegger* (Munich: C. H. Beck, 2001), p. 306.

95. *Ibid.*, p. 294.

96. Michel Serres, *The Troubadour of Knowledge* (Ann Arbor: University of Michigan Press, 1997), pp. 20–21.

97. *Ibid.*, p. 21.

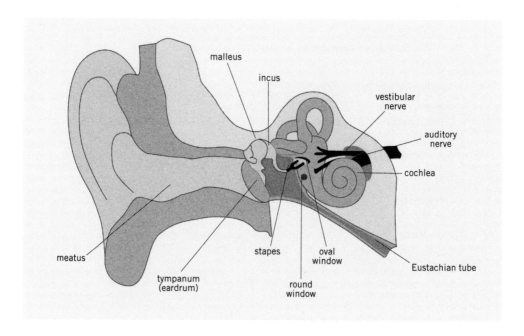

THE HUMAN EAR

Glossary

Air implantatus An airy substance also known as air ingenitus that was held to be contained in the tympanic cavity. The theory was disproved by Domenico Cotugno in 1760.

Basilar membrane A fibrous plate extending from the lamina spiralis to the spiral ligament on the outer wall of the cochlea. It separates the cochlear duct or scala media from the scala tympani and supports the organ of Corti.

Cochlea A spirally coiled, tapered bony tube of about two and three-quarters turns located within the internal ear. It contains the receptor organs essential to hearing.

Endolymph A watery fluid contained within the membranous labyrinth.

Eustachian tube The tube that runs from the middle ear to the pharynx. The function of the eustachian tube is to protect, aerate, and drain the middle ear.

Glottis The middle part of the larynx, the area where the vocal cords are located.

Helicotrema A narrow aperture within the apex of the cochlea that allows communication between the scala vestibuli and the scala tympani.

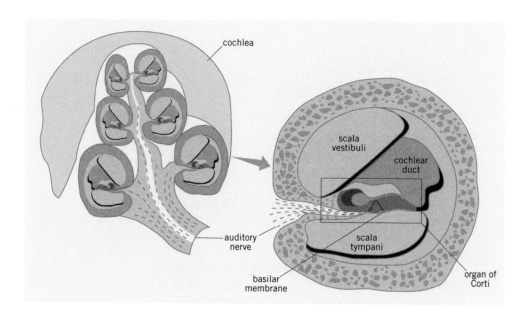

cochlea

scala
vestibuli

cochlear
duct

auditory
nerve

scala
tympani

basilar
membrane

organ of
Corti

CROSS SECTION OF THE COCHLEA

Lamina spiralis A double plate of bone dividing the spiral canal of the cochlea into the scala tympani and the scala vestibuli. Also known as the osseous spiral lamina.

Liquor cerebrospinalis The cerebrospinal fluid, which circulates through the ventricles to the spaces between the meninges about the brain and spinal cord.

Malleus The outermost of the three auditory ossicles that are located in the middle ear. Its shape resembles a club. The handle of the malleus is attached to the tympanic membrane, and the head of the malleus is attached to the body of the *incus*.

Nosology The classification of diseases.

Organ of Corti The organ of hearing proper lining the basilar membrane. It contains the auditory sensory cells or hair cells.

Oval window An opening through the bone that separates the middle ear from the scala vestibuli of the cochlea. It is closed by the footplate of the stapes.

Pericardial plexus A network of interlacing blood vessels or nerves surrounding the heart.

Peristalsis Successive waves of involuntary contraction passing along the walls of a hollow muscular structure such as the intestines.

Phrenitis An inflammation of the brain or of the meninges of the brain.

Phthisis Tubercolosis.

Reissner's membrane The membrane inside the cochlea that separates the cochlear duct from the scala vestibuli.

Round window An opening through the bone that separates the middle ear from the scala tympani of the cochlea and that is closed by a membrane; also called the fenestra rotunda.

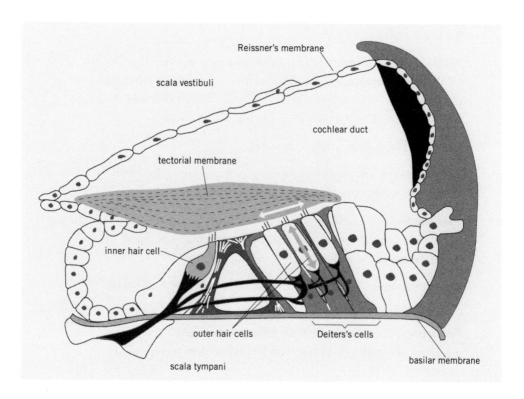

Reissner's membrane

scala vestibuli

cochlear duct

tectorial membrane

inner hair cell

outer hair cells

Deiters's cells

scala tympani

basilar membrane

ORGAN OF CORTI

Semicircular canals The three half-circular, interconnected tubes located inside the labyrinth.

Tectorial membrane A semigelatinous membrane covering the surface of the organ of Corti. It is in intimate contact with the cilia of the hair cells.

Tensor tympani The intraaural muscle attached to the handle of the malleus. Its reflex contraction, in response to intense sound or to tactile stimulation to parts of the face, draws the malleus inward, which increases tension on the eardrum.

Trachea The main trunk of the system of tubes by which air passes to and from the lungs.

Tympanum The conically shaped, semitransparent membrane that separates the external acoustic meatus from the middle ear cavity. The handle of the malleus is attached to it in the middle ear. Also called the tympanic membrane or eardrum.

Index

328, 339; existential ontology and,
337; philosophical, 317; teleology and,
323–24.
Antiquiertheit des Menschen, Die [The
Obsoleteness of Man] (Anders),
308–309.
Apperception, 220, 237, 244, 246, 247,
379 n.44.
Aqueduct, 60–61.
Arbeit und Rhythmus [Labor and Rhythm]
(Bücher), 289–91.
Arbuthnot, John, 127.
Arcades Project (Benjamin), 259, 266.
Architecture, 69, 70, 72, 266.
Architecture harmonique (Ouvrard), 105.
Ardinghello (Heinse), 152.
Arendt, Hannah, 307, 309, 311, 315, 338.
Aristotle, 32, 81, 97, 338.
Arithmetic, 13, 34–35, 40.
Art. *See* Aesthetics and art.
Art de ne point s'ennuyer, L' [The Art of Not
Getting Bored] (Boureau-Deslandes),
144.
Art history, 20.
Association, theory of, 130–31.
Astruc, Jean, 127.
Atomists, 33.
Atonality, 330.
Attention, 21, 242–43.
Attention-distraction dichotomy, 20–21.
Atys (Lully opera), 89.
Auditory culture, 17, 22, 308.
Auditory nerve, 64–66, 67, 152; in
anatomical illustrations, 398, 400;
cochlear resonance and, 222;
imagination and, 211; in Perrault's
physiology, 81; pitch perception and,
190; as quasi-autonomous agent, 214;
sign theory and, 249; sonic vibrations to
brain conducted by, 189; specific sensory
energies of, 216.
Auditory perception, 18, 238; of compound
sounds, 236; law of sensory energies and,
207; laws of physics and, 132; listener as
ego, 146; madness and, 45; mechanist
view of, 33; moral perspective and,
124; Perrault's theory of, 81; rhythmic
perception, 19; subjectivity and, 195;
temporal stabilization and, 279. *See also*

Hearing; Listening.
Auditory studies, 18.
Augustine, Saint, 316, 326, 328, 331.
Aurality, 14, 30, 47; Cartesian mechanism
and, 73; constitutive role of resonance
in history of, 11; eroticism and, 162–63,
165; listener function and, 24; self-
referential, 66–67.
Authenticity, 23.

BAADER, FRANZ VON, 158.
Baillet, Adrien, 38.
Baroque aesthetics, 126, 132; *folie de l'écoute*
and, 93; German Romanticism and, 161;
modern era and, 185, 186; neo-Baroque,
88; operatic arias, 125.
Barthes, Roland, 21, 187–88, 321.
Basilar membrane, 13–14, 121; in anatomical
illustrations, 400, 402; organ of Corti
and, 227, 232, 234; in Perrault's
physiology, 80; pitch perception and, 92;
structure of, 119; sympathetic resonance
and, 123; wave theory of hearing and, 313.
Bataille, Georges, 218, 394 n.46.
Bauhin, Gaspard, 62–64.
Baxt, Nikolai, 241.
Beats, theory of, 223, 293, 342.
Beeckman, Isaac, 36, 39, 45, 46, 101.
Beethoven, Ludwig van, 258, 270, 300,
301, 330.
Begriff der Kunstkritik in der deutschen Romantik
[The Concept of Criticism in German
Romanticism] (Benjamin), 186.
Békésy, Georg von, 13, 312–14.
Benedetti, Giovanni Battista, 99–101, 293.
Benjamin, Walter, 21, 192, 197, 216, 259,
288; critical *écriture* and, 309; on film
and the unconscious, 272; German
Romanticism and, 185–87; on Lotze's
pessimism, 266, 267; on mass media,
308; messianic tendencies, 186–87, 216,
272, 333; on radio, 319.
Bergson, Henri, 283.
Bernoulli, Daniel, 155, 189.
Besseler, Heinrich, 68, 72, 318, 328.
Billroth, Theodor, 25–26.
Binaries, 15, 23, 135, 138; rhythm and, 301;
time and, 326; tyranny of, 340.
Biology, 121, 159.

Meatus, 205, *398*.

Mechanism, Cartesian, 82, 119, 136, 190. *See also* Cartesianism.

Media technologies, 18, 114.

Mediation, 20, 90.

Medicine, 51, 159; aestheticization of, 146; birth of modern medicine, 139–40; healing powers of music, 133–41; "human harpsichord" and, 117; mechanist doctrines and, 74; pneumatology and, 126; vitalist, 141, 156. *See also* Montpellier school.

Meditations on First Philosophy (Descartes), 29–30, 31, 37, 43, 45, 66.

Medulla, 130.

Melancholia, 139, 140, 141–43, 145, 147, 148–49.

Melody, 125, 129; infinite, 281, 302; melodic affinity, 220; microrhythm (tonal rhythm) and, 294; musical therapy and, 148.

Mémoires pour servir à l'histoire naturelle des animaux, 71.

Memory, 29, 275, 286, 299; ego and, 37; location of, 82; melodic affinities and, 262, 263, 264; of musical listeners, 303; perception and, 283; in tripartite division of mental faculties, 11, 87.

Ménage, Gilles, 126.

Mendelssohn, Moses, 160, 161.

Menuret, Jean-Jacques, 146–49.

Menzel, Adolph, 259.

Mersenne, Marin, 35, 98, 101, 293.

Metaphysics, 52, 289, 333, 340; classical, 310; Leibnizian, 238; in Lully's operas, 72; materialism in balance with, 153; *Naturphilosophie* and, 159; ocular bias of, 333; of presence, 47, 48, 60, 331.

Meter, 42, 296, 300.

Meumann, Ernst, 273, 278–79, 284.

Meyer, Max Friedrich, 294.

Mézières, Jean Laurent de Béthizy, 129.

Michaelis, Christian F., 167, 367 n.37.

Middle Ages, 49, 52.

Middle ear, 60, 240–41.

Mill, John Stuart, 268–69.

Mimesis, 123, 170.

Mind, 20, 223; apperception and, 244; disembodied, 66; ear in relationship to, 10; galvanic action and, 196; invention of, 9; liberating role of, 142. *See also* Ego; Soul; Subject/subjectivity.

Mind–body relation, 13, 31, 73, 74, 98, 306; ambiguity of demarcation, 340; auditory perception and, 124; Cartesian view of, 135; happiness and, 115; Heinse's aural eroticism and, 163; Perrault's physiology and, 81–84; as unity, 73.

Miserere (Allegri), 169.

Mitchell, W.J.T., 16, 17, 20.

Mitvollzug (coperformance), 327–28, 338.

Modernism, 271, 272, 296.

Modernity, 11, 12, 17, 307; either-or logic of, 341; key elements of, 321; melancholia and, 143; as ocular era, 15; Schumann's music and, 188; vision as dominant sense and, 341.

Modernization, 26.

Moderns versus ancients. *See* Ancients versus moderns *(Querelle des anciens et des modernes).*

Molecules, motion of, 10.

Molière, 88.

Monde, Le [The World] (Descartes), 34, 98.

Mondonville, Jean-Joseph de, 119, 260 n.30.

Monism, 196, 278, 304.

Monochord, 34, 40, 116.

Montesquieu, Baron de, 117, 128, 130, 340.

Montpellier school, 113, 128, 129, 137, 146; *Naturphilosophie* and, 159; sensibility and, 147.

Moos, Paul, 295.

Moreno, Jairo, 42, 43.

Mozart, Wolfgang Amadeus, 170, 199, 329, 333.

Müller, Adam, 199.

Müller, Georg Elias, 242–43, 247.

Müller, Johannes, 27, 66, 321; on cochlear anatomy, 229, 232; Helmholtz and, 221; on internal and external reality, 275; on music, 211–14, 265; nervous breakdown of, 202, 208; "organic" subject and, 332; projection theory, 208; Romantic legacy and, 203, 209; theory of hearing, 204–207; on vision, 203. *See also* Specific sense energies, Müller's law of.

Müller-Tamm, Jutta, 210.

Music, 19, 20, 222; "absolute," 197, 202, 213, 214, 216; of ancient Greece, 92, 105,

Zone Books series design by Bruce Mau
Typesetting by Meighan Gale
Printed and bound by Thompson-Shore